A Field Guide to the Birds of Mexico and Adjacent Areas

Ernest Preston Edwards

A Field Guide
to the Birds of Mexico
and Adjacent Areas

Belize, Guatemala,
and El Salvador

Third Edition

Principal Illustrator
Edward Murrell Butler

University of Texas Press
Austin

Requests for permission to reproduce material from this work should be sent to Permissions, University of Texas Press, Box 7819, Austin, TX 78713–7819.

∞ The paper used in this publication meets the minimum requirements of American National Standard for Information Sciences—Permanence of Paper for Printed Library Materials, ANSI Z39.48–1984.

Library of Congress Cataloging-in-Publication Data

Edwards, Ernest Preston, 1919–
    A field guide to the birds of Mexico and Adjacent Areas: Belize, Guatemala, and El Salvador / Ernest Preston Edwards: principal illustrator Edward Murrell Butler. — 3rd ed.
        p.   cm.
    Rev. ed. of: Field guide to the birds of Mexico. 2nd ed. c1989.
    Includes bibliographical references (p.   ) and index.
    ISBN 0-292-72092-0 (cloth: alk. paper)
    ISBN 0-292-72091-2 (pbk.: alk. paper)
    1. Birds—Central America—Identification.   I. Edwards, Ernest Preston, 1919–   Field guide to the birds of Mexico.   II. Title.
QL687.A1E39   1998   97-19414
598′.0972—dc21

Dedicated to the memory of my wife,
Mabel Thacher Edwards

Contents

Illustrations

Acknowledgments

The gradual evolution of this book into its current form began fifty-one years ago with the publication, in the June 1947 issue of the *Wilson Bulletin,* of a scientific paper by Stephen W. Eaton and Ernest P. Edwards. It reported the discovery, on June 17, 1946, of two individuals of the Mangrove Cuckoo, *Coccyzus minor,* at the Mesa de Llera, in dry mesquite grassland, approximately halfway between Ciudad Victoria and Ciudad Mante, in the southern portion of the state of Tamaulipas, in Mexico, considerably outside what was then considered the normal range and preferred habitat of this cuckoo. Gathering the information for that paper, and thus laying the groundwork for all of my subsequent scientific and popular publications leading up to the publication of the current *Field Guide,* would not have been possible without the support and encouragement of Stephen W. Eaton, coleader of our (two-person) first trip to Mexico, and his mother, Esther Woodman Eaton; of my parents, Mabel Griffith Edwards and Preston Hampton Edwards; of my great-aunt Eleanor Griffith Quance, who helped to pay for my first year of graduate study at Cornell University in 1940–1941; of Mr. and Mrs. Colin Hardwicke, Ingeniero Luis Macías, and Everts Storms in Mexico; of Dwain Warner; and of Arthur A. Allen, Peter Paul Kellogg, and George Miksch Sutton in the Laboratory of Ornithology at Cornell University.

To outline the progress of the work culminating in the publication of this book, it is convenient to divide the fifty-one years into two periods: first, the twenty-five years that elapsed between the Mangrove Cuckoo report and the publication of the first edition of my book *A Field Guide to the Birds of Mexico* in 1972, and second, the twenty-six years that elapsed between publication of the first edition and of this third edition.

During the first twenty-five years I studied birds intensively and extensively in Mexico, Guatemala, and other Middle American countries, visiting all of the states of Mexico except Baja California Sur, visiting large bird collections in the United States and Mexico, and receiving valuable advice and instruction at Cornell University and the University of Michigan's Douglas Lake Biological Station. Among the persons to whom I am particularly indebted for assistance, support, and encouragement during that time are my wife, Mabel Thacher Edwards, in all phases of the work; Robert B. Lea in field, laboratory, and museum; Allan R. Phillips, who advised on many problems and carefully checked manuscripts; L. Irby Davis and his wife; and all of the persons named in the first paragraph. In addition I am indebted to Carl Aiken III, John Boehm, Roger Hurd, Douglas Lancaster, Virginia Lea, Paul Martin, Eugene S. Morton, Thomas Pulley, Stephen Russell, Mabel Slack, Richard Tashian, Katrina Thompson, J. Dan Webster, Arnold and Shirley Weinberg, and the several dozen participants in commercial bird-watching tours that I organized and led in the field. Miguel Alvarez del Toro, John Eiler, Mr. and Mrs. Dyfrig Forbes, Paul Gelrich, Frank Harrison, Don Jaime del Piño, Don Javier del Piño, David Vales and his family, and Bernardo Villa R. provided hospitality and assistance in Mexico. I am also grateful to Richard C. Banks, Allen Duvall, Lester Short, Richard Zusi, John Aldrich, Herbert Friedmann, and Alexander Wetmore at the U.S. National Museum of Natural History; Emmett R. Blake and Melvin A. Traylor of the Field Museum of Natural History; Harrison B. Tordoff, Robert Storer, Pierce Brodkorb, Robert M. Mengel, and Josselyn Van Tyne at the University of Michigan Museum of Zoology; Dean Amadon and Charles O'Brien at the American Museum of Natural History; Walter Dalquest, Jean and Richard Graber, John P. O'Neill, Douglas Pratt, George H. Lowery, Jr., and Robert J. Newman at the Louisiana State University Museum of Zoology; John William Hardy at the Moore Laboratory of Zoology at Occidental College; Kenneth C. Parkes at the Louis Agassiz Fuertes Collection at Cornell University; Olin Sewall Pettingill at the University of Michigan Biological Station; and artists and ornithologists Edward Murrell Butler and Frederick K. Hilton.

The efforts of all these persons, along with my efforts, resulted in the 1972 publication of a field guide that illustrated in color nearly every Mexican species that did not also occur in the United States (about 500); described in detail the behavior, habitat, and plumage of all the birds whether they were illustrated or not; and provided a Spanish name for each species.

Several of us, however, had realized even before publication that although this would be the most satisfactory single-volume Mexican field guide available or planned at the time, the ultimate goal should be to illustrate all of Mexico's birds (not just the approximately 50 percent of them that do not occur in the United States) in a book of a size and weight suitable for use, day after day, right out in the fields and forests. Therefore, Murrell Butler soon began painting additional plates covering as many as possible of the Mexican birds that also occur in the United States, while

I continued my field work in Mexico (including Baja California Sur) and went still farther afield in Belize, Costa Rica, Panama, Colombia, and Peru. In the course of this second period, of twenty-six years, we have come very close to our goal of producing a second edition in 1989 and now this third edition, a lightweight manual-size field guide illustrating more than 90 percent of the birds regularly occurring in Mexico and the adjacent countries of Belize, Guatemala, and El Salvador.

For their major efforts in helping to accomplish this I thank all of the persons named above and also the following persons who joined the effort after 1972: for special help with specific sections of this book, Chris Benesh (*Myiarchus* and field work), Oliver Komar (birds of El Salvador), Carolyn and Bruce Miller (birds of Belize), and Don Roberson (seabirds); for help in the field, Larry Lof, G. Michael McHugh, Charles R. Smith, Barbara Warburton, Fred S. Webster, Jr., and Marie Webster; for general advice and assistance or help in museums or libraries, John C. Arvin, Robert Behrstock, George and Janet Cobb, Ben B. Coffey, Jr., Lula Coffey, Celeste Delgado, Victor Emanuel, T. Ben Feltner, Barbara MacKinnon de Montes, Jerry Strickling, and Nancy Strickling.

Murrell Butler painted twenty-six new plates for the second edition, which are also used in this third edition, and has added paintings of several species not previously illustrated; F. P. Bennett, Jr., painted plate 11; and I painted plates III and 13, and parts of plates 5, 20, 23, and 48.

Lorraine Atherton's many hours of hard work in copy-editing the manuscript are much appreciated. Finally, I appreciate very much the patience, competence, and hard work of David Cavazos, Shannon Davies, Lois Rankin, and Mandy Woods, at the University of Texas Press, in guiding this book through the publishing process.

Introduction

The area covered by this book—Mexico, Belize, Guatemala, and El Salvador—is rich in bird life, readily accessible for the most part, and almost unique in its mixture of many typically temperate-zone species with many distinctively tropical birds. Although the area of Mexico, Belize, Guatemala, and El Salvador combined is considerably smaller than that of the United States, many more species of birds occur regularly in those countries than in the contiguous United States (the lower 48). The Atlantic lowlands of Mexico, Belize, and Guatemala (sometimes called the Gulf-Caribbean Lowlands) and the adjacent lower mountain slopes, up to about 5000 feet (1500 meters) above sea level, are richest in variety of species and numbers of typically tropical species, as compared with other parts of Mexico and Guatemala and as compared with El Salvador. Within these lowlands, especially from about 200 miles south of the U.S-Mexico border and farther south and southeast through northern Guatemala and Belize, the observer can encounter a host of distinctively tropical species, among them parrots, hummingbirds, motmots, toucans, woodcreepers, and tropical species of hawks, woodpeckers, jays, tanagers, grosbeaks, buntings, and orioles. Likewise, because of the varied topography, a birder in Mexico or Guatemala (and to a lesser extent a person in Belize or El Salvador) need travel only a couple of hours, up or down the mountain slopes, to find an assortment of birds quite different from those around the starting point.

Coverage

In contrast to the second edition, which covered only the birds of Mexico and all its islands and territorial waters, this third edition has extended full coverage to Belize, Guatemala, and El Salvador, in addition to Mexico, while restricting coverage of species that occur only on remote islands or over ocean waters far offshore. Birds in the latter category have been gathered, in this edition, in a special list at the end of the main text.

Specifically, the main text of this edition covers all the birds that we believe occur regularly (not casually or accidentally) on the mainlands of

Mexico, Belize, Guatemala, and El Salvador; in their coastal waters and islands out to a distance of three miles from the mainland; on Cozumel Island, Mexico; or on the readily accessible cayes of Belize.

How to Use This Book

It is important, first of all, for the user to develop a concept of the different physiographic features, the elevations, the types of vegetation, the behavior patterns of certain kinds of birds, the seasonal changes, and the distribution of various species within each country.

For example, a dull, brownish bird, slightly smaller than a robin, flying across the road in rather open, dry, highland areas in northern or central Mexico, may quite likely be a Canyon Towhee. A similarly plain brownish bird, about the same size, in the humid lowland forests of southeastern Mexico and Belize and Guatemala, might be a Rufous Piha, a Rufous Mourner, or one of the ovenbirds or woodcreepers. It is difficult to imagine even a remote possibility that a Canyon Towhee would ever be found in the lowland humid forests or that a Rufous Piha would ever be seen flying across the road in arid, semidesert, mountainous areas.

To assist you in making the necessary choices when attempting to identify a particular bird, we have divided Mexico and Guatemala into regions (and in Mexico, subregions), divided Belize by habitat types and location within the country, and divided El Salvador by location within the country.

The Regional System in Mexico and Guatemala

Within Mexico the regions, in sequence from west to east (followed by subregions from north to south, in parentheses), are: Baja California (nBajCal, sBajCal), Pacific (nPac, cPac, sPac), Highlands (nHi, cHi, sHi), Atlantic (nAtl, cAtl, sAtl), and Yucatan. (See map, plate IV.) Separate modifiers are also employed to make the subregional range statements more precise when appropriate, for example, n.nBajCal (northern nBajCal), s.nPac (southern nPac), and se.cAtl (southeastern cAtl). A period separates the directional modifier and the subregion.

The Baja California (BajCal) Region, in the northwestern part of Mexico, includes the entire Baja California Peninsula up to the U.S. border on the north and the Colorado River on the northeast and thus includes elevations from sea level to 10,000 feet or higher, on the tops of the highest mountains. The region is divided into the northern (nBajCal) subregion, from Tijuana south to Guerrero Negro, and the southern (sBajCal) subregion, from Guerrero Negro south to Cabo San Lucas.

The Pacific (Pac) Region in Mexico includes all of the Pacific coastal plain (outside Baja California) and the adjacent lower mountain slopes, up to approximately 5000 feet (1500 meters) elevation, and is divided into three successively smaller subregions: northern (nPac), extending from Puerto Peñasco and Nogales southward to Puerto Vallarta; central (cPac), from Puerto Vallarta southeastward to Tehuantepec; and southern (sPac), from Tehuantepec southeastward to Tapachula.

The Highlands (Hi) Region in Mexico includes the mountain ranges and relatively high plateaus above 5000 feet (1500 meters), except in a few lower areas in the northern part of the Central Plateau, forming the backbone that runs more or less northwest to southeast down the center of the country (and on through central Guatemala and parts of El Salvador). The Highlands is divided into three successively smaller subregions: northern (nHi), extending southward from the vicinity of Agua Prieta (opposite Douglas, Arizona), Ciudad Juárez (opposite El Paso, Texas), and the Sierra del Carmen (opposite Big Bend National Park, Texas) to Guadalajara, Guanajuato, and Pachuca; central (cHi), extending southeastward from there through Mexico City, Jalapa, and Oaxaca, almost to the Isthmus of Tehuantepec; and southern (sHi), divided into two narrow segments, one extending near the Pacific coast from the Isthmus of Tehuantepec to the Guatemala border and the other beginning near Tuxtla Gutiérrez and extending through San Cristóbal de las Casas to the vicinity of Comitán. Within those subregions the reader might frequently encounter the designations w+e.nHi (referring to the western and eastern mountain ranges of the northern Highlands), w.cHi (western portions of the central Highlands), or se.cHi (southeastern portions of the central Highlands).

The Atlantic (Atl) Region includes the shores and coastal plain of the Gulf of Mexico and the Caribbean Sea (except the northern half of the Yucatan Peninsula) and the lower slopes of the mountain backbone up to about 5000 feet elevation. Even though it is not nearly as extensive as the Pacific Region, it is divided into three subregions: northern (nAtl), extending from near Ciudad Acuña (opposite Del Rio, Texas) and Matamoros south to Ciudad Valles and Tampico; central (cAtl), extending from there southeastward to Coatzacoalcos; and southern (sAtl), extending from there (the Isthmus of Tehuantepec) to the Guatemalan border on the southeast, to Campeche on the north, and across the base of the Yucatan Peninsula to Belize and the Caribbean Sea.

The Yucatan (Yuc) Region includes the low flatlands of the northern part of the Yucatan Peninsula and extends from Champotón (south of Campeche) and Felipe Carrillo Puerto on the south to Progreso and the vicinity of Cancún on the north. Because of its relatively small size it is not divided into subregions, but there is a noticeable difference in vegetation, and therefore bird life, between the drier western half (w Yuc) and the wetter eastern half (e Yuc). (A space rather than a period separates directional modifiers and region abbreviations.)

Within Guatemala only three regions are designated: Pacific, Highlands, and Atlantic, with no subregions. Occasionally a modifier is used, such as ne Atl (the area around Puerto Barrios) or nw Atl (the Petén). The abbreviations Pac, Hi, and Atl represent the same locational and elevational data as they do in Mexico: Pac extends from the shores of the Pacific Ocean to the 5000-foot (1500-meter) level on the slopes of the mountains; Hi represents the highlands from there up to the tops of the highest mountains; and Atl extends from the 5000-foot (1500-meter) level on the other side (north side) of the mountains, on down to the shore of the Caribbean Sea, and to the Belize-Guatemala border and the Guatemala-Mexico border.

Bird Distribution in Belize and El Salvador

If we applied the same major regional designations to Belize (Blz) that we apply to Mexico and Guatemala, all of the country would fall into the southern Atlantic subregion, because it borders the Caribbean Sea and because the highest mountain in Belize falls considerably short of the 5000-foot (1500-meter) upper limit of the Atlantic Region. Most of the birds of the sAtl subregion of Mexico (and the Atlantic Region of Guatemala) are to be found in Belize, along with some of the birds that occur mainly in the Yucatan. Occasional parenthetical modifiers following "Blz" indicate that birds occur only in the coastal areas (cstl), only in the cayes, in both the coastal areas and the cayes (cstl + cayes), in the pine woods or pine ridge in general (pine), in the mountain pine woods only (mt pine), mainly in the north (n), or mainly in the south (s). If the country is listed without any modifiers, the bird is to be expected more or less throughout the country in suitable habitat.

El Salvador (El Sal) has one mountain peak rising about 9000 feet (about 2700 meters) above sea level and several above 6000 feet (about 1800 meters), as well as lowlands extending to the shores of the Pacific Ocean. It would fit into the regional system used in Mexico and Guatemala. For more precise designation of range the text sometimes uses parenthetical modifiers following the country abbreviation: (n) refers to birds occurring mainly or only in the northern part of the country; (w) to those restricted mainly to the western part; (e) to the very few species restricted to the eastern part; and (cstl) for birds restricted mainly to the coastal area (up to three miles inland or up to three miles offshore). As in the case of Belize, if no modifier is used, the bird can be expected in most parts of the country where suitable habitat exists. The affinities of the birds of El Salvador are mostly with the birds of the Pacific lowlands and adjacent lower-mountain to mid-mountain slopes of Guatemala and Mexico.

Reading the Species Write-ups

Most parts of the species write-ups, other than the range designations, are self-explanatory, but in case there is any doubt, here is a sample write-up, followed by an explanation of each portion in succession:

BLUE-CROWNED MOTMOT [19] Turco Real *Momotus momota*
   Range Mex–SAm. Res Mex (sPac, c.nAtl–sAtl, Yuc), Blz, Guat (Pac, Atl), ElSal.
   Habitat River-border woods, dry or humid forest, overgrown orchards.
   Voice A low pitched *hoot, hoot.*
   Field Marks 16″ Green above, or with some rufous; olive-green or rufous below; crown pale blue with black border (nAtl, n.cAtl) or crown with black center, then blue circle, then black border (s.cAtl, sAtl, sPac, Yuc); short bare space on racket-tipped tail; black ear streak and chest spot.

Blue-crowned Motmot Each entry begins with the English name (the common, or vernacular, name) for the species adopted by the American Ornithologists' Union (AOU). In a few cases, part of the name appears in parentheses, as in "**(Lesser Yellow-headed) Savanna Vulture**" or "**Ruddy (Crake) Rail.**" The parentheses in the first example indicate that the AOU currently uses the specific common name "Lesser Yellow-headed" for this vulture, but I prefer the name "Savanna." In the second example, it is the group name that differs: the AOU places this species in the group crake, but I prefer to call it a rail. In all such cases both names appear in the index. If the difference is *very* slight, for example between my usage of the more grammatically correct and precise "Spotted breasted Wren" and the AOU's "Spot breasted Wren" (does the wren have one spot or more than one?), parentheses are not used, and the AOU version of the name is not shown in the Index.

[19] A number in brackets following the English name indicates that the species is illustrated on that plate. The color plates are numbered 1 through 48. The black-and-white plates, numbered I, II, III, and IV, follow the color plates.

"Turco Real" This is the Spanish name for the species; in almost every case it is either the Spanish name I used in the second edition or the name used by Peterson and Chalif in their book *Aves de México.*

Momotus momota The scientific name of the species, in Latin form, corresponds to the name currently accepted by the AOU.

Range In this category, the overall range of the bird in the Western Hemisphere, excluding the Antilles, is given first. "Mex–SAm" indicates that this particular motmot occurs in Mexico, in all the countries between Mexico and South America (i.e., Belize, Guatemala, El Salvador, Honduras, Nicaragua, Costa Rica, and Panama), and on into South America. There is no attempt to indicate the details of its distribution in South America. If the bird occurs from the contiguous United States to some country in South America but is absent from El Salvador, this part would be written "US–SAm, exc ElSal." If the species is to be found from Alaska to western Nicaragua, but not in Belize and Honduras, it would be written "AK–Mex, Guat, ElSal, Nic."

The bird's seasonal status and distribution within its overall range are given next. "Res Mex (sPac, c.nAtl–sAtl, Yuc), Blz, Guat (Pac, Atl), ElSal" means, first, that the species is resident (found year-round) in Mexico, Belize, Guatemala, and El Salvador. Other seasonal status abbreviations are "sum" (found in the summer), "tr" (transient, travels through seasonally, as in the spring and /or fall), "win" (found in the winter). Second, the parenthetic abbreviations indicate that it does not occur throughout Mexico but only in the southern Pacific subregion (sPac), all of the Atlantic Region except the northernmost part of the northern Atlantic subregion (c.nAtl–sAtl, meaning central nAtl through the cAtl and sAtl subregions), and generally throughout the Yucatan Region (Yuc); and only in the Pac and Atl regions of Guatemala. (If the range included all the Pacific Region within Mexico, it would be abbreviated simply Pac. If it included only the central and southern Pacific subregions, it would be abbreviated csPac.) Third, the lack of parenthetic statements for Belize and El Salvador indicates that the bird is rather generally distributed throughout those countries in proper habitat. This statement doesn't attempt to provide any further details about the bird's occurrence in countries other than the four countries in our area of coverage. If the bird does not occur in a country, that country is not mentioned in this part of the species write-up.

Some range descriptions will end with a statement of relative abundance. To show how this works, let's compare the Blue-crowned Motmot's entry with the Keel-billed Motmot's ("Very rare, local"). The Blue-crowned Motmot write-up, by omitting any statement of relative abundance, indicates that the bird is likely to be seen often enough in the proper habitat and range that an average birder would not have to be told that someone else might think it is common, fairly common, or abundant. Expectations created by the use of such terms vary so widely from person to person that they are practically meaningless, especially when one word purports to cover the bird's status over its entire range in our area. The words "rare," "very rare," "local," or "irregular," on the other hand, are more likely to connote much the same status to each birder, regardless of the species being discussed or the background of the birder. Therefore, those terms are useful in describing the Keel-billed Motmot.

Habitat This category describes the bird's preferred habitat, concentrating on water features, geological features, and characteristic vegetation. Some write-ups also mention where the bird is likely to be seen within that habitat. For example, the White-breasted Hawk's habitat is described as "cloud forest or other dense humid forest, or partial clearings," and the bird can be seen "flying rapidly among the trees or perched in middle branches."

Voice A description of the voice (song, call, or alarm note) has been included for most birds that are secretive or nocturnal and those that have simple distinctive songs or calls. The reader is urged to purchase some of the commercially available recordings of birds of our area.

Field Marks This category begins with the length of the bird from tail tip to bill tip, in inches (in the Blue-crowned Motmot's case, 16 inches). The measurement is usually obtained from a museum specimen lying on its back; nevertheless, as an indicator of relative size, it can be very useful. For example, the smaller Keel-billed Motmot is listed at 13 inches, and the much smaller Tody Motmot is listed at 7 inches. When two measurements are listed in this space, the first refers to the size of the male and the second to the size of the female. Following the length is a brief physical description of the species, condensed from a much longer description in the first edition, retaining only the more important diagnostic features. In many species the male plumage differs from that of the female and of the immature birds, in which cases separate descriptions are included. Subheadings within the Field Marks category include M (male), F (female), adt (adult), imm (immature), sum (summer plumage), win (winter plumage), various morphs, and others. A few species have distinctive behavioral characteristics that may aid in field identification. In those cases the behavior is noted before the physical description.

Abbreviations

acc	accidental occurrence	nBajCal	northern Baja California sub-region
adj	adjacent		
adt	adult	nc	north-central
AK	Alaska	ncAtl	northern and central Atlantic subregions
AOU	American Ornithologists' Union		
		ncHi	northern and central Highlands subregions
Atl	Atlantic Region		
BajCal	Baja California Region	ncPac	northern and central Pacific subregions
Blz	Belize		
c	central	ne	northeastern
Can	Canada	nHi	northern Highlands sub-region
cas	casual occurrence		
cAtl	central Atlantic subregion	Nic	Nicaragua
cHi	central Highlands sub-region	nPac	northern Pacific subregion
		nsHi	northern and southern Highlands subregions
cPac	central Pacific subregion		
CRic	Costa Rica	nw	northwestern
csAtl	central and southern Atlantic subregions	Pac	Pacific Region
		Pan	Panama
csHi	central and southern Highlands subregions	pine	pine ridge
		res	resident
csPac	central and southern Pacific subregions	s	southern
		SAm	South America
cstl	coastal	sAtl	southern Atlantic subregion
e	eastern	sBajCal	southern Baja California sub-region
ec	east-central		
ElSal	El Salvador	sc	south-central
exc	except	se	southeastern
F	female	sHi	southern Highlands sub-region
Guat	Guatemala		
Hi	Highlands Region	sPac	southern Pacific subregion
Hon	Honduras	sum	summer
imm	immature	sw	southwestern
irr	irregular occurrence	tr	transient
juv	juvenile	untacs	under tail coverts
M	male	uptacs	upper tail coverts
Mex	Mexico	US	United States
mt pine	mountain pine woods or ridge	vis	visitor
		w	western
mts	mountains	wc	west-central
n	northern	win	winter
nAtl	northern Atlantic subregion	Yuc	Yucatan Region

A Field Guide to the Birds of Mexico and Adjacent Areas

TOPOGRAPHY OF A BIRD

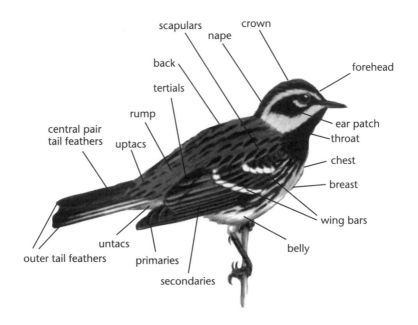

scapulars

crown

nape

back

tertials

forehead

rump

central pair
tail feathers

uptacs

ear patch

throat

chest

breast

wing bars

untacs

outer tail feathers

primaries

belly

secondaries

The Birds of Mexico, Belize, Guatemala, and El Salvador

TINAMOUS—PERDICES—TINAMIDAE

GREAT TINAMOU [4] Perdiz Mayor *Tinamus major*
Range Mex–SAm, exc ElSal. Res Mex (se.cAtl+sAtl), Blz, Guat (Atl). Rare.
Habitat Humid forest or dense woodland.
Voice A tremulous whistle, followed by short notes, often in pairs, some descending in pitch.
Field Marks 15″ Olive plumage, with bluish legs and feet.

LITTLE TINAMOU [4] Ponchita *Crypturellus soui*
Range Mex–SAm, exc ElSal. Res Mex (se.cAtl+sAtl), Blz, Guat (Atl). Rare.
Habitat Humid forest, woodlands, borders.
Voice A slow ascending series of tremulous notes; or a long, tremulous note ascending, then descending.
Field Marks 9″ Small size, grayish legs, and unbarred grayish brown or reddish brown plumage.

THICKET TINAMOU [4] Perdiz Canela *Crypturellus cinnamomeus*
Range Mex–CRic, SAm. Res Mex (s.nPac+nw.cPac+sPac, s.nAtl+csAtl, Yuc), Blz (n), Guat (Pac, Atl), ElSal.
Habitat Humid forest, scrubby woods, thorny thickets.
Voice A loud, clear, extended whistle, usually on one pitch, but may go down or up.
Field Marks 11″ Barred back (except male Mex, nPac); grayish or grayish brown (Mex, nPac) to rich reddish brown to dark olive-brown (Mex, sAtl); legs orange.

SLATY-BREASTED TINAMOU [4] Perdiz Jamuey *Crypturellus boucardi*
Range Mex–CRic, exc ElSal. Res Mex (se.cAtl+extreme s.sAtl), Blz, Guat (Atl). Rare.
Habitat Dense undergrowth of humid forest.
Voice Two extended, unobtrusive, low-pitched notes.
Field Marks 11″ Plumage (and leg color) like that of dark races of Thicket Tinamou, but mostly unbarred. M: very dark olive-brown to slaty. F: dark reddish brown; untacs barred.

LOONS—SOMORGUJOS—GAVIIDAE

RED-THROATED LOON Somorgujo Menor *Gavia stellata*
Range AK–Mex. Win Mex (w.BajCal, nw.nPac). Rare.

Habitat Mostly coastal salt water in winter.
Field Marks 25″ Like Pacific Loon, but bill more slender and upturned; Win: back more speckled; head and neck paler, less contrasty; Sum: throat rufous, *not* purplish; hindneck boldly streaked.

PACIFIC LOON [I] Somorgujo Pacífico *Gavia pacifica*
Range AK–Mex. Win Mex (BajCal, n.+c.nPac).
Habitat Ocean bays, coastal lagoons, estuaries.
Field Marks 25″ Smaller, and smaller-billed, than Common Loon. Win: contrasty blackish and white on head and neck; *no* back speckles. Sum: rows of large white spots above; throat purplish; head medium gray; sides of neck streaked.

COMMON LOON Somorgujo Común *Gavia immer*
Range AK–Mex. Win Mex (BajCal, nPac, ncHi, ncAtl). Rare.
Habitat Coastal, or inland lakes and rivers.
Field Marks 33″ Larger than Red-throated or Pacific Loon, with larger, straight, dark bill. Win: gray above, white below; less contrasty than Pacific Loon, more so than Red-throated Loon; *no* back speckles. Sum: rows of large white spots above; head and neck black with greenish gloss; two partial, striped collars.

GREBES—ZAMBULLIDORES—PODICIPEDIDAE

LEAST GREBE [I] Zambullidor Menor *Tachybaptus dominicus*
Range US–SAm. Res Mex (all, exc nBajCal and n.nPac), Blz (n), Guat, ElSal (rare and local Hi).
Habitat Ponds, lakes, marsh pools, lagoons.
Field Marks 9″ Darker, more slender-billed than Pied-billed Grebe. Plumage dark gray, except whitish belly and untacs. Win: whitish throat. Sum: blackish throat and crown.

PIED-BILLED GREBE [II] Zambullidor Piquipinto *Podilymbus podiceps*
Range AK–SAm. Res/win Mex, Blz, Guat, ElSal.
Habitat Pools, marshy ponds, lakes, rivers, lagoons.
Field Marks 12″ Mostly dark grayish brown, with whitish belly and untacs; bill short, stout, pale. Win: throat white; bill plain. Sum: throat and bill bar black.

HORNED GREBE Zambullidor Cornudo *Podiceps auritus*
Range AK–Mex. Win Mex (nBajCal, nw.nPac). Rare.
Habitat Mostly coastal waters.
Field Marks 13″ Like Eared Grebe, blackish gray above, with short, slender bill and red eyes, but Win: ear patch all white, hindneck and foreneck more contrasty blackish and white, Sum: neck chestnut, neat tawny face plumes extend backward mostly above eye.

EARED GREBE [II] Zambullidor Orejudo *Podiceps nigricollis*
Range Can–Mex, Guat, ElSal. Res/win Mex (irr res nBajCal+ncHi; win BajCal, Pac, Hi, ncAtl); win Guat (Pac, Hi), ElSal. Rare or local (summer), common (winter).

Habitat Lakes, ponds, rivers, lagoons.
Field Marks 13″ Bill short, slender, slightly upturned. Win: ear patch blackish, bordered below and behind by white crescent. Sum: head, neck, and chest black; tawny plumes fan out up and down behind eye.

WESTERN GREBE [I] Achichilique Occidental *Aechmophorus occidentalis*
Range AK–Mex. Res/win Mex (res nBajCal, ncHi; win BajCal, nPac). Rare.
Habitat Ponds, lakes, bays, lagoons.
Field Marks 28″ Contrasty black and white; long neck; black all around eye; bill mostly yellowish green.

CLARK'S GREBE [I] Achichilique de Clark *Aechmophorus clarkii*
Range AK–Mex. Res/win Mex (nBajCal, ncHi; win BajCal+nPac?). Rare.
Habitat Lakes, lagoons.
Field Marks 28″ Like Western Grebe, but white all around eye; bill mostly dull orange.

ALBATROSSES—ALBATROS—DIOMEDEIDAE

BLACK-FOOTED ALBATROSS [I] Albatros Oscuro *Phoebastria nigripes*
Range AK–Mex. Vis Mex (oceans off w.BajCal). Very rare to casual.
Habitat Open ocean and 3-mile waters.
Field Marks 30″ Mostly blackish brown; face, untacs, and uptacs usually white.

SHEARWATERS—PARDELAS—PROCELLARIIDAE

NORTHERN FULMAR Fulmar *Fulmarus glacialis*
Range AK–Mex. Vis Mex (w.BajCal; cas/acc nPac). Rare.
Habitat Open ocean and 3-mile waters.
Field Marks 17″ Flapping and long glides. Stouter, broader-winged than shearwaters; bill short, heavy, yellowish. Dark morph: uniform dark gray. Light morph: wings and back pale gray to medium gray with darker wingtips, and white head, tail, and underparts. Individuals intermediate between the two morphs may be seen also.

PINK-FOOTED SHEARWATER [III] Pardela Patirrosada *Puffinus creatopus*
Range AK–SAm. Vis Mex (BajCal, Pac), Guat (Pac), ElSal.
Habitat Open ocean and 3-mile waters.
Field Marks 16″ Slow, heavy flight. Grayish brown above; white below, with mottled sides and flanks; bill long, pinkish with black tip; feet pinkish.

WEDGE-TAILED SHEARWATER [45] Pardela Pacífica *Puffinus pacificus*
Range Mex–SAm, exc Blz, ElSal, Hon. Res/vis Mex (res off cPac; vis off sBajCal, csPac), Guat (Pac).
Habitat Open ocean, nest islands, and (very rarely) 3-mile waters.
Field Marks 16″ Tail rather long and wedge-shaped, *not* short and rounded; bill slender, pink with black tip; feet pink. Light morph: white below; contrasty dark above. Dark morph (very rare): uniform medium to dark brown.

SOOTY SHEARWATER [III] Pardela Gris *Puffinus griseus*
Range AK–SAm, exc ElSal, Hon. Vis Mex (BajCal, Pac; acc nAtl), Guat (Pac), ElSal.
Habitat Open ocean; rare in 3-mile waters.
Field Marks 17″ Blackish brown, with dark bill and feet; contrasty silver-white coverts on dark underwing.

SHORT-TAILED SHEARWATER Pardela Colicorta *Puffinus tenuirostris*
Range AK–Mex. Vis Mex (BajCal, nPac). Rare.
Habitat Over open ocean; very rare in 3-mile waters.
Field Marks 14″ Like Sooty Shearwater, but slightly smaller, shorter-billed, and may show less contrast of light grayish on dark underwing.

BLACK-VENTED SHEARWATER [III] Pardela Mexicana *Puffinus opisthomelas*
Range US–Mex. Res/vis Mex (res western islands nBajCal; vis BajCal+ncPac).
Habitat Open ocean and 3-mile waters.
Field Marks 14″ Blackish brown above; black bill, pink feet; underparts white except black untacs and blackish brown mottling on sides, flanks, and face.

TOWNSEND'S SHEARWATER Pardela de Townsend *Puffinus auricularis*
Range Mex, Guat, ElSal. Res/vis Mex (res off cPac: Revillagigedo Islands; vis off sBajCal, Pac); vis Guat (Pac), ElSal.
Habitat Open ocean, nest islands, and 3-mile waters.
Field Marks 14″ Like Black-vented Shearwater, but black legs and *little or no* mottling on sides and flanks.

AUDUBON'S SHEARWATER Pardela Chica *Puffinus lherminieri*
Range US–SAm, exc Blz, ElSal, Hon, Pan. Vis Mex (csPac, Yuc), Guat (Pac).
Habitat Open ocean and (very rarely) 3-mile waters.
Field Marks 12″ Blackish above; unmottled white below, except black primaries and blackish brown untacs; feet pinkish.

STORM-PETRELS—PAÍÑOS—HYDROBATIDAE

BLACK STORM-PETREL [45] Paíño Negro *Oceanodroma melania*
Range US–SAm, exc Blz, ElSal, Hon. Res/vis Mex (res islands BajCal+n.nPac; vis Pac), Guat (Pac).
Habitat Open ocean and 3-mile waters.
Field Marks 9″ Flapping and gliding, near the water surface. Large size. Appears black, except pale wing bar; tail forked; legs and feet black.

LEAST STORM-PETREL Paíño Mínimo *Oceanodroma microsoma*
Range US–SAm, exc Blz, ElSal, Hon. Res/vis Mex (res islands BajCal+n.nPac; vis Pac), Guat (Pac), ElSal (Pac).
Habitat Open ocean and 3-mile waters.
Field Marks 6″ Flies rapidly, erratically, with deep wingbeats. Like Black Storm-Petrel, but much smaller, with a short, wedge-shaped tail.

TROPICBIRDS—RABIJUNCOS—PHAETHONTIDAE

RED-BILLED TROPICBIRD [I] Rabijunco Piquirrojo *Phaethon aethereus*
  Range US–SAm, exc Blz. Res/vis Mex (res BajCal, ncPac; vis sPac), Guat (Pac), ElSal (acc cstl).
  Habitat Rocky headlands and islands, ranges over open ocean.
  Field Marks 35" Adt: white, with long, slender, white central tail feathers, fine black barring on back, black wingtips, and red bill. Imm: tail short; bill orange-yellow.

GANNETS, BOOBIES—SULAS—SULIDAE

MASKED BOOBY Sula Enmascarada *Sula dactylatra*
  Range US–SAm, exc ElSal. Res/vis Mex (res islands off sBajCal, cPac, Yuc; vis off csPac, Atl, Yuc), vis off Blz (acc), Guat. Rare.
  Habitat Over open ocean; very rare in 3-mile waters.
  Field Marks 32" Adt: white, except black wingtips, trailing edge of wing, tail, chin, and around eye; bill yellow; feet orange yellow. Imm: head, upperparts, and tail dark grayish brown, with white across hindneck; breast, belly, and untacs white.

BLUE-FOOTED BOOBY [III] Sula Piesazules *Sula nebouxii*
  Range US–SAm, exc Blz, ElSal. Res/vis Mex (res BajCal+nPac; vis cPac); vis Guat (Pac). Rare.
  Habitat Nest islands, coasts, open ocean.
  Field Marks 32" Feet bright blue; bill dark grayish blue. Adt: white below; blackish brown above with three white patches (on hindneck, back, and rump); head streaked. Imm: like Brown Booby, but head and throat darker, less streaky; rump dark; lower throat and chest much more streaked or whitish, *not* uniform dark brown.

BROWN BOOBY [III] Sula Cuellioscura *Sula leucogaster*
  Range US–SAm. Res/vis Mex (res BajCal, ncPac, Yuc; vis sPac); vis Blz (cstl + cayes), Guat (Pac), ElSal (cstl).
  Habitat Open ocean and 3-mile waters.
  Field Marks 28" Strong wingbeats and long, sweeping glides. Adt: feet and bill yellow; upperparts and entire head, neck, and chest dark brown in Atlantic birds (but head and anterior portion of neck whitish in Pacific males); belly and untacs white, underwing coverts white, flight feathers dark. Imm: like brown-headed adult, but duller, less contrasty; bill gray to dull yellow.

RED-FOOTED BOOBY [45] Sula Patirroja *Sula sula*
  Range Mex–SAm, exc ElSal. Res/vis Mex (res off ncPac, Yuc; vis off sBajCal, Pac, sAtl, Yuc), Blz (Half-Moon Caye); vis Guat (Pac).
  Habitat Mostly open ocean; very rare in 3-mile waters.
  Field Marks 27" Adt: feet red. White morph: white (tail may be dark with white

tip) but wingtip and trailing edge of wing black. Dark morph: dark brown, or dark brown with some white, such as white rump, uptacs, untacs, and/or tail. Imm: dark brownish, with orange to gray feet.

NORTHERN GANNET Sula Norteña *Morus bassanus*
Range US–Mex. Win Mex (ncAtl). Rare.
Habitat Open ocean; very rare in 3-mile waters.
Field Marks 38″ Flying strongly, gliding, diving. Adt: white, except black wingtips and tawny wash on head and neck. Subadult: mostly mottled dark brownish gray upperparts and head; whitish below, changing to more and more white intermixed on upperparts, and tawny on head.

PELICANS—ALCATRACES—PELECANIDAE

AMERICAN WHITE PELICAN Alcatraz Blanco *Pelecanus erythrorhynchos*
Range Can–CRic, exc Hon. Res/win Mex (res locally nHi, nAtl; win w.BajCal, Pac, ncHi, Atl, Yuc), Blz (acc), Guat (Pac), win ElSal. Rare, local.
Habitat Coastal bays and lagoons or inland lakes.
Field Marks 60″ Adt: white, except black flight feathers; very long, heavy, pouched orange-yellow bill; orange-yellow feet and legs. Imm: wings mottled, much gray on head and neck.

BROWN PELICAN [I] Alcatraz Pardo *Pelecanus occidentalis*
Range Can–SAm. Res/vis Mex (res cstl BajCal, nPac, csAtl, Yuc; vis csPac, nAtl), Blz (cstl + cayes); vis Guat (Pac, Atl), ElSal (cstl).
Habitat Mostly ocean beaches, rocky shores, bays.
Field Marks 50″ Groups fly in line, perch on rocks, or dive from the air. Mostly gray. Head and neck white in winter, white and brown in summer.

CORMORANTS—SARGENTOS—PHALACROCORACIDAE

DOUBLE-CRESTED CORMORANT [I] Cormorán Orejudo *Phalacrocorax auritus*
Range AK–Mex, Blz, Guat. Res/win Mex (res BajCal, n.nPac, Yuc; win nPac, Atl); res Blz (cstl + cayes).
Habitat Islands, headlands, bays, lagoons.
Field Marks 32″ Adt: black, with dark green sheen; rounded orange-yellow throat pouch. Imm: dark brown above and below, except whitish throat and breast; throat pouch yellow.

NEOTROPIC CORMORANT [I] Corvejón *Phalacrocorax brasilianus*
Range US–SAm. Res Mex (sBajCal, Pac, Hi, Atl, Yuc), Blz, Guat (Pac, Atl), ElSal.
Habitat Coastal lagoons, estuaries, ponds, rivers, marshes.
Field Marks 26″ Like Double-crested Cormorant, but smaller, longer-tailed; Adt: triangular yellow throat pouch with a white line border in breeding adults; Imm: throat and chest darker.

BRANDT'S CORMORANT [II] Cormorán de Brandt *Phalacrocorax penicillatus*
Range AK-Mex. Res/win Mex (BajCal, nPac).
Habitat Coastal waters, bays, inlets.
Field Marks 30" Adt: blackish (shows greenish sheen in summer), with scaly blackish brown back; blue throat pouch with broad buff band just behind it. Imm: dark grayish brown above; medium brown below, with V-shaped pale breast mark; throat pouch dull blue.

PELAGIC CORMORANT [II] Cormorán Pelágico *Phalacrocorax pelagicus*
Range AK-Mex. Res/win near sea level Mex (res nBajCal; win sBajCal). Rare.
Habitat Rocky headlands and islands, and nearby ocean waters.
Field Marks 27" Slender neck, small head, and slender bill. Adt: black, with green sheen; shaggy crests, red face, and white flank patch in summer. Imm: very dark grayish brown all over.

ANHINGAS—HUIZOTES—ANHINGIDAE

ANHINGA [I] Huizote *Anhinga anhinga*
Range US-SAm. Res Mex (s.nPac+csPac, Atl, Yuc), Blz, Guat (Pac, Atl), ElSal.
Habitat Swims, soars, in or near ponds, lagoons, estuaries, swamps.
Field Marks 32" Very slender neck; slender, sharp, straight bill; very small head; long, full tail; large silvery patch on wings and upper back. M: mostly glossy black. F: head, neck, and chest dark buffy brown.

FRIGATEBIRDS—FRAGATAS—FREGATIDAE

MAGNIFICENT FRIGATEBIRD [45] Fragata Común *Fregata magnificens*
Range US-SAm. Res Mex (BajCal, Pac, Atl, Yuc), Blz (cstl + cayes), Guat (Pac, Atl), ElSal.
Habitat Ocean, lagoons, estuaries, rarely inland.
Field Marks 39" Long, forked tail; hook-tipped bill. M: blackish; red throat sac not very prominent unless inflated. F: like male, but white breast and sides; no red throat sac. Imm: white head, throat, breast, and sides; less white in older immatures.

HERONS, EGRETS—GARZAS, PEDRETES—ARDEIDAE

PINNATED BITTERN [4] Pedrete Lineado *Botaurus pinnatus*
Range Mex-SAm, exc Pan. Res Mex (csAtl, Yuc), Blz, Guat (Atl), ElSal (cas e). Rare.
Habitat Marshes, marshy pond edges, lagoons, sluggish rivers.
Field Marks 25" Crown and back and sides of neck narrowly barred (*no* black patch on side of head); back and wings black-streaked and barred. See American Bittern.

AMERICAN BITTERN [1] Torcomón *Botaurus lentiginosus*
Range AK–Pan. Res/win Mex (res ncHi; win all); win Blz, Guat, ElSal (e). Rare, irregular.
Habitat Freshwater or brackish marshes.
Field Marks 26″ Heavy black streak on side of face and upper neck; heavy streaks of dark reddish brown on neck, breast, and back.

LEAST BITTERN [1] Garcita *Ixobrychus exilis*
Range Can–SAm. Sum/win Mex (res BajCal, Pac, cHi, Atl; tr nHi; win sHi, Yuc); res Blz (n), Guat (Pac, Atl), ElSal. Rare, local.
Habitat Marshes, marshy ponds and lakes.
Field Marks 12″ Secretive; when flushed flies farther and with slower wingbeats than rails. Rich buff wing patches contrast with black wingtips and tail. M: black back and crown. F: dark reddish brown back and crown.

BARE-THROATED TIGER-HERON [4] Garza Tigre Mexicana *Tigrisoma mexicanum*
Range Mex–SAm. Res Mex (Pac, Atl, Yuc), Blz, Guat (Pac, Atl), ElSal.
Habitat Wooded rivers, marshes, swamps, lagoons.
Field Marks 30″ Solitary. Adt: head mostly black and gray; throat bare, yellow; upperparts and sides of neck narrowly barred; black-bordered white streak down underside of neck; belly tawny brown. Imm: boldly barred buff and black.

GREAT BLUE HERON [1] Garzón Cenizo *Ardea herodias*
Range AK–SAm. Res/win Mex (res BajCal, nPac, Atl, Yuc; win csPac, Hi); vis Blz, Guat, ElSal. Dark morph common; white morph rare (Great White Heron, Garzón Albo, in our area occurs only in cstl Yuc).
Habitat Ocean beaches, lagoons, estuaries, lakes, ponds, marshes.
Field Marks 45″ Dark morph: much larger than other dark Mexican herons; bluish gray above; head whitish, with slender black plumes behind eye. White morph: white, with yellowish bill, like Great Egret, but larger, with yellowish, *not* blackish, legs.

GREAT EGRET [1] Garzón Blanco *Ardea alba*
Range Can–SAm. Res/win Mex (res Pac, w.cHi, Atl, Yuc; win BajCal, Hi), res Blz, Guat (res Pac; win all), res ElSal.
Habitat Coastal and inland waters, lagoons, marshes, lakes.
Field Marks 38″ White; note large size; mostly yellowish bill; blackish gray feet and legs.

SNOWY EGRET [1] Garza Nívea *Egretta thula*
Range Can–SAm. Res/win Mex (res sBajCal, Pac, w.cHi, Atl, Yuc; win BajCal, Hi), Blz, Guat (res Pac; win all), ElSal.
Habitat Lagoons, marshes, swamps, ponds, canals.
Field Marks 22″ Like immature Little Blue Heron, but black bill; black legs (or front of legs blackish and back of legs yellowish) and yellow or yellow-orange, *not* dark greenish, feet (toes).

LITTLE BLUE HERON [1] Garza Azul *Egretta caerulea*
Range Can–SAm. Res/win Mex (res sBajCal, Pac, w.cHi, nAtl, nw Yuc; win csHi, Atl, Yuc), Blz, Guat, ElSal.
Habitat Lagoons, tidal flats, marshes, ponds, canals.
Field Marks 25″ Bill bluish gray, broadly black-tipped. Adt: slaty blue, with greenish to blackish legs; purplish neck and head. Imm: white, or mottled white and blue; legs and feet dull greenish.

TRICOLORED HERON [1] Garza Flaca *Egretta tricolor*
Range Can–SAm. Res/win Mex (res BajCal, Pac, Atl, Yuc; win csHi), Blz, Guat (res Pac; win all), ElSal.
Habitat Lagoons, estuaries, mangrove swamps, marshes.
Field Marks 24″ Bill long, slender; underparts and stripe down front of neck white; neck and upperparts mostly dark blue. Imm: wings mottled with reddish brown; neck mostly dull tawny brown.

REDDISH EGRET [1] Garza Melenuda *Egretta rufescens*
Range US–SAm. Res Mex (BajCal, Pac, Atl, Yuc); res/vis Blz (cstl + cayes), Guat (Pac, Atl), ElSal (cstl). Rare, local.
Habitat Brackish lagoons, quiet bays and inlets, swamps.
Field Marks 30″ Moves about erratically when feeding. Bill mostly pink, with black tip; legs dark grayish blue. Dark morph: dark grayish blue, but shaggy head and entire neck rich reddish brown. White morph: plumage white. See Little Blue Heron.

CATTLE EGRET [1] Garza Ganadera *Bubulcus ibis*
Range AK–SAm. Res Mex, Blz, Guat, ElSal.
Habitat Usually with livestock in moist to wet grassy fields.
Field Marks 20″ Rather short, stout, yellow to red-orange bill; legs dark greenish to yellowish to orange-red. Breeding birds have tawny buff plumes on crown, chest, and back.

GREEN HERON [1] Garcita Oscura *Butorides virescens*
Range Can–Pan. Res/win Mex, Blz, Guat, ElSal.
Habitat Swamps, marshes, ponds, lagoons, estuaries.
Field Marks 16″ Adt: gray and dark green above; sides of neck reddish brown; legs yellow to orange. Imm: duller; streaked dark brown and white on sides of neck and underparts.

AGAMI HERON [4] Garza Agami *Agamia agami*
Range Mex–SAm, exc ElSal. Res Mex (se.cAtl+sAtl, sPac), Blz, Guat (Atl). Very rare, local.
Habitat Swamps, swampy streams, sluggish rivers, ponds.
Field Marks 28″ Adt: rich reddish brown below; iridescent dark green above; bill very long and slender. Imm: duller and browner above; streaked brown and buffy below.

BLACK-CROWNED NIGHT-HERON [1] Pedrete Gris *Nycticorax nycticorax*
Range Can–SAm. Res/win Mex (res BajCal, ncPac, ncHi, Atl; win sPac, sHi, Yuc), Blz, Guat, ElSal.
Habitat Swamps, marshes, ponds, lagoons.
Field Marks 26″ Head large. Adt: back black; wings light gray; underparts white. Imm: brown above, with pale spots; heavily streaked brown and buff below.

YELLOW-CROWNED NIGHT-HERON [1] Pedrete Enmascarado *Nyctanassa violacea*
Range Can–SAm. Res Mex (BajCal, Pac, cHi, Atl, Yuc), Blz, Guat (Pac, Atl), ElSal. Rare, local.
Habitat Wooded lagoons, mangrove or freshwater swamps, marshes.
Field Marks 26″ Head large. Adt: medium to dark gray body and wings; back streaked; head black and white, with tawny to yellowish plumed crown. Imm: streaked and mottled; slightly paler, grayer, and has smaller spots than immature Black-crowned Night-Heron.

BOAT-BILLED HERON [4] Garza Cucharón *Cochlearius cochlearius*
Range Mex–SAm. Res Mex (s.nPac+csPac, s.nAtl+csAtl, Yuc), Blz, Guat (Pac, Atl), ElSal. Rare, local.
Habitat Active at night; mangrove swamps, wooded rivers, ponds, brackish lagoons.
Voice A guttural *cah-cah-co.*
Field Marks 20″ Bill very broad, inflated. Adt: plumage reddish brown below, with black sides; pale gray above, with black back patch. Imm: brownish to gray above and buffy or whitish below.

IBISES, SPOONBILLS—IBIS—THRESKIORNITHIDAE

WHITE IBIS [1] Ibis Blanco *Eudocimus albus*
Range US–SAm. Res Mex (BajCal, Pac, Atl, Yuc), Blz (cstl + cayes), Guat (Pac, Atl), ElSal.
Habitat Marshes, wet meadows, mangroves.
Field Marks 23″ Long legs and long decurved bill pinkish. Adt: white, with black wingtips. Imm: white below; brown above (may be mottled); head and neck streaked.

GLOSSY IBIS [1] Ibis Morito *Plegadis falcinellus*
Range US, Mex, Blz, CRic, SAm. Res/win Mex (res c.sAtl; win cstl Yuc), Blz (win cstl). Rare.
Habitat Marshes, lagoons, flooded fields.
Field Marks 20″ Iris dark brown at all ages. Sum adt: purplish brown with bronzy and greenish gloss; reddish or grayish legs; bright blue lores. Imm+ win adt: dark bronzy gray-green to gray-brown; head and neck paler, more brownish and streaked whitish. Juv: like winter adult, but head and neck not streaked.

WHITE-FACED IBIS [1] Atotola *Plegadis chihi*
Range Can–SAm, exc Blz, Nic, Pan. Res/win Mex (res w.nHi–cHi; win BajCal, Pac, ncHi, ncAtl+w.sAtl); win Guat (Pac, Atl), ElSal (cas). Local.
Habitat Marshes, wet meadows, mud flats.
Field Marks 20″ Like Glossy Ibis, but bright red eyes (except juvenile, which has brownish eyes like Glossy Ibis) and Sum adt: white face border and red lores.

ROSEATE SPOONBILL [1] Espátula *Ajaia ajaja*
Range US–SAm. Res/vis Mex (res cstl Pac, Atl, Yuc; vis ncHi), Blz, Guat (Pac, Atl), ElSal.
Habitat Ponds, borrow pits, marshes, swamps.
Field Marks 30″ Much shorter-necked and shorter-legged than a flamingo. Bill long, heavy, with broad, flat tip. Adt: mostly pink, red, and white, with yellowish bill. Imm: mostly white; legs and bill yellowish.

STORKS—CIGÜEÑAS—CICONIIDAE

JABIRU [4] Jabirú *Jabiru mycteria*
Range Mex–SAm. Res/vis Mex (res sAtl; cas vis se.cPac+sPac, cAtl, Yuc), res Blz, Guat (res nw Atl; vis Pac), ElSal (cas e). Rare, local.
Habitat Secluded portions of large marshes, swamps, or wet meadows.
Field Marks 52″ No black in wings. Bill long, very heavy, black. Adt: neck bare, black with red collar at base; plumage all white. Imm: duller, with some brownish feathers. See Wood Stork.

WOOD STORK [1] Cigüeña Americana *Mycteria americana*
Range US–SAm. Res/vis Mex (res Pac, Atl, Yuc; vis cHi; cas BajCal), Blz, Guat (Pac, Atl), ElSal. Irregular.
Habitat Marshes, swamps, lagoons, wet fields.
Field Marks 36″ Mostly white, but flight feathers and tail black; head and upper neck bare, black; long bill slightly down-curved.

VULTURES—ZOPILOTES—CATHARTIDAE

BLACK VULTURE [5] Zopilote Común *Coragyps atratus*
Range US–SAm. Res Mex (Pac, Hi, Atl, Yuc), Blz, Guat, ElSal.
Habitat Pastures, beaches, rooftops, garbage dumps.
Field Marks 24″ Soars with wings straight out, often flaps rapidly several times, then glides. Like Turkey Vulture and Savanna Vulture, but tail short; wingtips whitish below; head black.

TURKEY VULTURE [5] Aura Común *Cathartes aura*
Range Can–SAm. Res Mex, Blz, Guat, ElSal.
Habitat Roadsides, pastures, semideserts, over woodland.
Field Marks 29″ Soars with wings up at an angle, rocking, seldom flapping.

Head red; plumage black; tail longer than Black Vulture's; no white in wing. Imm: head pale to dark gray.

(LESSER YELLOW-HEADED) SAVANNA VULTURE [4] Aura Sabanera *Cathartes burrovianus*
Range Mex – SAm. Res Mex (se.cPac+sPac, csAtl, Yuc), Blz, Guat (Pac). Rare.
Habitat Large marshes, wet savannas.
Field Marks 26" Usually flies low, rocking, gliding. Like Turkey Vulture, but Adt: head yellowish with some red and blue; upper surface of wing appears paler near tip; legs appear whitish, *not* dull reddish. Imm: head dark with pale nape.

KING VULTURE [4, 5] Zopilote Rey *Sarcoramphus papa*
Range Mex – SAm. Res Mex (se.cPac+sPac, se.cAtl+sAtl, Yuc), Blz, Guat (Pac, Atl), ElSal (w). Rare, local.
Habitat Dense humid forest, secluded partial clearings; usually seen high overhead.
Field Marks 31" Tail very short; wings very broad. Adt: tail, wingtips, and broad trailing edge of wing black; rest of plumage white except gray collar; bare head and neck red, orange, and blue. Imm: like Black Vulture, but much larger; usually splotched with white on underwing and belly.

FLAMINGOS—FLAMENCOS—PHOENICOPTERIDAE

GREATER FLAMINGO [1] Flamenco Común *Phoenicopterus ruber*
Range Mex, Blz. Res/vis Mex (extreme e.sAtl, Yuc), Blz (acc cstl). Abundant to very rare. (Almost all flamingo reports outside Yuc, and many in Yuc, pertain to Roseate Spoonbills.)
Habitat Coastal lagoons, inlets, estuaries.
Field Marks 45" Wading, feeding with bill upside down. Pink, with redder wings, but flight feathers black; neck and pink legs extended in flight. Imm: mostly dull whitish to pale grayish, with some pink.

DUCKS, GEESE, SWANS—PATOS, ANSARES—ANATIDAE

FULVOUS WHISTLING-DUCK [2] Chiquiote *Dendrocygna bicolor*
Range US – SAm, exc Nic. Res/win Mex (res Pac, cHi, Atl; win nBajCal, Yuc), Blz (vis cstl), Guat (vis Pac?), ElSal. Rare.
Habitat Wet grassy fields, marshes, rice fields.
Voice A shrill, whistled *kuh-wee.*
Field Marks 21" Head and underparts mostly rich tawny brown, streaked on neck and flanks; back and wings blackish with large tawny scallops; uptacs form a white U on top of black tail.

BLACK-BELLIED WHISTLING-DUCK [2] Pijije *Dendrocygna autumnalis*
Range US – SAm. Res Mex (res Pac, Atl, Yuc; win cHi), Blz, Guat (Pac, Atl), ElSal.
Habitat Marshes, swampy ponds, lagoons.

Voice A whistled *pe-he-he-he.*
Field Marks 21″ Adt: reddish brown breast; black belly; red bill and legs; much of wing white. Imm: paler, duller, with grayish bill and legs; dark brown belly.

TUNDRA SWAN [2] Cisne Menor *Cygnus columbianus*
Range AK–Mex. Win Mex (BajCal, nHi, nAtl). Very rare.
Habitat Irrigated grain fields, large lakes, marshes.
Voice A melodious *whoo.*
Field Marks 52″ Very long neck. Adt: all-white (including flight feathers), except black bill and feet and (usually) small yellow base-of-bill spot. Imm: pale gray, lighter below; bill grayish pink, blackish tipped.

WHITE-FRONTED GOOSE [2] Ganso Manchado *Anser albifrons*
Range AK–Mex. Win Mex (BajCal, Pac, ncHi, Atl; cas/very rare csPac, sAtl), acc Blz.
Habitat Flooded fields, large marshes, lakes.
Field Marks 29″ Uptacs form a white U on top of black tail. Adt: dark gray, with patchy black belly bands and white at base of bill; legs and bill pinkish to orange. Imm: *no* white on face; *no* black belly bands.

SNOW GOOSE [2] Ganso Real *Chen caerulescens*
Range AK–Mex, Blz, ElSal, Hon. Win Mex (nBajCal, nPac, ncHi, ncAtl; cas/very rare farther se); cas/acc Blz, ElSal. Irregular.
Habitat Wet or dry fields, large marshes, lakes.
Field Marks 28″ Closed bill shows noticeable gap; wingtips broadly black. White morph adt: mostly white; pinkish legs and bill. White morph imm: pale gray above; bill and legs black. Dark morph adt: white head and upper neck; dark gray back and belly; pale bluish gray wing patch. Dark morph imm: like immature White-fronted Goose, but pale wing patch and black bill and legs.

ROSS'S GOOSE [2] Ganso de Ross *Chen rossii*
Range AK–Mex. Win Mex (nBajCal, nHi, nAtl?). Very rare.
Habitat Wet fields, marshes, lakes.
Field Marks 24″ White morph adt: like white morph Snow Goose, but bill short, does not show a gap when closed. Dark morph adt: like dark morph Snow Goose, but neck all dark.

BRANT [2] Ganso de Collar *Branta bernicla*
Range AK–Mex. Win Mex (w.BajCal, nPac; acc n Yuc).
Habitat Estuaries, lagoons, tidal marshes.
Field Marks 26″ Bill, head, neck, and breast black; small white pattern on neck (*not* in immature); untacs white; long white uptacs almost cover black tail.

CANADA GOOSE [2] Ganso Canadiense *Branta canadensis*
Range AK–Mex. Win Mex (BajCal, nPac, nHi, ncAtl; cas/acc cHi, csPac).
Habitat Marshes, lakes, lagoons, estuaries; often grazing in grassy fields.
Field Marks 24″, **38″** Black neck and head, except broad white strap under chin; uptacs form white U on top of black tail. Races differ greatly in size and in color of underparts (from pale grayish to dark brownish gray).

MUSCOVY DUCK [4] Pato Real *Cairina moschata*
Range Mex–SAm. Res Mex (s.nPac+csPac, c.nAtl+csAtl, Yuc), Blz, Guat (Pac, Atl), ElSal. Rare.
Habitat Large swamps, sluggish wooded rivers.
Field Marks 32″, 26″ Glossy black, except white patch under and on top of wing; bill pale gray (or pinkish gray) and black. Imm: *little or no* white on wing.

WOOD DUCK [2] Pato Arcoiris *Aix sponsa*
Range Can–Mex. Win Mex (nPac, ncHi, ncAtl, Yuc; acc sBajCal). Rare.
Habitat Lakes, ponds, swamps, marshes.
Field Marks 18″ Floppy nape crest. M: white and black face, glossed green and purple; neck and breast chestnut. F: streaked below; head gray with white teardrop-shaped eye patch.

GREEN-WINGED TEAL [3] Cerceta Común *Anas crecca*
Range AK–Hon. Win Mex (all); very rare/acc Blz, Guat (Pac?), ElSal.
Habitat Lakes, marshes, lagoons.
Field Marks 14″ M: dark reddish brown head, with very large green eye patch; spotted breast; gray sides. F: streaked and mottled; green speculum; *no* blue patch on wing.

MOTTLED DUCK Pato Tejano *Anas fulvigula*
Range US–Mex. Res/win Mex (res nAtl; win Atl).
Habitat Ponds, lakes, marshes, estuaries.
Field Marks 24″ M+F: like female Mallard, but darker; white speculum border on trailing edge only (or may be absent); tail brown.

MALLARD [2] Pato de Collar *Anas platyrhynchos*
(Does not include Mexican Duck; see below)
Range AK–Mex, Guat? Res/win Mex (res nBajCal; win BajCal, nPac, ncHi, nAtl), Guat (Pac)? Rare.
Habitat Ponds, lakes, marshes.
Field Marks 24″ Tail white. M: green head, white collar, yellow bill. F: mottled yellowish brown; bill mostly dark, with reddish to yellowish base and tip; speculum white-bordered on leading *and* trailing edge; lateral tail feathers mostly white.

MEXICAN DUCK Pato Mexicano *Anas diazi*
(The AOU lumps this with Mallard; see above)
Range US–Mex. Res/win Mex (res w.nHi+cHi; win e.nHi).
Habitat Pond or lake borders, marshes.
Field Marks 24″ M+F: like female Mallard, but darker; bill yellow to orange; *not much* white in tail.

NORTHERN PINTAIL [2] Pato Golondrino *Anas acuta*
Range AK–SAm. Win Mex, Blz, Guat (Pac, Atl), ElSal.
Habitat Lakes, flooded fields, marshes, estuaries.
Field Marks 28″ Long neck, long tail. M: brown head; neck mostly white. F: mottled.

BLUE-WINGED TEAL [3] Cerceta Aliazul *Anas discors*
Range AK–SAm. Win Mex, Blz, Guat (Pac, Atl), ElSal.
Habitat Lakes, marshes, lagoons.
Field Marks 16" Green speculum; large blue wing patch (may be almost hidden). M: head dark blue, with white crescent. F: mottled grayish brown. See female Cinnamon Teal.

CINNAMON TEAL [3] Cerceta Café *Anas cyanoptera*
Range AK–SAm, exc ElSal. Res/win Mex (res nBajCal, ncHi; win BajCal, Pac, Atl, Yuc), Blz (?), Guat (Pac).
Habitat Lakes, marshes, lagoons.
Field Marks 16" Green speculum; large blue wing patch. M: reddish brown head, neck, and underparts. F: almost identical to female Blue-winged Teal, but bill slightly broader and flatter near tip.

NORTHERN SHOVELER [2] Pato Cucharón *Anas clypeata*
Range AK–SAm. Win Mex (all, exc sHi), Blz, Guat (Pac), ElSal.
Habitat Ponds, lakes, marshes, estuaries.
Field Marks 18" Bill dark, heavy, very broad near tip; large blue wing patch. M: green head, white breast, reddish brown flanks. F: mottled yellowish brown. See female teals.

GADWALL [2] Pato Pinto *Anas strepera*
Range AK–Mex. Win Mex (all, exc Yuc?).
Habitat Ponds, lakes, marshes, estuaries.
Field Marks 20" Reddish brown wing patch; speculum white. M: breast and sides finely mottled gray; head brownish; untacs and uptacs black. F: mottled brown; paler head.

EURASIAN WIGEON Pato Silbón *Anas penelope*
Range AK–Mex. Win Mex (w.BajCal, nPac, n.nAtl). Very rare.
Habitat Lakes, marshes, lagoons.
Field Marks 20" Like American Wigeon, but gray axillaries, *not* white; M: head and upper neck rich reddish brown, with buffy forehead and crown; back and flanks grayer; F: usually more uniform rusty brown (or grayish brown) head and neck.

AMERICAN WIGEON [2] Pato Chalcuán *Anas americana*
Range AK–SAm. Win Mex (all, exc sHi), Blz, Guat (Pac), ElSal.
Habitat Lakes, marshes, lagoons, estuaries.
Field Marks 20" M: white wing patch and crown; green eye patch. F: wing patch whitish; head grayish, finely streaked; sides *not* heavily mottled; breast tinged dull reddish brown.

CANVASBACK [3] Pato Coacoxtle *Aythya valisineria*
Range AK–Mex, Guat, Hon. Win Mex (all, exc sHi, Yuc?), Guat (Pac). Rare.
Habitat Large lakes or coastal waters.
Field Marks 22" Forehead slopes into long, black, heavy-based bill. M: red of

head darker and browner, back and sides whiter, than Redhead's. F: head, back, and sides pale gray.

REDHEAD [3] Pato Cabecirrojo *Aythya americana*
Range AK–Mex, Guat. Res/win Mex (res cHi; win all, exc sHi, Yuc?), Guat (Pac). Rare.
Habitat Marshes, large lakes, estuaries.
Field Marks 21″ Bill short, with white bar near tip, does *not* slope into forehead. M: reddish brown head; black breast. F: mostly brownish, with some white on face. See Ring-necked Duck and Canvasback.

RING-NECKED DUCK [3] Pato Piquianillado *Aythya collaris*
Range AK–Pan, exc Blz. Win Mex (BajCal, Pac, ncHi, Atl, Yuc), Guat (Pac, Atl). Rare.
Habitat Lakes, lagoons, estuaries.
Field Marks 17″ White bar near tip of bill. M: back black. F: darker than Redhead; area around base of bill whitish, but *not* contrasty. See Lesser Scaup.

GREATER SCAUP [3] Pato Boludo *Aythya marila*
Range AK–Mex. Win cstl Mex (BajCal, nPac). Very rare.
Habitat Bays, lagoons, estuaries.
Field Marks 19″ Long white wing stripe shows in flight. See Lesser Scaup. M: head, neck, and breast black; green gloss on head. F: darker than Redhead; like Lesser Scaup, except wing stripe.

LESSER SCAUP [3] Pato Bola *Aythya affinis*
Range AK–SAm. Win Mex (all), Blz, Guat (Pac), ElSal.
Habitat Lakes, lagoons, bays, estuaries.
Field Marks 17″ Short white wing stripe shows in flight; no white bar on bill. M: usually purplish gloss on head; much paler on back (gray) than Ring-necked Duck (black). F: dark brown; contrasty white area around base of bill.

BLACK SCOTER [3] Negreta Negra *Melanitta nigra*
Range AK–Mex. Win cstl Mex (nw.nBajCal). Rare.
Habitat Off beaches, on bays, ocean.
Field Marks 19″ M: all black, except orange knob on bill. F: blackish brown; side of head below eye to upper neck contrasty pale grayish brown; black bill. Imm M: like female, but less contrasty; yellow bill knob.

SURF SCOTER [3] Negreta de Marejada *Melanitta perspicillata*
Range AK–Mex. Win Mex (BajCal, nPac; cas/acc? e.nHi+n.nAtl).
Habitat Usually open ocean or deep bays.
Field Marks 20″ M: black, with white patch on hindneck and on forecrown; bill red, white, and black. F: blackish brown, with black bill; whitish face patches.

WHITE-WINGED SCOTER [3] Negreta Aliblanca *Melanitta fusca*
Range AK–Mex. Win cstl Mex (n.nBajCal, nw.nPac). Rare.
Habitat Off beaches or headlands, in bays.

Field Marks 22″ White wing patch. M: black, with white eye patch; black-knobbed orange bill. F: blackish brown, with whitish face patches; bill dull.

COMMON GOLDENEYE [3] Ojiamarillo Común *Bucephala clangula*
Range AK–Mex. Win Mex (BajCal, nPac, nHi, nAtl).
Habitat Ocean bays, inlets, lakes.
Field Marks 21″ Head appears puffy, high-crowned; bill short, dark. M: white below, black and white above; head dark green; rounded white patch below eye. F: grayish above and below, with white collar; head all dark brown. See Bufflehead and Common Merganser.

BUFFLEHEAD [3] Pato Crestiblanco *Bucephala albeola*
Range AK–Mex. Win Mex (BajCal, nPac, ncHi, ncAtl; sAtl?, Yuc?).
Habitat Ocean bays, estuaries, deep lakes.
Field Marks 14″ Head appears puffy, high crowned. M: white below, black and white above; much of head behind eye white, the rest mostly glossy black. F: whitish below; brown back and head; white patch behind eye.

HOODED MERGANSER [3] Mergo de Caperuza *Lophodytes cucullatus*
Range AK–Mex. Win Mex (BajCal, nPac, ncHi, nAtl; cas/acc cAtl, Yuc). Very rare.
Habitat Lakes, ponds, lagoons.
Field Marks 18″ Slender black bill. M: black-and-white head-and-breast pattern; fan-shaped crest; tawny sides. F: brown head; small tawny crest. See Bufflehead.

COMMON MERGANSER [3] Mergo Común *Mergus merganser*
Range AK–Mex. Win Mex (BajCal, n.nPac, n.nHi, n.nAtl). Rare.
Habitat Coastal waters, deep ponds, large lakes.
Field Marks 25″ M: head black, green-glossed; lower neck, breast, and sides white; bill slender, red; large white wing patch. F: head and neck tawny (except white throat), in marked contrast to white breast; smaller white wing patch.

RED-BREASTED MERGANSER [3] Mergo Copetón *Mergus serrator*
Range AK–Mex. Win cstl Mex (BajCal, nPac, ncAtl, w Yuc). Rare.
Habitat Bays, estuaries, inlets, lakes.
Field Marks 23″ Like Common Merganser, but much shaggier crest; M: breast dull reddish brown with spotty blackish streaks; grayish sides and flanks; F: sides of neck and foreneck whitish, *not* in marked contrast to whitish breast and throat.

MASKED DUCK [3] Pato Enmascarado *Nomonyx dominica*
Range US–SAm, exc Blz, Nic. Res Mex (s.nPac+csPac, Atl, Yuc), Guat (Pac, Atl), ElSal. Very rare.
Habitat Ponds, lagoons, sluggish rivers.
Field Marks 14″ M: black and reddish head, neck, and breast pattern; back and wings mottled, reddish brown; bill blue. F+imm: crown brown; two dark stripes on whitish face.

RUDDY DUCK [3] Pato Tepalcate *Oxyura jamaicensis*
Range AK–Mex, Guat, ElSal, Hon, SAm. Res/win Mex (res BajCal, nPac+ n.cPac, ncHi; win Pac, Atl, w Yuc?), Guat (Pac), ElSal.
Habitat Lakes, lagoons, estuaries.
Field Marks 16″ Sum M: reddish brown, with black-and-white head; blue bill. Win M: grayish brown; head dark brown and white, less contrasty; bill dull bluish gray. F: grayish brown above, much paler below; one dark stripe on whitish face.

OSPREYS—GAVILANES PESCADORES—PANDIONIDAE

OSPREY [6] Gavilán Pescador *Pandion haliaetus*
Range AK–SAm. Res/win Mex (res BajCal, nPac, e Yuc; win cSPac, Atl, Yuc; tr Hi), Blz; tr/win Guat (Pac, Atl), ElSal.
Habitat Over lakes, ponds, marshes, swamps, lagoons, bays, or on poles or in treetops near water.
Field Marks 23″ Blackish above, white below; long wings angled at wrist (which has a blackish patch); head whitish, with broad black line through eye (Yuc birds *lack* this black line).

HAWKS, EAGLES, KITES—GAVILANES—ACCIPITRIDAE

GRAY-HEADED KITE [4] Milano Cabecigris *Leptodon cayanensis*
Range Mex–SAm. Res Mex (sPac, csAtl, Yuc), Blz, Guat (Pac, Atl), ElSal. Rare.
Habitat Swamps, near lakes or marsh borders.
Field Marks 18″ Adt: blackish above, white below; gray head; two or three pale tail bars. Imm: white face and underparts; blackish crown, back, and wings; *or* head black, underparts streaked.

HOOK-BILLED KITE [4] Milano Pintado *Chondrohierax uncinatus*
Range US–SAm. Res Mex (s.nPac+csPac, cHi, Atl, Yuc), Blz, Guat (Pac, Atl), ElSal. Rare.
Habitat Forests, patchy low woods or scattered trees, borders, river borders, often near water.
Field Marks 16″ Spread wings narrow near body, broad near rounded tips; bill strongly hooked; two white to pale gray tail bars, basal bar sometimes hidden; eyes white to pale gray. Light morph M: medium to dark gray above; barred gray and whitish below; see Gray Hawk. Light morph F: blackish above; barred rufous and whitish below. Light morph imm: black and dark reddish brown above; usually whitish with some dark bars below, but may be clear white below; broad whitish collar in either case. Black morph: black, except white tail bars.

SWALLOW-TAILED KITE [7] Milano Tijereta *Elanoides forficatus*
Range US–SAm. Sum/tr Mex (sum sAtl; tr sPac, Atl, Yuc); sum Blz, Guat (Atl), ElSal (acc). Rare.
Habitat Swamps, marshes, humid forest.

Field Marks 24″ May maneuver overhead in small flocks, with long, sweeping glides, occasional strong wingbeats, catching aerial insects in its feet. Adt: glossy black, except white head, underparts, and underwing coverts; deeply forked tail. Imm: spotted or streaked.

WHITE-TAILED KITE [7] Milano Coliblanco *Elanus leucurus*
Range US–SAm. Res Mex (BajCal, Pac, ncHi, Atl, Yuc), Blz, Guat (Pac, Atl), ElSal.
Habitat Moist open country with scattered trees, tree-dotted pastures, marshes.
Field Marks 16″ Often hovers while hunting. Tail appears virtually all white. Adt: mostly white head and underparts; pearl gray above, with black wrist patch; eyes red. Imm: mottled brown back; dark wings; washed buffy below and on head, with faint dark streaks.

(SNAIL) EVERGLADE KITE [7] Milano Caracolero *Rostrhamus sociabilis*
Range US–SAm. Res Mex (c?sPac, csAtl, Yuc), Blz, Guat (Pac, Atl), ElSal (cas e). Local, irregular.
Habitat Large freshwater or brackish marshes.
Field Marks 18″ Bill very strongly hooked. Adt M: black, with white untacs, uptacs, tail base, and tail tip; legs red. F+Imm: mottled and streaked dark brown and white.

DOUBLE-TOOTHED KITE [4] Gavilán Bidentado *Harpagus bidentatus*
Range Mex–SAm. Res Mex (csPac, se.cAtl+sAtl, e Yuc), Blz, Guat (Atl), ElSal (cas e). Rare.
Habitat Humid forest, partial clearings.
Field Marks 13″ Dark streak down center of white throat. Adt: dark slaty gray above; whitish below with rufous bars; chest and sides nearly plain rufous; three narrow white bars on black tail. Imm: blackish brown above; whitish below, with heavy black streaks.

MISSISSIPPI KITE [6] Milano Migratorio *Ictinia mississippiensis*
Range US–SAm (exc Blz?). Tr Mex (sPac, Atl, Yuc), Guat (Pac?, Atl), ElSal (acc).
Habitat Open country, borders.
Field Marks 14″ Buoyant flight, much tail motion. Adt: dark gray above, pearly gray below; whitish head, unbarred black tail; slender, pointed dark wings. Imm: dark gray above; underparts and head whitish, streaked with dark brown; tail dark with several pale gray bars. See Plumbeous Kite.

PLUMBEOUS KITE [4] Milano Plomizo *Ictinia plumbea*
Range Mex–SAm. Sum Mex (se.cPac+sPac, s.nAtl+csAtl, e Yuc), Blz, Guat (Pac, Atl), ElSal.
Habitat Treetops in river-border woods, swamps, borders, partial clearings.
Field Marks 15″ Buoyant flight, with much tail motion. Adt+imm: like Mississippi Kite, but two broad whitish bars on black tail.

BALD EAGLE Águila Cabeciblanca *Haliaeetus leucocephalus*
Range AK–Mex. Res/win Mex (res sBajCal, n.nPac; win nPac, nHi, nAtl). Rare.
Habitat Scattered trees in coastal areas, bay shores, lagoons, estuaries, or along wooded shores of inland lakes.

Field Marks 33″ Adt: blackish brown except white head and white tail. Imm: blackish brown; dull white tail base; dull whitish mottling under wings. See Golden Eagle.

BLACK-COLLARED HAWK [5] Aguililla Canela *Busarellus nigricollis*
Range Mex–SAm. Res Mex (s.nPac+csPac, se.cAtl+sAtl, Yuc), Blz, Guat (Pac, Atl), ElSal. Rare.
Habitat Swamps, marshes, lagoons, swampy river-edge woods, secluded ponds.
Field Marks 19″ Reddish brown; very short-tailed and broad-winged. Adt: head mostly whitish; chest patch (partial collar) black; tips (broadly) and trailing edge of wings and broad tail tip black. Imm: barred and streaked dark brown, paler below, but head mostly white with scattered blackish streaks; trace of partial collar.

NORTHERN HARRIER [6] Gavilán Ratonero *Circus cyaneus*
Range AK–SAm. Res/win Mex (res n.nBajCal; win all), Blz, Guat, ElSal.
Habitat Tall-grass fields, large marshes, open grassy plains.
Field Marks 19″ Flapping and gliding irregularly close to the ground. Conspicuous white rump patch; long, barred tail; long wings. M: medium gray above; whitish below. F+imm: dark brown above; more cinnamon (and streaked) below.

SHARP-SHINNED HAWK [6] Gavilán Coludo *Accipiter striatus*
(Does not include White-breasted Hawk; see below)
Range AK–Pan. Res/win Mex (res ncHi; win all); win Blz, Guat, ElSal.
Habitat Mountain forest, borders, or hedgerows.
Field Marks 12″ Long, barred, square-tipped tail; rounded wings. Adt: dark gray above; narrow reddish bars below. Imm: dark grayish brown above; heavily streaked below. See Cooper's Hawk.

WHITE-BREASTED HAWK [5] Gavilán Pechiblanco *Accipiter chionogaster*
(The AOU lumps this with Sharp-shinned Hawk; see above)
Range Mex, Guat, ElSal, Hon, Nic. Res Mex (sPac, sHi), Guat (Hi), ElSal (n). Rare.
Habitat Cloud forest or other dense humid forest, or partial clearings; flying rapidly among the trees or perched in middle branches.
Field Marks 13″ Adt: blackish gray above, white below. Imm: a few fine black streaks on white breast.

COOPER'S HAWK [6] Gavilán de Cooper *Accipiter cooperii*
Range Can–CRic. Res/win Mex (res nBajCal, nPac, ncHi; win all exc Yuc); win Blz, Guat, ElSal. Rare.
Habitat Dense to open woods, scattered trees, woodland borders.
Field Marks 17″ Flies low (in forest) or overhead (in open). Like Sharp-shinned Hawk, but larger; tail rounded at tip.

BICOLORED HAWK [4] Gavilán Bicolor *Accipiter bicolor*
Range Mex–SAm, exc ElSal. Res Mex (s.nAtl+csAtl, e Yuc), Blz, Guat (Pac?, Atl). Rare.
Habitat Dense humid forest and small openings.

Field Marks 15" *Not* streaked in any plumage. Adt: dark gray above, pale gray below; reddish brown thighs; narrow whitish bars on blackish tail. Imm: dark grayish brown; collar and underparts buff.

NORTHERN GOSHAWK [6] Gavilán Azor *Accipiter gentilis*
Range AK–Mex. Res Mex (w.ncHi, cPac). Very rare.
Habitat Secluded high mountain forest, small openings, partial clearings.
Field Marks 22" Long, barred tail. Adt: medium bluish gray above; finely barred pale gray below; white line over eye; black patch behind eye. Imm: whitish line over eye; mottled dark brown above; whitish below, streaked and spotted blackish. See Gray Hawk.

CRANE HAWK [5] Aguililla Zancona *Geranospiza caerulescens*
Range Mex–SAm. Res Mex (c.nPac+csPac, c.nAtl+csAtl, Yuc), Blz, Guat (Pac, Atl), ElSal. Rare.
Habitat Swamps, forest, and borders, usually near water.
Field Marks 19" Crescent of large white spots under wing near tip. Adt: black; two broad white bars on long tail; legs long, orange-red. Imm: blackish, with white streaks on head; buffy bars on belly and flanks; whitish tail base.

WHITE HAWK [5] Aguililla Blanca *Leucopternis albicollis*
Range Mex–SAm. Res Mex (sPac, se.cAtl+s.sAtl), Blz (s), Guat (Pac, Atl), ElSal (w). Rare.
Habitat Dense forest, partial clearings, openings.
Field Marks 22" Adt (in Mexico): plumage all white, except black wingtip and narrow tail bar. Imm (and adults southeast of Mexico): more black on wing (wingtips, secondaries, and coverts mostly black); broad black tail bar.

COMMON BLACK-HAWK [5, 7] Aguililla Cangrejera *Buteogallus anthracinus*
Range US–SAm. Res/sum Mex (res c.nPac+csPac, c.nAtl+csAtl, Yuc; sum w.ncHi), Blz, Guat (Pac, Atl), ElSal.
Habitat Swamps, wooded riverbanks, tree-dotted fields, forest borders, partial clearings.
Field Marks 21" Adt: blackish; broad white tail bar and very narrow white tail tip; underwing may be heavily barred or show whitish wrist patch. Imm: heavily streaked dark brown, whitish, and tawny; may show dark mustache mark; several narrow gray tail bars.

MANGROVE BLACK-HAWK Aguililla Manglera *Buteogallus subtilis*
(May be part of Common Black-Hawk, above)
Range Mex–SAm, exc Blz. Res Mex (sPac), Guat (Pac), ElSal. Rare.
Habitat Mangrove swamps and coastal lagoons.
Field Marks 19" Like Common Black-Hawk, but averages smaller and frequents different type of habitat.

GREAT BLACK-HAWK [5] Aguililla Negra *Buteogallus urubitinga*
Range Mex–SAm. Res Mex (c.nPac+csPac, c.nAtl+csAtl, Yuc), Blz, Guat (Pac, Atl), ElSal.
Habitat Forest borders, wooded riverbanks, tall hedgerows.

Field Marks 24″ Like Common Black-Hawk, but larger; slightly longer-tailed and longer-legged; flight appears more labored; tail pattern differs (in adult). Adt: uptacs, narrow bar near tail base, broad bar farther out, and very narrow tail tip white; may appear to have one white tail bar and white rump patch.

HARRIS'S HAWK [7] Aguililla Cinchada *Parabuteo unicinctus*
Range US–SAm, exc Blz, Hon. Res Mex (BajCal, Pac, ncHi, nAtl), Guat (Pac), ElSal. Rare.
Habitat Dry or semidesert areas.
Field Marks 22″ In tops of low trees or large shrubs or flying rather low. Adt: black, with broadly rufous wrist patch and thighs; white untacs, uptacs, tail base, and tail tip. Imm: dark rich brown, and some tawny brown, above; heavily streaked below; reddish wrist patch and thighs; tail narrowly barred, white at base.

SOLITARY EAGLE [5] Águila Solitaria *Harpyhaliaetus solitarius*
Range Mex–SAm, exc Blz, ElSal, Nic. Res Mex (Pac, ncHi, csAtl), Guat (Hi?, Atl?). Very rare/casual.
Habitat Wooded foothills, midmountain slopes.
Field Marks 27″ Soars high overhead. Short tail; very broad wings. Adt: black; broad tail bar and very narrow tail tip whitish (band at base of tail hidden); uptacs finely scaled with whitish. Imm: like Common Black-Hawk, but much larger; blackish brown thighs and side-chest patches.

GRAY HAWK [7] Gavilán Gris *Asturina nitida*
Range US–SAm. Res Mex (Pac, csHi, Atl, Yuc), Blz, Guat (Pac, Atl), ElSal.
Habitat Open woods, partial clearings, riverbanks, borders.
Field Marks 17″ Adt: medium gray above; narrowly barred pale gray below; white tail bars. Imm: streaked below; *lacks* belly bars and large dark breast patch of adult Roadside Hawk.

ROADSIDE HAWK [5] Gavilán Caminera *Buteo magnirostris*
Range Mex–SAm. Res Mex (csPac, Atl, Yuc), Blz, Guat (Pac, Atl), ElSal.
Habitat Partial clearings, hedgerows, open woods, or borders; often perches on open branches, fence posts, or utility poles along highways.
Field Marks 16″ Several tail bars. Adt: gray or grayish brown above; broad grayish brown breast streaks, may form breast patch; belly barred. Imm: streaked breast, barred belly.

RED-SHOULDERED HAWK [6] Gavilán Ranero *Buteo lineatus*
Range Can–Mex. Res/win Mex (res BajCal, nAtl; win ncHi, nAtl+n.cAtl).
Habitat Tree-dotted pastures, woods, hedgerows, swamps; on low branches, utility poles, posts.
Field Marks 20″ Adt: mottled dark and white above; narrow reddish bars below; chestnut wrist patch; narrow white tail bars (two or three visible) on dark gray. Imm: browner and more heavily streaked below than Broad-winged Hawk, and whitish tail bars are narrower, fainter, and more numerous; also usually a trace of adult's wrist patch.

BROAD-WINGED HAWK [6] Gavilán Aludo *Buteo platypterus*
Range Can–SAm. Tr/win Mex (tr sPac, e.ncHi+sHi, ncAtl; win sBajCal, cSpac, sAtl), Blz (s), Guat, ElSal. Abundant tr, very rare and irregular win.
Habitat Woodlands but in Mex, Blz, Guat, and ElSal usually seen in flocks overhead.
Field Marks 17" Adt: dark grayish brown above, barred reddish below; broad white tail bars (one or two visible) on blackish tail. Imm: streaked above and below; narrow tail bands. See Red-shouldered Hawk.

SHORT-TAILED HAWK [7] Gavilán Colicorto *Buteo brachyurus*
Range US–SAm. Res Mex (Pac, e+w.nHi+s.cHi+sHi, Atl, Yuc), Blz, Guat, ElSal. Rare.
Habitat Scattered trees, forest borders, scrubby woods.
Field Marks 16" Soars overhead, hovers in updrafts. Several narrow whitish tail bands. Dark morph adt: black, except whitish tail bands. Light morph adt: throat and underparts white; sharp contrast with blackish sides of head and upperparts. Imm: blackish gray above; streaked or mottled buff and blackish brown below.

SWAINSON'S HAWK [7] Gavilán Chapulinero *Buteo swainsoni*
Range AK–SAm. Sum/win Mex (sum nPac, n.nHi; tr/win Pac, Hi, ncAtl); tr Blz, Guat (Pac), ElSal.
Habitat Dry sparsely wooded terrain, among or over scattered trees, open woods, tall hedgerows
Field Marks 21" Often migrating in flocks. Tail has several narrow dark bands and broader subterminal band. Dark morph adt: mostly dark brown to blackish brown, with barred untacs. Light morph adt: dark brown above; whitish below except dark brown chest band contrasting with whitish throat. Light morph imm: brown above; heavy streaks on buff below; patchy dark brown chest band.

WHITE-TAILED HAWK [7] Gavilán Coliblanco *Buteo albicaudatus*
Range US–SAm. Res Mex (Pac, Hi, nsAtl, Yuc), Blz (n), Guat (Pac, Hi), ElSal. Rare, irregular.
Habitat Partly wooded mountain slopes, open dry grassy plains, extensive scrubby woods, borders.
Field Marks 23" Adt: white below, gray above, with reddish wrist patch; dark tail bar. Imm: splotchy dark streaks on white below, blackish above; tail faintly, narrowly barred.

ZONE-TAILED HAWK [7] Gavilán Aura *Buteo albonotatus*
Range US–SAm, exc Blz?, ElSal? Res/win Mex (res nBajCal, nPac; sum ncHi; win BajCal, Pac, sHi, Atl, Yuc); win Blz?, Guat, ElSal?. Rare.
Habitat Tree-dotted shrubby fields, scrubby woods, borders, dry slopes.
Field Marks 21" In flight resembles Turkey Vulture, but has large *feathered* head; Adt: white tail bars (one or two below, two or three above); Imm: several whitish tail bars; breast speckled white on black.

RED-TAILED HAWK [6] Gavilán Colirrufa *Buteo jamaicensis*
Range AK–Pan. Res/win Mex (res BajCal, Pac, Hi, nAtl; win csAtl, Yuc); res Blz (cas? mt pine), Guat (Hi), ElSal.
Habitat Grassy plains, forests, woodlands, open brushy country, borders.
Field Marks 23″ Tail of typical adult is mostly rufous above with narrow black band near tip, then very narrow white band at tip; others may be whitish or grayish basally with more or less pale rufous toward tip. Typical light morph adt: dark above, white below, with patchy belly band; rufous tail. Typical light morph imm: streaked below (less on upper belly); narrow black tail bars on gray. Typical dark morph adt: mostly blackish brown; paler underwing; rufous tail.

FERRUGINOUS HAWK [6] Gavilán Real *Buteo regalis*
Range AK–Mex. Win Mex (BajCal, nPac, ncHi). Rare.
Habitat Open country, scrub woods, brushy plains.
Field Marks 23″ Flight feathers white below. Light morph adt: thighs, back, and large wing patch mottled reddish brown; uptacs, untacs, and tail base whitish; tail tip broadly pale grayish brown. Dark morph adt: mostly very dark brown, including underwing coverts; tail grayish above, white below. Imm: brown above, buff below; tail mottled near tip.

ROUGH-LEGGED HAWK [6] Gavilán Ártica *Buteo lagopus*
Range AK–Mex. Win Mex (nBajCal, n.nHi). Rare.
Habitat Open areas, open brushy plains.
Field Marks 22″ Broad dark subterminal tail band; basally tail mostly white (female) or barred gray and white (male); flight feathers mostly white with black tips, as seen from below; tarsi feathered. Light morph: heavily streaked head, back, and breast; black belly and flanks. Dark morph: head, back, underparts, and underwing coverts blackish brown.

GOLDEN EAGLE [6] Águila Real *Aquila chrysaetos*
Range AK–Mex. Res/win Mex (res nBajCal, ncHi; win sBajCal, nPac). Rare.
Habitat Dry mountain slopes, open woods and brushland.
Field Marks 34″ Wings long, tail rather short; tarsi feathered. Adt: dark brown with tawny crown and nape; faint grayish tail bars. Imm: rather contrasty white patch at base of inner primaries below; tail white basally, broadly black-tipped.

CRESTED EAGLE Águila Monera *Morphnus guianensis*
Range Blz–SAm, exc ElSal. Res Blz, Guat (Atl). Very rare.
Habitat Humid forest canopy.
Field Marks 30″ Like Harpy Eagle, but smaller, with single-pointed crest; Dark morph adt: blackish chest; much darker head and much heavier, darker barring below; Light morph adt: pale head and faint barring below; much paler chest; Imm: slightly more heavily barred below.

HARPY EAGLE [4] Águila Harpía *Harpia harpyja*
Range Mex–SAm, exc ElSal. Res Mex (sAtl), Blz, Guat (Atl). Very rare.
Habitat Secluded dense humid forest.

Field Marks 38″ Very large; very broad wings; powerful legs; rather long tail. Adt: ragged split crest; hindneck, upperparts, and broad breast band black; mostly white below; head mostly gray; heavy bill black; tail broadly barred black and pale gray. Imm: pale gray above, may be mottled; whitish below; crest dark and white; one broad black tail band. Birds acquire adult plumage in stages over several years.

BLACK-AND-WHITE HAWK-EAGLE [5] Aguililla Ventriblanca *Spizastur melanoleucus*
Range Mex–SAm, exc ElSal. Res Mex (sPac, csAtl, e Yuc), Blz, Guat (Pac, Atl). Very rare.
Habitat In or near dense humid forest.
Field Marks 24″ Tail long, barred. Adt: underparts, head, and hindneck clear white, with short black crest; upperparts black. Imm: dark brown above, white below; white wing bars.

BLACK HAWK-EAGLE [5] Aguililla Tirana *Spizaetus tyrannus*
Range Mex–SAm. Res Mex (csPac, csAtl, e Yuc), Blz, Guat (Pac, Atl), ElSal (w). Very rare.
Habitat Canopy in humid forest.
Field Marks 27″ Tail long, broadly barred. Adt: mostly black; narrow white bars on thighs and untacs; speckles and bars on lower belly; white crest streaks may be hidden. Imm: dark brown above; white below with black-barred thighs, belly, and untacs; may have faint streaks on breast; head mostly white, with some black streaks or patches.

ORNATE HAWK-EAGLE [5] Aguililla Elegante *Spizaetus ornatus*
Range Mex–SAm. Res Mex (csPac, s.nAtl+csAtl, e Yuc), Blz, Guat (Pac, Atl), ElSal. Rare.
Habitat Dense humid forest.
Field Marks 25″ Tail rather long, broadly barred black and pale gray. Adt: long black crest and (faintly barred) upperparts; rufous nape, sides of face and neck, and broad (usually partial) breast band; white throat, black-bordered; underparts heavily black-and-white barred. Imm: varies with age—mostly white below and on head and neck; sides, flanks, and thighs black-barred; usually faintly scalloped blackish brown above, with some black or brown in crest.

FALCONS—HALCONES—FALCONIDAE

CRESTED CARACARA [7] Caracara Común *Caracara plancus*
Range US–SAm. Res Mex (sBajCal, Pac, c.nHi+csHi, Atl, w Yuc), Blz (cas/acc n?), Guat (Pac, Atl?), ElSal.
Habitat Scrub woods, borders, roadsides.
Field Marks 23″ Often walks through farm fields, eats carrion. Long-legged. Adt: mostly blackish or dark brown, but throat, collar, untacs, tail base, and wing patch white. Imm: like adult, but browner; streaked below.

BARRED (FOREST-FALCON) MICRASTUR [5] Guaquillo Selvático *Micrastur ruficollis*
Range Mex–SAm. Res Mex (s.cPac+sPac, sHi, csAtl), Blz, Guat (Atl), ElSal. Very rare.
Habitat Dense humid forest or borders, midlevel.
Field Marks 14″ Four narrow pale bars on long, rounded tail. Adt: dark gray or brownish gray head, throat, and upperparts; narrow whitish and blackish bars below. Imm: dark brown or blackish above; may have whitish collar; buff below, more or less brown-barred, except white throat.

COLLARED (FOREST-FALCON) MICRASTUR [5] Guaquillo Collarejo *Micrastur semitorquatus*
Range Mex–SAm. Res Mex (s.nPac+csPac, s.nAtl+csAtl, Yuc), Blz, Guat (Pac, Atl), ElSal. Rare.
Habitat Open woods, swamps, forest borders, or partially open country.
Voice Loud and repeated single notes, *ow* or *wow*.
Field Marks 24″ Blackish above; tail long, black with several whitish bars. Light morph adt: underparts and collar white. Light morph imm: buffy below; more or less barred with dark brown. Buff morph adt: underparts and collar buffy or pale tawny brown. Dark morph adt: underparts and collar mostly blackish, like upperparts; belly may be barred whitish. Dark morph imm: like dark morph adult, but brown, *not* blackish, and belly and untacs barred light brown.

LAUGHING FALCON [5] Halcón Guaco *Herpetotheres cachinnans*
Range Mex–SAm. Res Mex (s.nPac+csPac, s.nAtl+csAtl, Yuc), Blz, Guat (Pac, Atl), ElSal.
Habitat Scrub forest, tree-dotted brushy fields; often perches on utility poles or open branches.
Voice Musical *ah* or *ha* notes, or series of notes like a human laugh.
Field Marks 22″ Crown, full collar, and underparts creamy buff; blackish brown face patch extends across nape; upperparts very dark brown; tail rather long, barred whitish or buffy and black.

AMERICAN KESTREL [6] Cernícalo Americano *Falco sparverius*
Range AK–SAm. Res/win Mex (res BajCal, nPac, Hi; win all), Blz (win), Guat (res Hi, win all), ElSal.
Habitat Rather dry open areas, tree-dotted fields, tall hedgerows, utility poles or wires.
Field Marks 11″ Tail (barred in female; plain with black bar near tip in male), rump, and barred back reddish brown; two black lines down side of face; whitish or buffy below, spotted (male) or streaked (female); wings bluish (male) or rufous barred with black (female).

MERLIN [6] Halcón Esmerejón *Falco columbarius*
Range AK–SAm. Win Mex, Blz, Guat, ElSal. Rare.
Habitat Large open areas, scattered trees, woodland borders.

Field Marks 12″ Streaked below. M: bluish gray above; tail barred black and gray. F+imm: brown above; tail dark brown and gray. See American Kestrel.

APLOMADO FALCON [7] Halcón Fajado *Falco femoralis*
Range Mex, Blz, Guat?, Nic, Pan, SAm. Res Mex (nw.nHi, csAtl), Blz, Guat (Pac?). Very rare.
Habitat Partial clearings, openings, forest borders, tree-dotted grassy fields.
Field Marks 16″ Flies rapidly, sometimes erratically. Adt: gray above; tail black with several fine white bars; pale line over black line behind eye; throat and breast white; sides and flanks broadly black, with white scaly marks; belly, thighs, and untacs tawny buff. Imm: like adult, but duller, browner; throat and breast buffy, streaked with blackish.

BAT FALCON [5] Halcón Enano *Falco rufigularis*
Range Mex–SAm. Res Mex (Pac, Atl, Yuc), Blz, Guat (Pac, Atl), ElSal.
Habitat Humid forest borders, partial clearings, tree-dotted pastures, dead treetops.
Field Marks 10″ Adt: black, with white throat; white bars on breast, sides, and tail; plain rufous belly, thighs, and untacs. Imm: duller, browner; unbarred dark brown breast and belly.

ORANGE-BREASTED FALCON [5] Halcón Pechirrufo *Falco deiroleucus*
Range Mex–SAm, exc ElSal. Res Mex (se.cAtl+s.sAtl), Blz, Guat (Pac, Atl). Very rare.
Habitat Humid forest canopy, small openings, secluded borders, partial clearings.
Field Marks 14″ Adt: Like Bat Falcon, but chest rufous; untacs barred with black. Imm: paler; blackish brown and buff; thighs heavily scaled or spotted.

PRAIRIE FALCON [6] Halcón Pálido *Falco mexicanus*
Range Can–Mex. Res/win Mex (BajCal, n.nPac, ncHi, w.nAtl). Rare.
Habitat Open, arid, or semiarid country; hilly, rocky, brushy areas; cliffs; dry, grassy tree-dotted plains.
Field Marks 18″ Mottled medium buffy brown above; heavy streaks below; not very contrasty tail bars; black line down from eye; dark hind border of ear patch. Imm: like immature Peregrine Falcon, but much paler; not so heavily streaked below; face lines more delicate.

PEREGRINE FALCON [6] Halcón Peregrino *Falco peregrinus*
Range AK–SAm. Res/win Mex (res BajCal, ncPac, ncHi, nAtl?; win all); win Blz, Guat, ElSal. Very rare.
Habitat Secluded cliffs or ledges, rocky canyons, and (especially winter) open country, coastal areas.
Field Marks 19″ Dark bluish gray above; black crown with broad black ear wedge down side of face; spotted and barred below, except whitish throat and breast; tail barred. Imm: like adult, but dark brown; heavily streaked below. See Prairie Falcon.

GUANS, CHACHALACAS—CHACHALACAS—CRACIDAE

PLAIN CHACHALACA Chachalaca Común *Ortalis vetula*
Range US–CRic, exc ElSal. Res Mex (sPac, Atl, Yuc), Blz, Guat (Atl).
Habitat Thickets, hedgerows, borders, or scrubby woods.
Voice A loud raucous chorus of *cha-cha-lac.*
Field Marks 24″ Often in groups. Brownish olive above; paler and buffier below; untacs pale dull tawny; tail long and (somewhat iridescent) blackish olive with whitish or buffy tip; head small, grayish.

RUFOUS-BELLIED CHACHALACA [8] Chachalaca Occidental *Ortalis wagleri*
Range Mex. Res Mex (nPac, w.nHi).
Habitat Overgrown clearings, brushy thorny woods, thickets, hedgerows.
Voice Four notes in a raucous chorus, *cha-cha-la-ca.*
Field Marks 24″ Like Plain Chachalaca, but belly, untacs, and tail tip rufous.

WEST MEXICAN CHACHALACA Chachalaca Pacífica *Ortalis poliocephala*
Range Mex. Res Mex (cPac+w.sPac, cHi).
Habitat Hedgerows, overgrown brushy fields, dense woodland borders, thickets.
Field Marks 24″ Dark grayish olive above; tail darker with greenish gloss; head gray; chest grayish brown, shading to whitish on belly; untacs pale reddish brown; tail tip buffy.

WHITE-BELLIED CHACHALACA [45] Chachalaca Ventriblanca *Ortalis leucogastra*
Range Mex–Nic, exc Blz. Res Mex (sPac), Guat (Pac), ElSal.
Habitat Brushy overgrown fields or clearings, borders, hedgerows, thickets.
Voice Four notes, *not* three, in a raucous chorus, *cha-cha-la-ca.*
Field Marks 24″ Like Plain Chachalaca, but somewhat browner overall; more contrasty grayish brown and white below, with white belly and untacs; tail-feather tips broadly white.

HIGHLAND GUAN [8] Pajuil *Penelopina nigra*
Range Mex–Nic, exc Blz. Res Mex (sPac, sHi, sAtl), Guat (Pac, Hi), ElSal (w). Rare.
Habitat Cloud forest or other humid forest; usually among lower branches.
Voice A high-pitched whistle.
Field Marks 24″ M: glossy black, with red legs and throat (bare skin). F: rich brown with many narrow black bars above and below.

CRESTED GUAN [8] Pava Cojolita *Penelope purpurascens*
Range Mex–SAm. Res Mex (s.nPac+csPac + adj Hi, s.nAtl+csAtl + adj Hi, e Yuc), Blz, Guat (Pac, Atl), ElSal (w). Rare.
Habitat Cloud forest or other dense, usually humid forest; high branches or canopy.
Field Marks 35″ Very large; blackish all over, somewhat glossy; long, rounded tail; bill and legs dark, but throat reddish (bare skin); faint whitish streaks on breast.

HORNED GUAN [8] Pavón Cornudo *Oreophasis derbianus*
Range Mex, Guat. Res Mex (s.sHi), Guat (Hi). Very rare.
Habitat On the ground in small openings or small partial clearings in cloud forest, or on higher branches in secluded portions of humid forest.
Field Marks 35" Mostly black plumage, but white breast (with very narrow black streaks) and bar on tail; red legs; red vertical "horn" projects from crown.

GREAT CURASSOW [8] Hocofaisán *Crax rubra*
Range Mex–SAm. Res Mex (sPac, s.nAtl+csAtl, e Yuc), Blz, Guat (Pac, Atl), ElSal (w). Rare.
Habitat Secluded dense humid forest; usually middle to upper branches.
Field Marks 36" M: mostly black, with curly black crest; yellow knob at base of bill; white belly and untacs. F: females vary greatly and have been placed in two or three morphs, with variants within each morph. All variants have the distinctive curly, more or less black-and-white crest, unlike any other comparable species in our area. Some variants are: blackish brown or rich reddish brown above; rufous to pale reddish brown below; head, upper neck, and curly crest spotted black and white; tail broadly barred. Other variants are: mostly barred black, brown, and white, except pale reddish brown belly and untacs; more white in crest. Imm: much like adult. Juv: much like adult female.

TURKEYS—GUAJOLOTES—PHASIANIDAE

WILD TURKEY Guajolote Norteño *Meleagris gallopavo*
Range US–Mex. Res Mex (e.nPac, w+e.nHi, w.nAtl?). Very rare.
Habitat Open pine or pine-oak woods, scrubby brushy areas, secluded borders, openings, clearings.
Field Marks 48", 34" Like Ocellated Turkey, but tail feathers bronzy, tipped buff or white; may have beard; bluish (*not* bright blue) head with red warts and wattles, including throat wattles; *no* blue subterminal spot on feathers of rump, uptacs, and tail; *not* as much white on secondaries.

OCELLATED TURKEY [8] Guajolote Ocelado *Meleagris ocellata*
Range Mex, Blz, Guat. Res Mex (sAtl, Yuc), Blz (n), Guat (nw Atl). Rare.
Habitat In or near dense forest or scrubby woods, secluded small openings, partial clearings, borders.
Field Marks 46", 32" Mostly blackish brown, with green, purple, and bronze reflections; bronzy rufous greater wing coverts; large white patch on secondaries; tail feathers and long uptacs grayish with blue subterminal spot and bronze tip; head bright blue with top-of-head wattles and orange-red warts.

PARTRIDGES, QUAILS—CODORNICES—ODONTOPHORIDAE

LONG-TAILED WOOD-PARTRIDGE [8] Perdiz Coluda *Dendrortyx macroura*
Range Mex. Res Mex (cHi + adj slopes down to cPac). Rare, local.
Habitat Secluded mountain forest undergrowth.

Voice A loud, rollicking whistle, *whip-er-will-a,* repeated rapidly.
Field Marks 15" Mottled rufous and gray; crest short; legs and tail rather long; bill, eye ring, and legs bright red; face black with white mustache mark and line over eye.

BEARDED WOOD-PARTRIDGE [8] Perdiz Veracruzana *Dendrortyx barbatus*
Range Mex. Res Mex (nw.cAtl). Very rare.
Habitat Secluded dense cloud forest.
Voice A loud, rollicking, whistled *chee-vee-sco-yo,* repeated rapidly.
Field Marks 11" Mostly rufous and grayish brown, mottled and streaked; throat broadly gray; breast mostly plain rufous; bill, legs, and eye ring red; very short crest.

BUFFY-CROWNED WOOD-PARTRIDGE [8] Perdiz Montañera *Dendrortyx leucophrys*
Range Mex – CRic, exc Blz. Res Mex (sHi), Guat (Hi + adj Pac, Atl), ElSal. Rare.
Habitat Undergrowth, borders, small openings of humid forest, or cloud forest.
Voice A loud, rollicking, repeated whistle.
Field Marks 13" Streaked rufous, gray, and olive-brown; forehead, forecrown, throat, and line over eye creamy buff; legs and eye ring red; bill mostly black.

SPOTTED WOOD-QUAIL [8] Codorniz Bolonchaco *Odontophorus guttatus*
Range Mex – Pan, exc ElSal. Res Mex (sPac, se.cAtl+sAtl), Blz, Guat (Pac, Atl).
Habitat Cloud forest and other dense humid forest.
Voice A loud, rollicking, mellow call, *bo-lon-cha-co,* repeated rapidly, with a chattering *cha-cha-cha* sometimes added.
Field Marks 11" Often in groups. Variable; sometimes divided into two morphs, olive-brown and reddish brown. M: floppy crest blackish or very dark brown, with orange or orange-buff streaks; mostly dark olive-brown or rufous-brown below, with small spotty streaks, but throat blackish with fine white streaks; blackish olive, or dark rufous-brown, above. F: duller, darker; little or no orange on crest.

SINGING QUAIL [8] Codorniz Silbadora *Dactylortyx thoracicus*
Range Mex – Hon. Res Mex (csPac + adj Hi, Atl + adj Hi, Yuc), Blz, Guat (Pac, Hi), ElSal.
Habitat Varied habitats, dense humid forest to open woods.
Voice Ascending series of loud notes, then *which-wheela,* repeated.
Field Marks 9" Races vary. M: black-mottled grayish olive-brown above; may be buffy brown or olive-brown below; throat and extended line over eye tawny rufous. F: like male above, but cinnamon to tawny buff below; gray and dark brown head pattern.

MONTEZUMA QUAIL [7] Codorniz de Moctezuma *Cyrtonyx montezumae*
Range US – Mex. Res Mex (ncHi).
Habitat Usually in open pine-oak woodland, or grassy brushy fields.
Field Marks 9" M: buff pompadour nape crest; swirling black-and-white pat-

tern on throat and head; white-spotted blackish sides and flanks; chestnut brown to blackish chestnut medially below. F: face pattern similar, but dull brown and buff; upperparts streaked brownish; underparts cinnamon-brown.

OCELLATED QUAIL [8] Codorniz Enmascarada *Cyrtonyx ocellatus*
Range Mex–Hon, exc Blz. Res Mex (sHi), Guat (Hi), ElSal (n).
Habitat Open woods, pine and pine-oak.
Field Marks 9″ Like Montezuma Quail, but M: some bluish gray on face, less black; mostly chestnut below, with fewer and duller spots and some blackish bars; F: darker above.

CRESTED BOBWHITE [48] Cuiche Centroamericano *Colinus cristatus*
White-breasted group [48] Cuiche Ventriblanco *Colinus c. hypoleucus*
Range Guat–ElSal. Res Guat (local e Pac, se Atl), ElSal (w).
Habitat Arid and semiarid brushy fields, hedgerows, patchy farms and scrubby woods, borders.
Voice A loud whistle like that of Northern Bobwhite.
Field Marks 8″ M: head contrasty rich brown and clear white, including white throat; underparts mostly white, usually with white-spotted reddish brown flanks; upperparts mottled and barred reddish brown, black, and white. F: much like Northern Bobwhite, but appears more light-spotted than dark-barred below; hindneck spotted or streaked black and white.
Spotted-bellied group Cuiche Ventrimanchado *Colinus c. leucopogon*
White-throated subgroup Cuiche Gorjiblanco *Colinus c. leucopogon*
Range ElSal, Hon. Res ElSal (e).
Habitat Semiarid brushy areas, borders, farm fields, hedgerows.
Voice A loud whistle like that of Northern Bobwhite.
Field Marks 8″ Like White-breasted group, with brown and white head and white throat, but remaining underparts dark grayish brown to cinnamon-brown with prominent white or pale buff spots.
Spotted-bellied subgroup Cuiche Ventrimanchado *Colinus c. sclateri*
Not in our area
Crested group Cuiche Crestado *Colinus c. cristatus*
Not in our area

NORTHERN BOBWHITE [7] Cuiche Común *Colinus virginianus*
Range Can–Mex, Guat. Res Mex (csPac, nw+ne,nHi+csHi, ncAtl+w.sAtl), Guat (extreme w Pac, Hi). Rare to common.
Habitat Open country with shrubs and grass, or woodland edge, pastures or cultivated fields.
Voice A loud *white* or *bob-white*.
Field Marks 9″ M: races vary. Northeastern birds are barred blackish and whitish below; others are dark rufous below; most have white throat and superciliary, but the throat is black in northwestern birds, and the entire head (including throat) is black in southeastern birds. F: streaked and spotted above; mostly barred dark brown and buff below; throat and line over eye buff.

(BLACK-THROATED) YUCATAN BOBWHITE [8] Cuiche Yucateco *Colinus nigrogularis*
Range Mex–Nic, exc ElSal. Res Mex (Yuc), Blz (n), Guat (nw Atl).
Habitat Semiarid brushy areas, hedgerows, farm fields, borders, scrub woods.
Voice A loud whistled *white* or *bob-white.*
Field Marks 8″ M: scaly black and white below; broadly black throat; white line over eye; ear patch mostly white. F: narrow bars below; throat and line over eye buff; like female Northern Bobwhite, but somewhat darker above.

BANDED QUAIL [8] Codorniz Listada *Philortyx fasciatus*
Range Mex. Res Mex (c.cPac, w+c.cHi).
Habitat Scattered trees, hedgerows, thick brush, semidesert.
Voice Cleek notes, a mellow *cwaw,* or barking *puk-cwaw.*
Field Marks 8″ Adt: heavily banded black and white below; lightly banded or scalloped above; black crest, rufous-tipped, tilts back. Imm: throat and sides of head black.

SCALED QUAIL [7] Codorniz Escamosa *Callipepla squamata*
Range US–Mex. Res Mex (nHi+n.cHi, nAtl).
Habitat Arid or semiarid grassy areas, thick brush, roadsides.
Voice A harsh *puk-cwaw* or *pe-co.*
Field Marks 11″ Mostly light to medium gray; short crest largely white; back and underparts appear scaly.

ELEGANT QUAIL [8] Codorniz Gris *Callipepla douglasii*
Range Mex. Res Mex (nPac).
Habitat Brushy areas, dry scrubby woods, hedgerows, thickets, shrubby borders.
Voice Cleek notes, also *puk-cwaw,* or *cwa-heet.*
Field Marks 10″ M: head and neck finely streaked black, on gray and rufous; crest plume rufous, tilts back; gray back and underparts; belly pale-spotted. F: mostly dark brown, including crest, with pale spots below and pale streaks on flanks and wings.

GAMBEL'S QUAIL [7] Codorniz Desértica *Callipepla gambelii*
Range US–Mex. Res Mex (ne.nBajCal, n+c.nPac, extreme n.nHi).
Habitat Dry brushy grassland, semidesert, borders, thickets, hedgerows.
Voice A loud *puk-cway-co-co.*
Field Marks 11″ M+F: like California Quail, but *not* scaly below; male has black forehead and creamy buff belly with black center patch.

CALIFORNIA QUAIL [7] Codorniz Californiana *Callipepla californica*
Range Can–Mex. Res Mex (BajCal).
Habitat Arid to moist scrub, woods edge, hedgerows, borders, thorny semidesert.
Voice A loud, mellow *cwaw,* or *puk-cwaw-cuk.*

Field Marks 10" Black crest plume curves forward. M: forehead broadly creamy buff; face and throat black, white-bordered; breast gray; belly appears scaly, cream-colored with brown center patch. F: head mostly gray, brown, and buff, faintly streaked; breast gray; belly appears scaly, creamy buff, but *no* dark center patch.

MOUNTAIN QUAIL [7] Codorniz de Montaña *Oreortyx picta*
Range Can–Mex. Res Mex (nBajCal).
Habitat Moist woods, open pine forests, grassy borders, hedgerows, or drier scrub, brushy hillsides.
Voice A loud *wuk* or *cuh-wuk*.
Field Marks 11" Long, slender, back-tilted, black crest plume; white-barred chestnut flanks; throat chestnut, bordered white; crown, hindneck, and breast gray; back brown.

RAILS, GALLINULES—RALITOS, RASCONES—RALLIDAE

RUDDY (CRAKE) RAIL [8] Ralito Rojizo *Laterallus ruber*
Range Mex–CRic. Res Mex (csPac, csAtl, Yuc), Blz, Guat (Pac, Atl), ElSal.
Habitat Freshwater or salty marshes, wet grassy or sedgy ditches or ponds; may call even when only a few feet away from a human observer.
Voice A chattering whinny.
Field Marks 6" Mostly rich reddish brown, but most of head dark gray; legs greenish.

GRAY-BREASTED (CRAKE) RAIL [48] Ralito Pechigrís *Laterallus exilis*
Range Blz–SAm, exc ElSal. Res Blz (s), Guat (ne Atl). Very rare.
Habitat Grassy ponds, marshes, wet meadows.
Field Marks 6" Like Black Rail, with barred flanks and chestnut patch on hind-neck and upper back, but head, neck, and breast much paler gray; back unspotted (has spots and spotty bars on wings); bill green at base.

BLACK RAIL [9] Ralito Negruzco *Laterallus jamaicensis*
Range US–SAm, exc ElSal, Nic. Res/vis Mex (n.nBajCal, s.nAtl+n.cAtl), Blz (cas? pine). Very rare and local.
Habitat Marshes, wet grassy fields, marshy ponds.
Voice A metallic *tikee-loo*, repeated, or a cooing *cro-cro-cro*.
Field Marks 5" Mostly blackish, spotted above; flanks barred black and white; nape and upper back dark chestnut; bill black.

CLAPPER RAIL [9] Rascón Picudo *Rallus longirostris*
Range US–Mex, Blz, SAm. Res cstl Mex (BajCal, nPac, nAtl, Yuc), Blz (cstl + cayes). Rare.
Habitat Marshes.
Field Marks 16" Like King Rail, but grayer, especially wrist patch; duller streaks and bars.

KING RAIL [9] Rascón Real *Rallus elegans*
Range Can–Mex. Res Mex (cPac, cHi, cAtl). Rare.
Habitat Usually large freshwater marshes, sometimes brackish areas.
Field Marks 17″ Grayish brown above, black-streaked; large wrist patch dark rufous; throat and breast bright rufous; flanks and untacs barred black and white; long bill.

VIRGINIA RAIL [9] Rascón Chico *Rallus limicola*
Range Can–Mex, Guat, SAm. Res/win Mex (res n.nBajCal, c.cHi+sHi; win BajCal, nPac, ncHi, nAtl+nw.cAtl), Guat (Hi + adj Pac). Irregular.
Habitat Marshes or marshy borders of ponds, lakes, and sluggish rivers.
Field Marks 8″ Adt: Like King Rail, but much smaller; paler, duller brown throat and breast; gray sides of face. Imm: darker; blurred blackish streaks on throat and breast.

GRAY-NECKED WOOD-RAIL [8] Rascón Cuelligris *Aramides cajanea*
Range Mex–SAm. Res Mex (se.cPac+sPac, csAtl, Yuc), Blz, Guat (Pac, Atl), ElSal (w).
Habitat Freshwater or salty swamps, wooded ponds, lakes and lagoons.
Voice A loud *tic-tic-tic-tic-tiree-tiree*.
Field Marks 16″ Gray or greenish gray upperparts, crown, neck, and breast; rufous nape and sides; black belly and untacs; bill red at base, yellowish near tip; red legs.

RUFOUS-NECKED WOOD-RAIL [8] Rascón Cuellirrufo *Aramides axillaris*
Range Mex–SAm, exc Guat? Res Mex (s.nPac+cPac, Yuc), Blz (cstl + cayes), ElSal (w). Rare.
Habitat Mostly flooded wooded areas, wooded brackish or salty lagoons, or mangrove swamps.
Field Marks 12″ Grayish above, but head, neck, breast, and sides reddish brown; belly and untacs black; bill yellowish; legs red.

UNIFORM (CRAKE) RAIL [8] Rascón Café *Amaurolimnas concolor*
Range Mex–SAm, exc ElSal. Res Mex (w.sPac, se.cAtl+w.sAtl), Blz (s), Guat (Atl). Very rare.
Habitat Freshwater swamps, sluggish streams in forest, swampy pond borders.
Field Marks 8″ Dark reddish brown above, bright rufous below; bill greenish; eyes red.

SORA [9] Polluela Sora *Porzana carolina*
Range Can–SAm. Res/win Mex (res nw.nBajCal; win all); win Blz, Guat, ElSal.
Habitat Freshwater or salty marshes, swamps, rice fields.
Voice A descending chatter or whinny.
Field Marks 8″ Adt: brownish gray above, streaked; pale gray below, with black throat to chest; flanks whitish barred. Juv: duller; brownish wash; throat *not* black.

YELLOW-BREASTED (CRAKE) RAIL [8] Polluela Pálida *Porzana flaviventer*
Range Mex–SAm, exc Hon? Res Mex (csPac, csAtl, Yuc), Blz (cas?), Guat (Pac), ElSal (e). Very rare.
Habitat Mostly in large freshwater marshes, marshy borders of lakes, ponds.
Field Marks 4.5″ Like Yellow Rail, but much paler below; white with buff wash on breast; black-barred flanks and untacs; sides of head gray; white line over eye; blackish crown.

SPOTTED RAIL [8] Rascón Pinto *Pardirallus maculatus*
Range Mex–SAm (exc Guat?, Hon, Nic?). Res Mex (s.nPac+csPac, w.cHi+sHi, csAtl, Yuc), Blz, ElSal (cas). Rare, range may be expanding.
Habitat Secluded areas in large marshes, mostly freshwater, or marshy lake borders.
Field Marks 10″ Blackish brown above with whitish streaks and spots; blackish gray below with whitish spots and bars; bill long, green with red base.

PURPLE GALLINULE [9] Gallareta Morada *Porphyrula martinica*
Range US–SAm. Res/win Mex (s.nPac+csPac, w.cHi+sHi, Atl, Yuc), Blz, Guat (Pac, Atl), ElSal.
Habitat Freshwater to salty marshes and swamps, or marshy borders of lagoons, lakes, ponds, sluggish rivers; often swims.
Field Marks 13″ Adt: head, neck, and underparts purplish, but lower belly and untacs white; greenish olive above; pale blue frontal shield; red bill, yellow-tipped. Imm: whitish to pale brown below; *no* white on head or side. See Common Moorhen.

COMMON MOORHEN [9] Gallareta Común *Gallinula chloropus*
Range Can–SAm. Res/win Mex, Blz, Guat, ElSal.
Habitat Ponds, marshes, swamps.
Field Marks 13″ Adt: blackish gray above; dark bluish gray below; white side stripe; lateral untacs white; frontal shield red; bill tip yellow. Imm: grayish; white side stripe.

AMERICAN COOT [9] Gallareta Gris *Fulica americana*
Range Can–SAm. Res/win Mex, Blz, Guat, ElSal.
Habitat Ponds, lakes, estuaries, lagoons, large freshwater or saltwater marshes or swamps; often walks on open shores.
Field Marks 15″ Adt: mostly blackish gray; bill white. Imm: paler; bill whitish.

SUNGREBES—PÁJAROS CANTIL—HELIORNITHIDAE

SUNGREBE [12] Pájaro Cantil *Heliornis fulica*
Range Mex–SAm, exc ElSal. Res Mex (sPac, s.nAtl+csAtl, se Yuc), Blz, Guat (Pac, Atl). Rare.
Habitat Secluded ponds, canals, lagoons, sluggish rivers.
Field Marks 12″ Mostly brownish gray above, pale gray below; heavy black

stripes on white to pale gray head and neck; bill rather long, reddish; toes lobed and broadly barred.

SUNBITTERNS—PAVITOS DE AGUA—EURYPYGIDAE

SUNBITTERN [12] Pavito de Agua *Eurypyga helias*
Range Mex–SAm, exc Blz, ElSal. Res Mex (extreme sc.sAtl), Guat (Atl). Very rare.
Habitat On the ground, near forest streams, in swamps; *not* a swimmer.
Field Marks 18″ Head blackish, with narrow white streaks; upperparts barred gray and black; neck and breast blackish; bill, legs, and neck long; two black and chestnut bars on gray tail; spread wings show chestnut, yellow, and black.

LIMPKINS—CARAOS—ARAMIDAE

LIMPKIN [9] Carao *Aramus guarauna*
Range US–SAm. Res Mex (sPac, csAtl, Yuc), Blz, Guat (Pac, Atl), ElSal.
Habitat Walking in swamps, moist or wet fields, swampy or marshy rivers or ponds.
Voice A loud, echoing, wailing or rolling *cyow,* or *cuk-cuk-cyow;* often at night.
Field Marks 28″ Streaked dark brown and buff; legs, neck, and bill long; bill dull yellowish, slightly decurved, rather blunt at tip.

CRANES—GRULLAS—GRUIDAE

SANDHILL CRANE [9] Grulla Gris *Grus canadensis*
Range AK–Mex. Win Mex (nBajCal, nPac, ncHi, nAtl; acc Yuc).
Habitat Large marshes, wet fields.
Voice A loud, rolling trumpeting.
Field Marks 45″ Extends neck and legs in flight. Adt: medium gray, may be stained brownish; crown red; throat whitish; bill, neck, and legs long. Imm: mostly brown or grayish brown.

THICK-KNEES—ALCARAVANES—BURHINIDAE

DOUBLE-STRIPED THICK-KNEE [12] Alcaraván *Burhinus bistriatus*
Range Mex–SAm, exc Blz, Pan. Res Mex (sPac, se.cAtl+w.sAtl), Guat (Pac), ElSal (e).
Habitat Mainly nocturnal; rough, scrubby areas, grassy fields, crop fields.
Voice Loud, echoing, cackling cries.
Field Marks 20″ Like a giant plover; mostly brown, striped and mottled; crown broadly striped; large yellow eyes; extended wing striped; short, heavy bill; long legs.

PLOVERS—CHORLOS—CHARADRIIDAE

BLACK-BELLIED PLOVER [10] Chorlo Gris *Pluvialis squatarola*
Range AK-SAm. Tr/win mostly cstl Mex, Blz (cstl + cayes), Guat (Pac), ElSal (cstl).
Habitat Coastal beaches, rocky shores, mud flats, rare on lakeshores.
Field Marks 12″ Win: mottled gray above; black patch under wing (shows in flight); pale gray below, faintly streaked; large head; thick black bill; black legs. Sum: more contrasty above; black face and underparts, but belly and untacs white.

AMERICAN GOLDEN-PLOVER [10] Chorlo Dorado *Pluvialis dominica*
Range AK-SAm. Tr Mex (all exc BajCal, nPac), Blz, Guat, ElSal. Rare.
Habitat Grassy fields, mud flats, marshes, estuaries.
Field Marks 11″ Like Black-bellied Plover, but more yellowish above; Win: buffier below; no black patch under wing; Sum: mostly black (*not* white) lower belly and untacs. (May show whitish flanks during molt; see Pacific Golden-Plover.)

PACIFIC GOLDEN-PLOVER Chorlo Pacifico *Pluvialis fulva*
Range AK-Mex. Win Mex (cstl nBajCal). Very rare.
Habitat Coastal marshes, estuaries, shores.
Field Marks 11″ Like American Golden-Plover, but more golden above; Win: more buffy to tawny buff on face and chest; Sum: in full breeding plumage shows broad white stripe along sides and flanks, *not* just whitish flanks during molt.

COLLARED PLOVER [45] Chorlito de Collar *Charadrius collaris*
Range Mex-SAm, exc Blz. Res Mex (s.nPac+csPac, cAtl+w.sAtl), Guat (Pac, Atl), ElSal (cstl).
Habitat Coastal beaches, mud flats, open shores of lagoons, estuaries, sometimes shores of large lakes.
Field Marks 6″ Adt: white forehead and throat and black crown patch and breast band all bordered behind or at sides by rufous; white belly; slender black bill; pinkish legs. Imm: crown *not* black; breast band duller, usually incomplete.

SNOWY PLOVER [10] Chorlito Alejandrino *Charadrius alexandrinus*
Range Mex-SAm, exc Blz, Nic? Res/win Mex (all exc sHi), Guat (Pac, Atl), ElSal (cstl).
Habitat Mostly coastal beaches, also mud flats, lagoon shores, lakeshores.
Field Marks 6.5″ Pale brownish gray above; white below; black or blackish brown forecrown; dark brown or black partial ear patch and patch on side of chest; *no* breast band; legs and bill blackish.

WILSON'S PLOVER [10] Chorlito Piquigrueso *Charadrius wilsonia*
Range US-SAm. Res/win Mex (BajCal, Pac, Atl, Yuc), Blz (cstl + cayes), Guat (Pac, Atl), ElSal (cstl).

Habitat Beaches, mud flats, coastal lagoons.

Field Marks 8" M: like summer Semipalmated Plover and F: like winter Semipalmated Plover, but larger; slightly paler above; bill much larger, heavier, and black; legs grayish.

SEMIPALMATED PLOVER [10] Chorlito Frailecillo *Charadrius semipalmatus*

Range AK–SAm. Tr/win Mex (BajCal, Pac, cHi, Atl, Yuc), Blz (cstl + cayes), Guat (Pac, Atl), ElSal.

Habitat Mainly ocean beaches, also lakeshores, lagoons, mud flats.

Field Marks 7" Medium brown above; forehead, throat, collar, and most of underparts white; legs orange. Sum: black forecrown, eye patch, and breast band; bill orange with black tip. Win: crown, eye patch, and breast band brown; bill dark. Piping Plover and Snowy Plover are much paler above; Wilson's Plover has a much larger bill.

PIPING PLOVER [10] Chorlito Chiflador *Charadrius melodus*

Range Can–Mex. Win Mex (nPac, ncAtl, n Yuc). Rare.

Habitat Coastal beaches, mud flats, lagoons.

Field Marks 7" Like Snowy Plover, but pale gray above; ear patch much paler; legs orange-yellow; bill heavier; Win: patch on side of chest much paler; Sum: breast band partial in front, or complete, and extends around the hindneck; bill orange with black tip.

KILLDEER [10] Tildío *Charadrius vociferus*

Range AK–SAm. Res/win Mex (res BajCal, ncPac, ncHi, nAtl; win all), Blz, Guat, ElSal.

Habitat Wet fields, open shores of ponds or lakes; often nests on gravel or pebbles.

Voice A loud, high-pitched, somewhat squeaky *kil-dee,* a musical *dee-it* and *dee-dee-dee-dee.*

Field Marks 11" Brown above; white forehead, throat, collar, and most of underparts; two black breast bands, the upper one forming a full collar; rump, uptacs, and much of tail salmon-colored; bill black.

MOUNTAIN PLOVER [10] Chorlo Llanero *Charadrius montanus*

Range Can–Mex. Win Mex (nBajCal, n.nPac, nHi, n.nAtl).

Habitat Farm fields, dry grassland, open plains.

Field Marks 9" Sum: brown above; white forehead, throat, and underparts; black crown patch and line through eye; breast washed with buff, *no* breast band. Win: *no* black on crown or through eye; usually buffier overall.

OYSTERCATCHERS—OSTREROS—HAEMATOPODIDAE

AMERICAN OYSTERCATCHER [9] Ostrero Americano *Haematopus palliatus*

Range US–SAm. Res/win Mex (BajCal, Pac, Atl, Yuc), Blz (cstl + cayes), Guat (Pac, Atl), ElSal.

Habitat Rocky ocean shores, gravel beaches, mud flats.
Field Marks 17" Long red bill; black head, neck, and chest; wing band, uptacs, and most of underparts white. BajCal and ncPac birds have some black spots or mottling on breast.

BLACK OYSTERCATCHER [9] Ostrero Negro *Haematopus bachmani*
Range AK–Mex. Res Mex (nBajCal+n.sBajCal; cas n.nPac).
Habitat Rocky ocean shores, headlands, beaches, mud flats.
Field Marks 17" Long red bill; plumage black to blackish olive-brown.

AVOCETS, STILTS—CANDELEROS—RECURVIROSTRIDAE

BLACK-NECKED STILT [9] Candelero Mexicano *Himantopus mexicanus*
Range US–SAm. Res/win Mex, Blz, Guat, ElSal.
Habitat Mud flats, lagoons, estuaries, marsh pools, lakeshores.
Field Marks 15" Often in noisy flocks. Black above, white below; slender black bill, may appear slightly up-curved; long legs red.

AMERICAN AVOCET [9] Piquicurvo *Recurvirostra americana*
Range Can–CRic, exc Nic. Res/win Mex (res nw.nBajCal, s.nHi+cHi, sw.nAtl; tr/win all exc sHi), Blz (cas/acc?), Guat (Pac), ElSal. Rare.
Habitat Lagoons, shallow ponds, wet meadows, marsh pools.
Field Marks 19" Sum adt: mostly black and white above; white below; head and neck cinnamon, bill slender, up curved; legs gray. Imm+win adt: head and neck pale gray.

JACANAS—CIRUJANOS—JACANIDAE

NORTHERN JACANA [9] Cirujano Mexicano *Jacana spinosa*
Range US–Pan. Res Mex (s.nPac+csPac, w.cHi, s.nAtl+csAtl, Yuc), Blz, Guat (Pac, Atl), ElSal.
Habitat Marshes, swamps, ditches, ponds, lakes, lagoons.
Voice A grating, cackling chatter.
Field Marks 9" Adt: mostly chestnut above and below; black head and neck; spread wing mostly lime-yellow. Imm: blackish above; face and underparts white; spread wing like adult's.

SANDPIPERS—PLAYEROS, CHORLETES—SCOLOPACIDAE

GREATER YELLOWLEGS [10] Tingüís Mayor *Tringa melanoleuca*
Range AK–SAm. Tr/win Mex, Blz, Guat, ElSal.
Habitat Mud flats, ponds, marshy fields, lagoons, lakeshores.
Voice A loud, three-noted *hew-hew-hew*.
Field Marks 14" Mottled gray above; white below with many fine neck streaks; spots and bars on sides; bill long, black, very slightly up-curved; uptacs white. See Lesser Yellowlegs.

LESSER YELLOWLEGS [10] Tingüís Menor *Tringa flavipes*
Range AK–SAm. Win/tr Mex, Blz, Guat, ElSal.
Habitat Coastal mud flats, lakeshores, marshes, lagoons.
Voice One or two whistled notes.
Field Marks 11″ Like Greater Yellowlegs, but smaller; bill shorter, straighter; usually not as heavily marked on neck, chest, and sides.

SOLITARY SANDPIPER [10] Playero Charquero *Tringa solitaria*
Range AK–SAm. Win/tr Mex, Blz, Guat, ElSal.
Habitat Mud flats, ponds, streams.
Field Marks 8″ Dark grayish brown above, speckled with white; neck and chest finely streaked; legs dull greenish, *not* yellow; much white on outer tail feathers.

WILLET [11] Playero Pihuihui *Catoptrophorus semipalmatus*
Range Can–SAm. Res/win Mex (res nAtl; win/tr BajCal, Pac, ncHi, Atl, Yuc), Blz (cstl + cayes), Guat (cstl), ElSal (cstl).
Habitat Coastal beaches, mud flats, rarely lakeshores.
Field Marks 15″ Striking black-and-white wing pattern in flight; bill long, straight, rather heavy. Win: mostly unstreaked gray neck and upperparts; unstreaked whitish below. Sum: mottled and streaked gray above; streaked neck and breast.

WANDERING TATTLER [11] Playero Sencillo *Heteroscelus incanus*
Range AK–SAm, exc Blz. Win Mex (BajCal, Pac), Guat (Pac), ElSal (cstl).
Habitat Rocky ocean shores and headlands.
Field Marks 10″ Win: plain medium gray above and on head and breast; white belly and untacs. Sum: fine wavy bars below; much longer bill than Surfbird.

SPOTTED SANDPIPER [11] Playero Alzacolita *Actitis macularia*
Range AK–SAm. Win Mex, Blz (cstl + cayes), Guat, ElSal.
Habitat Shores of ponds, lakes, streams, rivers, lagoons.
Field Marks 7″ Flies with rapid, stiff, shallow wingbeats. White wing stripe shows in flight. Win: gray above, white below; dark bill. Sum: heavy black spots below; bill orange, black-tipped; legs yellowish.

UPLAND SANDPIPER [10] Zarapito Ganga *Bartramia longicauda*
Range AK–SAm, exc ElSal. Tr Mex (csPac, Hi, Atl, Yuc), Blz (cas/acc?), Guat. Rare.
Habitat Open grassland, moist fields, open marshes.
Field Marks 12″ Mottled grayish brown above; neck buffy, finely streaked; belly and untacs white; long legs dull yellowish; short, straight, dark bill.

WHIMBREL [10] Zarapito Trinador *Numenius phaeopus*
Range AK–SAm. Win Mex (BajCal, Pac, Atl, Yuc), Blz (cstl + cayes), Guat (cstl), ElSal (cstl).
Habitat Coastal lagoons, mud flats, beaches (very rare on lakes, ponds).
Field Marks 17″ Mottled and spotted grayish brown above; whitish below; streaked on neck and chest; crown striped dark brown and whitish; bill long, decurved.

LONG-BILLED CURLEW [10] Zarapito Piquilargo *Numenius americanus*
Range Can–CRic. Win Mex (BajCal, Pac, ncHi, Atl, Yuc), Blz (cayes), Guat (Pac), ElSal (cas cstl).
Habitat Wet meadows, open marshes, coastal flats.
Field Marks 24″ Rich buffy brown; mottled with black above, and streaked on head, neck, and breast; bill very long, decurved; legs long, grayish.

HUDSONIAN GODWIT [10] Agachona Café *Limosa haemastica*
Range AK–Mex, Guat, CRic. Tr Mex (csPac, ncAtl; cas? cHi, Yuc), Guat (Pac). Very rare.
Habitat Coastal beaches, mud flats, lagoons.
Field Marks 16″ Black tail; white uptacs, outer part of tail base, and wing stripe; long, pinkish, black-tipped bill, slightly up-curved. Win: medium gray above; pale gray to whitish below. Sum: chestnut neck and underparts, with many narrow black bars; black above with white spots or scales.

MARBLED GODWIT [10] Agachona Real *Limosa fedoa*
Range Can–SAm. Win Mex (BajCal, Pac, Atl, Yuc), Blz (acc), Guat (Pac), ElSal (cstl).
Habitat Coastal beaches, lagoons, marshes, wet fields, ponds.
Field Marks 18″ Mostly rich buffy brown, mottled and barred above, streaked on neck, and finely barred below; very long, pinkish-based bill slightly up-curved.

RUDDY TURNSTONE [11] Chorlete Común *Arenaria interpres*
Range AK–SAm. Win/tr Mex (BajCal, Pac, cHi, Atl, Yuc), Blz (cstl + cayes), Guat (cstl), ElSal.
Habitat Beaches, mud flats, sand bars, lagoons.
Field Marks 9″ Bill short, black, with fine up-curved tip; legs orange; black-and-white wing, tail, and rump pattern, in all seasons. Win: mottled brownish gray above; white below with pale grayish patch on side of dark gray chest; usually shows traces of summer head pattern. Head paler than Black Turnstone's. Sum: intricate black-and-white head pattern; mostly bright rufous wings and back, with some black.

BLACK TURNSTONE [11] Chorlete Negro *Arenaria melanocephala*
Range AK–Mex. Win Mex (BajCal, nPac).
Habitat Mainly rocky shores and headlands.
Field Marks 9″ Bill and black-and-white flight pattern like Ruddy Turnstone's, but legs dark gray. Win: like Ruddy Turnstone, but much darker head and back; no trace of pattern on dark gray throat and breast. Sum: black back, head, and breast, with faint white streaks and bars; white line over eye and spot at base of bill. See Surfbird.

SURFBIRD [11] Playero de Marejada *Aphriza virgata*
Range AK–SAm, exc Blz. Win Mex (BajCal, Pac), Guat (Pac), ElSal (cas cstl).
Habitat Rocky ocean shores, jetties, headlands.
Field Marks 10″ Bill yellowish at base, *not* fine-tipped; legs dull yellowish;

black-and-white flight pattern, but rump and lower back gray, *not* white with black crossbar. Win: upperparts, head, and breast dark gray; throat and line over eye whiter than Black Turnstone's. Sum: gray, with streaked head, upperparts, and underparts.

RED KNOT [11] Playero Canuto *Calidris canutus*
Range AK–SAm, exc Blz. Win cstl Mex (BajCal, Pac, Atl, Yuc), Guat (cstl), ElSal (cstl).
Habitat Beaches, mud flats, lagoons.
Field Marks 10″ Head rather large; bill medium short, rather heavy, black; legs greenish. Win: grayish above; whitish below. Sum: streaked above; buffy reddish brown below; black-and-white barred rump and uptacs; faint white wing bar.

SANDERLING [11] Playerito Blanco *Calidris alba*
Range AK–SAm. Win Mex (BajCal, Pac; cas/very rare ncHi, Atl, Yuc), Blz (cstl + cayes), Guat (cstl), ElSal (cstl).
Habitat Mainly sandy ocean beaches.
Field Marks 7″ Runs into receding wave, then rapidly retreats from incoming wave. Legs black; bill medium length, black; white wing stripe; blackish wrist patch (may be hidden). Win: whiter, less streaked than other peeps; underparts pure white; back pale gray, faintly streaked. Sum: streaked head, neck, breast, and upperparts, with reddish brown wash.

SEMIPALMATED SANDPIPER [11] Playerito Semipalmeado *Calidris pusilla*
Range AK–SAm. Tr/win Mex (nBajCal, sPac, ncAtl, Yuc), Blz (cstl + cayes), Guat (cstl), ElSal.
Habitat Ocean beaches, mud flats, lagoons.
Field Marks 6″ Legs black; straight, short black bill; less brownish above and less streaked below than corresponding plumage of Western or Least Sandpiper.

WESTERN SANDPIPER [11] Playerito Occidental *Calidris mauri*
Range AK–SAm. Tr/win Mex (all exc sHi), Blz (cstl + cayes), Guat (cstl), ElSal.
Habitat Ocean beaches, mud flats, lakeshores.
Field Marks 6″ Legs black; longer, heavier bill (tip droops slightly) than Semipalmated Sandpiper or Least Sandpiper. Win: mottled gray above with slight brownish tinge; faint streaks below. Sum: mottled brownish gray above; pale rufous wash on scapulars, ear patch, and crown; many fine streaks below.

LEAST SANDPIPER [11] Playerito Mínimo *Calidris minutilla*
Range AK–SAm. Win/tr Mex, Blz (cstl + cayes), Guat, ElSal.
Habitat Ocean beaches, mud flats, lakeshores, estuaries.
Field Marks 6″ Legs dull yellowish; bill short, slender. Win: brownish gray above; white below, with finely streaked brownish breast band. Sum: mottled black and brownish above; fine streaks on brownish neck and breast. Browner than Semipalmated Sandpiper; more slender-billed than Western Sandpiper.

WHITE-RUMPED SANDPIPER [11] Playerito de Rabadilla Blanca *Calidris fuscicollis*
Range AK–SAm, exc ElSal. Tr Mex (Atl, Yuc), Blz, Guat (Atl). Rare.
Habitat Coastal beaches, mud flats; lakeshores, marsh pools.

Field Marks 7″ Rump and uptacs white; legs blackish. Win: grayer and paler than in summer. Sum: mottled brownish gray above; white below with streaked brownish gray breast.

BAIRD'S SANDPIPER [11] Playerito de Baird *Calidris bairdii*
Range AK–SAm, exc Blz. Tr Mex, Guat, ElSal (acc cstl). Rare.
Habitat Lakeshores, marshes, wet meadows, riverbeds.
Field Marks 7″ Longer-billed and larger than Least Sandpiper; bill and legs black; mottled above, scaly black and buffy; pale grayish brown streaked breast; folded wings extend well beyond tail tip.

PECTORAL SANDPIPER [11] Playero Manchado *Calidris melanotos*
Range AK–SAm. Tr Mex, Blz, Guat, ElSal. Rare.
Habitat Lakeshores, marsh pools, wet or dry grassy fields.
Field Marks 9″ Mottled grayish brown above; belly and untacs white; breast appears dark and contrasty, with narrow black streaks on pale brown; legs dull greenish.

DUNLIN [11] Playerito Lomo Rojo *Calidris alpina*
Range AK–Pan, exc ElSal, Hon, Nic. Win Mex (mainly BajCal, nPac, nAtl, Yuc), Guat (Pac).
Habitat Beaches, marshes, mud flats, wet grassy fields.
Field Marks 8″ Bill medium long, decurved near tip; legs black. Win: faintly streaked gray breast and upperparts; white belly. Sum: mottled rufous above; whitish below with fine black breast streaks and large black belly patch.

STILT SANDPIPER [10] Playero Zancón *Calidris himantopus*
Range AK–SAm, exc Blz? Tr/win Mex (all exc BajCal), Guat, ElSal.
Habitat Coastal mud flats, lagoons, lakeshores, marshes.
Field Marks 9″ Rather long slender black bill; long grayish green legs; small head. Win: gray above and on breast; mostly white below; uptacs white. Sum: mottled dark brown; heavily streaked breast; barred belly and uptacs; trace of rufous on head.

BUFF-BREASTED SANDPIPER [11] Playerito Pradero *Tryngites subruficollis*
Range AK–SAm. Tr Mex (Atl, Yuc), Blz, Guat (Atl), ElSal (acc). Rare.
Habitat Moist grassy fields, dry upland fields, open grassy marshes.
Field Marks 8″ Entire underparts rich buff; scaly black and buff mottling above; bill short, black; legs yellowish; underwings mostly white; head small. See Red Knot.

SHORT-BILLED DOWITCHER [10] Agachona Marino *Limnodromus griseus*
Range AK–SAm. Win Mex (BajCal, Pac, Atl, Yuc), Blz (cstl + cayes), Guat (cstl), ElSal.
Habitat Lagoons, coastal marshes, beaches.
Voice A loud *chew-chew-chew*. See Long-billed Dowitcher.
Field Marks 11″ Wedge-shaped, long, white rump-and-lower-back patch; very long bill. Win: gray upperparts and breast; whitish belly and untacs; faint bars on flanks. Sum: mottled black and buffy brown above; reddish brown below,

except whitish belly; spots and short bars on breast, sides, flanks; narrow black-and-white tail bars.

LONG-BILLED DOWITCHER [10] Agachona Piquilarga *Limnodromus scolopaceus*
Range AK–Pan, exc Hon, Nic. Win Mex (all exc sHi, Yuc), Blz (cstl + cayes), Guat (Pac), ElSal (acc).
Habitat Lakeshores, marshes, lagoons.
Voice A weak *tleek* or *tleek-tleek*.
Field Marks 12″ Like Short-billed Dowitcher, but bill averages longer; Sum: usually richer reddish brown below (including belly); more and longer bars (*not* spots) on breast, sides, and flanks; tail blacker (broader black bars).

COMMON SNIPE [11] Agachona Común *Gallinago gallinago*
Range AK–SAm. Win Mex, Blz, Guat, ElSal.
Habitat Marshes, wet fields, stream banks.
Voice A rasping *crepe* note.
Field Marks 10″ Erratic flight. Bill very long; legs short; head striped; neck, back, and breast heavily streaked black and white; tail orange and black.

WILSON'S PHALAROPE [11] Chorlillo Piquilargo *Phalaropus tricolor*
Range AK–SAm, exc Blz. Tr Mex, Guat, ElSal.
Habitat Walking or swimming in shallows of lakes, ponds, marsh pools.
Field Marks 9″ Bill long, very slender. Win: plain pale gray above, with dark gray wings; white below; pale gray eye stripe and crown; tail whitish, uptacs white; no wing stripes. Sum F: pale gray crown, hindneck, and most of back and scapulars; white below; black eye patch joins blackish and reddish brown streak down side of neck onto back and scapulars; pale rufous foreneck. Sum M: duller; rufous wash on neck, back.

RED-NECKED PHALAROPE [11] Chorlillo Piquifino *Phalaropus lobatus*
Range AK–SAm, exc Blz? Win/tr Mex (BajCal, Pac, very rare/cas ncHi, n Yuc), Blz (acc?), Guat (Pac), ElSal (cas cstl).
Habitat Mainly coastal, and in 3-mile waters; swimming in lagoons, estuaries, bays; rare far inland.
Field Marks 7″ Win: like Wilson's Phalarope, but bill shorter; central uptacs dark; whitish wing stripe and back stripes; black hindcrown and nape. Sum F: dark gray to blackish above with buffy to whitish stripes; white below with pale gray sides; blackish crown to ear patch; broadly white throat; rufous sides of neck and bib. Sum M: slightly paler, duller.

RED PHALAROPE [11] Chorlillo Piquigrueso *Phalaropus fulicaria*
Range AK–SAm, exc Blz, ElSal, Hon. Win/tr Mex (BajCal, Pac; very rare/cas ncHi), Guat (Pac).
Habitat Common at sea, rare near coast, very rare inland; swims in open ocean, bays, estuaries.
Field Marks 8″ Win: like Northern Phalarope, but plain gray above, wing stripe but *no* back stripes; forecrown white, *not* black; bill thicker. Sum F: mottled scaly black and buff above; black crown and throat; broadly white face; under-

parts and most of neck dark rufous; legs yellowish; bill yellowish, black-tipped. Sum M: paler and duller.

SKUAS, JAEGERS—SALTEADORES—STERCORARIIDAE

POMARINE JAEGER Salteador Pomarino *Stercorarius pomarinus*
Range AK–SAm, exc ElSal. Tr/win Mex (BajCal, Pac, Atl, Yuc; acc nHi), Blz (acc), Guat (cstl).
Habitat Open ocean, or near offshore islands; very rare in 3-mile waters.
Field Marks 22" Like Parasitic Jaeger, but larger, heavier, with heavier bill; more contrasty white at base of primaries above; Adt: extended central tail feathers twisted, with broad rounded tip. Light morph adt: heavier barring on sides, darker breast band. Dark morph adt: top and sides of head uniform blackish brown.

PARASITIC JAEGER [I] Salteador Parásito *Stercorarius parasiticus*
Range AK–SAm, exc ElSal. Tr/win Mex (BajCal, Pac, Atl, Yuc; acc nHi), Blz (acc), Guat (cstl).
Habitat Open ocean, or near offshore islands; rare in 3-mile waters.
Field Marks 20" Wings strongly angled in flight; whitish wing patch (white at base of primaries) more noticeable below than above. Light morph adt: dark grayish brown above; black crown; yellow and white side of face and collar; mostly white below, with plain pale gray sides and breast band; central tail feathers somewhat extended, narrow and pointed at tip. Dark morph adt: very dark brown; face and throat slightly paler; crown black. Imm: dark above; narrowly barred below; central tail feathers barely extended.

GULLS, TERNS—GAVIOTAS, CHARRANES—LARIDAE

LAUGHING GULL [I] Gaviota Risqueña *Larus atricilla*
Range Can–SAm. Res/win Mex (nPac+n.cPac, Atl, Yuc; win BajCal, csHi), Blz (cstl + cayes), Guat, ElSal.
Habitat Estuaries, bays, lagoons, large lakes.
Field Marks 16" No white on wingtip. Sum adt: mostly white, including tail; head all black; bill red; dark gray back and wings; black wingtips. Win adt: black bill; head mostly white, with gray around eye to nape. 1st win: dark brownish gray above; gray breast, white belly; mostly black tail (including outer tail feathers), with white tail base and uptacs.

FRANKLIN'S GULL Gaviota Apipizca *Larus pipixcan*
Range Can–SAm. Tr Mex (all, but rare BajCal, nPac, Yuc), Blz (cstl + cayes), Guat (Pac), ElSal.
Habitat Coastal waters, or ponds, lakes, or migrating in swirling flocks over open areas far from water.
Field Marks 15" Like Laughing Gull, but Sum adt: redder legs, black bar on white wingtip; Win adt: larger and darker dark area on hindcrown, nape, and

around eye; 1st win: paler and grayer above; white outer tail feathers; tail base more broadly white.

BONAPARTE'S GULL [III] Gaviota Menor *Larus philadelphia*
Range AK–Mex, ElSal, CRic, Pan. Win Mex (BajCal, nPac, nHi+n.cHi, Atl, Yuc), ElSal (cas cstl).
Habitat Coastal waters and large lakes.
Field Marks 14″ Like Laughing Gull, but Sum adt: much paler wings and back; very broadly white wingtips, edged black; black bill; bright red legs; Win adt: black bar on ear patch on otherwise white head; Imm: like winter adult, but tail white with narrow terminal band; pinkish legs; white and black wingtips, black trailing edge of wings, and blackish bar on upperwing coverts.

HEERMANN'S GULL [I] Gaviota Oscura *Larus heermanni*
Range Can–Mex, Guat. Res/win Mex (res BajCal, nPac; win csPac), Guat (Pac).
Habitat Coastal waters, lagoons, estuaries, beaches.
Field Marks 17″ Adt: dark pearly gray to blackish gray; paler below and on rump, with white head (mottled in winter) and red bill; blackish flight feathers; black tail with narrow white tip band. 1st win: very dark brown; bill flesh-colored with black tip.

MEW GULL [III] Gaviota Piquicorta *Larus canus*
Range AK–Mex. Win Mex (w.nBajCal). Rare.
Habitat Coastal waters, beaches, bays.
Field Marks 16″ Like Ring-billed Gull, but Adt: slender yellow bill *not* black-marked; eyes dark; more white on black wingtip; 1st win: paler and grayer back and wings; tail mostly blackish with grayish brown barred uptacs; 2nd win: bill duller; dark tail band narrower and spottier.

RING-BILLED GULL [I] Gaviota Pinta *Larus delawarensis*
Range Can–CRic, exc Nic. Win Mex (all exc sHi), Blz (acc), Guat (Pac), ElSal (cstl).
Habitat Coastal waters, harbors, bays; large inland lakes.
Field Marks 18″ Sum adt: white head, tail, and underparts; black patch on yellow bill; black wingtips with two white spots; legs yellow; eyes white. Win adt: crown and hindneck lightly mottled. 1st win: profusely small-spotted or mottled head, breast, and wing coverts; tail mottled grayish with broad black tail band. 2nd win: somewhat more heavily mottled than winter adult, and rather narrow black tail band near tip.

CALIFORNIA GULL [III] Gaviota Californiana *Larus californicus*
Range Can–Mex, ElSal. Win Mex (BajCal, ncPac), ElSal (cas cstl).
Habitat Beaches, lagoons, harbors, or over open ocean.
Field Marks 21″ Like Ring-billed Gull, but larger, slightly darker; Sum adt: bill has small red and black spot near tip, *not* a black patch; Win adt: more and heavier streaks on head and neck; 1st win: much darker, browner, and more mottled, especially on back and belly; tail blackish brown; feet pinkish; 2nd win: much darker on back and wings; all-blackish tail. See also Herring Gull.

HERRING GULL [III] Gaviota Plateada *Larus argentatus*
Range AK–Pan. Win Mex (BajCal, Pac, Atl, Yuc), Blz (cstl + cayes), Guat (cstl), ElSal (cstl).
Habitat Sandy or rocky seashores, lagoons, harbors, bays, lakes.
Field Marks 24" Legs and feet pink at all ages; adults much paler above than Western Gull, about the same as California Gull, and darker than Glaucous-winged Gull. Sum adt: small red bill spot; little white in wingtip; eyes yellow. Win adt: heavily mottled or streaked on head, neck, upper back, and breast; darker and browner than other large gulls in our area. 1st win: heavily streaked and mottled dark grayish brown; blackish tail; dark, barred uptacs; all-black bill. 2nd win: paler and slightly grayer than first winter, with whitish uptacs and tail base; bill yellowish with black patch at tip.

THAYER'S GULL Gaviota de Thayer *Larus thayeri*
Range AK–Mex. Win Mex (BajCal, nPac; acc n.nAtl).
Habitat Coastal waters, bays, lagoons, beaches.
Field Marks 23" Like Herring Gull, but all plumages paler and grayer; Sum adt: more white and little black on pale gray wingtips.

YELLOW-FOOTED GULL Gaviota de Cortez *Larus livens*
Range AK–Mex. Res/win Mex (res e BajCal, n.nPac; win cPac).
Habitat Mostly coastal bays, lagoons, beaches, rocky areas.
Field Marks 23" Like Western Gull, but Adt: yellow legs and feet; 1st win: much whiter head and underparts with much less mottling; blacker back; 2nd win: much blacker wings.

WESTERN GULL [III] Gaviota Occidental *Larus occidentalis*
Range Can–Mex. Res/win Mex (BajCal, n.nPac; cas ncPac).
Habitat Coastal waters, bays, lagoons, beaches.
Field Marks 23" Adt: white (with faint dark streaks on head and neck in winter), with blackish gray mantle; one white spot in black wingtip; red spot on yellow bill; pinkish legs; yellow eyes. 1st win: head, back, wings, and underparts heavily mottled dark grayish brown; legs dull pinkish; bill mostly black, paler at base; tail black. 2nd win: very dark gray to black on back; contrasty black secondaries and brownish wing coverts; bill yellow with black patch at tip.

GLAUCOUS-WINGED GULL [III] Gaviota Aliglauca *Larus glaucescens*
Range AK–Mex. Win Mex (BajCal, n.nPac).
Habitat Ocean bays, harbors, beaches, lagoons.
Field Marks 24" Like Herring Gull, but immature plumages much paler and grayer. Adt: slightly paler back and wings; wingtips pale gray like the rest of the wing, and white spots with *no* black. 1st and 2nd win: differ from all other similar large gulls in our area in having very pale brownish gray tail, *not* white or blackish.

BLACK-LEGGED KITTIWAKE [III] Rissa Patinegra *Rissa tridactyla*
Range AK–Mex. Win Mex (w BajCal; very rare/cas nPac).
Habitat Mainly open ocean waters; rare and irregular in 3-mile waters.

Field Marks 17″ Black legs; notched tail. Sum adt: white, except pale gray mantle and black wingtips; black legs; yellow bill; tail notched. Win adt: similar, but grayish smudge from ear patch to hindcrown. 1st win: blackish band across hindneck or upper back area; black-mottled wing coverts and black outer primaries forming a black M pattern from one wingtip to the other; black tail-tip band; black bill. See Bonaparte's Gull and Sabine's Gull.

SABINE'S GULL [III] Gaviota Colihendida *Xema sabini*
Range AK–SAm, exc Blz, Hon. Tr/win Mex (BajCal, Pac), Guat (Pac), ElSal (cstl).
Habitat Mainly open ocean and offshore islands; rare near shore.
Field Marks 14″ Buoyant flight. Tail forked; dark M pattern on spread wings; legs black. Adt: mostly white, but bill black with yellow tip; head dark slate gray (white with grayish hindcrown and nape smudge in winter); wing coverts and back mostly dark gray; long black patch from wrist to wingtip. 1st win: hindcrown, hindneck, back, and most wing coverts dark brownish gray; black tail-tip band; pale gray legs; all-black bill. See Bonaparte's Gull and Black-legged Kittiwake.

GULL-BILLED TERN [II] Charrán Piquigrueso *Sterna nilotica*
Range US–SAm. Res/win Mex (res nPac, ncAtl; win BajCal, csPac, sAtl, Yuc); vis Blz (cstl + cayes), Guat (cstl), ElSal (cstl). Rare, local.
Habitat Marshes, lagoons, tidal pools, sandbars, mainly coastal.
Field Marks 14″ Sum adt: mostly white, but crown, nape, legs, and heavy bill black; wings and back pale gray; tail notched. Win adt: forehead and most of crown white; faint gray streaks on hindcrown and nape. Juv: head and back white to pale gray, faintly streaked and mottled.

CASPIAN TERN [II] Charrán Cáspico *Sterna caspia*
Range Can–SAm, exc ElSal. Res/win Mex (res BajCal, Pac, Atl, Yuc; win cHi); win Blz (cstl + cayes), Guat (cstl), ElSal.
Habitat Beaches, sandbars, bays, lagoons, sandy islands in lakes.
Field Marks 22″ Like Royal Tern, but Sum adt: bill heavier, redder; outer primaries more broadly dark below; legs longer; tail *not* as deeply forked; wingtips extend well beyond tail tip in perched bird; Win+imm: forehead, forecrown, eye patch, as well as hindcrown and nape, mottled blackish, *not* white.

ROYAL TERN [I] Charrán Real *Sterna maxima*
Range US–SAm. Res/vis Mex, Blz (cstl + cayes), Guat (Pac, Atl), ElSal (cstl).
Habitat Lagoons, estuaries, sandbars, beaches.
Field Marks 20″ Sum adt: mostly white, with black forehead, crown, and nape; pale gray back and wings, but outer primaries dark gray above, mostly white below; legs short, black; bill rather heavy, bright orange. Win adt: forehead and forecrown white; black nape crest. Juv: like winter adult, but back and wings white with pale grayish brown mottling.

ELEGANT TERN [II] Charrán Elegante *Sterna elegans*
Range US–SAm, exc Blz, Hon. Sum/win Mex (sum BajCal, nPac; tr/win csPac); tr/win Guat (Pac), ElSal (cstl).

Habitat Coast or islands near shore, beaches, sandbars, lagoons.
Field Marks 17" Like Royal Tern, but slender bill; longer ragged crest; dark on hindneck in winter extends farther forward (to front of crown).

SANDWICH TERN [II] Charrán de Sandwich *Sterna sandvicensis*
Range US–SAm. Res/win cstl Mex (csPac, Atl, Yuc), Blz (cstl + cayes), Guat (Pac, Atl), ElSal (cstl). Rare.
Habitat Offshore islands, coastal waters, beaches, estuaries.
Field Marks 16" Like Royal Tern, but bill slender, black with yellow tip; very short rounded crest; Juv: pale gray back and wings.

ROSEATE TERN Charrán Rosado *Sterna dougallii*
Range US–Blz, ElSal, Hon. Tr Mex (ne Yuc), sum Blz (cayes), tr ElSal (acc). Rare.
Habitat Sandy islands, cayes, beaches, sandbars.
Field Marks 16" Like Forster's Tern, with deeply forked tail, but tail extends even farther beyond wingtips in perched bird and is white (tipped gray in juvenile), *not* all gray; bill mostly black, with orange only at base, *not* mostly orange with black tip; Win+juv: more black on crown and nape (as in winter Common Tern).

COMMON TERN [II] Charrán Común *Sterna hirundo*
Range AK SAm. Tr/win Mex, Blz (cstl + cayes), Guat (cstl), ElSal (cstl).
Habitat Coastal waters and ocean, bays, lagoons, estuaries.
Field Marks 15" Sum adt: mostly white, with pale gray back; upper surface of wings pale gray with a wedge-shaped blackish patch near wingtip; forehead, crown, and nape black; deeply forked tail; red legs; red bill with (usually) black tip. Imm+win adt: bill all black; black on head from eye to hindcrown to nape; blackish strip on upper side of leading edge of wing from wrist to shoulder.

FORSTER'S TERN [II] Charrán de Forster *Sterna forsteri*
Range Can–CRic. Res/win Mex (res n.nBajCal, n.nAtl; win BajCal, Pac, sw.nHi+cHi, Atl, Yuc), Blz (cas/acc), Guat (Pac), ElSal.
Habitat Lakes, ocean beaches, rocky shores, lagoons.
Field Marks 15" Like Common Tern, but tail grayish, more deeply forked, primaries whitish; *no* wedge-shaped patch near wingtip; Imm + win adt: *no* black wing bar from shoulder to wrist; black patch through eye, *not* on nape.

LEAST TERN [II] Charrán Mínimo *Sterna antillarum*
Range US–SAm, exc Nic. Res/sum/tr cstl Mex (res cPac; sum/tr BajCal, Pac, Atl, Yuc), Blz (cstl + cayes), Guat (Pac, Atl), ElSal. Rare.
Habitat Ocean beaches, lagoons, estuaries, lakeshores, sandbars.
Field Marks 9" Like Common Tern, but much smaller; outer primaries black; forehead white; Sum adt: bill almost all yellow, with small black area at tip; legs yellowish; Imm: Sum, legs black; Juv: legs yellowish.

BRIDLED TERN Charrán Collarejo *Sterna anaethetus*
Range Mex, Blz, CRic, Pan, SAm. Sum Mex (cstl s.nPac+cPac, e Yuc), Blz (cayes), ElSal (cas cstl).

Habitat Small rocky islands in 3-mile waters, beaches, estuaries, ocean. *Field Marks* 14″ Adt: like Sooty Tern, with a white forehead and (slightly paler and browner) dark crown and mantle, but white of forehead extending in a short line above and behind eye; outer tail feathers more whitish; usually a grayish collar around the hindneck. Juv: like adult, with all-whitish underparts and dark above, but back and upper surface of wing somewhat paler and rather scaly; crown and hindneck much paler. *Not* like the nearly all-dark juvenile Sooty Tern.

SOOTY TERN [II] Charrán Oscuro *Sterna fuscata*
Range US–SAm. Tr/sum Mex (sBajCal, s.nPac+csPac, n+e Yuc), Blz (cstl + cayes), Guat (cstl), ElSal (cas cstl).
Habitat Rare away from nest islands; over open ocean, rocky or sandy shores, small islands and cayes.
Field Marks 16″ Black above, except white forehead and white edges of deeply forked black tail; white below; bill and legs black. Juv: blackish brown, except whitish lower belly and untacs, faintly speckled back and wings, and pale gray underwing coverts.

BLACK TERN [I] Charrán Negro *Chlidonias niger*
Range Can–SAm. Tr/win Mex, Blz (cstl + cayes), Guat, ElSal (cstl).
Habitat 3-mile waters and offshore, also lakes, rivers, marshes.
Field Marks 10″ Medium gray back and wings and (forked) tail; black bill. Sum adt: black head and underparts, except white untacs. Win adt: mostly white, with black hindneck to ear patch and eye. Imm: like winter adult, but back mottled brownish. Patchy molting or subadult birds are numerous.

BROWN NODDY [II] Charrán Pardelo *Anous stolidus*
Range US–SAm. Sum Mex (s.nPac+nw.cPac, n+e Yuc), Blz (cayes), ElSal (acc), Guat (acc? Pac?, Atl?).
Habitat Mainly open ocean, offshore islands, also 3-mile waters; also bays, rocky headlands.
Field Marks 15″ Dark brown, with pale gray to whitish nape to forehead; wedge-shaped tail very long, tip slightly notched. Imm: forehead and crown much darker, with narrow whitish line from bill to eye.

BLACK SKIMMER [I] Rayador Negro *Rynchops niger*
Range US–SAm. Res/win Mex (BajCal, Pac, ncHi, Atl, Yuc), Blz (cstl), Guat, ElSal.
Habitat Mainly quiet coastal waters, lagoons, estuaries, sandbars; also lakes, rivers.
Field Marks 18″ To catch small fish or invertebrates, the bird holds bill open as it flies along with knifelike lower mandible cutting the water surface. Mostly black above, white below; bill long, bladelike, red with black tip, lower mandible longer than upper; legs red. Imm: mottled brown and gray above.

AUKLETS, MURRES—ALCUELAS, ALCITAS—ALCIDAE

COMMON MURRE Alcuela Grande *Uria aalge*
Range AK–Mex. Win Mex (nw.nBajCal).
Habitat Open ocean or offshore islands; very rare in 3-mile waters.
Field Marks 17″ Sum: black above, white below, with all-black head and upper neck. Win: throat and sides of head and neck white; narrow black line down from eye and along rear of ear patch.

XANTUS'S MURRELET [I] Alcita de Xantus *Synthliboramphus hypoleucus*
Range Can–Mex. Res/win off Mex (res BajCal; win nPac).
Habitat Open ocean or islands; very rare in 3-mile waters.
Field Marks 10″ Black above; white below (including underwings) except narrowly blackish sides, which show best when wings are raised; ear patch, eye crescents, and partial line above eye white in Mexican race (*hypoleucus*), but mostly black, except white eye crescents, in California race (*scrippsi*).

CRAVERI'S MURRELET Alcita de Craveri *Synthliboramphus craveri*
Range US–Mex. Res/win off Mex (BajCal, nPac).
Habitat Open ocean (or Gulf of California) or islands; very rare in 3-mile waters.
Field Marks 10″ Like Xantus's Murrelet, but more extensively black on sides; much darker, and mottled, underwings; bill longer.

CASSIN'S AUKLET Alcita Oscura *Ptychoramphus aleuticus*
Range AK–Mex. Res off Mex (w BajCal).
Habitat Mostly open ocean or islands; very rare in 3-mile waters, rocky coasts.
Field Marks 9″ Compact, stub-tailed; blackish gray above; dark gray throat, breast, sides, and flanks; belly and untacs white; bill short, thick, with pale spot at base of lower mandible; eye crescents white and eyes whitish.

RHINOCEROS AUKLET Alcuela Rinoceronte *Cerorhinca monocerata*
Range AK–Mex. Win Mex (w BajCal).
Habitat Mostly open ocean; rare in 3-mile waters, bays, headlands; surface diving, seldom flying.
Field Marks 14″ Win adt: dark gray, with lighter gray throat, breast, and sides; belly whitish; thick yellowish bill. Sum adt: two white face plumes; bill orange-yellow, with basal knob.

PIGEONS, DOVES—PALOMAS—COLUMBIDAE

ROCK DOVE Paloma Doméstica *Columba livia*
Range AK–SAm. Res Mex, Blz, Guat, ElSal.
Habitat Cities, towns, villages, farms.
Field Marks 13″ Variable; white to nearly black, variegated or uniform; many individuals are close to the wild type—mostly medium bluish gray, with irides-

cent green and purple collar; two broad black wing bars; white rump; broad black tail-tip band; legs red.

PALE-VENTED PIGEON [12] Paloma Ventriclara *Columba cayennensis*
Range Mex–SAm, exc ElSal. Res Mex (sAtl, se Yuc), Blz, Guat (Atl). Rare.
Habitat Treetops in humid forest or flying over large cleared areas in patchy forest.
Field Marks 13″ M: purplish red; shading to dark bluish gray on rump; hindneck bronzy green; sides of head gray; throat, belly, and untacs whitish. F: duller. See Short-billed Pigeon.

SCALED PIGEON [12] Paloma Escamosa *Columba speciosa*
Range Mex–SAm, exc ElSal. Res Mex (se.cAtl+sAtl, e Yuc), Blz, Guat (Atl).
Habitat Treetops or flying over dense forest.
Field Marks 13″ M: head and most of upperparts purplish and chestnut; upper back, collar, and breast scaly black and rufous; belly and untacs scaly white and purplish; legs purplish. F: duller; more reddish brown above; less reddish tinge below.

WHITE-CROWNED PIGEON [18] Paloma Coroniblanca *Columba leucocephala*
Range US–Mex, Blz, Hon, Pan. Res Mex (cstl e Yuc), Blz (cstl + cayes).
Habitat Mangroves, humid forest, second growth.
Field Marks 13″ M: blackish purple, but crown and forehead white; hindneck barred green; bill red, pale-tipped. F: crown whitish. Imm: crown dark.

RED-BILLED PIGEON [18] Paloma Morada *Columba flavirostris*
Range US–CRic. Res Mex (Pac, Atl, Yuc), Blz, Guat (Pac, Atl), ElSal.
Habitat Woodlots, forest borders, hedgerows, scrubby woods.
Field Marks 13″ Head, neck, and breast purplish rufous, shading to grayish brown back and to dark bluish gray wings, rump, belly, untacs, and tail; bill red, with yellow tip; legs red.

BAND-TAILED PIGEON [18] Paloma Ocotera *Columba fasciata*
Range Can–SAm, exc Blz. Res Mex (n.nBajCal, Hi), Guat (Hi), ElSal.
Habitat Mountain pine or pine-oak woods.
Field Marks 14″ Dark bluish gray and paler gray above, with greenish scaled upper back; white band across nape; head and breast purplish gray; tail black, with somewhat indistinct broad gray tail-tip band; belly and untacs white; legs and black-tipped bill yellow.

SHORT-BILLED PIGEON [12] Paloma Oscura *Columba nigrirostris*
Range Mex–SAm, exc ElSal. Res Mex (se.cAtl+s.sAtl), Blz, Guat (Atl).
Habitat Treetops, in dense humid forest.
Voice Like human voices murmuring *waddle, wat-wat-waddle;* pitch of last *waddle* may be higher or lower.
Field Marks 12″ Dull grayish purple head and underparts; tail and upperparts dark grayish brown; bill black; eyes red; legs dull red.

SPOTTED DOVE Paloma Pintada *Streptopelia chinensis*
Range US–Mex. Res Mex (extreme n.nBajCal).
Habitat Suburban gardens, borders, hedgerows.
Field Marks 12″ Like Mourning Dove, but darker above; more contrasty maroon breast and pale gray head; more rounded tail with broader white feather tips; Adt: hindneck and sides of neck black with many small white spots; Imm: faint spotting on hindneck.

WHITE-WINGED DOVE [18] Paloma Aliblanca *Zenaida asiatica*
Range US–SAm. Res/win Mex, Blz (n), Guat, ElSal.
Habitat Semidesert, scrubby woods, hedgerows, farm fields.
Voice Hoo-hoot-hoo-hoo-oo ("who cooks for you?").
Field Marks 12″ Grayish brown above; paler, buffier head and underparts; white patch shows on folded wing and even more prominently on extended wing; tail broadly white-cornered; bill black.

ZENAIDA DOVE [12] Paloma Zenaida *Zenaida aurita*
Range Mex (+Antilles). Res Mex (cstl n Yuc).
Habitat Scrubby woods, palm groves, mangroves.
Field Marks 11″ Like Mourning Dove, but white wing bar; shorter, rounded tail gray-tipped, *not* white-tipped. Like White-winged Dove, but more reddish brown; white wing bar, but *no* white wing patch; tail corners gray, *not* white.

MOURNING DOVE Paloma Huilota *Zenaida macroura*
Range Can–Pan. Res/win Mex (res BajCal, ncPac, ncIIi, nAtl; win all), Blz, Guat, ElSal.
Habitat Scattered trees, hedgerows, patchy woods and farms, semidesert, grassy brushy plains.
Field Marks 12″ Brownish gray above, with darker wings; grayish buff below; long, narrow wedge-shaped tail, with tail feathers gray at base, white-tipped.

INCA DOVE [18] Tortolita Colilarga *Columbina inca*
Range US–CRic, exc Blz. Res Mex (Pac, Hi, ncAtl+w.sAtl), Guat (exc n), ElSal.
Habitat Gardens, farmyards, hedgerows, woodland borders.
Voice An abrupt *coo-cote.*
Field Marks 8″ Brownish gray above, paler below; liberally scaly above and below; tip and sides of long tail white; rufous wing patch.

COMMON GROUND-DOVE [18] Tortolita Común *Columbina passerina*
Range US–SAm. Res Mex (all exc some nHi and most sAtl), Blz (n), Guat (exc n), ElSal.
Habitat Scrubby woods, borders, hedgerows, vacant lots, farmyards.
Voice Repeated *hoo-ut.*
Field Marks 6.5″ Grayish; paler on head and below; slightly scaly head and breast; tail short, rounded, with little white; rufous and black flight feathers; folded wings spotted; red bill black-tipped. M: bluish on nape, pinkish on face and below.

PLAIN-BREASTED GROUND-DOVE [12] Tortolita Pechilisa *Columbina minuta*
Range Mex–SAm, exc Hon. Res Mex (csPac, se.cAtl+w.sAtl), Blz, Guat (Pac, Atl), ElSal (w). Rare, local, irregular.
Habitat Hedgerows, savannas, woodland borders.
Field Marks 6″ Plumage and voice like Common Ground-Dove's, but *no* scaly marks or spots on head or breast; few spots on folded wing.

RUDDY GROUND-DOVE [12] Tortolita Rojiza *Columbina talpacoti*
Range Mex–SAm. Res Mex (c.nPac–sPac, s.nAtl+csAtl, Yuc), Blz, Guat (Pac, Atl), ElSal.
Habitat Parks, gardens, woodland borders, farms, orchards, hedgerows, open brushy grassy fields.
Field Marks 7″ Like Plain-breasted and Common Ground-Doves, but much more rufous and lacks breast marks of the latter. M: rich reddish brown with bluish head. F: paler, more grayish brown; head *not* bluish; wing spots black. Birds of ncAtl paler, duller.

BLUE GROUND-DOVE [12] Tórtola Azul *Claravis pretiosa*
Range Mex–SAm. Res Mex (sPac, s.nAtl+csAtl, Yuc), Blz, Guat (Pac, Atl), ElSal. Rare.
Habitat Patchy humid forest and fields; flies rapidly near ground, usually paired.
Voice A series of quiet single *hoot* notes and long pauses.
Field Marks 8″ M: pale powder blue-gray, with black tail sides and wing spots. F: brownish; like female Ruddy Ground-Dove, but wing spots reddish brown; seldom seen apart from male.

(MAROON-CHESTED) MONDETOURA GROUND-DOVE [12] Tórtola Oscura *Claravis mondetoura*
Range Mex–SAm, exc Blz, Nic. Res Mex (sPac, csHi, csAtl), Guat (Hi + adj Pac, Atl), ElSal (acc n). Very rare, irregular.
Habitat Cloud forest or other humid forest undergrowth.
Field Marks 8″ Like Blue Ground-Dove, but tail broadly white-cornered; M: purplish breast; gray sides and flanks; white belly; F: dark purplish wing spots.

WHITE-TIPPED DOVE [18] Paloma Perdiz *Leptotila verreauxi*
Range US–SAm. Res Mex (Pac+Atl + adj Hi, Yuc), Blz, Guat, ElSal.
Habitat Undergrowth, from scrubby woods to dense forest.
Voice A very low-pitched, unobtrusive, mournful *oo-ooo*, ascending slightly.
Field Marks 11″ Grayish brown above; pinkish buff breast and sides of head; whitish belly and untacs; pale pinkish forehead to pale purplish gray crown to iridescent purplish hindneck; tail corners white; bill black; legs red.

GRAY-FRONTED DOVE [12] Paloma Cabeciploma *Leptotila rufaxilla*
Range Mex–SAm, exc ElSal. Res Mex (Atl), Blz, Guat (Atl). Rare.
Habitat Undergrowth, woods to dense forest.
Field Marks 10″ Like White-tipped Dove, but forehead pale bluish gray; crown and hindneck medium gray; belly and untacs whiter.

CARIBBEAN DOVE [12] Paloma Caribeña *Leptotila jamaicensis*
Range Mex, Blz (+ Antilles). Res Mex (n.sAtl, s+e Yuc), Blz (n cstl). Rare (common on Cozumel Island).
Habitat Scrub woods, humid forest, borders.
Voice Four-noted, slow, last note higher, *hoo-hoo hoo-hoo* ("Who, who, poor Pooh?").
Field Marks 10″ Like White-tipped Dove, but whiter belly and untacs; more broadly iridescent purplish on hindneck and sides of neck. Best distinguished by voice.

GRAY-CHESTED DOVE [12] Paloma Pechigrís *Leptotila cassini*
Range Mex–SAm, exc ElSal. Res Mex (s.c.sAtl), Blz (s), Guat (Atl). Very rare.
Habitat Undergrowth of dense humid lowland forest.
Field Marks 10″ Like White-tipped Dove, but upper belly, breast, neck, and head much darker, medium purplish gray, not pinkish buff, flanks brownish; less white on tail.

WHITE-FACED QUAIL-DOVE [12] Paloma Codorniz *Geotrygon albifacies*
Range Mex–Nic, exc Blz. Res Mex (csPac, csIIi, csAtl), Guat (Hi + adj Pac, Atl), ElSal (w). Rare, local, irregular.
Habitat Undergrowth of dense cloud forest or overgrown mountain coffee plantations.
Field Marks 12″ Rich reddish brown to purplish above; crown and nape pale bluish gray; forehead, chin, and sides of face whitish; lines of "scales" on sides of neck; bill black.

TUXTLA QUAIL-DOVE [12] Paloma Morena *Geotrygon carrikeri*
Range Mex. Res Mex (cAtl: mts se Veracruz). Rare.
Habitat Undergrowth in humid forest.
Field Marks 10″ Above olive-brown and violet; gray crown to dark greenish hindneck; forehead and black-rimmed ear patch white; breast bluish gray; bill red with black tip.

RUDDY QUAIL-DOVE [12] Paloma Rojiza *Geotrygon montana*
Range Mex–SAm. Res Mex (s.nPac I csPac, s.nAtl+csAtl, Yuc), Blz, Guat (Pac, Atl), ElSal (w). Rare.
Habitat Ground or low shrubs in humid forest undergrowth.
Field Marks 9″ M: rich rufous above; pinkish buff below; ear patch buff out lined with dark reddish brown; streaked reddish brown and buff below eye. F: like male, but duller and more olive above; duller and somewhat darker than male below.

PARROTS, PARAKEETS, MACAWS—PERIQUITOS, COTORRAS—PSITTACIDAE

GREEN PARAKEET [13] Periquito Verde *Aratinga holochlora*
(Does not include Red-throated Parakeet; see below)
Range Mex. Res Mex (c.nPac+sPac, nAtl+n.cAtl).

Habitat Patchy farms and woods, open forest, borders.
Field Marks 11″ Green, may be tinged yellowish below; tail long, pointed.

RED-THROATED PARAKEET [13] Periquito Hondureño *Aratinga rubritorquis*
(The AOU lumps this with Green Parakeet; see above)
Range Guat, ElSal, Hon, Nic. Res Guat (ec Guat), win ElSal.
Habitat Pine-oak woods, borders, deciduous forest.
Field Marks 11″ Like Green Parakeet, but throat orange-red or patchy red and green.

PACIFIC PARAKEET Periquito Pacífico *Aratinga strenua*
Range Mex – Nic, exc Blz. Res Mex (sPac), Guat (Pac), ElSal.
Habitat Woods, borders, farmlands, orchards.
Field Marks 11″ Like Green Parakeet, but bill thicker and legs heavier.

OLIVE-THROATED PARAKEET *Aratinga nana*
(See Aztec Parakeet, next)

AZTEC PARAKEET [13] Periquito Azteco *Aratinga astec*
(The AOU lumps this with *A. nana*, Jamaican Parakeet, which does not occur in our area, and calls the combined species Olive-throated Parakeet)
Range Mex – SAm, exc ElSal. Res Mex (s.nAtl+csAtl, Yuc), Blz, Guat (Atl).
Habitat Forest borders, farms, open woods.
Field Marks 10″ Like Green Parakeet, but smaller, with blue and black flight feathers; pale olive (nAtl) to darker brownish olive (sAtl+Yuc) throat and breast.

ORANGE-FRONTED PARAKEET [13] Periquito Común *Aratinga canicularis*
Range Mex – CRic, exc Blz. Res Mex (s.nPac+csPac), Guat (Pac), ElSal.
Habitat Arid scrub, woodland borders, farms.
Field Marks 9″ Yellowish green, with orange forehead; whitish eye ring; flight feathers blue and black.

MILITARY MACAW [13] Guacamaya Verde *Ara militaris*
Range Mex + SAm. Res Mex (nPac+n.cPac + adj Hi, nAtl + adj Hi). Rare.
Habitat Cliffs, canyons, secluded forests, and river borders.
Field Marks 30″ Mostly dull yellowish green; forehead red; flight feathers, untacs, uptacs, and tail tip (above) blue; basal half of tail red above; bill black.

SCARLET MACAW [13] Guacamaya Roja *Ara macao*
Range Mex – SAm, exc ElSal. Res Mex (se.sAtl), Blz (s), Guat (Atl). Very rare.
Habitat Secluded dense forest and patchy clearings; disappearing in most of Middle America.
Field Marks 36″ Red; some wing coverts yellow; flight feathers, untacs, and uptacs blue.

THICK-BILLED PARROT [13] Cotorra Serrana *Rhynchopsitta pachyrhyncha*
Range Mex. Res Mex (w.ncHi). Rare.
Habitat Secluded mountain pine-oak or pine forests.
Field Marks 16″ Often flies high. Green, but forehead, short superciliary line,

wrist patch, and thighs red; underwing patch yellow; medium-long pointed tail; black bill.

MAROON-FRONTED PARROT [13] Cotorra Oriental *Rhynchopsitta terrisi*
Range Mex. Res Mex (ce.nHi). Rare, local.
Habitat Cliffs, canyons, in pine-oak or pine forests.
Voice A loud high-pitched rolling *cra-ak.*
Field Marks 16" Often in flocks. Like Thick-billed Parrot, but forehead maroon; underwings dark gray.

BARRED PARAKEET [13] Periquito Serrano *Bolborhynchus lineola*
Range Mex–SAm, exc Blz, ElSal. Res Mex (sPac, e.cHi+sHi + adj Atl), Guat (Hi). Very rare, local.
Habitat Treetops in secluded cloud forest, or high over canyons or deep valleys.
Field Marks 6.5" Green; heavy black bars above, narrow bars below; tail short, pointed.

MEXICAN PARROTLET [13] Periquito Mexicano *Forpus cyanopygius*
Range Mex. Res Mex (c+s.nPac+nw.cPac). Irregular.
Habitat Scrubby woods, orchards, borders, large parks.
Voice A thin, tinkling *cree.*
Field Marks 5.5" Often in flocks. M: green; rump and wing patch blue; tail very short. F: *no* blue.

(ORANGE-CHINNED) TOVI PARAKEET [13] Periquito Aliamarillo *Brotogeris juqularis*
Range Mex–SAm, exc Blz. Res Mex (sPac), Guat (Pac), ElSal.
Habitat Farms, woodlots, borders, parks.
Voice *Scree* and *ji-ji-ji-jit.*
Field Marks 7" Rapid flight in flocks—flaps then sails. Shades of green; more brownish and bluish above, more yellowish below; orange chin not prominent; brown wrist patch; underwing coverts bright yellow; tail short, pointed.

BROWN-HOODED PARROT [13] Perico Orejirrojo *Pionopsitta haematotis*
Range Mex–SAm, exc ElSal. Res Mex (se.cAtl+sAtl), Blz, Guat (Atl). Rare.
Habitat Canopy to midlevels in humid forest or borders.
Field Marks 8" Mostly green, with mostly olive-brown and dark gray head and red ear patch; breast yellow-olive; red sides under wings.

WHITE-CROWNED PARROT [13] Perico Chilillo *Pionus senilis*
Range Mex–SAm, exc ElSal. Res Mex (sPac, s.nAtl+csAtl), Blz, Guat (Atl). Rare.
Habitat Canopy in humid or mixed forests.
Voice A rasping *cleek* or *scree, culey, culey.*
Field Marks 9" Strong flight high overhead. Green, but may appear blackish, and back, breast, and head very dark bluish, except white crown and throat; red eye ring; wing patch brown; untacs red.

WHITE-FRONTED PARROT [13] Loro Frentiblanco *Amazona albifrons*
Range Mex–CRic. Res Mex (c+s.nPac+csPac, sAtl, Yuc), Blz, Guat (Pac, Atl), ElSal (w).

Habitat Open forest, patchy woods and farmlands, scrub, borders.
Field Marks 10″ Green with white forehead, red lores and eye ring; somewhat scaly breast, back, and hindneck. M: red wing patch. F: *no* red on wing. See Yucatan Parrot.

(YELLOW-LORED) YUCATAN PARROT [13] Loro Yucateco *Amazona xantholora*
Range Mex, Blz. Res Mex (n.+e.sAtl, Yuc), Blz (n).
Habitat Patchy forest and clearings, scrubby woodland, borders, or overhead.
Field Marks 10″ M+F: like White-fronted Parrot, but more scaly; blackish ear patch; yellow lores; M: less red on wing (alula green, *not* red); F: blue, *not* white, on head; *no* red around eye or on wing.

RED-CROWNED PARROT [13] Loro Tamaulipeco *Amazona viridigenalis*
Range US–Mex. Res Mex (nAtl+n.cAtl).
Habitat River-border woods, forest borders, ranches, second growth.
Voice *Clee-u,* then a harsh *crack-crack-crack.*
Field Marks 12″ Mostly dull yellowish green, somewhat scaly; crown red and forehead red; cheeks pale green; red wing patch; tail short, rounded.

LILAC-CROWNED PARROT [13] Loro Occidental *Amazona finschi*
Range Mex. Res Mex (s.nPac+cPac + adj Hi).
Habitat Patchy woods and farms, orchards, borders; rare in highland pine-oak or pine forest.
Field Marks 12″ Mostly green; forehead dark red; crown pale bluish; wing patch red.

RED-LORED PARROT [13] Loro Frentirrojo *Amazona autumnalis*
Range Mex–SAm, exc ElSal. Res Mex (s.nAtl+csAtl), Blz, Guat (Atl).
Habitat Forest, patchy woods, farms, borders.
Voice A loud, harsh *be-brick* or *she-currick,* or soft, rasping petulant *ca-crra-cra.*
Field Marks 12″ Mostly green; forehead and lores red; ear patch yellow (north of Costa Rica); pale bluish green crown; red wing patch; bill gray; tail short, rounded. Imm: *no* yellow on ear patch.

MEALY PARROT [13] Loro Verde *Amazona farinosa*
Range Mex–SAm, exc ElSal. Res Mex (se.cAtl+sAtl), Blz, Guat (Atl). Rare.
Habitat Middle to upper branches in humid forest near openings; often flies below forest crown.
Voice A quiet *crack* or *sreek;* loud *rack.*
Field Marks 15″ More grayish or bluish green than most other parrots in our area; broadly pale blue crown; dark bill; tail rather short, rounded, with broadly yellowish green tip.

YELLOW-HEADED PARROT [13] Loro Cabeciamarillo *Amazona oratrix*
Range Mex–SAm, exc ElSal. Res Mex (cPac, c.nAtl–w.sAtl), Blz (n). Very rare, local.
Habitat Patchy forest, river borders.
Voice A loud *wow* or *ow,* like a human voice.

Field Marks 14" Mostly green, but entire head yellow (except in Belize, where the nape, throat, and lower sides of face are green, and the northeastern Atlantic region of Guatemala, where nape and throat are green); bill pale yellowish. Imm: head all green or nearly so; *no* red on wings; bill pale dull yellowish.

YELLOW-NAPED PARROT [13] Loro Nuquiamarillo *Amazona auropalliata*
Range Mex–CRic, exc Blz. Res Mex (sPac), Guat (Pac), ElSal. Rare, local.
Habitat Humid forest, patchy woods, partial clearings.
Field Marks 14" Like Yellow-headed Parrot, but head green, except broadly yellow hindneck and sometimes crown; bill dark; one red wing patch.

CUCKOOS, ANIS—CUCOS, CUCLILLOS—CUCULIDAE

BLACK-BILLED CUCKOO [15] Cuclillo Piquinegro *Coccyzus erythropthalmus*
Range Can–SAm. Tr Mex (all exc BajCal, nPac), Blz, Guat, ElSal (cas).
Habitat Borders, hedgerows, scrubby woods.
Field Marks 12" Like Yellow-billed Cuckoo, but bill black; eye ring red; *no* rufous on wing; white tips on tail feathers very narrow, form narrow bars across tail.

YELLOW-BILLED CUCKOO [15] Cuclillo Piquiamarillo *Coccyzus americanus*
Range Can–SAm. Sum/tr Mex (sum s.sBajCal, nPac, nAtl, Yuc; tr all exc BajCal); tr Blz, Guat, ElSal. Rare, local.
Habitat Patchy thickets, trees, and overgrown fields, brushy borders, hedgerows.
Field Marks 12" Brown above, white below; bill black above, buffy yellow below, slightly decurved; inner webs of primaries rufous, forming a wing patch in flight; tail graduated, black with long white feather-tip spots.

MANGROVE CUCKOO [15] Cuclillo Manglero *Coccyzus minor*
Range US–SAm. Res Mex (s.nPac+csPac, s.nAtl+csAtl, cstl Yuc), Blz (cstl), Guat (cstl), ElSal. Rare.
Habitat Patchy woods and thickets, river-edge woods, mangrove swamps.
Voice A slow *cuk-cuk-cuk, co, co, co.*
Field Marks 12" Like Yellow-billed Cuckoo, but with black mask; tawny buff belly and untacs; *no* rufous markings on wing.

SQUIRREL CUCKOO [14] Cuco Vaquero *Playa cayana*
Range Mex–SAm. Res Mex (c.nPac–sPac, peripheral cHi, s.nAtl+csAtl, Yuc), Blz, Guat (Pac, Atl), ElSal.
Habitat Very rare in highlands; moist forest, tree-dotted fields, borders, woodlots.
Voice A sharp *peek* or *peek-purr-rr.*
Field Marks 19" Races vary. nPac and cPac: rich rufous above; throat broadly pale pinkish brown; lower breast, belly, and untacs pale gray; tail feathers mostly chestnut, with subterminal black bar and broad white tip; eyes red; bill and eye ring green; sPac, Atl, and Yuc: like previous birds, but lower breast, belly, and untacs blackish gray; tail feathers (from below) mostly blackish, with white tip.

STRIPED CUCKOO [14] Chiflador Rayado *Tapera naevia*
Range Mex–SAm. Res Mex (sPac, se.cAtl+sw.sAtl+e.sAtl, se Yuc), Blz, Guat
(Pac, Atl), ElSal. Rare.
Habitat Pastures, grassy scrub, borders, open woods.
Voice A deliberate far-carrying whistle, of two or three to five notes.
Field Marks 11″ Brownish above; back heavily streaked and crown (slightly
crested) finely streaked with black; face striped whitish and brown; white below
except broadly pale buff throat.

PHEASANT CUCKOO [14] Cuco Faisán *Dromococcyx phasianellus*
Range Mex–SAm. Res Mex (se.cPac+sPac, se.cAtl+sAtl, Yuc), Blz, Guat (Pac,
Atl), ElSal. Very rare.
Habitat Humid forest, scrubby woods, thickets, borders.
Voice A slow, loud, clear *haw-haw-ha-ha, haw,* or tremolo *ho-haw-ho-o-o-o.*
Field Marks 15″ Blackish brown above, spotted and scaled; white below, except
black-spotted buffy throat and breast; head small, with short dark brown crest;
white line behind eye; tail long, graduated; uptacs very long, plumelike.

LESSER GROUND-CUCKOO [14] Chiflador Terrestre *Morococcyx erythropygus*
Range Mex–CRic, exc Blz. Res Mex (s.nPac+csPac), Guat (Pac), ElSal.
Habitat Scrubby woods, thickets, borders, brushy fields.
Voice One rasping hoot or several, slowing.
Field Marks 11″ Green-glossed grayish brown above, with blackish and rufous
rump; tawny rufous below, with blackish untacs; face lines buff and black; blue
eye ring.

LESSER ROADRUNNER [14] Correcamino Tropical *Geococcyx velox*
Range Mex–Nic, exc Blz. Res Mex (c.nPac–sPac, sw.csHi, n Yuc), Guat (Pac +
adj Hi), ElSal.
Habitat Overgrown brushy fields, dry thorny woods, dry sandy coastal areas.
Field Marks 18″ Like Greater Roadrunner, with sides of neck streaked, but un-
derparts *not* streaked.

GREATER ROADRUNNER [15] Correcamino Norteño *Geococcyx californianus*
Range US–Mex. Res Mex (BajCal, n.nPac, ncHi, nAtl).
Habitat Brushy fields, scrubby borders, mesquite grassland, semideserts.
Voice A low mournful *coo* or *hoot.*
Field Marks 22″ Heavily streaked above and on lower throat, neck, and chest;
ragged crest; long tail, with white feather tips.

SMOOTH-BILLED ANI [15] Garrapatero Piquiliso *Crotophaga ani*
Range US–Mex, Blz, Hon, CRic–SAm. Res Mex (ne Yuc), Blz (acc).
Habitat Scrubby woods, orchards, thickets, brushy fields.
Voice A harsh *peu-ut.*
Field Marks 13″ Like Groove-billed Ani, but bill arch higher, no grooves on bill.

GROOVE-BILLED ANI [15] Garrapatero Pijuy *Crotophaga sulcirostris*
Range US–SAm. Res Mex (c.nPac–sPac, Atl, Yuc), Blz, Guat, ElSal.

Habitat Brushy fields, farms, hedgerows, gardens, borders.
Voice A somewhat musical *pee-clue*.
Field Marks 12″ Black all over, appears scaly; tail rather long, rounded, floppy; bill laterally compressed, very high, sides grooved.

BARN OWLS—LECHUZAS—TYTONIDAE

BARN OWL [15] Lechuza de Campanario *Tyto alba*
Range Can–SAm. Res Mex, Blz, Guat, ElSal. Rare.
Habitat Old buildings, towers, wells, ruins, patchy woods and fields.
Voice A raspy, hisslike screech.
Field Marks 15″ Buffy brown above, mottled and barred; white or buff below, with scattered small spots; face heart-shaped, white or buff.

TYPICAL OWLS—TECOLOTES, LECHUZAS—STRIGIDAE

FLAMMULATED OWL [15] Tecolotito Ojioscuro *Otus flammeolus*
Range Can–Mex, Guat. Res/win Mex (res/sum ncIIi; win sIIi); win Guat (IIi), ElSal. Rare.
Habitat Pine forest or pine-oak woods.
Voice A low *hoot* or paired hoots, repeated slowly.
Field Marks 7″ Like Western Screech-Owl, but eyes dark brown; ear tufts very short; facial disk redder than other feathers.

EASTERN SCREECH-OWL [15] Tecolote Chillón *Otus asio*
Range Can–Mex. Res Mex (nAtl).
Habitat Dry woods, river borders, patchy woods and thickets.
Voice A mellow or wailing tremolo, descending or not.
Field Marks 8″ Gray morph: pale to medium gray all over; streaked, mottled, barred, and spotted; facial disk has black border and white V above bill, leading to prominent ear tufts; eyes bright yellow. Red morph: like gray morph, but rufous replaces most of gray; *not* as heavily streaked.

WESTERN SCREECH-OWL [14] Tecolote Occidental *Otus kennicottii*
Range AK–Mex. Res Mex (BajCal, n.nPac, ncHi).
Habitat Pine or pine-oak woods, semidesert, openings.
Voice A bouncing *hoot, hoot, hoot-hoo-hoo-oo-o*.
Field Marks 8″ Like Eastern Screech-Owl, but red morph dull brown, *not* rufous. Vinaceous Screech Owl has a pinkish wash above and below and fewer dark streaks but nevertheless is now considered a race of Western Screech-Owl.

BALSAS SCREECH-OWL Tecolote de Balsas *Otus seductus*
Range Mex. Res Mex (w+c.cPac).
Habitat Scrubby woods, cactus, semidesert.
Voice Like Western Screech-Owl, but rougher.
Field Marks 8″ Like gray morph of Western Screech-Owl, but eyes brown.

PACIFIC SCREECH-OWL Tecolote Manglero *Otus cooperi*
Range Mex–CRic, exc Blz. Res Mex (se.cPac+sPac), Guat (Pac), ElSal. Rare.
Habitat Palm groves, open woods, mangrove swamps.
Voice A rather rough, uniformly low-pitched, short trill.
Field Marks 8″ Like Western Screech-Owl, but toes and lower tarsus *not* feathered.

WHISKERED SCREECH-OWL Tecolote Rítmico *Otus trichopsis*
Range US–Nic, exc Blz. Res Mex (csPac, w.+se.nHi+csHi), Guat (Hi), ElSal (n).
Habitat Dry oak, pine-oak, or pine woods.
Voice Low-pitched hoots on one pitch—*hoohoohoo, hoo, hoo* or *hoohoohoo, hoo.*
Field Marks 8″ Like Eastern Screech-Owl, with gray morph and red morph, but facial bristles longer, voice different.

VERMICULATED SCREECH-OWL [14] Tecolote Crescendo *Otus guatemalae*
Range Mex–SAm, exc ElSal. Res Mex (c.nPac–cPac, s.nAtl+csAtl, Yuc), Blz, Guat (Atl). Rare.
Habitat Scrubby woods, humid forest, borders.
Voice A long, rather low-pitched trill on one pitch, beginning quietly, gradually becoming louder, ending abruptly.
Field Marks 8″ Like Western Screech-Owl, but fewer dark streaks and more narrow bars below; eyebrow lines *not* as contrasty; toes *not* feathered; voice different.

BEARDED SCREECH-OWL [14] Tecolote Grillo *Otus barbarus*
Range Mex, Guat. Res Mex (sHi), Guat (Hi). Rare.
Habitat Midmountain pine or pine-oak woodlands and borders.
Voice A short, quiet, high-pitched trill.
Field Marks 7″ Like Western Screech-Owl, but smaller; more contrasty black-streaked on whitish below; eyebrow marks and whisker marks more contrasty white; toes and lower tarsus *not* feathered; voice different.

CRESTED OWL [14] Búho Corniblanco *Lophostrix cristata*
Range Mex–SAm. Res Mex (sPac, se.cAtl+s.sAtl), Blz (s), Guat (Pac, Atl), ElSal (acc). Rare.
Habitat Humid forest, woodlots, partial clearings.
Field Marks 16″ Brown above, with large white wing spots; underparts vermiculated dark brown and paler tawny brown; face dark reddish brown, with white line over eye and long white ear tufts.

SPECTACLED OWL [14] Búho de Anteojos *Pulsatrix perspicillata*
Range Mex–SAm. Res Mex (sPac, se.cAtl+s.sAtl), Blz (s), Guat (Pac, Atl), ElSal. Rare.
Habitat Dense humid lowland forest, forest borders, openings, partial clearings.
Voice A rapid series of low-pitched, thumping notes.
Field Marks 19″ *No* ear tufts; blackish brown above and on breast; belly and un-

tacs tawny; face blackish brown, with white throat, whisker marks, and eyebrow lines.

GREAT HORNED OWL [15] Búho Cornudo *Bubo virginianus*
Range AK–SAm. Res Mex, Blz, Guat (Hi + adj Pac), ElSal.
Habitat Semidesert to moist forest.
Field Marks 20″ Races vary greatly; most brownish, streaked and mottled above, mostly barred below; face rufous with black border; white throat; medium ear tufts.

NORTHERN PYGMY-OWL [15] Tecolotito Norteño *Glaucidium gnoma*
Range AK–Mex, Guat, Hon. Res Mex (sBajCal, w+e.nHi+csHi), Guat (Hi).
Habitat Upland pine forest, pine-oak woods.
Voice A long slow series of high piping notes on one pitch—*ho, ho, ho, ho, ho, ho, ho,* etc.
Field Marks 7″ Gray or reddish above, with pale spots; mostly white below with blackish streaks; two eye spots on nape; five or six bars on tail; tiny spots on crown.

COLIMA PYGMY-OWL Tecolotito Colimense *Glaucidium palmarum*
Range Mex. Res Mex (ncPac). Rare.
Habitat Humid woodland, mixed pine-oak woods, dry deciduous forest.
Voice Like that of Ferruginous Pygmy-Owl, but usually in much shorter and more irregular series.
Field Marks 6″ Like Ferruginous Pygmy-Owl, but tail shorter, with only two or three bars.

TAMAULIPAS PYGMY-OWL Tecolotito Tamaulipeco *Glaucidium sanchezi*
Range Mex. Res Mex (e.nHi). Rare.
Habitat Cloud forest, humid pine-oak woods.
Voice Like that of Northern Pygmy-Owl, but has only two or three notes in a series.
Field Marks 6″ Like Northern Pygmy-Owl, but has only two or three bars on its short tail.

CENTRAL AMERICAN PYGMY-OWL [14] Tecolotito Centroamericano *Glaucidium griseiceps*
Range Mex–SAm, exc ElSal. Res Mex (se.cAtl+s.sAtl), Blz, Guat (Pac, Atl). Rare.
Habitat Humid lowland forest.
Voice Like that of Ferruginous Pygmy-Owl, but usually only a few notes in a series.
Field Marks 6″ Like Ferruginous Pygmy-Owl, *but tail shorter,* with only three or four bars. In ncPac Mex, see Colima Pygmy-Owl; in e.nHi Mex, see Tamaulipas Pygmy-Owl.

FERRUGINOUS PYGMY-OWL [15] Tecolotito Bajeño *Glaucidium brasilianum*
Range US–SAm. Res Mex (Pac, Atl, Yuc), Blz, Guat (Pac, Atl), ElSal.
Habitat Humid forest borders, scrub woods, riverbank forest, thickets.

Voice Like that of Northern Pygmy-Owl, but faster; may begin with *cwirt* notes.
Field Marks 7″ Like Northern and Least Pygmy-Owls, but faint streaks, *not* spots, on crown; six to eight tail bars.

ELF OWL [15] Tecolotito Enano *Micrathene whitneyi*
Range US–Mex. Res/win Mex (res sBajCal; sum/win ncPac, ncHi). Rare.
Habitat Semidesert scrub, scrubby woods, rocky slopes with cactus.
Field Marks 6″ Grayish brown above, with white nape band; whitish and buffy brown below; no ear tufts; tail much shorter than Pygmy-Owl's.

BURROWING OWL [15] Tecolote Llanero *Athene cunicularia*
Range Can–SAm, exc Blz, Nic. Res/win Mex (res BajCal, nPac, nHi; win csPac, csHi, ncAtl; cas Yuc); win Guat (Pac + adj Hi), ElSal (cas). Rare.
Habitat Usually on ground or fence post or utility pole in grassy plains, dry brush, rocky areas; often active by day.
Voice A loud piping *toot-too.*
Field Marks 9″ Reddish to grayish, spotted above; whitish below, with barred sides and flanks; black band across white throat; legs long; tail short.

MOTTLED OWL [14] Mochuelo Café *Ciccaba virgata*
Range Mex–SAm. Res Mex (Pac, e.+w.ncHi, Atl, Yuc), Blz, Guat (Pac, Atl), ElSal.
Habitat Very rare in highlands; humid forest, partial clearings, borders, orchards, plantations.
Voice A slow descending, burred *hroot, hroot, hroot, hroot.*
Field Marks 14″ Blackish brown above, mottled and dotted; buffy or tawny below, with heavy streaks; facial disks rimmed with white or buff; eyes brown; tail with four or five dark bars; *no* ear tufts.

BLACK-AND-WHITE OWL [14] Mochuelo Zarado *Ciccaba nigrolineata*
Range Mex–SAm. Res Mex (csAtl, sPac, s+e Yuc), Blz, Guat (Pac, Atl), ElSal (w). Rare.
Habitat Dense humid forest, tall river-border woods, partial clearings.
Field Marks 15″ Black above, but hindneck barred with whitish; underparts narrowly barred black and white; usually only four or five narrow white tail bars; *no* ear tufts.

SPOTTED OWL [15] Búho Manchado *Strix occidentalis*
Range Can–Mex. Res Mex (local nBajCal, w.+e.nHi+w.cHi). Rare.
Habitat Highland pine forest, pine-oak woods.
Voice Like first three or four notes of Barred Owl's call.
Field Marks 19″ Like Barred Owl, but large whitish spots above, *not* bars; barred and spotted below, *not* streaked.

BARRED OWL [15] Búho Serrano *Strix varia*
Range AK–Mex. Res Mex (w.ncHi+se.cHi). Rare.
Habitat Pine or pine-oak forests.
Voice A loud *ho-hoo ho-hoo, ho-hoo ho-hoo-ah.*

Field Marks 20" Brownish gray, barred above and on chest; rest of underparts heavily streaked; *no* ear tufts; eyes brown.

FULVOUS OWL [14] Lechuzón *Strix fulvescens*
Range Mex, Guat, ElSal, Hon. Res Mex (sHi), Guat (Hi), ElSal (n). Rare.
Habitat Open pine forest or humid pine-oak woods.
Voice A loud four-noted *huho, huhoo;* may be repeated a second time quickly.
Field Marks 17" Like Barred Owl, but much more reddish brown and buff or tawny, above and below.

LONG-EARED OWL [15] Lechuza Caricafé *Asio otus*
Range Can–Mex. Res/win Mex (res n.nBajCal, local e.nHi; win ncPac, ncHi). Rare.
Habitat River valleys, dense hedgerows, pine forest, pine-oak woods.
Voice Often three low-pitched hoots.
Field Marks 15" Like Great Horned Owl, but smaller and more slender; ear tufts proportionally longer and attached closer to center of (reddish) face.

STYGIAN OWL [14] Lechuza Oscura *Asio stygius*
Range Mex, Blz, Guat, Hon, Nic, SAm. Res Mex (w.nHi, w+s+e.cHi, Yuc), Blz, Guat (Pac, Hi). Very rare.
Habitat Pine forest, pine-oak woods, thickets, scrubby woods.
Voice *Hoo* or *hoo-hoo.*
Field Marks 17" Heavy black streaks and narrow crossbars on pale gray below, appears whitish-spotted in some lights; head, ear tufts, and upperparts blackish, with a prominent whitish urn-shaped patch between the yellow eyes and base of centrally located ear tufts.

SHORT-EARED OWL [15] Lechuza Llanera *Asio flammeus*
Range AK–Mex, Guat. Win Mex (BajCal, nPac+nw.cPac, ncHi, nAtl+n.cAtl), Guat (acc). Rare.
Habitat Grassy, open country; marshy, grassy, or sedgy fields.
Field Marks 16" Often hunts in daylight, flight buoyant and somewhat erratic. Streaked tawny and brown above and below, but whitish belly and untacs; sooty around eyes; white between eyes; ear tufts very short, close together.

STRIPED OWL [14] Lechuza Cariblanca *Pseudoscops clamator*
Range Mex–SAm. Res Mex (se.cAtl+w.sAtl, sPac), Blz (s), Guat (Pac, Atl), ElSal. Rare.
Habitat Patchy woods and grassy fields, thickets, forest borders.
Voice A rapid series of rather rough notes, *ho-ho-ho-ho-ho-ho.*
Field Marks 14" Streaked dark brown and tawny above; tawny buff below, with sharp brown streaks; face whitish, black-bordered; ear tufts long, from near center of face.

NORTHERN SAW-WHET OWL [15] Tecolotito Cabezón *Aegolius acadicus*
Range AK–Mex. Res Mex (w+e.nHi+cHi). Very rare, local.
Habitat Mountain forest of fir, pine-oak, or pine.

Voice Like Ferruginous Pygmy-Owl's, but slightly slower, more mellow.
Field Marks 7″ Adt: dark brown above, with white spots; whitish below, with rufous streaks; head appears square; tail short, barred. Juv: reddish brown above, spotted; head and breast chocolate brown; belly and untacs tawny rufous; white between eyes.

UNSPOTTED SAW-WHET OWL [14] Tecolotito Volcanero *Aegolius ridgwayi*
Range Mex, Guat, ElSal, CRic, Pan. Res Mex (sHi), Guat (Hi), ElSal (n). Very rare.
Habitat Mountain pine-oak woods, high cloud forest, partial clearings, borders.
Field Marks 7″ Like Northern Saw-whet Owl, but *no* spots on upperparts; *no* bars on tail; toes partly bare. Juv: rich brown above, buffy below.

NIGHTJARS — TAPACAMINOS — CAPRIMULGIDAE

SHORT-TAILED NIGHTHAWK Chotacabra Colicorta *Lurocalis semitorquatus*
Range Mex – SAm, exc Blz, ElSal. Res Mex (extreme se.sAtl), Guat (Atl). Rare.
Habitat Humid forest, partial clearings, borders, openings.
Field Marks 8″ Mostly blackish brown all over, spotted and mottled with rufous and whitish, or narrowly barred (belly, untacs, and tail) pale dull reddish brown; white patch on throat; tail short and slightly notched.

LESSER NIGHTHAWK [15] Chotacabra Halcón *Chordeiles acutipennis*
Range US – SAm. Res/win Mex, Blz, Guat, ElSal.
Habitat Scrubby woods, semidesert, patchy thorny woods and fields.
Voice A low-pitched, unobtrusive tremolo.
Field Marks 8″ M: mottled grayish above; buffy-gray barred below and on tail; white throat; white bar near wingtip crosses four outermost primaries. F: wingtip bar buffy; throat white or buff.

COMMON NIGHTHAWK [15] Chotacabra Zumbón *Chordeiles minor*
Range US – SAm. Sum/tr Mex (sum w.ncHi+sHi + adj Pac, ncAtl; tr csPac, Hi, sAtl, Yuc), Blz, Guat.
Habitat Open areas, brushy short-grass fields, patchy farms and woods.
Voice A nasal, rasping *peent.*
Field Marks 9″ Flies high. Like Lesser Nighthawk, but darker and grayer; white bar farther from wingtip, crosses five outermost primaries; may have unbarred whitish lower belly and untacs.

PAURAQUE Pachacua Pucuya *Nyctidromus albicollis*
Range US – SAm. Res Mex (c.nPac – sPac, Atl, Yuc), Blz, Guat (Pac, Atl), ElSal.
Habitat Patchy farms and woods, brushy fields, hedgerows, semidesert, orchards, borders.
Voice A repeated, rasping whistle, *pur-weer* or *wee-o.*
Field Marks 11″ M: mottled grayish brown, buff, and black above; barred black-

ish and dull tawny below; white patches on tail; white bar on wing. F: little white in tail; wing bar buff.

COMMON POORWILL Pachacua Tevíi *Phalaenoptilus nuttallii*
Range Can–Mex. Res Mex (BajCal, n.nPac, nHi, nAtl).
Habitat Low scrubby woods, semidesert, rocky slopes, borders.
Voice A mellow whistle, *pur-will* or *cor-yillup*.
Field Marks 8″ Mostly mottled gray above and below. M: broad white bar on blackish throat and upper breast; white tail corners. F: throat bar buff; tail patches buff or whitish.

EARED POORWILL [14] Pachacua Orejón *Nyctiphrynus mcleodii*
Range Mex. Res Mex (ncPac + adj Hi). Rare, local.
Habitat Mountain pine forest and pine-oak woods, open woods, borders.
Voice A loud, abrupt *pyeeoo*.
Field Marks 7″ M: mostly dark brown and tawny above and below, with black-spotted scapulars, white-spotted wing coverts, and white band on throat; tail corners white; feathers of chest and side of crown elongated. F: more reddish.

YUCATAN POORWILL [14] Pachacua Yucateca *Nyctiphrynus yucatanicus*
Range Mex, Blz, Guat. Res Mex (e.sAtl, Yuc), Blz, Guat (n Atl). Rare.
Habitat Patchy woods and fields, thorny woods, borders.
Voice An abrupt *whee-oo* or *will*.
Field Marks 7″ Like Eared Poorwill, but much darker and more mottled above and below.

CHUCK-WILL'S-WIDOW Tapacamino de Paso *Caprimulgus carolinensis*
Range US–SAm. Tr/win Mex (sPac, Atl, Yuc), Blz (n), Guat, ElSal (tr). Rare.
Habitat Thickets, undergrowth, river-valley woods, borders, hedgerows.
Voice A loud whistle, *yuc-wheeoo-witto*.
Field Marks 11″ Seldom calls in winter. Mottled dark buffy reddish brown; white throat bar; two large tail patches white above, buffy below. F: *no* tail patches.

(TAWNY-COLLARED NIGHTJAR) CHIP-WILLOW [14] Tapacamino Ti-cuer
Caprimulgus salvini
Range Mex, Nic? Res Mex (ncAtl+w.sAtl).
Habitat Semidesert, scrubby woods, patchy farms and fields, borders.
Voice A clear, loud *yip-willow*.
Field Marks 9″ M: mostly mottled rich blackish brown; collar pale tawny rufous behind, pale buff in front; tail blackish with broadly white corners. F: tail has small buff corners.

YUCATAN NIGHTJAR Tapacamino Yucateco *Caprimulgus badius*
Range Mex, Blz, Guat, Hon. Res Mex (n.sAtl, Yuc), Blz, Guat (Atl). Rare.
Habitat Patchy woods, overgrown fields, borders.
Voice A rolling *yip-willo-reeo*.

Field Marks 9" Like Chip-willow, but collar paler; face darker; tail patches white in female as well as in male, and much larger; voice different.

(BUFF-COLLARED NIGHTJAR) TUCUCHILLO Préstame-tu-cuchillo *Caprimulgus ridgwayi*
Range US, Mex, Guat, Hon. Res/sum Mex (Pac + adj Hi, c.cAtl), Guat (e). Rare.
Habitat Thickets, borders, brushy fields, pine-oak woods.
Voice A rapid chatter, *cu-cu-cu-cu-cu-cu-whee-o,* rising then falling sharply and ending in a whistle.
Field Marks 9" M: mostly dark grayish brown above, paler below; collar reddish buff behind, whitish in front; tail barred, with large white corner patches. F: tail patches much smaller, dull buffy white.

WHIP-POOR-WILL Tapacamino Cuerporruín *Caprimulgus vociferus*
Northern group Cuerporruín Norteño *Caprimulgus v. vociferus*
Range Can–Pan. Win Mex (sPac, sHi, Atl), Blz (s), Guat, ElSal.
Habitat Hedgerows, patchy woods and brush, partial clearings, forest borders.
Voice A loud, rhythmic, repeated whistle, *whip-pur-wee-o.*
Field Marks 10" M: mottled grayish brown above; barred brownish gray below; throat bar and very large tail corners white. F: throat bar and very small tail patches pale dull buffy.
Mexican group Cuerporruín Mexicano *Caprimulgus v. arizonae*
Range US–Hon, exc Blz, ElSal? Res/sum Mex (s.sBajCal, w.+e.nHi+csHi + adj Pac), Guat (Hi), ElSal (n?).
Habitat Pine forest, pine-oak woods, partial clearings, borders.
Voice *Wheer-pur-weer,* like call of Northern group birds, but more rolling and burred, and phrases repeated more slowly.
Field Marks 10" Like Northern group, but usually darker and more reddish buff; smaller white patches on tail corners in male.

(SPOT-TAILED NIGHTJAR) PIT-SWEET [14] Tapacamino Pit-suit *Caprimulgus maculicaudus*
Range Mex, Hon, Nic, SAm. Sum Mex (se.cAtl+sw.sAtl). Rare.
Habitat Patchy grassland and scrubby woods, savannas.
Voice A very high-pitched *keep-sweep, not* repeated rapidly.
Field Marks 7" M: mottled blackish brown above; reddish nape collar; mottled buff and black below, but plain buff lower belly and untacs; tail black with white tail corners and white spots below. F: *no* white in tail.

POTOOS—JOJÚS—NYCTIBIIDAE

GREAT POTOO Jojú Grande *Nyctibius grandis*
Range Mex–SAm, exc Blz, ElSal. Res Mex (s.c.sAtl), Guat (Atl). Very rare.
Habitat Humid forest, partial clearings, borders.
Field Marks 21" Like Northern Potoo, but larger and larger-headed; entire head and throat grayish with fine vermiculations, *not* streaked dark brown and

whitish; underparts generally more vermiculated or narrowly barred, *not* streaked; eyes dark brown, *not* yellow (but eyes of both species glow reddish orange in a light beam).

NORTHERN POTOO [14] Jojú Norteño *Nyctibius jamaicensis*
Range Mex–CRic. Res Mex (s.nPac+csPac, s.nAtl+csAtl, Yuc), Blz, Guat (Pac, Atl), ElSal. Rare.
Habitat Patchy woods and shrubby fields, pastures, forest borders; perches upright on posts, dead trees.
Voice A loud *baw;* loud rasping notes.
Field Marks **14"** Mottled, blotched, and streaked brownish gray and blackish; more blackish blotches on breast; head striped black, brown, and whitish; tail long; mouth large, but bill small; eyes yellow (but glow reddish orange in a light beam).

SWIFTS—VENCEJOS—APODIDAE

BLACK SWIFT [18] Vencejo Negro *Cypseloides niger*
Range AK–CRic, exc Blz. Sum/tr Mex (BajCal, Pac, w.nHi+csHi), Guat (Pac + adj Hi), ElSal (cas). Rare.
Habitat Over open areas, dry rocky slopes, shrubby grassy plains, waterfalls.
Field Marks **7"** M: black, often with faint white frosting on forehead; tail medium, usually slightly notched. F: belly may be faintly scalloped with white.

(WHITE-FRONTED) SIERRA MADRE SWIFT [23] Vencejo Mexicano *Cypseloides storeri*
(Some authorities lump this with White-chinned Swift; see below)
Range Mex. Res/sum Mex (nw–sc.cHi). Very rare.
Habitat *Barrancas,* steep-sided valleys, mountain slopes, waterfalls.
Field Marks **6"** Like female Chestnut-collared Swift, appears black all over, but slightly larger; tail shorter; in the hand, shows white frosting all around base of bill (chin, lores, forehead, etc.). Like Black Swift, but wing and tail relatively shorter; more white frosting on chin and all around base of bill.

WHITE-CHINNED SWIFT [23] Vencejo Sombrío *Cypseloides cryptus*
Range Blz–SAm. Res/sum Blz (s), Guat (Atl). Rare.
Habitat Open country, mountainsides, wooded ravines, waterfalls.
Field Marks **6"** Like Sierra Madre Swift, but white frosting mostly on chin and around base of lower mandible, *not* reaching center of forehead.

CHESTNUT-COLLARED SWIFT [23] Vencejo Cuellicastaño *Streptoprocne rutila*
Range Mex–SAm, exc Blz, Nic. Res/win Mex (wc.nHi–se.sHi + adj Pac), Guat (Hi + adj Pac), ElSal. Rare.
Habitat Over open or wooded slopes or deep ravines.
Voice A rasping *zee-zee-zee.*
Field Marks **5.5"** Blackish brown; appears round-headed. M: inconspicuous, broad, dark reddish brown full collar. F: *no* reddish brown collar.

WHITE-COLLARED SWIFT [23] Vencejo Cuelliblanco *Streptoprocne zonaris*
Range Mex–SAm. Res Mex (csPac, s.nAtl–sc.sAtl), Blz (s), Guat, ElSal.
Habitat Cliffs, caves, over wet fields, stream valleys, humid forest, partial clearings.
Voice A loud *cleek, cleek, cleek.*
Field Marks 8″ Blackish, except white full collar (broader below); tail medium, notched.

WHITE-NAPED SWIFT [23] Vencejo Nuquiblanco *Streptoprocne semicollaris*
Range Mex. Res/vis Mex (s.nPac, sw.nHi, sw.+sc.cHi; cas/acc sPac). Rare.
Habitat Over deep ravines, rocky wooded slopes, or brushy flatlands.
Voice A harsh, extended *chi-ik, chi-ik.*
Field Marks 9″ Blackish, except white nape band; tail square or slightly notched.

CHIMNEY SWIFT [18] Vencejillo de Chimenea *Chaetura pelagica*
Range Can–SAm. Tr Mex (Atl, Yuc), Blz, Guat (Atl), ElSal.
Habitat Over open country, wooded slopes, humid forest, savanna.
Voice High-pitched, rather musical, rapid, chipping notes.
Field Marks 5″ Blackish brown; throat pale gray; tail short, square, spiny. See Vaux's Swift.

VAUX'S SWIFT [18] Vencejillo Común *Chaetura vauxi*
Range AK–SAm. Res/tr Mex (res s.nPac–sPac, csHi, s.nAtl–sc.sAtl, Yuc; tr nBajCal, nPac, w.nHi), Blz, Guat, ElSal.
Habitat Caves, *cenotes,* clearings, patchy woods and fields, orchards.
Voice Like Chimney Swift's, but somewhat less musical and not as loud.
Field Marks 4″ Like Chimney Swift, but paler below and on rump; throat whitish (but both Chimney Swift and Vaux's Swift may be blackened with soot); tail short, square, spiny.

WHITE-THROATED SWIFT [18] Vencejo Pechiblanco *Aeronautes saxatalis*
Range Can–Hon, exc Blz. Res Mex (BajCal, s.nPac+cPac, Hi), Guat (Hi + adj Pac), Guat (Hi), ElSal. Rare.
Habitat Usually over mountainous terrain, deep ravines, wooded or open rocky slopes.
Field Marks 6.5″ Black and white like Geronimo Swift, but white line over eye; breast and center of belly white; tail much shorter, only slightly forked.

(LESSER SWALLOW-TAILED) CAYENNE SWIFT [23] Vencejillo Tijereta *Panyptila cayennensis*
Range Mex–SAm. Res Mex (sPac, c.cAtl–sc.sAtl), Blz, Guat (Pac, Atl), ElSal (w). Very rare.
Habitat High over humid forest, archaeological sites, partial clearings, borders, and openings; long, vertical fibrous tube nest glued (with saliva) against tree trunk or to walls of buildings.
Field Marks 5″ Like Geronimo Swift, but much smaller; flight somewhat more like that of Chimney Swift or Vaux's Swift.

GREAT BLUE HERON
p. 8

GREEN HERON
p. 9

Imm

LITTLE BLUE
HERON
p. 9

Molting
Imm

Imm

White
morph

DISH EGRET
p. 9

White
morph

CATTLE EGRET
p. 9

Imm

GREAT EGRET
p. 8

SNOWY EGRET
p. 8

OLORED
RON
. 9

Imm

BLACK-
CROWNED
NIGHT-HERON
p. 10

BCNH
Imm

YCNH

Imm

YELLOW-
CROWNED
NIGHT-HERON
p. 10

RICAN
TERN
. 8

WHITE IBIS
p. 10

LEAST
BITTERN
p. 8

ROSEATE SPOONBILL
p. 11

Imm

Imm

WHITE-FACED
IBIS
p. 11

GREATER
FLAMINGO
p. 12

Imm

WOOD STORK
p. 11

GLOSSY
IBIS
p. 10

Murrell
Butler

2

TUNDRA SWAN
p. 13

Imm

CANADA GOOSE
p. 13

BRANT
p. 13

WHITE-FRONTED
GOOSE
p. 13

Imm

Imm

ROS
GOO
p. 1

Imm

Dark morph

SNOW
GOOSE
p. 13

White morph

BLACK-BELLIED
WHISTLING-DUCK
p. 12

Imm

MALLARD
p. 14

F

M

FULVOUS
WHISTLING-DUCK
p. 12

F

NORTHERN
PINTAIL
p. 14

F

M

F

M

GADWALL
p. 15

F

M

WOOD DUCK
p. 14

F

M

NORTHERN
SHOVELER
p. 15

F

M

AMERICAN
WIGEON
p. 15

F

M

Mu
Bu

3

GREEN-WINGED TEAL p. 14   M   F

BLUE-WINGED TEAL p. 15   F   M

CINNAMON TEAL p. 15   M

REDHEAD p. 16   F   M

RING-NECKED DUCK p. 16   F   M

GREATER SCAUP p. 16   M

CANVASBACK p. 15   F   M

BUFFLEHEAD p. 17   F   M

LESSER SCAUP p. 16   F   M

COMMON GOLDENEYE p. 17   F   M

MASKED DUCK p. 17   F   M

RUDDY DUCK p. 18

HOODED MERGANSER p. 17   F   M

WHITE-WINGED SCOTER p. 16   Adt M   Adt F   Imm M

Imm F

OLDSQUAW p. 186   F Win   Adt M Win   Adt M Sum

SURF SCOTER p. 16   Adt M   Adt F

BLACK SCOTER p. 16   M   F   F

RED-BREASTED MERGANSER p. 17   M

COMMON MERGANSER p. 17   M   F

Murrell Butler

4

GREAT TINAMOU
p. 1

LITTLE
TINAMOU
p. 1

SLATY-BREASTED
TINAMOU
p. 1

THICKET
TINAMOU
p. 1

BARE-THROATED
TIGER-HERON
p. 8

PINNATED
BITTERN
p. 7

AGAMI HERON
p. 9

BOAT-BILLED
HERON
p. 10

M

MUSCOVY
DUCK
p. 14

JABIRU
p. 11

(Lesser Yellow-he
SAVANNA VULT
p. 12

KING
VULTURE
p. 12

DOUBLE-TOO
KITE
p. 19

PLUMBEOUS
KITE
p. 19

M

F

GRAY-HEADED
KITE
p. 18

HOOK-BILLED KITE
p. 18

HARPY EAGLE
p. 24

BICOLORED HAWK
p. 20

Murie
Butle

5

VULTURES

TURKEY p. 11

BLACK p. 11   KING p. 12

CRANE HAWK   BLACK-HAWKS

WHITE HAWK
p. 21

p. 21   GREAT p. 22   COMMON p. 21

GREAT BLACK-HAWK
p. 22

ITARY EAGLE
p. 22

BLACK-COLLARED
HAWK
p. 20

Imm

ORNATE
HAWK-EAGLE
p. 25

BLACK-AND-WHITE
HAWK-EAGLE
p. 25

Imm

Underwing

COLLARED
(Forest-Falcon)
MICRASTUR
p. 26

Buff morph

BLACK
HAWK-EAGLE
p. 25

CRANE HAWK
p. 21

LAUGHING FALCON
p. 26

BARRED (Forest-Falcon)
MICRASTUR
p. 26

WHITE-BREASTED
HAWK
p. 20

ROADSIDE HAWK
p. 22

Imm

ORANGE-BREASTED
FALCON
p. 27

BAT FALCON
p. 27

Murrell
Butler

6

MISSISSIPPI
KITE
p. 19

Imm

NORTHERN
GOSHAWK
p. 21

COOPER'S HAWK
p. 20

Imm

Imm

BROAD-WINGED
HAWK
p. 23

Imm

Dark
morph

ROUGH-
LEGGED HAWK
p. 24

SHARP-SHIN...
HAWK
p. 20

FERRUGINOUS
HAWK
p. 24

Imm

Dark
morph

RED-TAIL...
HAWK p...

Im

RED-SHOULDERED
HAWK p. 22

MERL...
p. 26

NORTHERN
HARRIER
p. 20

GOLDEN EAGLE
p. 24

Tail of
imm

M

Imm

F

AMERICAN KESTREL
p. 26

PRAIRIE
FALCON
p. 27

PEREGRINE
FALCON
p. 27

OSPREY
p. 18

F

Murrell
Butler

WHITE-TAILED KITE
p. 19

SWALLOW-TAILED
KITE
p. 18

M

(Snail)
EVERGLADE
KITE
p. 19

F

WHITE-TAILED
HAWK
p. 23

ZONE-TAILED
HAWK
p. 23

SHORT-TAILED
HAWK
p. 23

Black
morph

GRAY HAWK
p. 21

SWAINSON'S HAWK
p. 23

COMMON
BLACK-HAWK
p. 21

CRESTED
CARACARA
p. 25

HARRIS'S HAWK
p. 22

APLOMADO
FALCON
p. 27

GAMBEL'S
QUAIL
p. 32

M

MOUNTAIN
QUAIL
p. 33

SCALED
QUAIL
p. 32

CALIFORNIA
QUAIL
p. 32

M

F

F

MONTEZUMA
QUAIL
p. 30

M

F

NORTHERN
BOBWHITE
p. 31

M

F

Northern Bobwhite: Males of
some other Mexican races

Murrell
Butler

8

GREAT CURASSOW
p. 29

M

F

CRESTED GUAN
p. 28

RUFOUS-BELLIED
CHACHALACA
p. 28

OCELLATED TURKEY
p. 29

M

HIGHLAND GUAN
p. 28

F

HORNED GUAN
p. 29

BEARDED
WOOD-PARTRIDGE
p. 30

LONG-TAILED
WOOD-PARTRIDGE
p. 29

BUFFY-CROWNED
WOOD-PARTRIDGE
p. 30

M

F

ELEGANT
p. 3

SPOTTED
WOOD-QUAIL
p. 30

GRAY-NECKED WOOD-RAIL
p. 34

RUFOUS-NE
WOOD-R
p. 34

OCELLATED QUAIL
p. 31

M

F

(Black-throated)
YUCATAN BOBWHITE
p. 32

M

F

SINGING QUAIL
p. 30

M

F

BANDED QUAIL
p. 32

YELLOW-BREASTED
(Crake) RAIL
p. 35

RUDDY (Crake) RAIL
p. 33

SPOTTED RAIL
p. 35

UNIFORM (Crake)
p. 34

Murrell
Butler

SORA
p. 34

Imm

VIRGINIA RAIL
p. 34

Imm

YELLOW RAIL   p. 187   BLACK RAIL   p. 33   **9**

PURPLE
GALLINULE
p. 35

COMMON
MOORHEN
p. 35

AMERICAN COOT   p. 35

BLACK-NECKED STILT
p. 39

Win

BLACK OYSTERCATCHER
p. 39

AMERICAN
AVOCET
p. 39

Imm

AMERICAN
OYSTERCATCHER
p. 38

NORTHERN
JACANA
p. 39

KING RAIL
p. 34

CLAPPER RAIL
p. 33

WHOOPING CRANE
p. 187

SANDHILL CRANE
p. 36

Imm

Imm

LIMPKIN
p. 36

Murrell
Butler

10

BLACK-BELLIED
PLOVER
p. 37

AMERICAN
GOLDEN-PLOVER
p. 37

SEMIPALMATED
PLOVER
p. 38

Win

Win

WILSON'S PLOVER
p. 37

M

MOUNTAIN
PLOVER
p. 38

SNOWY PLOV
p. 37

F

KILLDEER
p. 38

F

M

Win

PIPING P
p. 3

F

UPLAND
SANDPIPER
p. 40

WHIMBREL
p. 40

LONG-BILLED
CURLEW
p. 41

Win

SOLITARY
SANDPIPER
p. 40

HUDSONIAN
GODWIT
p. 41

MARBLED GODWIT
p. 41

LONG-BIL
DOWITCH
p. 44

Win

LESSER
YELLOWLEGS
p. 40

GREATER
YELLOWLEGS
p. 39

SHORT-BILLED
DOWITCHER
p. 43

STILT
SANDPIPER
p. 43

Win

Murrell
Butler

11

SPOTTED SANDPIPER p. 40

WILLET p. 40

Win

WANDERING TATTLER p. 40

Win

Win

RUDDY TURNSTONE p. 41

Win

Win

BLACK TURNSTONE p. 41

KNOT p. 42

SURF-BIRD p. 41

Win

COMMON SNIPE p. 44

SANDERLING p. 42

Win

SEMIPALMATED SANDPIPER p. 42

Win

Win

p. 42

Win

LEAST SANDPIPER p. 42

Win

Sum

Sum

BAIRD'S SANDPIPER p. 43

TERN PIPER 42

Win

Win

WHITE-RUMPED SANDPIPER p. 12

PECTORAL SANDPIPER p. 43

DUNLIN p. 43

BUFF-BREASTED SANDPIPER p. 43

F

RED PHALAROPE p. 44

M

RED-NECKED PHALAROPE p. 44

F

WILSON'S PALAROPE p. 44

F

M

M

Win

M

Win

Win

Murrell Butler

12

DOUBLE-STRIPED
THICK-KNEE
p. 36

SUNBITTERN
p. 36

PALE-VENTED PIGEON
p. 52

SUNGREBE
p. 35

SHORT-BILLED
PIGEON
p. 52

SCALED PIGEON
p. 52

SOCORRO DOVE
p. 188

ZENAIDA DOVE
p. 53

PLAIN-BREASTED
GROUND-DOVE
p. 54

RUDDY
GROUND-DOVE
p. 54

M

BLUE
GROUND-DOVE
p. 54

M

F

(Maroon-chested)
MONDETOURA
GROUND-DOVE
p. 54

F

M

CARIBBEAN DOVE
p. 55

GRAY-FRONTED
DOVE
p. 54

GRAY-CHESTED
DOVE
p. 55

TUXTLA
QUAIL-DOVE
p. 55

RUDDY
QUAIL-DOVE
p. 55

M

F

WHITE-FACED
QUAIL-DOVE
p. 55

Murrell
Butler

13

SCARLET MACAW
p. 56

MILITARY MACAW
p. 56

4.

1.
M

6.

2.
M

F

1.&2.

5.

3.

AZTEC PARAKEET
p. 56

1. WHITE-FRONTED
p. 57

M

F

2. (Yellow-Lored)
YUCATAN
p. 58

3. BROWN-HOODED
p. 57

MEALY
p. 58

4. RED-LORED
p. 58

YELLOW-HEADED p. 58

5. WHITE-CROWNED
p. 57

MAROON-FRONTED
p. 57

PARROTS

LILAC-CROWNED
p. 58

RED-CROWNED
p. 58

YELLOW-NAPED
p. 59

6. THICK-BILLED p. 56

ED-THROATED
p. 56

(Orange-chinned)
TOVI
p. 57

GREEN
p. 55

MEXICAN
PARROTLET
p. 57

AZTEC
p. 56

ORANGE-FRONTED
p. 56

BARRED
p. 57

PARAKEETS

14

SQUIRREL
CUCKOO
p. 59

STRIPED
CUCKOO
p. 60

PHEASANT
CUCKOO
p. 60

LESSER GROUND-CUCKOO
p. 60

LESSER
ROADRUNNER
p. 60

WESTERN SCREECH-OWL
"Vinaceous" race
p. 61

VERMICULAT
SCREECH-OW
p. 62

SPECTACLED OWL
p. 62

BEARDED
SCREECH-OWL
p. 62

CRESTED
OWL
p. 62

MOTTLED
OWL
p. 64

CENTRAL AMERICAN
PYGMY OWL
p. 63

BLACK-AND-WHITE
OWL
p. 64

FULVOUS OWL
p. 65

STRIPED
OWL
p. 65

STYGIAN
OWL
p. 65

UNSPOT
SAW-WI
OWL
p. 66

NORTHERN
POTOO
p. 69

(Spot-tailed Nightja
PIT-SWEET
p. 68

YUCATAN
POORWILL
p. 67

F

M

EARED
POORWILL
p. 67

F

M

Murrell
Butler

(Tawny-collared Nightjar)
CHIP-WILLOW
p. 67

15

BLACK-BILLED
CUCKOO
p. 59

YELLOW-BILLED
CUCKOO
p. 59

MANGROVE
CUCKOO
p. 59

GROOVE-BILLED
ANI
p. 60

SMOOTH-BILLED
ANI
p. 60

MMULATED OWL
p. 61

EASTERN SCREECH-OWL p. 61

Gray morph   Red morph

NORTHERN
PYGMY-OWL
p. 63

FERRUGINOUS
PYGMY-OWL
p. 63

CONI Wing

COMMON
NIGHTHAWK
p. 66

ELF OWL
p. 64

Imm

LENI Wing

LESSER
NIGHTHAWK
p. 66

NORTHERN
SAW-WHET
OWL
p. 65

BURROWING OWL p. 64

BARN OWL
p. 61

GREATER
OADRUNNER
p. 60

GREAT HORNED
OWL
p. 63

LONG-EARED
OWL
p. 65

Murrell
Butler

SPOTTED OWL
p. 64

BARRED OWL
p. 64

SHORT-EARED OWL
p. 65

16

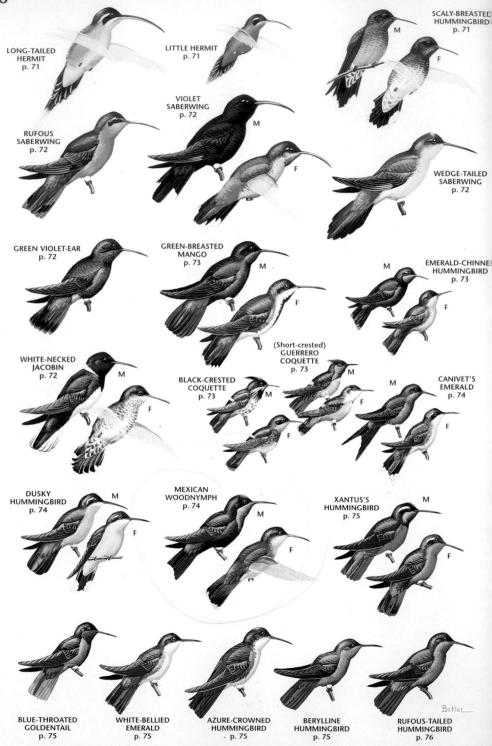

LONG-TAILED
HERMIT
p. 71

LITTLE HERMIT
p. 71

SCALY-BREASTED
HUMMINGBIRD
p. 71

M

F

VIOLET
SABERWING
p. 72

M

F

RUFOUS
SABERWING
p. 72

WEDGE-TAILED
SABERWING
p. 72

GREEN VIOLET-EAR
p. 72

GREEN-BREASTED
MANGO
p. 73

M

F

EMERALD-CHINNED
HUMMINGBIRD
p. 73

M

F

WHITE-NECKED
JACOBIN
p. 72

M

F

BLACK-CRESTED
COQUETTE
p. 73

M

F

(Short-crested)
GUERRERO
COQUETTE
p. 73

M

F

CANIVET'S
EMERALD
p. 74

M

F

DUSKY
HUMMINGBIRD
p. 74

M

F

MEXICAN
WOODNYMPH
p. 74

M

F

XANTUS'S
HUMMINGBIRD
p. 75

M

F

BLUE-THROATED
GOLDENTAIL
p. 75

WHITE-BELLIED
EMERALD
p. 75

AZURE-CROWNED
HUMMINGBIRD
p. 75

BERYLLINE
HUMMINGBIRD
p. 75

RUFOUS-TAILED
HUMMINGBIRD
p. 76

Butler

BLUE-TAILED
HUMMINGBIRD
p. 76

CINNAMON
HUMMINGBIRD
p. 76

GREEN-FRONTED
HUMMINGBIRD
p. 76

STRIPED-TAILED
HUMMINGBIRD
p. 77

M

F

(Blue-capped)
OAXACA
HUMMINGBIRD
p. 77

(White-tailed) GUERRERO
HUMMINGBIRD
p. 77

M

M

F

(Amethyst-throated)
CACIQUE HUMMINGBIRD
p. 77

M

F

GREEN-THROATED
MOUNTAIN-GEM
p. 77

M

F

GARNET-THROATED
HUMMINGBIRD
p. 78

M

F

PURPLE-CROWNED
FAIRY
p. 78

M

F

PLAIN-CAPPED
STARTHROAT
p. 78

LONG-BILLED
STARTHROAT
p. 78

M

F

SLENDER
SHEARTAIL
p. 79

M

F

MEXICAN
SHEARTAIL
p. 79

M

F

SPARKLING-TAILED
HUMMINGBIRD
p. 79

M

F

BEAUTIFUL
HUMMINGBIRD
p. 79

M

F

BUMBLEBEE
HUMMINGBIRD
p. 81

M

F

Murrell
Butler

18

COMMON GROUND-DOVE
p. 53
M
F

WHITE-TIPPED DOVE
p. 54

WHITE-CROWNED PIGEON
p. 52

BAND-TAILED PIGEON
p. 52

RED-BILLED PIGEON
p. 52

WHITE-WINGED DOVE
p. 53

INCA DOVE
p. 53

VAUX'S SWIFT
p. 70

BLACK SWIFT
p. 69

WHITE-THROATED SWIFT
p. 70

CHIMNEY SWIFT
p. 70

BROAD-BILLED
p. 74
M
F

M
F
WHITE-EARED
p. 75

BUFF-BELLIED
p. 76

VIOLET-CROWNED
p. 76

BLUE-THROATED
p. 77
M
F

M
MAGNIFICENT
p. 78
F

M
F
LUCIFER
p. 79

M
F
BLACK-CHINNED
p. 80

M
F
ANNA'S
p. 80

M
COSTA'S
p. 80
F

M
F
CALLIOPE
p. 80

M
BROAD-TAILED
p. 81
F

M
RUFOUS
p. 81
F

Butler

HUMMINGBIRDS

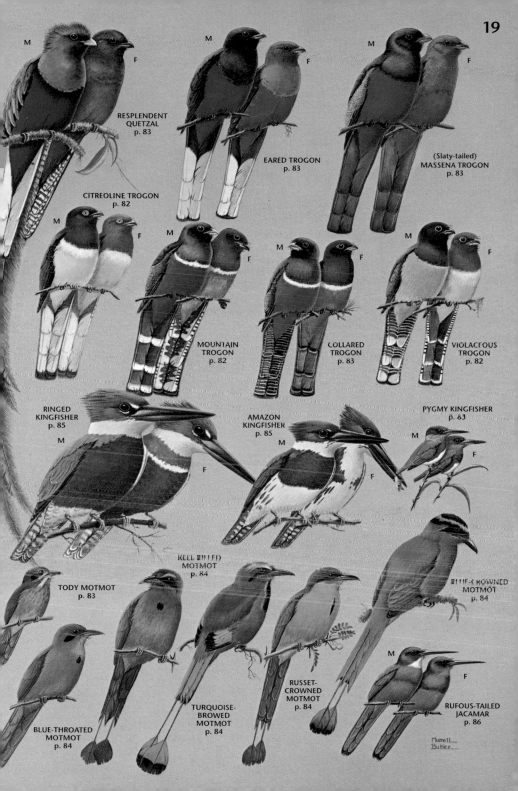

19

M
F

RESPLENDENT
QUETZAL
p. 83

M
F

EARED TROGON
p. 83

M
F

(Slaty-tailed)
MASSENA TROGON
p. 83

CITREOLINE TROGON
p. 82

M
F

M
F

MOUNTAIN
TROGON
p. 82

M
F

COLLARED
TROGON
p. 83

M
F

VIOLACEOUS
TROGON
p. 82

RINGED
KINGFISHER
p. 85
M

F

AMAZON
KINGFISHER
p. 85
M

F

PYGMY KINGFISHER
p. 83

M

F

KEEL-BILLED
MOTMOT
p. 84

TODY MOTMOT
p. 83

BLUE-CROWNED
MOTMOT
p. 84

BLUE-THROATED
MOTMOT
p. 84

TURQUOISE-
BROWED
MOTMOT
p. 84

RUSSET-
CROWNED
MOTMOT
p. 84

M
F

RUFOUS-TAILED
JACAMAR
p. 86

Murrell
Butler

20

RUBY-THROATED
HUMMINGBIRD
p. 80

M
F

M

F

(Golden-crowned)
MEXICAN
EMERALD
p. 73

ALLEN'S
HUMMINGBIRD
p. 81

M

GRAY KINGBIRD
p. 109

EASTERN
KINGBIRD
p. 109

EASTERN
PHOEBE
p. 105

BLACK-HEADED
TROGON
p. 82

M

F

HAIRY
WOODPECKER
p. 89

M

F

CORDILLERAN
FLYCATCHER
p. 104

TREE SWALLOW
p. 122

BANK
SWALLOW
p. 123

Imm

MYIARCHUS FLYCATCHERS

GREAT CRESTED
FLYCATCHER
p. 106

Great crested
p. 106

Brown-crested
p. 107

Ash-throated
p. 106

Nutting's
p. 106

Yucatan
p. 105

Dusky-
p. 1

BELTED KINGFISHER
p. 85

F

M

WILLIAMSON'S
p. 89

Im

LEWIS'S
WOODPECKER
p. 87

YELLOW-
BELLIED
p. 89

M

RED-NAPED
p. 89

RED-BREASTED
p. 89

YELLOW-
BELLIED
p. 88

F

Butler

SAPSUCKERS

ELEGANT TROGON
p. 82

M

F

GREEN KINGFISHER
p. 85

M

F

NORTHERN FLICKER
Red-shafted group
p. 91

M

F

ACORN
WOODPECKER
p. 97

M

NORTHERN
FLICKER
Yellow-shafted
group
p. 91

F

GILDED
FLICKER
p. 91

M

F

F

M

GILA W.
p. 88

M

F

GOLDEN-
FRONTED
WOODPECKER
p. 88

M

M

F

HAIRY WOODPECKER
p. 89

M

LADDER-BACKED W.
p. 89

F

ARIZONA W.
p. 90

M

F

ROSE-THROATED
BECARD
p. 110

M

F

NUTTALL'S
WOODPECKER
p. 89

HORNED LARK
p. 121

PURPLE MARTIN
p. 121

M

F

BARN SWALLOW
p. 123

CLIFF SWALLOW
p. 123

CAVE SWALLOW
p. 123

N. ROUGH-WINGED
SWALLOW
p. 122

VIOLET-GREEN
SWALLOW
p. 122

WHITE-NECKED
PUFFBIRD
p. 85

WHITE-WHISKERED
PUFFBIRD
p. 86

F

M

EMERALD
TOUCANET
p. 86

COLLARED ARACARI
p. 86

KEEL-BILLED
TOUCAN
p. 86

GRAY-CROWNED
p. 91

M

F

BRONZE-WINGED
p. 90

M

F

WOODPECKERS

M

F

GOLDEN-OLIVE
p. 90

M

F

CHESTNUT-COLORED
p. 91

M

F

LINEATED
p. 91

M

F

(Gray-breasted) BALSAS
p. 88

M

F

GOLDEN-CHEEKED
p. 87

M

F

(Red-vented) YUCATAN
p. 88

M

F

PALE-BILLED
p. 92

M

F

BLACK-CHEEKED
p. 87

M

F

SMOKY-BROWN
p. 90

M

F

STRICKLAND'S
p. 90

Murrell
Butler

23

WHITE-COLLARED SWIFT
p. 70

WHITE-NAPED SWIFT
p. 70

CHESTNUT-COLLARED SWIFT
p. 69

(White-fronted)
SIERRA MADRE SWIFT
p. 69

WHITE-CHINNED
SWIFT
p. 69

M

F

(Great Swallow-tailed)
GERONIMO SWIFT
p. 71

(Lesser Swallow-tailed)
CAYENNE SWIFT
p. 70

TAWNY-WINGED
p. 93

RUDDY
p. 93

BLACK-BANDED
p. 94

OLIVACEOUS
p. 93

WEDGE-BILLED
p. 94

NORTHERN
BARRED
WOODCREEPER
p. 94

SPOTTED p. 95

(Strong-billed)
GIANT p. 94

WHITE-
STRIPED
p. 95

STREAKED-
HEADED
p. 95

(Ivory-billed)
LAUGHING p. 94

Murrell
Butler

SPOTTED-CROWNED
p. 95

WOODCREEPERS

24

RUFOUS-BREASTED
SPINETAIL
p. 92

SCALY-THROATED
(Foliage-gleaner)
LEAFGLEANER
p. 92

RUDDY (Foliage-gleaner)
LEAFGLEANER
p. 92

BUFF-THROATED
(Foliage-gleaner)
LEAFGLEANER
p. 92

PLAIN
XENOPS
p. 93

M

TAWNY-THROATED
LEAFTOSSER
p. 93

M

SCALY-THROATED
LEAFTOSSER
p. 93

GREAT ANTSHRIKE
p. 95

F

F

BARRED
ANTSHRIKE
p. 95

M

M

F

M

M

F

RUSSET ANTSHRIKE
p. 96

F

PLAIN ANTVIREO
p. 96

SLATY ANTWREN
p. 96

DOTTED-WINGED
ANTWREN
p. 96

M

BLACK-FACED
ANTTHRUSH
p. 97

SCALED ANTPITTA
p. 97

DUSKY ANTBIRD
p. 96

F

M

F

M

F

M

RED-CAPPED
MANAKIN
p. 112

F

LONG-TAILED
MANAKIN
p. 112

WHITE-COLLARED
MANAKIN
p. 112

THRUSH-LIKE
MOURNER
p. 111

Murrell
Butler

TUFTED FLYCATCHER
p. 101

BELTED FLYCATCHER
p. 100

PILEATED
FLYCATCHER
p. 101

RUDDY-TAILED
FLYCATCHER
p. 100

SULPHUR-
RUMPED
FLYCATCHER
p. 100

ROYAL
FLYCATCHER
p. 100

M

F

STUB-TAILED
SPADEBILL
p. 100

YELLOW-OLIVE
FLYCATCHER
p. 99

EYE-RINGED
FLATBILL
p. 99

COMMON
TODY-FLYCATCHER
p. 99

SLATE-HEADED
TODY-
FLYCATCHER
p. 99

NORTHERN
BENTBILL
p. 99

YELLOW-BELLIED
ELAENIA
p. 98

CARIBBEAN
ELAENIA
p. 98

GREENISH
ELAENIA
p. 98

PALTRY
TYRANNULET
p. 97

YELLOW-BELLIED
TYRANNULET
p. 97

SEPIA-CAPPED
FLYCATCHER
p. 98

OCHRE-BELLIED
FLYCATCHER
p. 98

Murrell
Butler

26

LOVELY COTINGA
p. 112

M

F

BRIGHT-RUMPED
ATTILA
p. 105

SPECKLED
MOURNER
p. 111

RUFOUS
MOURNER
p. 105

RUFOUS PIHA
p. 111

CINNAM
BECAR
p. 11

GRAY-COLLARED
BECARD
p. 110

M

F

BLACK-CROWNED
TITYRA
p. 111

MASKED TITYRA
p. 111

M

M

FORK-TAI
FLYCATCH
p. 110

F

F

STREAKED
FLYCATCHER
p. 108

PIRATIC
FLYCATCHER
p. 108

BOAT
FLYC
p.

SOCIAL
FLYCATCHER
p. 107

NUTTING'S
FLYCATCHER
p. 106

YUCATAN
FLYCATCHER
p. 105

FLAMMU
FLYCAT
p. 1

TROPICAL
PEWEE
p. 102

WHITE-THROATED
FLYCATCHER
p. 103

PINE
FLYCATCHER
p. 104

YELLOWISH
FLYCATCHER
p. 104

Murrell
Butler

27

VERMILION FLYCATCHER
p. 105

M   F

BLACK PHOEBE
p. 105

SAY'S PHOEBE
p. 105

SCISSOR-TAILED
FLYCATCHER
p. 109

CASSIN'S
KINGBIRD
p. 109

WESTERN
KINGBIRD
p. 109

TROPICAL
KINGBIRD
p. 108

THICK-BILLED
KINGBIRD
p. 109

SULPHUR-
BELLIED
FLYCATCHER
p. 108

GREAT KISKADEE
p. 107

DUSKY-
CAPPED
FLYCATCHER
p. 106

WESTERN
WOOD PEWEE
p. 101

ASH-
OATED
ATCHER
106

BROWN-
CRESTED
FLYCATCHER
p. 107

OLIVE-SIDED
FLYCATCHER
p. 101

GREATER PEWEE
p. 101

DUSKY FLYCATCHER
p. 103

GRAY FLYCATCHER
p. 104

BUFF-BREASTED
FLYCATCHER
p. 104

Butler 73 NORTHERN
BEARDLESS-TYRANNULET
p. 97

28

SINALOA
MARTIN
p. 121

M

F

GRAY-BREASTED
MARTIN
p. 121

BLACK-CAPPED
SWALLOW
p. 122

MANGROVE
SWALLOW
p. 122

WHITE-THROATED MAGPIE-JAY
p. 117

TAMAULIPAS CROW
SINALOA CROW
p. 120

BLACK-THROATED
MAGPIE-JAY
p. 117

Imm

BROWN JAY
p. 118

Imm

Plain-tipped
morph

White-tipped
morph

Adt

Imm

TUFTED JAY
p. 117

SAN BLAS JAY
p. 118

Juv

YUCATAN JAY
p. 118

AZURE-HOODED
JAY
p. 119

(White-throated)
OMILTEMI JAY
p. 119

PURPLISH-BACKED
JAY
p. 118

DWARF JAY
p. 119

BLACK-THROATED
JAY
p. 119

UNICOLORED JAY
p. 120

Murrell
Butler

CLARK'S NUTCRACKER
p. 120

COMMON RAVEN
p. 121

CHIHUAHUAN RAVEN
p. 120

GREEN JAY
p. 118

PINYON JAY
p. 120

MEXICAN JAY
p. 119

WESTERN SCRUB-JAY
p. 119

STELLER'S JAY
p. 117

MEXICAN CHICKADEE
p. 123

MOUNTAIN CHICKADEE
p. 123

JUNIPER
TITMOUSE
p. 124

...ED TITMOUSE
p. 123

TUFTED TITMOUSE
Black-crested group
p. 124

M

M

F

VERDIN
p. 124

Imm

BUSHTIT
p. 124

WHITE-BREASTED
NUTHATCH
p. 125

PYGMY
NUTHATCH
p. 125

Murrell
Butler

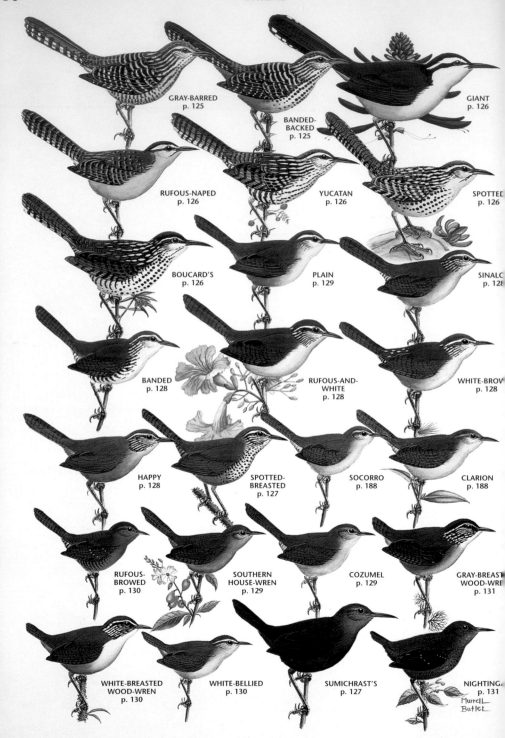

GRAY-BARRED
p. 125

BANDED-
BACKED
p. 125

GIANT
p. 126

RUFOUS-NAPED
p. 126

YUCATAN
p. 126

SPOTTED
p. 126

BOUCARD'S
p. 126

PLAIN
p. 129

SINALO
p. 128

BANDED
p. 128

RUFOUS-AND-
WHITE
p. 128

WHITE-BROW
p. 128

HAPPY
p. 128

SPOTTED-
BREASTED
p. 127

SOCORRO
p. 188

CLARION
p. 188

RUFOUS-
BROWED
p. 130

SOUTHERN
HOUSE-WREN
p. 129

COZUMEL
p. 129

GRAY-BREAST
WOOD-WRE
p. 131

WHITE-BREASTED
WOOD-WREN
p. 130

WHITE-BELLIED
p. 130

SUMICHRAST'S
p. 127

NIGHTING
p. 131

Murrell
Butler

BROWN CREEPER
p. 125

WRENTIT
p. 137

AMERICAN
DIPPER
p. 131

SEDGE WREN
p. 130

MARSH WREN
p. 130

CACTUS WREN
p. 126

CAROLINA
WREN
p. 128

BEWICK'S WREN
p. 129

NORTHERN
HOUSE-WREN
p. 129

LONG-BILLED
THRASHER
p. 138

ROCK WREN
p. 127

CANYON
WREN
p. 127

CURVE-BILLED
THRASHER
p. 139

BENDIRE'S
THRASHER
p. 138

CALIFORNIA
THRASHER
p. 139

LE CONTE'S THRASHER
p. 139

NORTHERN
MOCKINGBIRD
p. 137

CRISSAL THRASHER
p. 139

TOWNSEND'S
SOLITAIRE
p. 133

AMERICAN ROBIN
American group
p. 136

Murrell
Butler

32

COZUMEL THRASHER
p. 138

OCELLATED THRASHER
p. 139

GRAY THRASHER
p. 138

BLUE MOCKINGBIRD
p. 139

BLUE-AND-WHITE
MOCKINGBIRD
p. 139

BLACK CATBIRD
p. 137

SOCORRO
MOCKINGBIRD
p. 188

TROPICAL
MOCKINGBIRD
p. 138

AMERICAN ROBIN
San Lucas group
p. 137

M

RUFOUS-
COLLARED ROBIN
p. 136

RUFOUS-BACKED
ROBIN
p. 136

WHITE-THROATED
ROBIN
p. 136

F

MOUNTAIN ROBIN
p. 135

M

CLAY-COLORED
ROBIN
p. 135

F

BLACK ROBIN
p. 135

M

BROWN-BACKED
SOLITAIRE
p. 133

SLATE-COLORED
SOLITAIRE
p. 134

F

AZTEC THRUSH
p. 137

RUSSET
p. 134

RUDDY-
CAPPED
p. 134

ORANGE-
BILLED
p. 134

BLACK-
HEADED
p. 134

Murrell
Butler

SPOTTED
p. 134

NIGHTINGALE-THRUSHES

WINTER WREN
p. 130

ROCK WREN
p. 127

CANYON WREN
p. 127

GRAY CATBIRD
p. 137

SAGE THRASHER
p. 138

WOOD THRUSH
p. 135

HERMIT THRUSH
p. 135

SWAINSON'S
THRUSH
p. 135

VEERY
p. 135

M

EASTERN BLUEBIRD
p. 133

GRAY-CHEEKED THRUSH
p. 135

M

F

MOUNTAIN
BLUEBIRD
p. 133

M

WESTERN BLUEBIRD
p. 133

F

F

AMERICAN PIPIT
p. 140

DAR
WING
140

Adt

Win

SPRAGUE'S PIPIT
p. 140

EUROPEAN STARLING
p. 140

M

USE
RROW
183

F

Win

Imm

Murrell
Butler

34

WHITE-LORED
GNATCATCHER
p. 132

F

M

M Win

TROPICAL
GNATCATCHER
p. 133

F

M

BLACK-CAPPED
GNATCATCHER
p. 132

F

M

M Win

GRAY SILKY-FLYCATCHER
p. 140

M

F

LONG-BILLED
GNATWREN
p. 132

RUFOUS-BROWED
PEPPERSHRIKE
p. 117

CHESTNUT-SIDED
SHRIKE-VIREO
p. 116

GREEN SHRIKE-VIREO
p. 116

COZUMEL VIREO
p. 113

MANGROVE VIREO
p. 113

GOLDEN
VIREO
p. 115

DWARF
VIREO
p. 114

YUCATAN VIREO
p. 116

SLATY VIREO
p. 113

TAWNY-CROWNED
GREENLET
p. 116

LESSER GREENLET
p. 116

Murrell
Butler

35

M
F
BLACK-CAPPED
VIREO
p. 114

WHITE-EYED VIREO
p. 113

HUTTON'S VIREO
p. 115

GRAY VIREO
p. 114

L'S VIREO
p. 113

BLUE-HEADED VIREO
p. 114

RED-EYED VIREO
p. 115

WARBLING
VIREO
p. 115

RANGE-
OWNED
ARBLER
p. 141

VIRGINIA'S
WARBLER
p. 142

COLIMA WARBLER
p. 142

LUCY'S WARBLER
p. 142

M
F
OLIVE WARBLER
p. 141

Win
YELLOW-RUMPED WARBLER
Audubon's group
p. 144

M
F
BLACK-THROATED
GRAY WARBLER
p. 144

GRACE'S
WARBLER
p. 145

F M
MACGILLIVRAY'S
WARBLER
p. 148

M
F
GRAY-CROWNED
YELLOWTHROAT
p. 149

RED-FACED WARBLER
p. 150

PAINTED REDSTART
p. 150

BANANAQUIT
p. 152

Butler

36

BLACK-AND-WHITE
WARBLER
p. 147

M

F

PROTHONOTARY
WARBLER
p. 147

M

F

SWAINSON'S
WARBLER
p. 147

WORM-EATING
WARBLER
p. 147

"Brewster's"
p. 141

"Lawrence's" p. 141

Golden-winged
p. 141

BLUE-WINGED
WARBLER
p. 141

GOLDEN-WINGED
WARBLER
p. 141

M

M

F

TENNESSEE WARBLER
p. 141

M

F

M

F

M

F

NASHVILLE WARBLER
p. 142

M

NORTHERN
PARULA
p. 142

TROPICAL PARULA
p. 142

M

F

YELLOW WARBLER
p. 143

M

MAGNOLIA
WARBLER
p. 143

M

F

GOLDEN
WARBLER
p. 143

M

PINE WARBLER
p. 146

CAPE MAY
WARBLER
p. 144

F

M

F

TOWNSEND'S
WARBLER
p. 144

M

F

BLACK-THROATED
BLUE WARBLER
p. 144

M

M

F

Win

M

HERMIT WARBLER
p. 145

BLACK-THROATED
GREEN WARBLER
p. 145

GOLDEN-CHEEKED
WARBLER
p. 145

Murrell
Butler

37

M

M

YELLOW-THROATED
WARBLER
p. 145

F

F

ERULEAN WARBLER
p. 147

BLACKBURNIAN
WARBLER
p. 145

M

F

M

F

CHESTNUT-SIDED
WARBLER
p. 143

BAY-BREASTED WARBLER
p. 146

Win

BLACKPOLL WARBLER
p. 146

M

Eastern

Western

Win

PRAIRIE WARBLER
p. 146

PALM WARBLER
p. 146

OVENBIRD
p. 147

KENTUCKY WARBLER
p. 148

NORTHERN
WATERTHRUSH
p. 148

LOUISIANA
WATERTHRUSH
p. 148

M

F

M

M

F

ELLOW-BREASTED
CHAT
p. 151

HOODED WARBLER
p. 149

WILSON'S WARBLER
p. 150

MOURNING WARBLER
p. 148

M

F

M

F

M

CANADA WARBLER
p. 150

AMERICAN REDSTART
p. 147

F

38

(Crescent-chested)
SPOT-BREASTED
WARBLER
p. 143

TROPICAL PARULA
p. 142

MANGROVE WARBLER
p. 143

BELDING'S
YELLOWTHROAT
p. 149

COMMON YELLOWTHROAT
Common group
p. 148

ALTAMIRA
YELLOWTHROAT
p. 149

BLACK-POLLED
YELLOWTHROAT
p. 149

HOODED
YELLOWTHROAT
p. 149

RED-BREASTED
CHAT
p. 152

GRAY-THROATED
CHAT
p. 152

SLATE-THROATED
REDSTART
p. 150

FAN-TAILED WARBLER
p. 151

RED WARBLER
p. 150

PINK-HEADED WARBLER
p. 150

GOLDEN-CROWNED
WARBLER
p. 151

GOLDEN-BROWED
WARBLER
p. 151

RUFOUS-CAPPED WARBLER
Rufous-capped group
p. 151

RUFOUS-CAPPED WARBLER
Chestnut-capped group
p. 151

Murrell
Butler '71

BLUE-CROWNED
CHLOROPHONIA
p. 156

ELEGANT EUPHONIA
p. 156
M
F

SCRUB EUPHONIA
Scrub group
p. 155
M
F

YELLOW-THROATED
EUPHONIA
p. 156
M
F

OLIVE-BACKED
EUPHONIA
p. 156
M
F

GOLDEN-HOODED
TANAGER
p. 157

(Azure-rumped)
CABANIS'S
TANAGER
p. 156

YELLOW-WINGED
TANAGER
p. 155

RED-HEADED
TANAGER
p. 155
M
F

PASSERINI'S
TANAGER
p. 155
M
F

CRIMSON-
COLLARED
TANAGER
p. 154

ROSE-THROATED
TANAGER
p. 153
M
F

WHITE-WINGED
TANAGER
p. 154
M
F

(Flame-colored)
STRIPED TANAGER
p. 154
M
F

RED-HEADED
TANAGER
p. 154
M
F

RED-CROWNED
ANT-TANAGER
p. 153
M

RED-THROATED
ANT-TANAGER
p. 153
M
F

BLACK-THROATED
SHRIKE-TANAGER
p. 153
M

M

COMMON
BUSH-TANAGER
p. 152

GRAY-HEADED
TANAGER
p. 153

ROSY THRUSH-TANAGER
p. 152
F

Murrell
Butler '71

40

PHAINOPEPLA
p. 140

M   F

LOGGERHEAD SHRIKE
p. 112

SUMMER TANAGER
p. 153

M

F

HEPATIC TANAGER
p. 153

M

F

NORTHERN CARDINAL
p. 172

M

F

WESTERN TANAGER
p. 154

M

F

PYRRHULOXIA
p. 172

M

F

BLUE GROSBEAK
p. 173

M

F

BLACK-HEADED
GROSBEAK
p. 172

M

F

PAINTED BUNTING
p. 174

M

F

LAZULI BUNTING
p. 173

M

F

VARIED BUNTING
p. 174

M

F

EVENING GROSBEAK
p. 183

M

M

F

PURPLE FINCH
p. 181

M

F

HOUSE FINCH
p. 181

M

F

CASSIN'S FINCH
p. 181

M

F

WHITE-COLLARED
SEADEATER
Sharpe's group
Cinnamon-rumped group
p. 158

F

M

PINE SISKIN
p. 181

Butler

41

BUFF-THROATED SALTATOR
p. 171

BLACK-HEADED SALTATOR
p. 171

(Grayish) GRAY
SALTATOR
p. 171

BLACK-FACED
SALTATOR
p. 171

...SON-COLLARED
GROSBEAK
p. 171

BLUE BUNTING
p. 173

M

F

M

F

M

BLUE BLACK
GROSBEAK
p. 173

F

YELLOW
M GROSBEAK
p. 172

F

...bellied)
...TA'S
...TING
...73

M

F

M

ORANGE-BREASTED
BUNTING
p. 174

M

M

YELLOW-FACED
GRASSQUIT
p. 159

F

...OODED
...ROSBEAK
p. 183

VARIABLE
SEEDEATER
p. 158

M

F

BLUE SEEDEATER
p. 159

M

BLUE-BLACK
GRASSQUIT
p. 157

M

RUDDY-BREASTED
SEEDEATER
p. 158

M

F

M

I

F

M

F

M

M

GRASSLAND
YELLOW-FINCH
p. 159

F

Murrell
Butler

THICK-BILLED SEED-FINCH
p. 158

BLACK-CAPPED SISKIN
p. 182

BLACK-HEADED SISKIN
p. 182

42

SLATY FINCH
p. 159

M   F

RUFOUS-CAPPED
BRUSH-FINCH
p. 160

WHITE-NAPED
BRUSH-FINCH
p. 160

YELLOW-THROATED
BRUSH-FINCH
p. 160

CHESTNUT-CAPPED
BRUSH-FINCH
p. 160

(Plain-breasted)
TUXTLA
BRUSH-FINCH
p. 160

GREEN-STRIPED
BRUSH-FINCH
p. 160

COLLARED TOWHEE
p. 162

1   2   3

SPOTTED TOWHEE
p. 162

4   5   6

Hybrids of Collared Towhee and Spotted Towhee
(see p. 162)

WHITE-THROATED
TOWHEE
p. 163

ORANGE-BILLED
SPARROW
p. 161

GREEN-BACKED
SPARROW
p. 161

RUSTY-CROWNED
GROUND-SPARROW
p. 161

SIERRA MADRE
SPARROW
p. 167

PREVOST'S
GROUND-SPARROW
p. 161

WHITE-EARED
GROUND-SPARROW
p. 161

STRIPED SPARROW
p. 165

Murrell
Butler

43

ROSE-BREASTED
GROSBEAK
p. 172
M
F

INDIGO BUNTING
p. 173
M
F

DICKCISSEL
p. 174
M
F

AMERICAN
GOLDFINCH
p. 182
M
F

GREEN-TAILED TOWHEE
p. 162

LARK BUNTING
p. 167
F
M

SPER SPARROW
p. 166

CHIPPING SPARROW
p. 165
Sum
Win

FIELD SPARROW
p. 165
Adt
Juv

WHITE-CROWNED
SPARROW
p. 169
Adt
Imm

GOLDEN CROWNED
SPARROW
p. 169
Adt
Imm

WHITE-THROATED
SPARROW
p. 168
Bright
Dull

FOX SPARROW
p. 167

LINCOLN'S
SPARROW
p. 168

SWAMP SPARROW
p. 168

M Sum
F
M Win

CHESTNUT-COLLARED
LONGSPUR
p. 170

M Sum
F Win
M Win

MCCOWN'S LONGSPUR
p. 170

Murrell
Butler

44

LESSER GOLDFINCH
p. 182

M

F

M

Green-backed
group

LAWRENCE'S
GOLDFINCH
p. 182

M

F

RED CROSSBILL
p. 181

M

F

CALIFORNIA TOWHEE
p. 162

ABERT'S TOWHEE
p. 163

OLIVE SPARROW
p. 161

SAVANNAH SPARROW
p. 167

GRASSHOPPER
SPARROW
p. 167

LARK SPARROW
p. 166

RUFOUS-WINGED
SPARROW
p. 164

RUFOUS-CROWNED
SPARROW
p. 164

BOTTERI'S
SPARROW
p. 164

CASSIN'S
SPARROW
p. 164

BLACK-THROATED
SPARROW
p. 166

SAGE
SPARROW
p. 166

DARK-EYED
JUNCO
p. 169

Slate-colored
group

Gray-headed
group

Oregon
subgroup

BREWER'S SPARROW
p. 165

YELLOW-EYED
JUNCO
p. 170

M

F

BLACK-CHINNED
SPARROW
p. 166

SONG SPARROW
p. 168

Imm

CLAY-COLORED SPARROW
p. 165

Murrell
Butler

45

VE-STRIPED SPARROW
p. 165

BRIDLED SPARROW
p. 163

BLACK-CHESTED
SPARROW
p. 163

STRIPED-HEADED
SPARROW
p. 163

SUMICHRAST'S
SPARROW
p. 163

OAXACA
SPARROW
p. 164

RUSTY
SPARROW
p. 164

(Rufous-collared)
ANDEAN SPARROW
p. 168

BLACK
RM-PETREL
p. 4

COLLARED
PLOVER
p. 37

SPOTTED-BREASTED
ORIOLE
p. 178

BLUE-GRAY
TANAGER
p. 155

WORTHEN'S
SPARROW
p. 166

MAGNIFICENT
FRIGATEBIRD
p. 7

WHITE-BELLIED
CHACHALACA
p. 28

TAILED
VATER
3

F

M

M

F

RED-FOOTED BOOBY
p. 5

IMPERIAL
WOODPECKER
p. 188

MURRELL
BUTLER

46

BLUE-GRAY GNATCATCHER
p. 132

BLACK-TAILED GNATCATCHER
p. 132

GOLDEN-CROWNED KINGLET
p. 131

RUBY-CROWNED KIN
p. 131

F

M

F

M

F

M Sum

M Win

F

M

BRONZED COWBIRD
p. 176

M

GREAT-TAILED GRACKLE
p. 176

M

M

BROWN-H
COWB
p. 17

F

F

F

BALTIMORE
ORIOLE
p. 179

M

ORCHARD
p.

F

BREWER'S
BLACKBIRD
p. 93

M

F

M

M

ALTA
ORI
p.

F

SCOTT'S ORIOLE
p. 186

M

BULLOCK'S
ORIOLE
p. 179

AUDUBON'S ORIOLE
p. 179

M

F

RED-WINGED
BLACKBIRD
p. 175

F

HOODED ORIOLE
p. 177

M

F

M

TRICOLORED BLACKBIRD
p. 175

M

F

M

F

EASTERN
MEADOWLA
p. 175

YELLOW-HEADED
BLACKBIRD
p. 175

MB

47

(Chestnut-headed)
WAGLER'S OROPENDOLA
p. 180

MONTEZUMA
OROPENDOLA
p. 180

YELLOW-BILLED
CACIQUE
p. 180

(Yellow-winged)
MEXICAN CACIQUE
p. 180

M

GIANT COWBIRD
p. 176

F

F

(Melodious)
SINGING BLACKBIRD
p. 176

(Black-backed)
ABEILLE'S ORIOLE
p. 179

M

OCHRE ORIOLE
p. 177

F

BLACK-COWLED
ORIOLE
p. 176

(Black-vented)
WAGLER'S ORIOLE
p. 177

M

BAR-WINGED ORIOLE
p. 177

F

YELLOW-TAILED
ORIOLE
p. 178

YELLOW-BACKED
ORIOLE
p. 178

ORANGE
ORIOLE
p. 178

M

M

STREAKED-
BACKED ORIOLE
p. 178

F

F

M

F

M

F

M

F

M

F

CINNAMON-BELLIED
FLOWERPIERCER
p. 159

GREEN HONEYCREEPER
p. 157

RED-LEGGED
HONEYCREEPER
p. 157

SHINING HONEYCREEPER
p. 157

Murrell
Butler '71

48

VIOLET-CROWNED
WOODNYMPH
p. 74

BARE-CROWNED
ANTBIRD
p. 96
M

WESTERN
SLATY- ANTSHRIKE
p. 96
F

GRAY-BREASTED
(Crake) RAIL
p. 33

F

M

BROWN
VIOLET-EAR
p. 72

WHITE-WINGED
BECARD
p. 110

M

M

F

BAND-TAILED
BARBTHROAT
p. 71

OLIVACEOUS
PICULET
p. 87

SLATE-COLORED
SEEDEATER
p. 158

COCOA
WOODCREEPER
p. 94

MOUNTAIN
ELAENIA
p. 98

GRAY-H
PIPR
p.

M

BUSHY-CRESTED
JAY
p. 118

CRESTED BOBWHITE
White-breasted group
p. 31

F

SOUTHEASTERN SPECIALTIES

PACIFIC LOON
p. 2

Win

WESTERN GREBE
p. 3

CLARK'S GREBE
p. 3

BROWN PELICAN
p. 6

Imm

I

RED-BILLED TROPICBIRD
p. 5

Adt

Sum

NEOTROPIC CORMORANT
p. 6

Imm

DOUBLE-CRESTED CORMORANT
p. 6

Imm

ACK SKIMMER
p. 50

BLACK-FOOTED ALBATROSS
p. 3

ANHINGA p. 7

M

F

Imm

HEERMANN'S GULL
p. 46

ASITIC
GER
45

Win

Imm

rk
rph

LAUGHING GULL
p. 45

Sum

XANTUS'S MURRELET
p. 51

BajCal
race

Sum

Cal race

BLACK TERN
p. 50

Imm

Win

Win

Win

G-BILLED
GULL
p. 46

ROYAL TERN
p. 48

LEAST GREBE
p. 2

Murrell
Butler

II

PIED-BILLED GREBE
p. 2

Sum

Win

EARED GREBE
p. 2

Sum

Win

BRANDT'S CORMORANT
p. 7

Sum

Win

PELAGIC CORMORANT
p. 7

Sum

Sum

Win

GULL-BILLED
TERN
p. 48

Win

Sum

SANDWICH
TERN
p. 49

Win

Sum

CASPIAN
TERN
p. 48

Win

Sum

Win

Sum

ELEGANT TERN
p. 48

SOOTY TERN
p. 50

Imm

Adt

Win

COMMON TERN
p. 49

Win

Sum

LEAST TERN
p. 49

Win

Win

Sum

BROWN NODDY
p. 50

FORSTER'S TERN
p. 49

Sum

ARCTIC TERN
p. 187

F.P.BENNETT

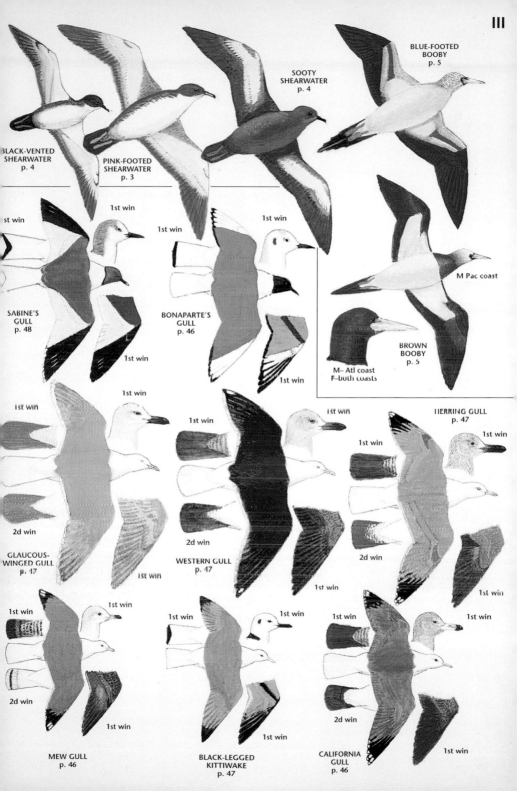

III

BLUE-FOOTED
BOOBY
p. 5

SOOTY
SHEARWATER
p. 4

BLACK-VENTED
SHEARWATER
p. 4

PINK-FOOTED
SHEARWATER
p. 3

1st win

1st win

1st win

1st win

st win

SABINE'S
GULL
p. 48

BONAPARTE'S
GULL
p. 46

M Pac coast

1st win

BROWN
BOOBY
p. 5

1st win

M– Atl coast
F–both coasts

1st win

1st win

1st win

1st win

HERRING GULL
p. 47

1st win

1st win

2d win

GLAUCOUS-
WINGED GULL
p. 47

WESTERN GULL
p. 47

2d win

2d win

1st win

1st win

1st win

1st win

1st win

1st win

1st win

1st win

2d win

2d win

MEW GULL
p. 46

BLACK-LEGGED
KITTIWAKE
p. 47

CALIFORNIA
GULL
p. 46

1st win

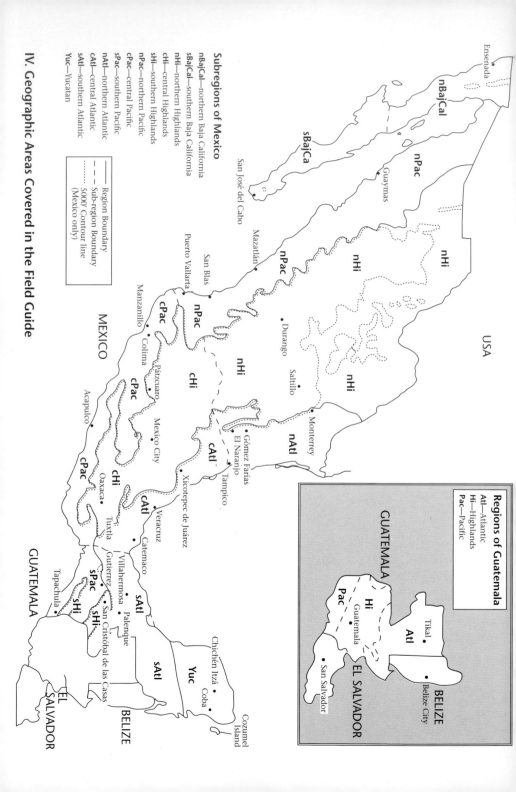

IV. Geographic Areas Covered in the Field Guide

Subregions of Mexico

nBajCal—northern Baja California
sBajCal—southern Baja California
nHi—northern Highlands
cHi—central Highlands
sHi—southern Highlands
nPac—northern Pacific
cPac—central Pacific
sPac—southern Pacific
nAtl—northern Atlantic
cAtl—central Atlantic
sAtl—southern Atlantic
Yuc—Yucatan

——	Region Boundary
– – –	Sub-region Boundary
⋯⋯	5000' Contour line (Mexico only)

Regions of Guatemala

Atl—Atlantic
Hi—Highlands
Pac—Pacific

(GREAT SWALLOW-TAILED) GERONIMO SWIFT [23] Vencejo Tijereta *Panyptila sanctihieronymi*
Range Mex, Guat, ElSal, Hon, Nic. Res Mex (s.nPac+csPac + adj csHi), Guat (Hi + adj Pac), ElSal (w). Rare.
Habitat Usually seen in spectacular flight over rugged terrain, canyons, steep slopes, mountain forests, waterfalls.
Voice A plaintive *tyee-ew.*
Field Marks 8″ Glossy black, but throat, sides of neck, upper breast, flank patch, and narrow band on hind border of long slender wing white; tail long, deeply forked.

HUMMINGBIRDS—CHUPAFLORES—TROCHILIDAE

BAND-TAILED BARBTHROAT [48] Ermitaño Barbudo *Threnetes ruckeri*
Range Blz, Guat, Hon–SAm. Res Blz (s), Guat (Atl). Rare.
Habitat Humid forest undergrowth, thickets, borders.
Field Marks 4.5″ Like Long-tailed Hermit, with whitish-bordered black mask and long, decurved bill, but chin and upper throat black, *not* pale buff; rufous chest; deeply rounded, mostly black-and-white tail, *not* a long and slender-pointed, less contrasty tail. See also Rufous Saberwing.

LONG-TAILED HERMIT [16] Ermitaño Común *Phaethornis superciliosus*
(Includes Mexican Hermit, *P. s. mexicanus*)
Range Mex–SAm, exc ElSal. Res Mex (s.nPac+cPac, c.cAtl– sc.cAtl), Blz (s), Guat (Atl); *P. s. mexicanus* Mex (s.nPac+cPac).
Habitat Humid forest undergrowth, borders, river-edge woods, ravines.
Voice A rasping *creep.*
Field Marks 6″ Bronzy back; blackish ear patch; buffy eye line and mustache mark; mostly buffy below; grayer on throat and breast; bill very long, decurved; tail Y-shaped, with very long white tips of central feathers extended far beyond other feathers. See Little Hermit.

LITTLE HERMIT [16] Ermitaño Chico *Phaethornis longuemareus*
Range Mex–SAm, exc ElSal. Res Mex (se.cAtl+sAtl), Blz, Guat (Atl).
Habitat Humid forest undergrowth, dense humid forest.
Field Marks 3.5″ Crown and back bronzy; rump and uptacs dark rufous; rich tawny buff below; blackish ear patch with buffy border above and below; bill very long, decurved; tail graduated, long wedge shape, with reddish brown feather tips. See Long-tailed Hermit.

SCALY-BREASTED HUMMINGBIRD [16] Chupaflor Escamado *Phaeochroa cuvierii*
Range Mex–SAm, exc ElSal. Cas/irr res? Mex (sc.sAtl); res Blz (s), Guat (Atl). Very rare.
Habitat Humid forest, partial clearings, borders.
Field Marks 5″ M: greenish above; throat and breast scaly dull greenish; tail black below, broadly white-cornered; belly buff. F: belly whitish. See White-necked Jacobin.

WEDGE-TAILED SABERWING [16] Fandanguero Gritón *Campylopterus curvipennis*
Range Mex, Blz, Guat, Hon. Res Mex (s.nAtl+csAtl, Yuc), Blz, Guat (Atl).
Habitat Humid forest, borders, partial clearings, gardens.
Field Marks 5" Greenish above, with violet forehead; pale gray to whitish below; tail rather long, wedge-shaped. M: tail blackish, especially toward tip. F: outer tail feathers broadly whitish at tip.

LONG-TAILED SABERWING Fandanguero Colilargo *Campylopterus excellens*
Range Mex. Res Mex (se.cAtl).
Habitat Humid forest, gardens, orchards, partial clearings.
Field Marks 5.5" Like Wedge-tailed Saberwing, but larger; tail notably longer.

RUFOUS SABERWING [16] Fandanguero Rojizo *Campylopterus rufus*
Range Mex, Guat, ElSal. Res Mex (sPac + adj Hi), Guat (Pac), ElSal. Rare.
Habitat Humid forest undergrowth, partial clearings, *cafetales,* borders.
Field Marks 5" Greenish above; dark patch through eye; underparts rufous; tail square, mostly rufous from below, with black bar near tip; bill long, slightly decurved, black. See Little Hermit and Band-tailed Barbthroat.

VIOLET SABERWING [16] Fandanguero Morado *Campylopterus hemileucurus*
Range Mex–Pan. Res Mex (local c.cPac+sPac, c.cAtl–s.c.sAtl), Blz (s), Guat (Pac+Atl + adj Hi), ElSal. Rare.
Habitat Humid forest undergrowth, overgrown coffee or banana plantations, shrubby partial clearings.
Field Marks 5.5" Tail black below with prominent white corners; bill medium long, strongly decurved. M: mostly dark purple, appears black in poor light, with green wrist patch and uptacs. F: greenish above, pale gray below; small violet throat patch (or spots in immature female). Imm M: like female, but much darker and greener below.

WHITE-NECKED JACOBIN [16] Chupaflor Nuquiblanco *Florisuga mellivora*
Range Mex–SAm, exc ElSal. Res Mex (c.cAtl–sc.sAtl), Blz (s), Guat (Atl). Rare.
Habitat Middle branches in humid forest, borders, partial clearings.
Field Marks 4.5" Bill medium, black, straight. M: dark blue head, throat, and chest; white hindneck band; bright green back and rump; white belly, untacs, and most of tail. F: Like female Scaly-breasted Hummingbird, but more contrastingly scaled blackish or greenish on white; white tail corners much smaller, on greenish, *not* black, tail.

BROWN VIOLET-EAR [48] Chupaflor Café *Colibri delphinae*
Range Blz, Guat, Hon, Nic–SAm. Res Blz, Guat (Atl). Rare.
Habitat Canopy of humid forest or middle branches in partial clearings, borders.
Field Marks 4.5" Mostly brownish; bill short, straight; dull whitish stripe on side of face, between purplish ear patch and bluish green throat.

GREEN VIOLET-EAR [16] Chupaflor Verdemar *Colibri thalassinus*
Range Mex–SAm, exc Blz. Res Mex (csHi + adj cPac; acc sBajCal, Yuc), Guat (Hi + adj Pac), ElSal.

Habitat Moist mountain pine-oak, fir, or pine forest, borders, partial clearings.
Field Marks 4.5″ Bill medium length, slightly decurved. M: mostly dark iridescent green, with purplish ear patch; may have purplish chest patch; some buff on untacs; dull blackish band on bluish tail.

GREEN-BREASTED MANGO [16] Chupaflor Gorjinegro *Anthracothorax prevostii*
Range Mex–SAm. Res/win Mex (csPac, s.nAtl+csAtl, Yuc), Blz (s), Guat (Pac, Atl), ElSal.
Habitat Humid open woods, partial clearings, borders, gardens.
Field Marks 4.5″ Bill black, medium long, slightly decurved. M: mostly bright green, with darker ear patch; narrow black patch on throat and chest; most of tail bright purple. F: like male, but white below, with jagged black median stripe; dark tail white-tipped.

EMERALD-CHINNED HUMMINGBIRD [16] Colibrí Piquicorto *Abeillia abeillei*
Range Mex–Nic. Res/vis Mex (e.cHi+sHi + adj sPac+csAtl), Guat (Hi), ElSal (w). Very rare.
Habitat Cloud forest, partial clearings in humid forest, borders.
Field Marks 3″ White spot or short line behind eye; dark square tail gray-tipped; very short straight black bill. M: iridescent green; throat brighter green; breast black. F: bright greenish above; whitish or pale gray below.

(SHORT-CRESTED) GUERRERO COQUETTE [16] Coqueta de Guerrero *Lophornis brachylopha*
Range Mex. Res Mex (c.cPac). Rare, local.
Habitat Humid forest, partial clearings, borders.
Field Marks 2.5″ Bronzy above; short straight bill; buff or whitish bar on lower back. M: elongated rufous crest feathers; grayish underparts, with bright green gorget; square, rufous tail; black bill. F: mostly grayish buff below, but throat white; crown rufous, *not* crested; bill dark; tail square, blackish, with cinnamon tip.

BLACK-CRESTED COQUETTE [16] Coqueta Crestinegra *Lophornis helenae*
Range Mex–CRic, exc ElSal. Res Mex (sPac, se.cAtl+s.sAtl), Blz (s), Guat (Pac, Atl), Rare.
Habitat Humid forest, second growth, partial clearings, borders.
Field Marks 2.5″ Bronzy above; bill short, straight; white bar on lower back. M: long black crest; chin broadly green with buff and black throat plumes, bronzy rufous speckles on white breast and belly; tail short, reddish brown. F: *no* crest; buffy below with many dark breast speckles; tail reddish brown, with broad black bar.

(GOLDEN-CROWNED) MEXICAN EMERALD [20] Esmeralda Mexicana *Chlorostilbon auriceps*
Range Mex. Res Mex (c.nPac–cPac).
Habitat Scrubby woods, partial clearings, gardens, borders.
Field Marks 3.8″ Like Canivet's Emerald, but tail much more deeply forked, in male and female.

COZUMEL EMERALD Esmeralda Cozumeleña *Chlorostilbon forficatus*
Range Mex. Res Mex (ne Yuc: Cozumel Island).
Habitat Scrubby woods, borders, overgrown clearings, gardens.
Field Marks **3.8″** Like Canivet's Emerald, but tail much more deeply forked in male and female.

CANIVET'S EMERALD [16] Esmeralda Verde *Chlorostilbon canivetii*
(Includes Salvin's Emerald, *C. canivetii salvini*)
Range Mex–CRic. Res Mex (sPac + adj Hi, s.nAtl+csAtl + adj Hi, Yuc), Blz, Guat, ElSal; *C. c. salvini* Guat (Hi, Pac), ElSal.
Habitat Humid to dry forest, partial clearings, borders, gardens.
Field Marks **3.4″** M: bright iridescent green, with brighter green throat; bill short, straight, red at base, black-tipped; tail black, deeply forked. F: dull greenish above; whitish below; tail slightly forked, with white corners; white line behind eye; black ear patch.

DUSKY HUMMINGBIRD [16] Colibrí Prieto *Cynanthus sordidus*
Range Mex. Res Mex (s.cHi + adj Pac). Irregular.
Habitat River-border woods, gardens, parks, orchards, overgrown vacant lots.
Field Marks **3.5″** Like female Broad-billed Hummingbird, but slender bill; darker underparts; duller, more bronzy green, *not* blackish blue, tail; M: *no* small gray tail corners; F: rather large white tail corners.

BROAD-BILLED HUMMINGBIRD [18] Colibrí Piquiancho *Cynanthus latirostris*
(Includes Doubleday's Hummingbird, *C. doubledayi*)
Range US–Mex. Res/sum Mex (ncPac, w.nHi+cHi + adj Atl; cas sBajCal); *C. doubledayi* Mex (cstl c+se.cPac).
Habitat Gardens, brushy woods, partial clearings, thickets.
Field Marks **3.5″** Bill mostly broad, red with black tip; tail blackish blue. M: iridescent green; gorget greenish blue; untacs pale gray or whitish; tail forked. F: greenish above, pale gray below; tail square, with small gray corners.

MEXICAN WOODNYMPH [16] Ninfa Mexicana *Thalurania ridgwayi*
Range Mex. Res Mex (s.nPac+nw.cPac). Rare.
Habitat Humid forest, overgrown clearings, wooded ravines.
Field Marks **4″** Bill medium, black, slightly decurved; tail notched. M: dark iridescent green above, but forehead and forecrown violet-blue; blackish below, but gorget to center of breast bright bluish green; tail blackish. F: greenish above, pale grayish below, with dull gray-green breast; tail dark with whitish tail corners.

VIOLET-CROWNED WOODNYMPH [48] Ninfa Violeta *Thalurania townsendi*
Range Blz–Pan, exc ElSal. Res Blz (s), Guat (se Atl). Rare.
Habitat Humid forest, borders, partial clearings.
Field Marks **4″** Like Mexican Woodnymph, but M: much more deeply forked tail; mostly green, *not* black, breast, belly, and untacs, with some purplish on sides, flanks, and upper back.

BLUE-THROATED GOLDENTAIL [16] Chupaflor Colidorado *Hylocharis eliciae*
Range Mex–SAm. Res/vis Mex (sPac, se.cAtl+sc.sAtl), Blz, Guat (Pac, Atl), ElSal. Rare.
Habitat Forest, river-border woods, partial clearings.
Field Marks **3.5"** Iridescent green, with reddish bronze uptacs; cinnamon-brown untacs; iridescent greenish gold tail; purplish blue throat; bill straight, red with black tip.

WHITE-EARED HUMMINGBIRD [18] Chupaflor Orejiblanco *Hylocharis leucotis*
Range US–Nic, exc Blz. Res Mex (Hi), Guat (Hi), ElSal (n).
Habitat Gardens, borders, pine-oak woods, mountain pine forest.
Field Marks **3.5"** Square tail; slender bill red with black tip; white line behind eye. M: crown broadly dark purple; blackish ear patch; iridescent green throat; pale gray untacs. F: crown and upperparts dull greenish; whitish below, with variable green speckling on throat, sides, and flanks.

XANTUS'S HUMMINGBIRD [16] Chupaflor Peninsular *Hylocharis xantusii*
Range Mex. Res Mex (sBajCal).
Habitat Rocky hillsides with scrubby shrubs, gardens, borders, open dry woods.
Field Marks **3.5"** Like White-eared Hummingbird, but M: forehead and chin black; breast, belly, untacs, and tail rich rufous below; F: all-rufous underparts; tail rufous below, with dull black bar near tip.

WHITE-BELLIED EMERALD [16] Chupaflor Esmeralda *Amazilia candida*
Range Mex–Nic, exc ElSal. Res Mex (sPac, csAtl, Yuc), Blz, Guat (Pac, Atl).
Habitat Humid forest, borders, partial clearings, overgrown fields.
Field Marks **3.5"** Greenish crown and upperparts; clear white below, except lightly mottled green sides; tail gray, with dull dark band near tip; bill medium short, dark above, red below. See Azure-crowned Hummingbird.

AZURE-CROWNED HUMMINGBIRD [16] Chupaflor Coroniazul *Amazilia cyanocephala*
Range Mex–Nic. Res Mex (s.nAtl+cAtl+sw.sAtl + adj Hi), Blz (plne), Guat (Hi + adj Pac), ElSal (n).
Habitat Cloud forest, gardens, pine or pine-oak woods, borders.
Field Marks **4"** Like White-bellied Emerald, but crown iridescent blue; sides more broadly (and more grayish) green; *no* dark tail band; bill darker, mostly blackish.

BERYLLINE HUMMINGBIRD [16] Chupaflor de Berilo *Amazilia beryllina*
Range Mex, Guat, ElSal, Hon. Res Mex (Pac + adj nHi, csHi + adj Atl), Guat (Hi + adj Pac), ElSal.
Habitat Scrubby pine-oak woods, borders, overgrown clearings.
Field Marks **3.5"** M: iridescent green; folded wings, uptacs, and tail rufous; lower belly and untacs pale dull rufous; bill reddish below, dark above. F: belly and untacs grayish.

BLUE-TAILED HUMMINGBIRD [17] Chupaflor Coliazul *Amazilia cyanura*
Range Mex – Nic, exc Blz. Res Mex (se.sPac), Guat (Pac), ElSal (e).
Habitat Humid forest, *cafetales*, partial clearings, borders.
Field Marks **3.7"** Bright iridescent green above and below, with coppery rump; blackish blue tail and uptacs; dark purplish folded wings, with rufous patch (mostly secondaries); untacs whitish.

RUFOUS-TAILED HUMMINGBIRD [16] Chupaflor Tzácatl *Amazilia tzacatl*
Range Mex – SAm, exc ElSal. Res Mex (s.nAtl+csAtl, s Yuc), Blz, Guat (Atl).
Habitat Borders, gardens, hedgerows, clearings, forest.
Field Marks **3.5"** Iridescent green, but lower breast and belly gray; untacs, uptacs, and tail rich reddish brown, with tail tinged purple; wings blackish; red bill black-tipped.

BUFF-BELLIED HUMMINGBIRD [18] Chupaflor Yucateco *Amazilia yucatanensis*
Range US, Mex, Blz, Guat. Res Mex (Atl, Yuc), Blz (n), Guat (nw Atl).
Habitat Scrubby woods, gardens, borders.
Field Marks **3.5"** Like Rufous-tailed Hummingbird, but buffy rufous, *not* gray, lower breast, belly, and untacs; slightly notched tail tinged bronzy green, *not* purplish.

CINNAMON HUMMINGBIRD [17] Chupaflor Canelo *Amazilia rutila*
Range Mex – CRic. Res Mex (s.nPac+csPac, n+e Yuc), Blz (cstl + cayes), Guat (Pac), ElSal.
Habitat Scrubby woods, thickets, borders, gardens.
Field Marks **4"** Dull greenish above; uptacs, tail (darker near tip), sides of face, and underparts rich reddish brown; bill bright red, black-tipped.

VIOLET-CROWNED HUMMINGBIRD [18] Chupaflor Occidental *Amazilia violiceps*
Range US – Mex. Res Mex (ncPac, w.ncHi).
Habitat Scrubby open woods, river borders, partial clearings.
Field Marks **4"** Contrasty white below, dull greenish bronze to grayish bronze above, tail greener; crown broadly violet (dull in some immatures); bill red, black-tipped. See Green-fronted Hummingbird.

GREEN-FRONTED HUMMINGBIRD [17] Chupaflor Corona Verde *Amazilia viridifrons*
Green-fronted group *A. v. viridifrons*
Range Mex. Res Mex (sc – se.cPac+sPac).
Habitat Open woods, parks, gardens, overgrown clearings.
Field Marks **4"** Like Violet-crowned Hummingbird, especially dull-crowned immatures, but crown green or blackish; sides and flanks gray; uptacs and tail *not* greenish, but M: rufous-bronze, F: dull grayish brown.
Cinnamon-sided group [17] Chupaflor Flanquicanelo *A. v. wagneri*
Range Mex. Res Mex (se.cPac).
Habitat Scrubby thorny woods, wooded river valleys.
Field Marks **4"** Like Green-fronted group, but bright reddish brown stripe down side of neck and on sides and flanks.

STRIPED-TAILED HUMMINGBIRD [17] Chupaflor Colirrayado *Eupherusa eximia*
Range Mex–Pan. Res Mex (s.csAtl + adj Hi), Blz (s), Guat (Atl).
Habitat Cloud forest, borders, humid ravines.
Field Marks 3.5″ Bill black, medium length; rufous patch (secondaries) on folded blackish wing; tail (from below) contrasty white-based, black-tipped. M: iridescent green; lower belly buff; untacs white. F: pale to medium gray below, with whiter untacs and greenish sides. See Oaxaca Hummingbird.

(BLUE-CAPPED) OAXACA HUMMINGBIRD [17] Chupaflor Oaxaqueño *Eupherusa cyanophrys*
Range Mex. Res Mex (se.cPac + adj Hi).
Habitat Humid ravines, dense borders, in mixed mountain forest.
Field Marks 3.5″ Like Striped-tailed Hummingbird, but additional rufous on wings (on inner primaries) and M: crown iridescent blue; belly all green, *not* partly buffy; tail mostly whitish below, shading to gray tip and F: paler gray below; tail appears all white or whitish below.

(WHITE-TAILED) GUERRERO HUMMINGBIRD [17] Chupaflor Guerrerense *Eupherusa poliocerca*
Range Mex. Res Mex (c.cPac). Local.
Habitat Humid and mixed forest, borders, moist ravines.
Field Marks 3.5″ Like Oaxaca Hummingbird, but M: crown green, *not* blue.

GREEN-THROATED MOUNTAIN-GEM [17] Chupaflor Montañero *Lampornis viridipallens*
Range Mex, Guat, ElSal, Hon. Res Mex (sHi + adj Pac+Atl), Guat (Hi), ElSal (w).
Habitat Mountain pine-oak or cloud forest.
Field Marks 4″ M: bright green crown to greenish back to coppery rump to black uptacs and tail; underparts whitish, throat speckled green on white; sides mottled green and pale gray; ear patch black; line behind eye white; bill medium long, straight, black. F: similar, but uniformly bright green above; sides of tail pale gray; *no* speckles on throat.

(AMETHYST-THROATED) CACIQUE HUMMINGBIRD [17] Chupaflor Amatista *Lampornis amethystinus*
(Includes Margaret's Hummingbird, *L. margaritae*)
Range Mex, Guat, ElSal, Hon. Res Mex (Hi + adj csPac+Atl), Guat (Hi), ElSal (n); *L. margaritae* Mex (cHi + adj Pac).
Habitat Pine-oak woods, fir forest, clearings, cloud forest.
Field Marks 5″ Bill medium short, black, straight. M: iridescent green above and on sides; black ear patch; iridescent red throat (bluish violet in *L. margaritae*); blackish gray breast, belly, and untacs; gray-cornered black tail. F: paler below; throat rich buff; tail corners paler gray.

BLUE-THROATED HUMMINGBIRD [18] Chupaflor Gorjiazul *Lampornis clemenciae*
Range US–Mex. Res/sum Mex (w+e.nHi+cHi). Local.
Habitat Grassy meadows, moist ravines, open pine forest, pine-oak woods.
Field Marks 5″ Bill medium long, slightly decurved, black. M: mostly bronzy

green above; large white corners on rounded black tail; blue throat; gray breast and belly; white line behind eye; black ear patch. F: throat pale gray.

GARNET-THROATED HUMMINGBIRD [17] Chupaflor Alicastaño *Lamprolaima rhami*
Range Mex, Guat, ElSal, Hon. Res Mex (local csHi + adj Pac+Atl), Guat (Hi), ElSal (n). Rare.
Habitat Cloud forest, humid pine forest, borders.
Field Marks 4.5″ Dark iridescent green above; rufous wings with some black feather edgings; short black bill; blackish purple tail; underparts and border of red throat black; chest violet. F: duller; dark gray below, with traces of red on throat; tail gray-cornered.

MAGNIFICENT HUMMINGBIRD [18] Chupaflor Magnífico *Eugenes fulgens*
Range Mex–Pan. Res Mex (Hi + adj Pac, Atl), Blz (acc), Guat (Hi), ElSal.
Habitat Rocky slopes, pine-oak woods, partial clearings, pine forest.
Field Marks 4.5″ M: dark green above; crown purple; tail dark green; wings blackish; mostly blackish below, but iridescent green throat. F: dull greenish above; tail dark green, with black bar near tip and pale gray corners; underparts pale gray; throat speckled.

PURPLE-CROWNED FAIRY [17] Chupaflor Pechinevado *Heliothryx barroti*
Range Mex–SAm, exc ElSal. Res Mex (sc.sAtl), Blz (s), Guat (Atl). Very rare.
Habitat Humid forest, small openings, woodland pools, flowering epiphytes.
Field Marks 5″, 6″ Shining pale bluish green above, but black central tail feathers; underparts and tail (below) clear white; black patch through eye; short, straight, black bill. M: crown purple. F: crown green; tail much longer than male's, graduated.

LONG-BILLED STARTHROAT [17] Chupaflor Piquilargo *Heliomaster longirostris*
Range Mex–SAm, exc Blz. Res Mex (csPac, se.cAtl+s.sAtl), Guat (Pac, Atl), ElSal.
Habitat Humid forest borders, partial clearings, openings.
Field Marks 4.5″ Like Plain-capped Starthroat, but line behind eye pale grayish olive, *not* contrasty white; base of tail (below) dark greenish, blending to black; Adt: forehead and forecrown bright blue (all males and cPac females) or bronzy green (other females); *not as much* black on chin and upper throat; Imm: may have some red speckles on throat.

PLAIN-CAPPED STARTHROAT [17] Chupaflor Pochotero *Heliomaster constantii*
Range Mex–CRic, exc Blz. Res Mex (Pac), Guat (Pac), ElSal.
Habitat Dry scrubby woods, borders, hedgerows.
Field Marks 4.5″ Bill long, rather stout, straight, black; tail pale gray at base (seen from below), then contrasty broad black bar, and prominent whitish corners. Adt: greenish above, bill to tail, with a whitish streak down center of rump; white mustache mark and line behind eye; black ear patch; blackish chin and upper throat; iridescent red lower throat; grayish breast and belly. Imm: entire throat blackish.

SLENDER SHEARTAIL [17] Tijereta Sureña *Doricha enicura*
Range Mex, Guat, ElSal, Hon. Res Mex (sHi + adj upper slopes Pac), Guat (Hi), ElSal (w).
Habitat Humid forest, lush borders, *cafetales,* overgrown partial clearings.
Field Marks **4.5″,** *2.5″* Bill medium length, somewhat decurved, black. M: iridescent green above; very deeply forked tail all black; white below, except violet gorget and bronzy green sides. F: underparts and line behind eye buff; black mask; slightly forked tail, rufous at base, then a black bar and white tip. See Sparkling-tailed Hummingbird.

MEXICAN SHEARTAIL [17] Tijereta Yucateca *Doricha eliza*
Range Mex. Res Mex (near-coast c.cAtl, n Yuc). Very rare cAtl, common cstl n Yuc.
Habitat Low thorny woods, brushy fields, hedgerows, gardens.
Field Marks **4″,** *2.5″* Bill long, slightly decurved, black. M: iridescent green above; white below, with broadly green sides and purplish red gorget with pointed corners; tail very deeply forked, feathers square-tipped, black with brown stripe. F: greenish above, mostly white below; rounded tail buffy at base (below), then broadly black, with white corners.

SPARKLING-TAILED HUMMINGBIRD [17] Chupaflor Moscón *Tilmatura dupontii*
Range Mex–Nic, exc Blz. Res Mex (s.nPac+csPac, csHi), Guat (Hi + adj Pac, Atl), ElSal (w). Rare.
Habitat Parks, gardens, open pine-oak woods, humid forest, *cafetales.*
Field Marks **4″,** *2.5″* Drifting, supersmooth flight is like that of a large bee; tail of male sparkles. Bill short, straight, black. M: mostly iridescent green, with white patch on each side of rump; blue throat; white chest; tail very deeply forked; tail feathers black and brown, with white tips. F: greenish above; buff patch each side of rump; dark tawny rufous below. Darker rufous below (and straighter-billed) than female Slender Sheartail, Mexican Sheartail, Lucifer Hummingbird, or Beautiful Hummingbird.

LUCIFER HUMMINGBIRD [18] Tijereta Altiplanero *Calothorax lucifer*
Range US–Mex. Res/win Mex (ncHi + adj slopes Pac). Rare.
Habitat Dry brushy grassland, open pine or pine-oak woods, borders.
Field Marks **3.5″,** *3″* Greenish above; bill medium length, black, decurved. M: whitish below with long-cornered, reddish violet gorget; broadly grayish green sides and flanks; tail black, medium long, deeply forked. F: pale buffy below; whitish untacs; tail double-rounded, with rufous base below, then broadly black, then white corners; pale streak behind eye. See Beautiful Hummingbird, female Sparkling-tailed Hummingbird, and female Slender Sheartail.

BEAUTIFUL HUMMINGBIRD [17] Tijereta Oaxaqueño *Calothorax pulcher*
Range Mex. Res Mex (se.cHi + adj upper slopes Pac). Rare.
Habitat Brushy areas, scrubby woods, semidesert.
Field Marks **3.5″,** *3″* Like Lucifer Hummingbird, but bill slightly shorter, more

slender, not as strongly decurved; M: tail longer, outer feathers broader, with more rounded tips.

RUBY-THROATED HUMMINGBIRD [20] Chupaflor Rubí *Archilochus colubris*
Range Can–Pan. Win/tr Mex (s.nPac+csPac, Hi, Atl, Yuc; acc sBajCal), Blz, Guat, ElSal. Rare.
Habitat Patchy woods and pastures, gardens, woodlots, borders.
Field Marks **3.5″** Greenish above; bill medium length, slender, black, straight; tail feathers pointed. M: tail forked, blackish; front of face blackish; whitish below, with iridescent red gorget, and broadly greenish sides. F: black tail double-rounded, white-tipped; underparts whitish, sides tinged brownish. See Black-chinned, Anna's, and Broad-tailed Hummingbirds.

BLACK-CHINNED HUMMINGBIRD [18] Chupaflor Barbinegro *Archilochus alexandri*
Range Can–Mex. Sum/win Mex (BajCal, ncPac, ncHi, nAtl). Rare.
Habitat Gardens, dry brushy areas, river valleys, semidesert.
Field Marks **3.5″** Like Ruby-throated Hummingbird, but M: gorget black and (lower part) violet and F: may be *not* as brownish below; crown *not* as greenish. See Costa's Hummingbird.

ANNA'S HUMMINGBIRD [18] Chupaflor Coronirrojo *Calypte anna*
Range Can–Mex. Res/win Mex (res nw.nBajCal; win nBajCal, n.nPac, n.nHi).
Habitat Open areas with scattered trees, semidesert, gardens, overgrown fields, river-border woods.
Field Marks **4″** Bill black, short, straight. M: greenish above, with red forehead and crown; dull greenish gray below, with white chest and short-cornered red gorget; tail notched, black. F: greenish above, pale gray below; red and gray specks on throat; dark ear patch; tail rounded, greenish (below) to black, with white tips. See Costa's and Broad-tailed Hummingbirds.

COSTA'S HUMMINGBIRD [18] Chupaflor Coronivioleta *Calypte costae*
Range US–Mex. Res/win Mex (BajCal, n.nPac; win s.nPac).
Habitat Scrubby thorny semidesert, scattered trees and shrubs, gardens, dry streambeds.
Field Marks **3.5″** Like Anna's Hummingbird but smaller; *not* as much greenish gray below; M: crown and longer-cornered gorget violet, *not* red; F: white underparts, *no* specks on throat. See Black-chinned Hummingbird.

CALLIOPE HUMMINGBIRD [18] Chupaflor Rafaguitas *Stellula calliope*
Range Can–Mex. Sum/win Mex (sum/tr nBajCal; tr/win ncPac + adj lower slopes Hi). Rare.
Habitat Woodland edge, open pine-oak or pine woods, wooded stream valleys, thickets, brush.
Field Marks **2.5″** Greenish above, mostly whitish below. M: gorget ragged, streaked white and violet-red; tail short, blackish. F: whitish below; red and gray throat specks; tinged cinnamon on sides, flanks, and untacs; *little* rufous on

tail, which is short, rounded, green at base (below) to black, with white corners. See Anna's and Broad-tailed Hummingbirds.

BUMBLEBEE HUMMINGBIRD [17] Chupaflor Zumbador *Atthis heloisa*
Range Mex. Res Mex (w+e.nHi+c+s.cHi). Rare.
Habitat Cloud forest, open pine or pine-oak woods, partial clearings.
Field Marks 2.3" Greenish above, mostly white below; bill short, straight, black; tail rounded, rufous at base, to contrasty black, with white corners. M: sides greenish; gorget violet-red, with medium long corners. F: gray specks on throat; pale rufous sides; buffy untacs; white line behind eye. See Wine-throated and larger Allen's and Rufous Hummingbirds.

WINE-THROATED HUMMINGBIRD Chupaflor Enano *Atthis ellioti*
Range Mex, Guat, ElSal, Hon. Res Mex (sHi), Guat (Hi), ElSal (w). Rare.
Habitat Cloud forest, humid mixed forest, partial clearings, borders.
Field Marks 2.3" Like Bumblebee Hummingbird, but slightly smaller, bill shorter; M: gorget redder.

BROAD-TAILED HUMMINGBIRD [18] Chupaflor Vibrador *Selasphorus platycercus*
Range Can - Mex, Guat. Res/win Mex (ncHi), Guat (Hi).
Habitat High-mountain meadows, open grassy pine woods, large openings in oak woods.
Field Marks 3.5" Greenish above, mostly whitish below; bill straight, medium length, black. M: gorget bright red; sides broadly grayish green; tail black be low. Wings produce high-pitched trill in flight. F: gray throat speckles; buffy wash on sides and flanks; larger than Calliope; more rufous on (rounded) tail above than Calliope, less than Allen's or Rufous Hummingbirds. See Ruby-throated Hummingbird.

RUFOUS HUMMINGBIRD [18] Chupaflor Dorado *Selasphorus rufus*
Range AK Mex, Blz Tr/win Mex (tr nBajCal, nPac, ncHi; win cPac, cHi), Blz (acc).
Habitat Shrubby pine woods, gardens, parks, partial clearings.
Field Marks 3.5" White below, but pale rufous sides, flanks, and untacs; bill medium short, straight, black. M: rich rufous above; short-cornered gorget dark red (young males and some adults have much green on back and crown, somewhat like Allen's Hummingbird). F: greenish above; tail from below shows much rufous at base, then black, then white corners; gray or red throat speckles. See Allen's, Calliope, and Broad-tailed Hummingbirds.

ALLEN'S HUMMINGBIRD [20] Chupaflor Sasin *Selasphorus sasin*
Range US–Mex. Tr/win Mex (nBajCal, nPac+nw.cPac, w.nHi+cHi).
Habitat Scrubby woods, overgrown clearings, borders.
Field Marks 3.5" Like Rufous Hummingbird, but M: green back, nape, and crown; F: much narrower outer tail feathers. More rufous on rounded tail than Calliope and Broad-tailed Hummingbirds.

TROGONS—TROGONES—TROGONIDAE

BLACK-HEADED TROGON [20] Trogón Cabecinegro *Trogon melanocephalus*
Range Mex–CRic. Res Mex (se.cAtl+sAtl, Yuc), Blz, Guat (Atl), ElSal. Rare.
Habitat Woodlands, humid forest, orchards, borders.
Voice Like that of Citreoline Trogon (see also Barred Antshrike voice).
Field Marks 11″ Yellow-bellied. Like Citreoline Trogon, but underside of female's tail shows two black bars across white (some males may show this pattern also); eyes dark brown, not yellow; and eye ring lighter blue; and M: blacker head and chest and bluish tail (above) and back.

CITREOLINE TROGON [19] Trogón Pacífico *Trogon citreolus*
Range Mex. Res Mex (s.nPac–w.sPac).
Habitat Dense thorny woods, borders, thickets, hedgerows.
Voice An accelerating series of croaks, ending in a rattle, *co—co—co—co—co-co-co-kr-r-r-r-r.* See Barred Antshrike voice.
Field Marks 11″ Yellow-bellied. Tail white below, except black base and tip; eyes yellow; eye ring bluish. M: tail (above) and back green; head blackish. F: head slaty gray; tail (above) and back blackish. See Black-headed and Violaceous Trogon.

VIOLACEOUS TROGON [19] Trogón Violáceo *Trogon violaceus*
Range Mex–SAm. Res Mex (sPac, csAtl, Yuc), Blz, Guat (Pac, Atl), ElSal. Rare.
Habitat Dense forest, open humid woods, borders, partial clearings.
Voice A musical series, *cyo, cyo, cyo, cyo,* etc.
Field Marks 10″ Yellow-bellied. Like Citreoline Trogon, but eye ring greenish yellow; M: upper breast, back, tail (above) more purplish and most of tail narrowly barred black and white below; F: tail black below, with narrow white feather tips and barred margins.

MOUNTAIN TROGON [19] Trogón Mexicano *Trogon mexicanus*
Range Mex, Guat, Hon. Res Mex (Hi), Guat (Hi + adj Pac).
Habitat Open or dense pine-oak, pine, or fir forest.
Voice A regular ringing series *co, co, co,* etc., or *cah-oo,* etc.
Field Marks 12″ Red-bellied, with white chest bar. M: tail black below, with three broad white bars; tail bluish green above, with black tip; head and back iridescent greenish; bill yellow. F: tail feathers black below, with white tips and barred margins; upperparts and tail (above) brown. See Elegant and Collared Trogon.

ELEGANT TROGON [21] Trogón Elegante *Trogon elegans*
Range US–CRic, exc Blz. Res Mex (ncPac, e+w.nHi+cHi, s.nAtl+nw.cAtl), Guat (e Pac), ElSal. Irregular.
Habitat Rocky ravines, dry oak or pine-oak woods, thorny scrub, humid river borders.
Voice A hoarse, clucking, croaking series, *co-wy, co-wy, co-wy, co-wy.*
Field Marks 11″ Red-bellied. Like Mountain and Collared Trogon, but tail gray

(finely vermiculated black and white) below, with white feather tips; M: tail copper-colored above, with black tip; F: tail brown above with black tip; white patch behind and below eye.

COLLARED TROGON [19] Trogón Collarejo *Trogon collaris*
Range Mex–SAm. Res Mex (csPac+csAtl + adj Hi, Yuc), Blz, Guat (Pac, Atl + adj Hi), ElSal (n).
Habitat Humid forest, river-border woods, scrub woods, *cafetales*.
Voice A slightly descending musical two-noted call, *cyo-cyo*.
Field Marks 10″ Red-bellied. Like Mountain Trogon, but M: back more golden green; tail black below with fine white bars, golden green above and F: tail dull grayish below with narrow dark bar near each feather tip.

(SLATY-TAILED) MASSENA TROGON [19] Trogón Grande *Trogon massena*
Range Mex–SAm, exc ElSal. Res Mex (se.cAtl+sAtl), Blz, Guat (Atl).
Habitat Humid forest, overgrown clearings, lush gardens, *cafetales*.
Voice Loud barking notes.
Field Marks 13″ Red-bellied. *No* white breast bar; tail black below. M: orange bill and eye ring; head, chest, and upperparts, including tail above, bluish green. F: slaty gray head, chest, upperparts, and tail; upper mandible mostly dark.

EARED TROGON [19] Trogón Silbador *Euptilotis neoxenus*
Range US–Mex. Res Mex (nw.nHi–wc.cHi). Rare, irregular.
Habitat Mountain pine forest, open pine-oak woods.
Voice Higher-pitched and more trilled than that of other trogons *tree-tree-tree-tree*.
Field Marks 14″ Red-bellied. Like Massena Trogon, but tail mostly white below; bill dark gray; M: tail blackish blue above; F: upperparts bluish green, *not* slaty gray.

RESPLENDENT QUETZAL [19] Quetzal Norteño *Pharomachrus mocinno*
Range Mex–Pan, exc Blz. Res Mex (sHi + adj Pac+Atl), Guat (Hi + adj Pac, Atl), ElSal (n). Rare.
Habitat Cloud forest, other dense humid mountain forest.
Field Marks 35″, 15″ Red-bellied. Wing coverts and uptacs form plumes. M: tail white below; uptacs very long, extending up to a foot or two beyond tip of tail. F. head medium gray; chest to uptacs green to gray to dull red; tail barred blackish gray and whitish below; uptacs reach tip of tail.

MOTMOTS—MOMOTOS—MOMOTIDAE

TODY MOTMOT [19] Momoto Enano *Hylomanes momotula*
Range Mex–SAm. Res Mex (sPac, se.cAtl+sAtl), Blz, Guat (Pac, Atl), ElSal (w). Rare.
Habitat Low branches in dense humid forest.
Voice A slow series of *cwook* or *cwonk* notes.

Field Marks 7" Sits quietly, flies directly, with rapid wingbeats. Tail *not* racket-tipped; *no* black chest spot; crown rufous; short pale blue line over eye; mostly blackish ear patch, with white and olive lines below; back and wings green; underparts mostly pale buffy greenish, with faint streaks; center of belly white.

BLUE-THROATED MOTMOT [19] Momoto Gorjiazul *Aspatha gularis*
Range Mex, Guat, ElSal, Hon. Res Mex (sHi), Guat (Hi), ElSal (n). Very rare.
Habitat Humid pine, pine-oak, or cloud forest.
Voice Coot or *took*, singly or series.
Field Marks 11" Tail *not* racket-tipped; plumage mostly olive-green, with pale blue throat; small black ear patch; small black chest spot; tail long, graduated, and dull rufous below.

BLUE-CROWNED MOTMOT [19] Turco Real *Momotus momota*
Range Mex–SAm. Res Mex (sPac, c.nAtl–sAtl, Yuc), Blz, Guat (Pac, Atl), ElSal.
Habitat River-border woods, dry or humid forest, overgrown orchards.
Voice A low-pitched *hoot, hoot.*
Field Marks 16" Green above, or with some rufous; olive-green or rufous below; crown pale blue with black border (nAtl, n.cAtl) or crown with black center, then blue circle, then black border (s.cAtl, sAtl, sPac, Yuc); short bare space on racket-tipped tail; black ear streak and chest spot.

RUSSET-CROWNED MOTMOT [19] Momoto Coronicafé *Momotus mexicanus*
Range Mex–Guat. Res Mex (Pac + adj Hi), Guat (local, interior Atl).
Habitat Open arid slopes, low thorny woodland, semidesert scrub.
Voice A burred, low-pitched *h-rr-oot.*
Field Marks 13" Pale olive-green above, pale bluish green below; crown rufous; short bare space on racket-tipped tail; black ear streak and chest spot.

KEEL-BILLED MOTMOT [19] Gallinola *Electron carinatum*
Range Mex–CRic, exc ElSal. Res Mex (s.sAtl), Blz (s), Guat (Atl). Very rare, local.
Habitat Humid forest, partial clearings.
Voice Like part of cackle of chicken, a loud, nasal *donk* or *conk.*
Field Marks 13" Olive-green above, dull brownish below; bill broad, flat, keeled on top; forehead rufous; blue streak over eye; short bare space on racket-tipped tail; black ear streak and chest spot.

TURQUOISE-BROWED MOTMOT [19] Momoto Corbatinegro *Eumomota superciliosa*
Range Mex–CRic, exc Blz. Res Mex (sPac, n.sAtl, Yuc), Guat (Pac), ElSal.
Habitat Dry thorny woods, humid forest borders, farms, gardens, archaeological sites.
Voice A mellow or harsh *toke* or *tuck* or *tuck-a-loke.*
Field Marks 14" Brownish green above, with dull rufous back patch; greenish breast, with long blue-bordered black streak down throat to chest; rufous belly and untacs; pale blue plumelike stripe over eye; black ear patch; long bare space on racket-tipped tail.

KINGFISHERS—PESCADORES—ALCEDINIDAE

RINGED KINGFISHER [19] Pescador Grande *Ceryle torquata*
Range US-SAm. Res Mex (s.nPac+csPac, Atl), Blz, Guat (Pac, Atl), ElSal. Rare.
Habitat Rivers, canals, ponds, estuaries, lagoons, marshes, swamps.
Field Marks 17″ Gray-blue above (collar white), reddish brown below; ragged crest; bill stout. M: untacs whitish. F: broad blue breast band, bordered above and below by white; belly and untacs reddish brown. See Belted Kingfisher.

BELTED KINGFISHER [20] Pescador Norteño *Ceryle alcyon*
Range AK-SAm. Tr/win Mex, Blz, Guat, ElSal. Rare.
Habitat Rivers, lakes, ponds, lagoons, marshes, estuaries.
Field Marks 13″ Like Ringed Kingfisher, but M: white below with blue chest band and F: three breast bands—blue upper, white middle, rufous lower; belly and untacs white.

AMAZON KINGFISHER [19] Pescador Amazonas *Chloroceryle amazona*
Range Mex-SAm. Res Mex (s.nPac+csPac, s.nAtl+csAtl), Blz, Guat (Pac, Atl), ElSal (?). Rare.
Habitat Wooded rivers, ponds, lakes, lagoons, estuaries.
Field Marks 11″ Like Green Kingfisher, dark green above, with broad white collar, but plain, *not* heavily white spotted, dark green wings; larger, with heavier bill; larger and shaggier crest and F: only one breast band, often or usually incomplete.

GREEN KINGFISHER [21] Pescador Menor *Chloroceryle americana*
Range US-SAm. Res Mex (Pac, Hi, Atl, Yuc), Blz, Guat, ElSal.
Habitat Streams, rivers, ponds, coastal lagoons.
Field Marks 8″ Dark green above, somewhat rounded crest, broad white collar, many white spots and spotty bars on wings and tail. M: broad chest band rufous; flanks spotted dark green. F: usually two spotty green breast bands on white (lower band may be incomplete).

PYGMY KINGFISHER [19] Pescador Enano *Chloroceryle aenea*
Range Mex-SAm. Res Mex (sPac, se.cAtl+sAtl, Yuc), Blz, Guat (Pac, Atl), ElSal (cstl). Rare.
Habitat Wooded stream banks, small ponds, mangrove swamps, marsh pools.
Field Marks 5″ Flies with buzzy wingbeats. Dark green above; much smaller than any other kingfisher in our area. M: throat (and partial collar, more or less), breast, sides, and flanks tawny buff to rufous; belly and untacs white. F: *not as much* rufous below; dark green chest band.

PUFFBIRDS—BOCONES—BUCCONIDAE

WHITE-NECKED PUFFBIRD [22] Bocón *Notharchus macrorhynchos*
Range Mex-SAm. Res Mex (sPac, se.cAtl+sAtl, e Yuc), Blz, Guat (Pac, Atl), ElSal. Rare.

Habitat Upper branches along forest borders, open woods, partial clearings.
Field Marks 9″ Perches upright, flies out to catch insects. Large head; heavy black bill; crown, back, and wings black; forehead, cheeks, collar, and underparts white, except broad black chest band; short, graduated tail.

WHITE-WHISKERED PUFFBIRD [22] Barbón *Malacoptila panamensis*
Range Mex–SAm, exc ElSal. Res Mex (sc.sAtl), Blz (s), Guat (Atl). Rare.
Habitat Humid forest, thickets, partial clearings, borders.
Field Marks 8″ Streaked below, spotted above; whitish shaggy mustache mark; heavy bill; graduated tail. M: brown head and upperparts; rufous below; buffy untacs. F: brownish gray head and upperparts; pale buffy and whitish below.

JACAMARS—PICOLARGOS—GALBULIDAE

RUFOUS-TAILED JACAMAR [19] Picolargo Común *Galbula ruficauda*
Range Mex–SAm, exc ElSal. Res Mex (se.cAtl+sAtl), Blz, Guat (Atl). Rare.
Habitat Humid forest, stream banks, lush borders.
Voice A loud, clear *wheet* or *tyoop*, or a trill.
Field Marks 9″ Perches quietly, flies out to catch insects. Top and sides of head, breast, and upperparts, including top of tail, shiny green; belly, untacs, and tail (below) rufous; throat white (male) or rufous (female).

TOUCANS—TUCANES—RAMPHASTIDAE

EMERALD TOUCANET [22] Tucancillo Verde *Aulacorhynchus prasinus*
Range Mex–SAm. Res Mex (csPac + adj Hi, csAtl + adj Hi), Blz, Guat, ElSal.
Habitat Dense humid forest, cloud forest, openings, partial clearings.
Voice A long, slow series, *wok, wok, wok,* etc.
Field Marks 14″ Bright green, darker above; throat white; untacs rufous; tail graduated, feathers blackish below with broad rufous tips; very large bill mostly yellow above, black below.

COLLARED ARACARI [22] Tucancillo Collarejo *Pteroglossus torquatus*
Range Mex–SAm. Res Mex (sPac, se.cAtl+sAtl, Yuc), Blz, Guat (Pac, Atl), ElSal. Irregular.
Habitat Dense humid forest, river-valley forest, partial clearings, borders.
Voice An abrupt whistle, *see-ah* or *pee-ah*.
Field Marks 16″ Mostly blackish green above and on throat and chest; red rump; patchy bright yellow, red, and black below; bill very large, whitish above, black below, appears many-toothed; eyes white.

KEEL-BILLED TOUCAN [22] Tucán Piquiverde *Ramphastos sulfuratus*
Range Mex–SAm, exc ElSal. Res Mex (csAtl, s+e Yuc), Blz, Guat (Atl). Irregular.
Habitat Humid forest, partial clearings, borders, mixed farms and woods.
Voice A croaking series, *r-rak, r-rak, r-rak,* or *crak, crak,* etc.
Field Marks 20″ Mostly black; throat, face, sides of neck, and chest yellow; un-

tacs bright red; uptacs white; extremely large bill yellowish green, with orange patch and red tip.

WOODPECKERS—CARPINTEROS—PICIDAE

OLIVACEOUS PICULET [48] Carpinterito Oliváceo *Picumnus olivaceus*
Range Guat–SAm, exc ElSal. Res Guat (e Atl). Rare.
Habitat Humid forest, borders, partial clearings.
Field Marks 3.5" Brownish; crown and nape spotted white on blackish; tail short, *not* sharp-tipped, black with a prominent yellow center stripe; M: red-streaked forehead; F: white-spotted forehead.

LEWIS'S WOODPECKER [20] Carpintero Ventrirrosado *Melanerpes lewis*
Range Can–Mex. Wm Mex (nBajCal, n.nPac, n.nHi). Casual/rare, irregular.
Habitat Scattered trees and shrubs, dry river-valley woods, open pine or oak woods.
Field Marks 10" Front of face maroon-red; rear of face (and upper throat) black; collar and breast silvery gray; belly deep pink; untacs blackish; upperparts black with greenish gloss.

ACORN WOODPECKER [21] Carpintero Arlequín *Melanerpes formicivorus*
Range US–SAm. Res Mex (BajCal, Pac, Hi, Atl), Blz (pine), Guat, ElSal (n).
Habitat Mostly in mountain oak or pine-oak woods, but also down to near sea level, in mixed grass-palmetto-oak-pine habitat.
Voice A nasal rhythmic *wick-y, wick-y, wick-y*, or a single crenk.
Field Marks 8" Often in groups, packs acorns into rows of holes drilled in trees or posts. M: black, but white rump, uptacs, forehead, cheek patch, throat band (tinged yellowish), and small wing patch; forecrown and hindcrown red; belly and untacs white with some black streaks; eyes white. F: forecrown black; hind-crown red.

BLACK-CHEEKED WOODPECKER [22] Carpintero Selvático *Melanerpes pucherani*
Range Mex–SAm, exc ElSal. Res Mex (sc.cAtl+s.sAtl), Blz (s), Guat (Atl). Rare.
Habitat Humid forest, borders, partial clearings.
Field Marks 7.5" Darker-backed than similar species; small white patch behind eye, within long, broad black eye streak. M: narrow white bars on black back; dark bars on pale gray sides and untacs; throat and breast pale gray; reddish belly patch; white rump; red crown and nape. F: nape red; crown mostly black and pale gray.

GOLDEN-CHEEKED WOODPECKER [22] Carpintero Cariamarillo *Melanerpes chrysogenys*
Range Mex. Res Mex (c.nPac–cPac).
Habitat Scrubby thorny woods, overgrown river valleys, borders, mixed farms and woods.
Field Marks 8" Black-and-white barred back, rump, and untacs; mostly pale gray underparts with yellow-tinged belly; small black eye patch; faint yellowish

wash on ear patch (cheeks); red crown; yellow forehead and nape. F: similar, but crown pale gray and black, *not* red.

(GRAY-BREASTED) BALSAS WOODPECKER [22] Carpintero del Balsas *Melanerpes hypopolius*
Range Mex. Res Mex (c+se.cPac).
Habitat Semidesert, saguaro-covered hillsides, dry river valleys, scrubby thorny woods.
Voice A harsh *cherr.*
Field Marks 10″ Like Gila Woodpecker (male has round red crown patch), but pale red on cheek; short black line over eye; much darker and grayer below and on head.

(RED-VENTED) YUCATAN WOODPECKER [22] Carpintero Yucateco *Melanerpes pygmaeus*
Range Mex, Blz, Hon. Res Mex (ne.sAtl, Yuc), Blz (n). Rare.
Habitat Scrubby woods, borders, partial clearings, mixed fields and woods.
Field Marks 6″ Like Yucatan (narrow-barred) form of Golden-fronted Woodpecker, but smaller and smaller-billed, darker and yellower around base of bill, and more white on forehead; F: only a very small patch of red on nape.

GILA WOODPECKER [21] Carpintero Desértico *Melanerpes uropygialis*
Range US–Mex. Res Mex (BajCal, nPac + adj ncHi).
Habitat Desert or semidesert, cactus-covered slopes, thorny scrubby borders.
Field Marks 9″ Paler than Balsas Woodpecker—*no* range overlap. Barred back and rump; pale grayish to whitish below and on face; untacs barred. M: round red crown patch. F: crown pale brownish gray.

GOLDEN-FRONTED WOODPECKER [21] Carpintero Común *Melanerpes aurifrons*
Range US–Nic. Res Mex (sPac, ncHi, Atl, Yuc), Blz, Guat, ElSal.
Habitat Scrubby woods, humid forest borders, dry river valleys, gardens, clearings.
Field Marks 9″ Wide-barred type **[21]**, M: barred black and white above, white bars about as wide as black bars; rump and uptacs white; tail black or barred black and white; forehead pale gray or whitish; crown red; nape or hindcrown gray; hindneck yellow or orange; pale gray below, with yellow or orange wash on belly; white patch on extended wing; F: yellow hindneck, but entire crown grayish to whitish, *not* red. Narrow-barred type (not illustrated): black bars narrow, and white bars very narrow; tail usually black, but may be barred with white; yellow-orange or red wash on belly; M: large red patch on crown, continuing down nape and hindneck; F: red hindneck, but entire crown gray, *not* red.

YELLOW-BELLIED SAPSUCKER [20] Chupasavia Común *Sphyrapicus varius*
Range AK–Pan. Win Mex (csPac, Hi, Atl, Yuc; cas n.nBajCal, nPac), Blz, Guat, ElSal.
Habitat Various wooded habitats, but rare to casual in very dry or very wet forest.

Field Marks 9″ Digs small holes in bark, eats sap. M: crown and throat red; black throat border and chest band; black above, liberally barred with whitish and with long white patch on wing; rump patch white. F: like male, but chin and upper throat white. Juv + part of 1st win: mostly barred blackish and brown above and below, with little or no trace of adult pattern, except on wing; gradually acquires adult pattern and colors through winter and early spring.

RED-NAPED SAPSUCKER [20] Chupasavia Nuquirroja *Sphyrapicus nuchalis*
Range Can–Mex. Win Mex (BajCal, nPac, nHi). Rare.
Habitat Varied wooded habitats, pine-oak woods, deciduous forest.
Field Marks 9″ Like Yellow-bellied Sapsucker, with red throat in male, but female throat red also, *not* white; male and female nape patch red, *not* black; Juv: adult plumage by late fall or early winter.

RED-BREASTED SAPSUCKER [20] Chupasavia Cabecirroja *Sphyrapicus ruber*
Range AK–Mex. Win vis Mex (n.nBajCal). Very rare.
Habitat Conifers and other woodland.
Field Marks 9″ Like Yellow-bellied Sapsucker, but darker-backed, with fewer whitish bars, and head and chest nearly all red, with short diagonal white streak below eye.

WILLIAMSON'S SAPSUCKER [20] Chupasavia Oscura *Sphyrapicus thyroideus*
Range Can–Mex. Res/win Mex (res mts n.nBajCal; win w.ncHi + adj Pac). Rare.
Habitat Mountain pine forest or pine-oak woods.
Field Marks 9″ M: black, except two white head stripes, wing patch, rump, and uptacs; red throat; yellow belly; black-and-white barred sides. F: mostly heavily barred blackish brown and white; black breast patch; yellow belly patch; brownish head and throat; white rump and uptacs; *no* large white patch on wing.

LADDER-BACKED WOODPECKER [21] Carpinterillo Mexicano *Picoides scalaris*
Range US–Nic. Res Mex, local Blz, Guat, ElSal (cas e).
Habitat Desert, semidesert, scrubby woods, borders, clearings.
Field Marks 7″ Barred black-and-white back; pale gray below with streaked sides; narrowly black-bordered white ear patch; heavily spotted wings. M: red crown patch. F: crown black, *no* red. See Nuttall's Woodpecker.

NUTTALL'S WOODPECKER [21] Carpinterillo Californiano *Picoides nuttallii*
Range US–Mex. Res Mex (n.nBajCal).
Habitat Dry wooded river valleys, thorny scrubby woods, hedgerows, borders.
Field Marks 7″ Like Ladder-backed Woodpecker, but broadly black ear patch; large black patch below nape and on sides of neck. (Ranges overlap only in n.nBajCal.)

HAIRY WOODPECKER [20, 21] Carpintero Ocotero *Picoides villosus*
Range AK–Pan, exc Blz. Res Mex (n.nBajCal, Hi), Guat (Hi), ElSal (n).
Habitat Mountain forests or open woods of pine, pine-oak, or fir.
Field Marks 9″–7″ Back stripe, wing spots, part of cheek, line over eye, and

outer tail feathers white or whitish; wings, scapulars, some head markings, and central tail feathers black. M: small red nape patch. F: *no* red. Birds of northwestern Mexico whitish below; birds of northeastern, central, and southern Mexico, Guatemala, and El Salvador medium grayish brown below. Progressively smaller from northwest Mexico to Panama.

ARIZONA WOODPECKER [21] Carpintero de Arizona *Picoides arizonae*
(The AOU lumps this with Strickland's Woodpecker; see below)
Range US–Mex. Res Mex (w.ncHi). Rare.
Habitat Oak or pine-oak woods.
Field Marks 8″ Plain dark brown above; brown spots below, on white; brown ear patch and malar streak on white face. M: red nape patch. F: *no* red.

STRICKLAND'S WOODPECKER [22] Carpintero Volcanero *Picoides stricklandi*
(Does not include Arizona Woodpecker; see above)
Range Mex. Res Mex (c.cHi). Rare.
Habitat High-mountain woodlands.
Field Marks 8″ Like Arizona Woodpecker, but back barred and underparts heavily streaked.

SMOKY-BROWN WOODPECKER [22] Carpinterillo Café *Veniliornis fumigatus*
Range Mex–SAm. Res Mex (s.nPac+csPac [rare and local], s.nAtl+csAtl, s+e Yuc), Blz, Guat (Pac, Atl), ElSal.
Habitat Humid areas, dense forest, wooded river valleys, partial clearings, hedgerows.
Field Marks 6″ Dark brown; throat and face grayish. M: nape red, crown streaked red. F: crown and nape brown, *not* red.

BRONZE-WINGED WOODPECKER [22] Carpintero Verde *Piculus aeruginosus*
(The AOU lumps this with Golden-olive Woodpecker; see below)
Range Mex. Res Mex (c.nAtl–c.cAtl + adj Hi). Rare.
Habitat Dense humid forest, cloud forest, wooded river valleys.
Voice One call is a petulant *kweer*.
Field Marks 10″ Like Golden-olive Woodpecker, but grayer and greener, *not* as yellowish below or as bronzy above; appears more scaly than barred below; *no* red on sides of forecrown or forehead.

GOLDEN-OLIVE WOODPECKER [22] Carpintero Oliváceo *Piculus rubiginosus*
(Does not include Bronze-winged Woodpecker; see above)
Range Mex–SAm. Res Mex (sPac, sHi, se.cAtl+sAtl, Yuc), Blz, Guat, ElSal. Rare.
Habitat Cloud forest, borders, humid pine-oak or pine woods.
Voice Like Northern Flicker's, *clee* and *kick-kick-kick-kick*. Also a weak, chattering trill, on one pitch.
Field Marks 9″ M: red border all around crown joins red patch on nape; mustache mark red; dark olive to brownish olive above; barred yellowish and dark olive-green below. F: red nape patch, but *little or no* red on sides of crown or forehead; *no* red mustache mark.

GRAY-CROWNED WOODPECKER [22] Carpintero Occidental *Piculus auricularis*
Range Mex. Res Mex (c.nPac–cPac + adj Hi). Rare.
Habitat Humid pine-oak or pine forest, borders, partial clearings.
Field Marks 9″ Like Golden-olive Woodpecker, with red mustache mark in male, but more grayish green overall; only faint traces of red, or none, on nape or border of crown.

NORTHERN FLICKER [21] Carpintero Norteño *Colaptes auratus*
Yellow-shafted group [21] Carpintero Aliamarillo *Colaptes a. auratus*
Range AK–Mex. Win Mex (nw+ne.nHi + adj Pac+Atl). Very rare.
Habitat Pine forest, pine-oak woods, borders, partial clearings.
Voice Clee or *clee-o*. Also a high-pitched chatter, *kick-kick-kick-kick*.
Field Marks 11″ Brown above, barred black, with white rump; grayish crown and nape, with red nape patch; throat and face buffy gray; black chest band; black-spotted whitish breast and belly; yellow underwings and tail base. M: black mustache mark. F: *no* mustache mark.
Red-shafted group [21] Carpintero Alirrojo *Colaptes a. cafer*
(Includes *C. a. mexicanoides*)
Range AK–Nic, exc Blz. Res Mex (nBajCal, e+w.ncHi+sHi + adj ncPac+ncAtl), Guat (Hi), ElSal.
Habitat Open or dense pine or pine-oak or fir forests, partial clearings.
Field Marks 12″ Like Gilded Flicker, with red mustache mark (male only) and no red nape patch, but brown of crown, nape, and back darker and more reddish; underwings and tail base red, *not* yellow.

GILDED FLICKER [21] Carpintero Dorado *Colaptes chrysoides*
Range US–Mex. Res Mex (BajCal, n.nPac).
Habitat Desert or semidesert, saguaro-covered hillsides.
Field Marks 11″ Like Yellow-shafted group of Northern Flicker, with tail base and underwings yellow, but pale buffy brown crown; pale gray face and throat; *no* red nape patch; M: mustache mark red, *not* black.

CHESTNUT-COLORED WOODPECKER [22] Carpintero Castaño *Celeus castaneus*
Range Mex–Pan, exc ElSal. Res Mex (s.cAtl+sAtl, s+e Yuc), Blz, Guat (Atl). Rare.
Habitat Dense humid forest.
Voice A mellow but slightly metallic *cleek*.
Field Marks 10″ Appears very dark, with many V-shaped black marks on rich chestnut above and below; crested head creamy brown; bill greenish ivory. M: broad mustache mark, part of ear patch, and (sometimes) lores red.

LINEATED WOODPECKER [22] Carpintero Real *Dryocopus lineatus*
Range Mex–SAm. Res Mex (c.nPac–sPac, c.nAtl–sAtl, Yuc), Blz, Guat (Pac, Atl), ElSal. Rare.
Habitat Humid forest borders, openings, open scrubby woods, river-border woods, large trees in mixed pastures and hedgerows.
Field Marks 12″ Eyes pale yellow. M: black, except broadly red forehead, crest, and mustache mark; black-and-whitish barred belly, sides, and untacs; whitish

chin; white streak from scapulars up along side of neck and (in most areas) under eye to base of bill. F: forehead and mustache mark black, *not* red.

PALE-BILLED WOODPECKER [22] Carpintero Picotero *Campephilus guatemalensis*
Range Mex–SAm. Res Mex (c.nPac–sPac, c.nAtl–sAtl, Yuc), Blz, Guat (Pac, Atl), ElSal. Rare.
Habitat Humid forest, borders, partial clearings, wooded river valleys.
Field Marks 14″ Double-rap pecking is distinctive. Like Lineated Woodpecker, but sides of face all red (except very small black bare-skin patch around eye), *not* black and white or black, white, and red; and M: chin and upper throat red, *not* whitish; F: chin, upper throat, and front and top of crest black.

OVENBIRDS—TREPAMUSGOS—FURNARIIDAE

RUFOUS-BREASTED SPINETAIL [24] Colaespina Chepita *Synallaxis erythrothorax*
Range Mex–Hon. Res Mex (sPac, se.cAtl+sAtl, Yuc), Blz, Guat (Pac, Atl), ElSal. Rare.
Habitat Hedgerows, thickets, brushy forest borders and openings.
Voice Rasping, *one-two-three-kick.*
Field Marks 6″ Olive-brown back; gray head; rich reddish brown breast; gray belly; throat finely streaked; tail rather long, spine-tipped.

SCALY-THROATED (FOLIAGE-GLEANER) LEAFGLEANER [24] Trepamusgo Cejudo *Anabacerthia variegaticeps*
Range Mex–SAm. Res Mex (csHi + adj Pac+Atl), Blz (s), Guat (Hi + adj Pac+ Atl), ElSal (n). Rare.
Habitat Cloud forest or humid oak or pine-oak woods; mostly in middle or upper branches.
Field Marks 6″ Brown above, slightly paler below; throat broadly creamy, faintly scaled; spectacles (prominent eye ring and line behind eye) buff, with broad dark line below eye. See Buff-throated Leafgleaner.

BUFF-THROATED (FOLIAGE-GLEANER) LEAFGLEANER [24] Trepamusgo Gorjipálido *Automolus ochrolaemus*
Range Mex–SAm, exc ElSal. Res Mex (se.cAtl+sAtl), Blz (s), Guat (Atl). Rare.
Habitat Undergrowth to middle branches of dense lowland humid forest.
Field Marks 7″ Like Spectacled Leafgleaner, but notably larger; *no* eye ring; throat, sides of face, and line behind eye rich tawny buff with brown line behind eye.

RUDDY (FOLIAGE-GLEANER) LEAFGLEANER [24] Trepamusgo Castaño *Automolus rubiginosus*
Range Mex–SAm, exc Blz. Res Mex (sw+ne.cHi+sHi + adj Pac+Atl), Guat (Hi + adj Pac, Atl), ElSal (n). Rare.
Habitat Undergrowth in humid forest.
Field Marks 8″ Mostly rich brown; throat bright tawny rufous; bill straight, sharp, dark; *no* contrasty face pattern.

PLAIN XENOPS [24] Picolezna Sencillo *Xenops minutus*
Range Mex–SAm, exc ElSal. Res Mex (se.cAtl+sAtl, s+e Yuc), Blz, Guat (Atl). Rare.
Habitat Humid forest, partial clearings.
Field Marks 4.5″ Mostly dull olive-brown to reddish brown; pale buffy eye stripe, and white mustache mark; short, up-turned, wedge-shaped bill; black and rufous tail. Usually does *not* perch upright as illustrated; looks and acts more like a small woodcreeper, wren, or piculet, but note white mustache mark and black and rufous tail.

TAWNY-THROATED LEAFTOSSER [24] Breñero Gorjirrufo *Sclerurus mexicanus*
Range Mex–SAm, exc Blz, ElSal. Res Mex (e.cHi+sHi + adj sPac+csAtl), Guat (Hi + adj Pac, Atl). Rare.
Habitat Ravines or stream banks in humid forest, on ground or in low shrubs.
Voice A sharp, loud *chip*.
Field Marks 6″ Like Ruddy Leafgleaner, but darker and more olive-brown; tail shorter, more rounded, and much darker; bill longer and slightly decurved.

SCALY-THROATED LEAFTOSSER [24] Breñero Oscuro *Sclerurus guatemalensis*
Range Mex–SAm, exc Blz, ElSal. Res Mex (sAtl), Guat (Atl). Very rare.
Habitat Rocky areas or ravines in dense humid forest, on ground or in low shrubs.
Field Marks 6″ Like Tawny-throated Leaftosser, but even darker, duller brown; throat scalloped dark brown and buffy to whitish; bill slightly shorter and straight.

WOODCREEPERS—TREPADORES—DENDROCOLAPTIDAE

TAWNY-WINGED WOODCREEPER [23] Trepador Sepia *Dendrocincla anabatina*
Range Mex–Pan, exc ElSal. Res Mex (se.cAtl+sAtl, s+e Yuc), Blz, Guat (Atl). Rare.
Habitat Dense humid forest, partial clearings.
Field Marks 7″ Mostly unstreaked dull olive-brown; tail and large patch on wing contrasty rufous; pale buff line over eye; throat whitish; chest faintly streaked.

RUDDY WOODCREEPER [23] Trepador Rojizo *Dendrocincla homochroa*
Range Mex–SAm. Res Mex (sPac, se.cAtl+sAtl, Yuc), Blz, Guat (Pac, Atl), ElSal (w). Rare.
Habitat Cloud forest or other humid forest, near or on ground near army ants.
Field Marks 7″ Plain dark dull rufous; throat paler, tawnier; bill straight, grayish brown.

OLIVACEOUS WOODCREEPER [23] Trepador Oliváceo *Sittasomus griseicapillus*
Range Mex–SAm. Res Mex (csPac + adj Hi, s.nAtl+csAtl, Yuc), Blz, Guat (Pac, Atl), ElSal.
Habitat Humid forest, dense scrubby woods, borders.

Field Marks 6″ Olive-gray, with rufous wings and spine-tipped tail; bill short, straight, slender.

WEDGE-BILLED WOODCREEPER [23] Trepador Pico de Cuña *Glyphorhynchus spirurus*
Range Mex–SAm, exc ElSal. Res Mex (se.cAtl–sc.sAtl), Blz (s), Guat (Atl). Rare.
Habitat Humid forest, partial clearings.
Field Marks 6″ Ear patch, throat, and breast lightly streaked buff; line behind eye buff; bill short, wedge-shaped. See Plain Xenops.

(STRONG-BILLED) GIANT WOODCREEPER [23] Trepador Gigante *Xiphocolaptes promeropirhynchus*
Range Mex–SAm. Res Mex (c.cPac, csHi), Blz, Guat (Atl + adj Hi), ElSal. Rare (very rare and local cPac).
Habitat Pine forest, humid pine-oak woods, piney ridgetops in cloud forest.
Field Marks 12″ Plain buffy throat; lightly streaked head and breast; bill long, rather heavy, slightly decurved.

NORTHERN BARRED-WOODCREEPER [23] Trepador Barrado *Dendrocolaptes sanctithomae*
Range Mex–SAm. Res Mex (cPac, se.cAtl+sAtl, s+e Yuc), Blz, Guat (Atl), ElSal. Rare (very rare and local cPac).
Habitat Humid forest, borders, dense river-border woods, usually near ground.
Field Marks 11″ Narrow black bars all over, except bright rufous wings and tail; bill heavy, black, or (cPac) very pale brownish buff.

BLACK-BANDED WOODCREEPER [23] Trepador Ocotero *Dendrocolaptes picumnus*
Range Mex, Guat, Hon, CRic–SAm. Res Mex (sHi), Guat (Hi). Very rare.
Habitat Humid pine forest or pine-oak woods.
Field Marks 10″ Only woodcreeper in our area both streaked (head, throat, breast) and barred (belly, flanks, untacs); bill long, straight, blackish.

COCOA WOODCREEPER [48] Trepador Cacao *Xiphorhynchus susurrans*
Range Guat–SAm, exc ElSal. Res Guat (ne Atl).
Habitat Humid forest, partial clearings, borders.
Field Marks 10″ Like Laughing Woodcreeper, but streaking does not extend as far down on belly; bill mostly blackish and straight, *not* slightly decurved.

(IVORY-BILLED) LAUGHING WOODCREEPER [23] Trepador Piquiclaro *Xiphorhynchus flavigaster*
Range Mex–CRic. Res Mex (Pac + adj cHi, s.nAtl+csAtl, Yuc), Blz, Guat (Pac, Atl), ElSal.
Habitat Mangrove swamps, deciduous woods, humid forest, partial clearings, borders.
Voice A mellow descending *tyew-tyew-tyew;* also a mellow, descending, laughing whinny.
Field Marks 8″ Rather heavily streaked, except nearly plain buffy throat; bill long, slender, decurved, pale.

SPOTTED WOODCREEPER [23] Trepador Manchado *Xiphorhynchus erythropygius*
Range Mex–SAm. Res Mex (c.cPac+sPac, e.cHi + adj Atl, sHi + adj Pac+Atl),
Blz (s), Guat (Hi + adj Pac), ElSal (n).
Habitat Cloud forest or other dense humid forest.
Field Marks 9″ Mostly olive-brown with light spotty streaking above and many
buffy spots below; rufous wings and tail; bill mostly dark, rather long.

WHITE-STRIPED WOODCREEPER [23] Trepador Gorjiblanco *Lepidocolaptes leucogaster*
Range Mex. Res Mex (w.ncHi + adj Pac, se.cHi). Rare.
Habitat Pine, pine-oak, or fir forest, dry scrubby woods.
Field Marks 9″ Plain dull reddish brown back; rufous wings and tail; head and
underparts heavily streaked contrasty black (to dark olive) and white; chin, up-
per throat, and line over eye white.

STREAKED-HEADED WOODCREEPER [23] Trepador Dorsirrayado *Lepidocolaptes souleyetii*
Range Mex–SAm. Res Mex (csPac, se.cAtl–s.c.sAtl), Blz (s), Guat (Pac, Atl),
ElSal.
Habitat Humid forest, partial clearings, borders, lower-slope pine woods.
Voice A descending, rolling chatter.
Field Marks 8″ Like Laughing Woodcreeper, but smaller; only faintly streaked
above; bill not as long and heavy. See Spot-crowned Woodcreeper.

SPOTTED-CROWNED WOODCREEPER [23] Trepador Montés *Lepidocolaptes affinis*
Range Mex–SAm, exc Blz. Res Mex (s.cHi+e.ncHi+sHi + adj csPac+csAtl),
Guat (Hi + adj Pac), ElSal.
Habitat Cloud forest or humid pine or pine-oak forest.
Field Marks 8″ Like Streaked-headed Woodcreeper (which does not range nearly
as far north, and seldom as far up into the mountains), but crown has rows of
fine spots, *not* streaks.

ANTSHRIKES, ANTBIRDS—
PUPEROS, HORMIGUEROS—THAMNOPHILIDAE

GREAT ANTSHRIKE [24] Batará Mayor *Taraba major*
Range Mex–SAm, exc ElSal. Res Mex (se.cAtl+sAtl), Blz (s), Guat (Atl). Rare.
Habitat Humid thickets, partial clearings, forest borders.
Field Marks 8″ Contrasty white below, black (male) or rufous (female) above;
eyes red; bill thick, black, hook-tipped; shaggy crest.

BARRED ANTSHRIKE [24] Batará Barrado *Thamnophilus doliatus*
Range Mex–SAm. Res Mex (sPac, s.nAtl+csAtl, Yuc), Blz, Guat (Pac, Atl), ElSal.
Habitat Thickets, scrubby woods, forest borders, hedgerows.
Voice An accelerating clucking chatter ends in an abrupt slurred note, as if the
bird were inhaling on that note. See Citreoline Trogon.
Field Marks 6″ Eyes white. M: body and wings barred and head streaked black

and white; floppy crest with partly hidden white patch. F: rufous above, tawny below; face streaked blackish on buffy.

WESTERN SLATY-ANTSHRIKE [48] Batará Pizarra *Thamnophilus atrinucha*
Range Blz–SAm, exc ElSal. Res Blz (s), Guat (ne Atl). Very rare.
Habitat Humid forest, thickets, overgrown clearings.
Field Marks 6″ M: slaty gray to black above, with spotty white wing bars; mostly medium gray to slaty gray below. F: similar, but in shades of grayish brown, buff, and rufous-brown.

RUSSET ANTSHRIKE [24] Pupero Café *Thamnistes anabatinus*
Range Mex–SAm, exc ElSal. Res Mex (se.cAtl–sc.sAtl), Blz, Guat (Atl). Very rare.
Habitat Humid forest.
Field Marks 6″ Much paler below and on face than similar reddish brown birds, such as mourners, pihas, cotingas. M: dull tawny brown above, with rufous wings and tail; face and underparts pale tawny buff; bill rather heavy. F: duller.

PLAIN ANTVIREO [24] Hormiguerito Sencillo *Dysithamnus mentalis*
Range Mex–SAm, exc ElSal, Nic. Res Mex (sc.sAtl), Blz (s), Guat (Atl). Very rare.
Habitat Humid forest.
Field Marks 4″ Faint wing bars; short tail; dark eyes. M: plain medium to dark gray above and on breast; throat whitish; belly whitish to pale yellow. F: browner above, crown rufous.

SLATY ANTWREN [24] Hormiguerito Apizarrado *Myrmotherula schisticolor*
Range Mex–SAm, exc Blz, ElSal. Res Mex (extreme sc.sAtl), Blz (cas), Guat (Atl). Rare.
Habitat Humid forest, mostly in undergrowth.
Field Marks 4″ Bill short, rather slender; tail rather short. M: gray, with black throat and breast; spotty wing bars. F: dark brown above; buffy wing bars; pale buff to tawny buff below.

DOTTED-WINGED ANTWREN [24] Hormiguerito Alipunteado *Microrhopias quixensis*
Range Mex–SAm, exc ElSal. Res Mex (se.cAtl+s.sAtl), Blz, Guat (Atl). Rare.
Habitat Humid forest, second growth, partial clearings.
Field Marks 4.5″ M: black, with spotty white wing bars and tail corners. F: contrasty rufous below and slaty gray above, with spotty wing bars and tail corners.

DUSKY ANTBIRD [24] Hormiguero Tirano *Cercomacra tyrannina*
Range Mex–SAm, exc ElSal. Res Mex (se.cAtl+s.sAtl), Blz, Guat (Atl). Rare.
Habitat Humid forest borders, overgrown partial clearings, thickets.
Field Marks 6″ M: dark slaty gray all over; faint spotty pale wing bars and narrow tail tip. F: olive-brown above, rich tawny rufous below.

BARE-CROWNED ANTBIRD [48] Hormiguero Calvo *Gymnocichla nudiceps*
Range Blz–SAm, exc ElSal. Res Blz (s), Guat (ne Atl). Very rare.
Habitat Thickets, undergrowth in humid forest or second growth, overgrown clearings.

Field Marks 6" M: black all over except pale blue bare skin on forehead, forecrown, lores, and around eye; white wing bars, tail-feather tips, and wrist spots. F: similar, but medium to dark reddish brown and buff, and not as much blue bare skin.

ANTTHRUSHES, ANTPITTAS—GALLITOS, CHOLINOS—FORMICARIIDAE

BLACK-FACED ANTTHRUSH [24] Hormiguero Carinegro *Formicarius analis*
Range Mex–SAm, exc ElSal. Res Mex (se.cAtl+sAtl, s+e Yuc), Blz, Guat (Atl). Rare.
Habitat Humid forest or dense patchy second growth.
Voice A deliberate whistle, first note higher-pitched, *haa, ha-ha-ha-ha*—or a mellow rolling *tch-ha-ba-ba-ba-ba-ba-ba-ba*, last three notes higher.
Field Marks 7" On ground (tail pointing up) or perched low while singing. Dark reddish brown above, dark gray below; pale blue eye ring; black throat and part of face, bordered by rufous; very short black tail.

SCALED ANTPITTA [24] Cholino Escamoso *Grallaria guatimalensis*
Range Mex–SAm, exc Blz. Res Mex (cHi [local] + shi + adj cspac+csAtl), Guat (Hi + adj Pac+Atl), ElSal (w). Rare.
Habitat Dense undergrowth in cloud forest or other humid forest.
Field Marks 8" Hops on ground, logs, or shrubs. Scalloped blackish on olive back and bluish gray crown; tawny rufous (cHi birds are much paler) below; throat and malar area striped, with black necklace; tail very short, rufous; bill rather heavy, blackish.

FLYCATCHERS—MOSQUEROS—TYRANNIDAE

PALTRY TYRANNULET [25] Mosquerito Gritón *Zimmerius vilissimus*
Range Mex–SAm. Res Mex (sHl + adj Pac+Atl), Blz (s), Guat (Hi + adj Pac, Atl), ElSal (w). Rare.
Habitat Humid forest, partial clearings, borders, plantations.
Voice A quiet *peer-deer* or *pee-wee*.
Field Marks 4.5" Greenish olive above, grayer on crown and nape; pale gray below, with very faint breast streaks and yellowish wash on belly and untacs; white forehead and line over eye; bill very short, small.

YELLOW-BELLIED TYRANNULET [25] Mosquerito Pequeñito *Ornithion semiflavum*
Range Mex–CRic, exc ElSal. Res Mex (se.cAtl+s.sAtl), Blz (s), Guat (Atl). Rare.
Habitat Humid forest, wooded river valleys.
Field Marks 3.5" Olive above; crown dark gray; prominent white line over eye; yellow below, faintly streaked; tail and bill very short.

NORTHERN BEARDLESS-TYRANNULET [27] Mosquerito Lampiño *Camptostoma imberbe*
Range US–CRic. Res Mex (Pac, Hi, Atl, Yuc), Blz, Guat (Pac+Atl + adj Hi), ElSal.
Habitat Tree-dotted pastures, hedgerows, thickets, scrubby woods, borders.

Voice A descending, high-pitched, mournful *pee-pee-pee-pee-pee* or a sad squealed *pee-ut.*

Field Marks 4" Pale grayish olive, with dark wings (whitish to pale brown wing bars) and tail; whitish to yellowish belly and untacs; white chin and short line over eye; bill very small, with pale dull orange to pinkish lower mandible.

GREENISH ELAENIA [25] Elenia Verdosa *Myiopagis viridicata*
Range Mex–SAm. Res Mex (s.nPac+csPac + adj Hi, s.nAtl+csAtl + adj Hi, Yuc), Blz, Guat (Pac, Atl), ElSal. Rare.
Habitat Borders, scrubby woods, thickets, pine-oak woods.
Voice A high-pitched *zeet* or *pee-wee.*
Field Marks 5.5" Olive-green above; blackish wings and tail; throat and faintly streaked breast pale gray; belly and untacs yellowish; bill small.

CARIBBEAN ELAENIA [25] Parlotero Antillano *Elaenia martinica*
Range Mex, Blz. Res Mex (extreme e.sAtl, extreme e Yuc), Blz (cstl + cayes).
Habitat Hedgerows, scrubby woods, borders, partial clearings.
Voice A rasping *whee-oo* and a harsh *pee-ree.*
Field Marks 6" Like Yellow-bellied Elaenia, but browner above; little or no yellow below; lower mandible brighter orange.

YELLOW-BELLIED ELAENIA [25] Parlotero Grande *Elaenia flavogaster*
Range Mex–SAm. Res Mex (sPac, se.cAtl+sAtl, Yuc), Blz, Guat (Pac, Atl), ElSal.
Habitat Tree-dotted pastures, old fields, hedgerows, forest borders.
Voice A rasping *bee-ee-r,* harsh *clip-it, clip-beer,* or *clip-clip-peer.*
Field Marks 6" Noisy agitated pairs fly tree to tree, catch insects, pick berries. Olive above, grayer on head; blackish wings, pale wing bars; throat whitish; breast pale grayish olive; belly and untacs yellowish; partly hidden white patch in small ragged crest; tail rather long.

MOUNTAIN ELAENIA [48] Parlotero Serrano *Elaenia frantzii*
Range Guat–SAm. Res Guat (local, Hi + adj Pac?, Atl), ElSal. Rare.
Habitat Open woods, scattered trees, borders, partial clearings.
Field Marks 6" Olive above; feathers of crown barely elongated, usually no concealed white in crown; narrow white spectacle lines and eye ring; whitish or yellowish wing bars and wing-feather edgings; whitish to pale yellowish below, grayer on breast.

OCHRE-BELLIED FLYCATCHER [25] Mosquerito Ventriocre *Mionectes oleagineus*
Range Mex–SAm. Res Mex (sPac, csAtl, Yuc), Blz, Guat (Pac, Atl), ElSal (w). Rare.
Habitat Humid forest, borders, partial clearings, *cafetales.*
Field Marks 5" Flicks one wing at a time, eats insects and berries. Dark greenish olive above; throat, chest, and sides grayish olive; lower breast, belly, and untacs dull rufous tawny; bill slender.

SEPIA-CAPPED FLYCATCHER [25] Mosquerito Gorripardo *Leptopogon amaurocephalus*
Range Mex–SAm, exc ElSal. Res Mex (se.cAtl+s.sAtl; cas se Yuc), Blz, Guat (Atl). Rare.

Habitat Humid forest, borders, partial clearings.
Field Marks 5" Greenish olive above; crown and nape dark olive-brown; face and breast faintly streaked; throat whitish; breast pale olive; belly yellow; buff wing bars.

NORTHERN BENTBILL [25] Mosquerito Piquicurvo *Oncostoma cinereigulare*
Range Mex–Pan. Res Mex (sPac, se.cAtl+sAtl, Yuc), Blz, Guat (Pac, Atl), ElSal. Rare.
Habitat Dense humid forest, borders, partial clearings.
Voice A short, quiet metallic trill, *bir-r-r-r.*
Field Marks 4" Perches upright, quietly, usually in lower branches. Olive-green above, with gray crown and nape; dark wings, two white wing bars; throat, breast, and ear patch faintly streaked; yellow belly and untacs; bill arched, bent down at tip; eyes white; tail short. See Yellow-olive Flycatcher.

SLATE-HEADED TODY-FLYCATCHER [25] Espatulilla Gris *Poecilotriccus sylvia*
Range Mex–SAm, exc ElSal. Res Mex (se.cAtl+sAtl, s+e Yuc), Blz, Guat (Atl). Very rare.
Habitat Lower inner branches in dense humid forest, scrubby woods, thickets.
Voice A quiet mellow *took.*
Field Marks 3.5" Grayish olive-green above, whitish below, with grayish breast; crown and nape dark gray; wing bars and wing-feather edgings yellowish, tail short, narrow, graduated; bill somewhat spatulate; eyes pale grayish brown.

COMMON TODY-FLYCATCHER [25] Espatulilla Común *Todirostrum cinereum*
Range Mex–SAm. Res Mex (sPac, se.cAtl+sAtl, Yuc), Blz, Guat (Pac, Atl), ElSal. Rare.
Habitat Brushy pastures, overgrown clearings, forest borders, scrubby woods.
Voice A musical, whistled trill and a repeated, dry *tick.*
Field Marks 3.5" Holds tail high, waves it from side to side, hops actively from twig to twig. Blackish olive above, with paler rump and black crown, nape, and ear patch; underparts bright yellow; wings black with yellowish bars and feather edgings; black tail narrow at base, white-tipped; bill spatulate, black; eyes whitish.

EYE-RINGED FLATBILL [25] Piquichato de Anteojos *Rhynchocyclus brevirostris*
Range Mex–SAm. Res Mex (c.cPac–sPac + adj Hi, c.cAtl–sAtl + adj Hi, s+e Yuc), Blz, Guat (Pac, Atl), ElSal (w). Rare.
Habitat Dense humid lowland forest, cloud forest.
Voice A high-pitched *wees.*
Field Marks 6" Dark olive-green; breast faintly streaked; belly and untacs yellow; prominent white eye ring; bill very broad and flat, dark above and pale below.

YELLOW-OLIVE FLYCATCHER [25] Piquichato Ojiblanco *Tolmomyias sulphurescens*
Range Mex–SAm. Res Mex (sPac, se.cAtl+sAtl, Yuc), Blz, Guat (Pac, Atl), ElSal. Rare.

Habitat Humid forest, borders, scrubby woods, partial clearings.
Voice A very high-pitched *weet, weet, weet.*
Field Marks 5″ Like Northern Bentbill, but larger; broad, flat bill; longer tail; rather prominent spectacles and moves around actively, seldom perches quietly upright.

STUB-TAILED SPADEBILL [25] Piquichato Mexicano *Platyrinchus cancrominus*
Range Mex–CRic. Res Mex (sPac, se.cAtl+sAtl, s+e Yuc), Blz, Guat (Pac, Atl), ElSal. Rare.
Habitat Dense undergrowth of humid forest, thickets, borders, overgrown clearings.
Voice Two to five notes, a petulant, abrupt chatter, *ki-di-di-di-dit.*
Field Marks 4″ Usually turns around abruptly on its perch just before flying. Brownish above, with white throat and tawny breast; very short flat bill; extremely short tail; white eye ring; buffy spot on dark ear patch.

ROYAL FLYCATCHER [25] Mosquero Real *Onychorhynchus coronatus*
Range Mex–SAm. Res Mex (sPac, se.cAtl+sAtl, s+e Yuc), Blz, Guat (Pac, Atl), ElSal. Very rare.
Habitat Dense humid forest; nest usually hangs over small stream or pool.
Field Marks 7″ Mostly olive-brown above, with tawny tail and underparts; bill long, broad, flat; legs yellow to yellow-orange; crest extends back and down when folded, flares crossways when open, red in male, tawny buff in female, bordered and spotted iridescent bluish.

RUDDY-TAILED FLYCATCHER [25] Mosquerito Colirrojizo *Terenotriccus erythrurus*
Range Mex–SAm, exc ElSal. Res Mex (s.sAtl), Blz (s), Guat (Atl). Very rare.
Habitat Humid forest, overgrown clearings.
Field Marks 3.5″ Olive above, with rufous and black wings; pale tawny rufous rump, uptacs, tail, and underparts.

SULPHUR-RUMPED FLYCATCHER [25] Papamoscas Saltarín *Myiobius sulphureipygius*
Range Mex–SAm, exc ElSal. Res Mex (se.cAtl+sAtl, s+e Yuc), Blz, Guat (Atl). Rare.
Habitat Lower branches in dense humid forest or overgrown partial clearings.
Voice A harsh *chip* or *pick* or a musical *ter-ter-ter.*
Field Marks 5″ Moves often, wings drooping, tail partly spread, bright rump patch usually very conspicuous. Brownish olive above; blackish wings and tail; underparts tawny to whitish on throat and yellowish on belly; rump bright creamy yellow.

BELTED FLYCATCHER [25] Papamoscas Chiapaneco *Xenotriccus callizonus*
Range Mex, Guat, ElSal. Res Mex (sHi + upper slopes sPac), Guat (Hi), ElSal. Very rare, local.
Habitat Low inner branches in thickets, hedgerows, dense brush along borders.

Voice A petulant *cheer* or *chip pirr-rr* or a *pert, pert, pick-chi-chew.*
Field Marks 5" Jerks tail up, flicks wings, seldom *lowers* crest. Brownish olive above; crown and long crest brownish gray; blackish wings with buffy brown bars and feather edgings; underparts mostly yellow, with tawny rufous breast band and whitish throat.

PILEATED FLYCATCHER [25] Papamoscas del Balsas *Xenotriccus mexicanus*
Range Mex. Res Mex (cPac + adj Hi). Rare, local, irregular.
Habitat Arid scrubby woods, rocky hillsides or ravines.
Voice A two-phrased song, a whistled *twheeyu,* then a rolling trill and abrupt whistle *tr-r-r-eet-yu;* also a *chee-up.*
Field Marks 5.5" Often flies to ground to pick up insects, flicks tail up, flicks wings, raises and lowers crest. Grayish to brownish olive above; whitish below, darker on breast; long, pointed but ragged, grayish crest; white wing bars, eye ring, and lores; wings blackish.

TUFTED FLYCATCHER [25] Papamoscas Penachudo *Mitrephanes phaeocercus*
Range Mex–SAm, exc Blz. Res/win Mex (res e+w.ncHi+sHi; win ncPac, ncAtl), Guat (Hi), ElSal (n).
Habitat Open pine, pine-oak, oak, or fir forest; or (winter) borders, riverbanks.
Voice A rolling *churree, churree.*
Field Marks 5" Rufous-olive above, with buffy rufous wing bars on blackish wings; prominent crest; rich tawny rufous below. See Buff-breasted Flycatcher.

OLIVE-SIDED FLYCATCHER [27] Mosquero Boreal *Contopus cooperi*
Range AK–SAm. Sum/win Mex (sum mts nBajCal; tr/win Pac, Hi, Atl), tr/win Blz, Guat, ElSal. Rare.
Habitat Upper branches of pine forests, pine-oak woods, river-border woods, partial clearings.
Field Marks 7" Grayish olive above and on sides and flanks; throat and center of breast and belly white; partly hidden white patch on each side of rump. See Greater Pewee.

GREATER PEWEE [27] Tengofrío Grande *Contopus pertinax*
Range US–Nic. Res Mex (Hi + adj Pac+Atl), Blz (pine), Guat (Hi), ElSal (res/win n).
Habitat Upper branches, open pine woods, pine-oak or fir forest, or lowland forests, river borders.
Voice *Pert* or *pert-pert,* or a sad hesitant *ree-deet, ree-oo (José María* or *Tengofrío)* or *ree-deet, ree-deet, ree-deet, ree-oo.* See Bright-rumped Attila.
Field Marks 7" Grayish olive, paler below; slight crest. Like Olive-sided Flycatcher, but lower mandible orange; *no* broad white center streak below.

WESTERN WOOD-PEWEE [27] Tengofrío Occidental *Contopus sordidulus*
Range AK–SAm, exc Blz? Sum/tr Mex (BajCal, Pac, Hi), Guat (Pac + adj Hi), ElSal.
Habitat Scrubby open woods, borders, partial clearings, open pine woods.

Voice A rasping *weer* or *peer.*
Field Marks 5" Dark grayish olive above and on breast and sides; whitish throat, belly, and untacs; blackish wings, white wing bars; bill may be yellow-brown below. See Eastern Wood-Pewee.

EASTERN WOOD-PEWEE Tengofrío Verdoso *Contopus virens*
Range Can–SAm, exc ElSal? Tr Mex (sPac, sHi, Atl, Yuc), Blz, Guat. Rare.
Habitat River-border woods, forest borders, partial clearings, hedgerows, open woods.
Voice A plaintive *pee-a-wee* or *pe-wee* (seldom heard in Mexico).
Field Marks 5" Like Western Wood-Pewee (except voice), but slightly paler below; lower mandible pale yellowish.

TROPICAL PEWEE [26] Tengofrío Tropical *Contopus cinereus*
Range Mex–SAm. Res Mex (sPac, se.cAtl+sAtl, Yuc), Blz, Guat (Pac, Atl), ElSal. Rare.
Habitat Partial clearings, openings in humid forest, borders, tree-dotted pastures.
Voice A liquid, twittering series or a single *peet.*
Field Marks 5" Like Western Wood-Pewee (except voice), but lores appear whiter, center of belly yellower.

YELLOW-BELLIED FLYCATCHER Mosquerito Oliva *Empidonax flaviventris*
Range Can–Pan. Tr/win Mex (e.cPac+sPac, Atl, Yuc), Blz, Guat, ElSal. Rare.
Habitat Usually low in open woods, humid forest, borders.
Voice A quiet, rising *cur-lee.*
Field Marks 5" Brownish olive above; prominent yellowish eye ring and wing bars; throat pale yellowish; breast yellowish olive; belly and untacs yellow; bill nearly as wide (at base) as it is long, yellowish orange below.

ACADIAN FLYCATCHER Mosquerito Verdoso *Empidonax virescens*
Range Can–SAm. Tr Mex (sPac + adj Hi, Atl + adj Hi, Yuc), Blz, Guat, ElSal. Rare.
Habitat Wooded stream valleys, humid forest, borders.
Voice A rising, abrupt *wheet;* also a quiet chatter.
Field Marks 5.5" Mostly olive above, but wings blackish brown with whitish bars; pale yellowish to whitish eye ring; throat and lower breast whitish; chest and sides grayish olive; belly and untacs pale yellow to whitish; bill nearly as wide (at base) as it is long, yellowish below.

ALDER FLYCATCHER Mosquerito Alnoro *Empidonax alnorum*
Range AK–SAm, exc Blz?, ElSal? Tr Mex (sPac + adj Hi, Atl + adj Hi), Guat. Migration poorly understood. Rare.
Habitat Thickets, borders, hedgerows; in summer in alder swamps or thickets in bogs or near ponds.
Voice *Fee-bee-o.*
Field Marks 5" Like Acadian Flycatcher, but darker and browner above and on

chest (contrasts more with white throat); duller belly and untacs; eye ring less distinct; bill more orange below.

WILLOW FLYCATCHER Mosquerito Saucero *Empidonax traillii*
Range Can-Pan. Tr/win Mex (BajCal, Pac, Hi, Atl), Blz (cas), Guat, ElSal. Migration poorly understood. Rare.
Habitat Moist thickets, partial clearings, borders; in summer in wet meadows, drier brushy areas.
Voice An abrupt *fitz-bew*.
Field Marks 5″ Like Alder Flycatcher, but slightly browner above; eye ring even less prominent.

WHITE-THROATED FLYCATCHER [26] Mosquerito Gorjiblanco *Empidonax albigularis*
Range Mex-Pan. Res/win Mex (res cHi; sum w+e.ncHi+sHi; win csPac, csAtl), Blz (s), Guat, ElSal. Rare, local.
Habitat Wet meadows, shrub-dotted moist fields, brushy marshes, borders, dry brush.
Voice An abrupt, sneezelike *er-rick-er*.
Field Marks 5″ Like Alder Flycatcher, but slightly browner, white throat more contrasty; breast may appear vaguely streaked; wing bars and eye ring buffier; flanks and untacs may be buffy; thighs and underwing coverts cinnamon-buff; bill flesh color below.

LEAST FLYCATCHER Mosquerito Mínimo *Empidonax minimus*
Range Can-CRic. Tr/win Mex (s.nPac+csPac, Hi, Atl, Yuc); win Blz, Guat, ElSal.
Habitat Open woods, thickets, borders, wooded parks, large suburban gardens.
Voice An abrupt, unmusical *chi-bec*.
Field Marks 4.5″ Like Hammond's Flycatcher, but head and upperparts darker; belly and untacs slightly yellower; throat slightly whiter; bill paler below.

HAMMOND'S FLYCATCHER Mosquerito Pasajero *Empidonax hammondii*
Range AK-Nic, exc Blz. Tr/win Mex (nBajCal, Pac, Hi, ucAtl), Guat (Pac, Hi), ElSal (n).
Habitat Pine or fir forest or pine-oak woods, borders.
Voice Three parts, *si-pit, sup, tre-ip*.
Field Marks 5″ Like Dusky Flycatcher, but head relatively larger, paler, contrasts more with back; tail shorter, grayish margin on outer tail feathers; bill slightly shorter, darker below.

DUSKY FLYCATCHER [27] Mosquerito Oscuro *Empidonax oberholseri*
Range Can-Mex. Res/win Mex (res mts nBajCal; tr/win nBajCal, Pac, Hi).
Habitat Scrubby woods, hedgerows, borders, open woods.
Voice Several phrases in sequence, *chippy, chi-wee, tslip*.
Field Marks 5″ Flicks tail up. Like Gray Flycatcher, but slightly darker and more olive, with more contrasty wing bars and eye ring; yellower below; bill darker below.

GRAY FLYCATCHER [27] Mosquerito Gris *Empidonax wrightii*
Range US-Mex. Tr/win Mex (sBajCal, ncPac, ncHi).
Habitat Hedgerows, borders, semidesert, dry pine or piñon-juniper woods.
Voice An abrupt *chi-bic.*
Field Marks 5" Pushes tail downward. Gray above, wings darker; whitish wing bars and eye ring; whitish below (yellower in winter), with pale grayish chest; tail notched, outer feathers white-edged; bill about twice as long as wide, pale orange at base below, dark-tipped.

PINE FLYCATCHER [26] Mosquerito Pinero *Empidonax affinis*
Range Mex, Guat. Res Mex (Hi), Guat (Hi).
Habitat Dense or open pine, pine-oak, or fir forest, borders, partial clearings.
Voice A mellow, loud *peet* or *pert.*
Field Marks 5" Like Gray Flycatcher, but browner; wings darker; wing bars (tinged olive) and eye ring more prominent; yellower below with more olive tinge on chest.

PACIFIC-SLOPE FLYCATCHER Mosquerito Occidental *Empidonax difficilis*
Range US-Mex. Sum/win Mex (sum local BajCal; win BajCal, ncPac).
Habitat Shrubby ravines in pine or pine-oak forests.
Voice Several *se-weet* phrases.
Field Marks 5" Like Cordilleran Flycatcher in appearance and behavior, except for voice. Not expected in northern and central highlands.

CORDILLERAN FLYCATCHER [20] Mosquerito Barranqueño *Empidonax occidentalis*
Range AK-Mex. Res Mex (ncPac, w+e.nHi+cHi).
Habitat Shrubby ravines in pine, pine-oak, fir, or other mountain forest.
Voice An abrupt *hree-deet.*
Field Marks 5" Like Yellow-bellied Flycatcher, but somewhat browner above and on breast; bill more orange below; wing bars buffier, not so prominent; tail somewhat longer.

YELLOWISH FLYCATCHER [26] Mosquerito Amarillento *Empidonax flavescens*
Range Mex-Pan, exc Blz. Res/win Mex (sHi + adj Pac+Atl; local se.cAtl [Tuxtla Mts.]), Guat (Hi + adj Pac), ElSal.
Habitat Cloud forest and other humid forest; also pine-oak woods.
Voice A high-pitched *hree-deet.*
Field Marks 5" Like Cordilleran Flycatcher (may be same species), but yellower above and below.

BUFF-BREASTED FLYCATCHER [27] Mosquerito Canelo *Empidonax fulvifrons*
Range US-Hon, exc Blz. Res/win Mex (Hi + adj ncPac), Guat (Hi + adj Pac), ElSal (n).
Habitat Open pine, pine-oak, or fir forest, or (winter) river-border woods.
Voice A musical, rolling *pulleet-yew.*
Field Marks 4.5" Grayish brown above, darker on crown; pale buff wing bars and wing-feather edgings; eye ring white; pale tawny below, to whitish belly and untacs.

BLACK PHOEBE [27] Mosquero Negro *Sayornis nigricans*
Range US–SAm. Res Mex (BajCal, Pac, Hi, s.nAtl–sc.sAtl), Blz (s), Guat, ElSal (w). Rare.
Habitat Near pools, streams, lakes.
Voice A harsh *fee-bee.*
Field Marks 6″ Black, but belly, untacs, and some feather edgings white.

EASTERN PHOEBE [20] Mosquero Fibí *Sayornis phoebe*
Range Can–Mex. Win Mex (ncHi, ncAtl; cas/very rare BajCal, Pac, Yuc). Rare.
Habitat Hedgerows, borders.
Voice Fee-bee.
Field Marks 6″ Like Eastern Wood-Pewee, but yellower below; head darker; *no* wing bars; bill black.

SAY'S PHOEBE [27] Mosquero Llanero *Sayornis saya*
Range AK–Mex. Res/win Mex (BajCal, ncPac, Hi, ncAtl). Rare.
Habitat Arid grassy fields, open semidesert, rocky ravines or hillsides.
Field Marks 7″ Dull medium gray above; darker head, wings, and tail; mostly tawny buff below.

VERMILION FLYCATCHER [27] Mosquero Cardenalito *Pyrocephalus rubinus*
Range US–SAm, exc ElSal, CRic. Res Mex, Blz, Guat (Atl).
Habitat Arid open areas, semideserts, brushy overgrown fields, parks, gardens; on weeds, fences, wires
Field Marks 5.5″ M: black, except scarlet crown and underparts F+Imm: dull grayish brown above; dark ear patch; white throat; white breast streaked gray or brown; belly and untacs pale yellow, pink, or red.

BRIGHT-RUMPED ATTILA [26] Atila Bigotón *Attila spadiceus*
Range Mex–SAm. Res Mex (c.nPac–sPac + adj Hi, c.cAtl–sAtl + adj Hi, Yuc), Blz, Guat (Pac, Atl), ElSal. Rare.
Habitat Humid forest, borders, openings, scrubby woods, river borders, tree-dotted pastures.
Voice Like Greater Pewee's, but louder, more abrupt, *wheed-ut, wheed-ut, wheed-ut, whee-oo.*
Field Marks 8″ Variable; usually brown or olive above; rump and uptacs yellow or tawny; underparts whitish or tawny; face, throat, and breast streaked; eyes whitish, tan, brown, or red.

RUFOUS MOURNER [26] Llorona Alazán *Rhytipterna holerythra*
Range Mex–SAm, exc ElSal. Res Mex (sc.cAtl–sc.sAtl), Blz (s), Guat (Atl). Rare.
Habitat Dense humid forest, partial clearings, dense borders.
Voice A sad *wheep* or *wheep-wee.*
Field Marks 8″ Dull reddish brown above, tawny brown below. See Speckled Mourner.

YUCATAN FLYCATCHER [20, 26] Copetón Yucateco *Myiarchus yucatanensis*
Range Mex, Blz, Guat. Res Mex (c+e.sAtl, Yuc), Blz (n), Guat (nw Atl). Rare.

Habitat Forest, open scrubby woods, borders, hedgerows.
Voice A long, rising, somewhat plaintive, whistled note, *hueeee,* and a rapid descending series of short whistles.
Field Marks 7″ Like Dusky-capped Flycatcher, with tail feathers mostly dark gray below with only a narrow fringe of dull rufous on inner web, but slightly paler overall, especially on crown; voice different.

DUSKY-CAPPED FLYCATCHER [20, 27] Copetón Triste *Myiarchus tuberculifer*
Range US–SAm. Res Mex (Pac, Hi, Atl, Yuc; acc sBajCal), Blz, Guat (Pac, Atl + adj Hi), ElSal.
Habitat Tree-dotted pastures, humid to dry forests, partial clearings, borders, hedgerows.
Voice A mournful *whee-oo* or a slow, rolling trill, *peer-r-r,* often with a preceding note, *drew-peer-r-r.*
Field Marks 6.5″ Brownish olive above, with blackish brown to dark brown crown; rufous-buff wing bars; pale gray throat, slightly darker gray breast; pale yellow belly; tail feathers blackish below, with only a narrow fringe of rufous (or none) on inner web.

ASH-THROATED FLYCATCHER [20, 27] Copetón Gorjicenizo *Myiarchus cinerascens*
Range US–CRic, exc Blz. Res/win Mex (res/sum BajCal, nPac, ncHi; win csPac, sHi, ncAtl), Guat (Pac), ElSal (cas).
Habitat Overgrown grassy fields, open woods, hedgerows, borders.
Voice A soft *ker-peer* or *ka-breer,* and a rasping *pert.*
Field Marks 7.5″ Crown dull brown; nape and sides of face pale brownish gray; whitish throat and very pale gray breast; pale yellow belly and untacs; whitish wing bars; nearly entire inner web of tail feathers rufous below, but tips broadly dark gray; rufous primary edgings contrast sharply with whitish secondary edgings.

NUTTING'S FLYCATCHER [20, 26] Copetón Acahualero *Myiarchus nuttingi*
Range Mex–CRic, exc Blz. Res Mex (Pac + adj Hi, local sw.nAtl), Guat (Pac + adj Hi), ElSal.
Habitat Scrubby woods, borders, dry open woods, partial clearings.
Voice An emphatic *wheet* or *whee-whee.*
Field Marks 7″ Like Ash-throated Flycatcher, with broad rufous inner web of tail feathers below, but rufous of tail continues to tip, *not* cut off by a dark gray band at tip; less contrast between primary edgings and secondary edgings; voice different.

GREAT CRESTED FLYCATCHER [20] Copetón Viajero *Myiarchus crinitus*
Range Can–SAm. Tr/win Mex (sPac, sHi, Atl, Yuc), Blz, Guat, ElSal.
Habitat Borders, open woods, overgrown fields, partial clearings.
Voice A loud, rolling *ree-eep;* a rolling, slowing *kree-kree-kree-kree.*
Field Marks 8.5″ Like Brown-crested Flycatcher, but much more rufous on tail, with only a narrow stripe of dark gray on each tail-feather shaft; throat, chest, and head darker gray, contrasting sharply with bright yellow belly and untacs; bill orange at base below.

BROWN-CRESTED FLYCATCHER [20, 27] Copetón Tiranillo *Myiarchus tyrannulus*
Range US–CRic, SAm. Res/sum Mex (Pac+Atl + adj Hi, Yuc; cas sBajCal), Blz, Guat (Pac, Atl), ElSal.
Habitat Open woods, borders, brushy pastures, partial clearings.
Voice A mellow *whit* and a raspy *breer.*
Field Marks 8.5″ Like Ash-throated Flycatcher, but larger; larger-billed; brighter yellow on belly and untacs; somewhat more rufous on tail. Like Great Crested Flycatcher, but bill dark, heavier; chest paler gray, contrasting less with yellow belly; tail less rufous, with broader shaft stripes of dark gray.

FLAMMULATED FLYCATCHER [26] Copetón Piquiplano *Deltarhynchus flammulatus*
Range Mex. Res Mex (c.nPac–w.sPac). Very rare.
Habitat Dense scrubby dry woods, overgrown fields, thickets, hedgerows.
Voice A quiet querulous *wee-eet,* sliding down then up; a quiet rolling *pr-r-reet.*
Field Marks 6.5″ Resembles Ash-throated Flycatcher somewhat, but more grayish above, with cinnamon-rufous uptacs, wing bars, and wing-feather edgings; pale gray eye ring; whitish lores prominent at times; chest pale gray faintly streaked whitish; belly and untacs pale yellow; tail dark brown and rufous; bill rather short, broad, flat.

GREAT KISKADEE [27] Luis Bienteveo *Pitangus sulphuratus*
Range US–SAm. Res Mex (Pac+Atl + adj Hi, Yuc), Blz, Guat (Pac, Atl + adj Hi), ElSal.
Habitat River-border woods, forest borders, open woods, partial clearings, hedgerows; often over water, may catch small fish.
Voice A very loud nasal *ree* or *kurree* or *keep-kurree.*
Field Marks 9″ Reddish brown above, with rufous wings and tail; head broadly striped black and white; underparts bright yellow, except white throat; medium heavy bill.

BOAT-BILLED FLYCATCHER [26] Luis Piquigrueso *Megarynchus pitangua*
Range Mex–SAm. Res Mex (s.nPac+csPac, s.nAtl+csAtl, Yuc), Blz, Guat (Pac, Atl), ElSal. Rare.
Habitat Higher branches in tree-dotted fields, forest borders, river-border woods, partial clearings.
Voice A high-pitched *gü-lick, gü-lick,* a whining *kee-rr-r* or *mew-e-r-r,* or a dry *chee-r-r.*
Field Marks 9″ Like Great Kiskadee, but voice different, and wings and tail more grayish olive, *not* rufous; bill heavier.

SOCIAL FLYCATCHER [26] Luis Gregario *Myiozetetes similis*
Range Mex–SAm. Res Mex (c.nPac–sPac, s.nAtl+csAtl, Yuc), Blz, Guat (Pac, Atl), ElSal.
Habitat Often in (family?) groups on branches overhanging rivers or ponds, or in forest borders, tree-dotted fields, partial clearings.
Voice Ki-tee, ki-tee, ki-tee or a petulant *chee-ee.*
Field Marks 7″ Often flutters wings while perched, seems excitable. Like Great

Kiskadee, but much smaller and smaller-billed; more grayish olive above; *no* rufous on wing.

STREAKED FLYCATCHER [26] Ventura Pinta *Myiodynastes maculatus*
Range Mex–SAm, exc ElSal. Sum Mex (s.nAtl+csAtl, s+e Yuc), Blz, Guat (Atl).
Rare.
Habitat Partly cleared pastures, woods along rivers, humid forest borders or openings.
Voice A melodious *tyew;* a whining *wa-a-a.*
Field Marks 8″ Like Sulphur-bellied Flycatcher, but head stripes yellower; underparts whiter; bill heavier.

SULPHUR-BELLIED FLYCATCHER [27] Ventura Meca *Myiodynastes luteiventris*
Range US–SAm. Sum Mex (Pac+Atl + adj Hi, Yuc), Blz, Guat (Pac, Atl + adj Hi), ElSal.
Habitat Partly cleared pastures, forest borders and openings, orchards, woods along rivers.
Voice A high-pitched *peet-chee.*
Field Marks 8″ Streaked dark brown and buff above, with rich rufous rump, uptacs, and tail; yellow below with heavy dark streaks; head streaked white and blackish gray.

PIRATIC FLYCATCHER [26] Ventura Pirata *Legatus leucophaius*
Range Mex–SAm, exc ElSal. Sum Mex (sPac, csAtl), Blz, Guat (Atl). Rare.
Habitat Partial clearings, overgrown pastures, luxuriant hedgerows, borders; often seen on outer branches or utility wires near a hanging nest, which it uses after driving away the original occupants.
Voice A loud whistled *whee-oo* (pause), then three softer musical notes, *te-te-te.*
Field Marks 6.5″ Like Streaked and Sulphur-bellied Flycatchers, but smaller and smaller-billed; darker and *not* streaked above.

TROPICAL KINGBIRD [27] Tirano Tropical *Tyrannus melancholicus*
Range US–SAm. Res/sum Mex (Pac+Atl + adj Hi, Yuc; rare/cas BajCal), Blz, Guat (Pac+Atl + adj Hi), ElSal.
Habitat Hedgerows, partly wooded pastures, scrub woods, forest borders, mixed woods and farms.
Voice Chipping, trilling notes, higher-pitched than Couch's Kingbird's; also high-pitched *kittick* notes.
Field Marks 8″ Grayish olive above, with bluish gray crown; blackish wings; yellow below, except white throat and pale grayish wash on chest; tail blackish brown, notched. See Couch's Kingbird.

COUCH'S KINGBIRD Tirano Mexicano *Tyrannus couchii*
Range US, Mex, Blz, Guat. Res Mex (Atl, Yuc), Blz, Guat (Atl).
Habitat Overgrown pastures, open woods, ranches, forest borders, partial clearings.
Voice A mellow *pert* or *pit;* a rolling *whee-ee-rr-r* or *ti-peer.*

Field Marks 8″ Like Tropical Kingbird, but voice different, and tail may be more brownish. See Cassin's and Western Kingbirds.

CASSIN'S KINGBIRD [27] Tirano Gritón *Tyrannus vociferans*
Range US, Mex, Blz?, Guat, Hon. Res/win Mex (res/sum nBajCal, ncPac, ncHi; win BajCal, sPac, sHi), Blz (cas?), Guat (Pac?).
Habitat Shrubby pastures, open mesquite grassland, hedgerows, thickets; perches on wires, posts, shrubtops.
Voice A chipping *kiteer, kiteer, kiteer, kiteer.*
Field Marks 8″ Like Tropical Kingbird, but more contrasty; chest much darker gray; tail blacker, square with pale tip band.

THICK-BILLED KINGBIRD [27] Tirano Piquigrueso *Tyrannus crassirostris*
Range US, Mex, Guat. Res Mex (ncPac + adj Hi), very rare/cas Guat (Pac).
Habitat Upper branches in scrubby woods, borders, partial clearings.
Voice A loud harsh *bur-ree,* or *kit-er-keer.*
Field Marks 8″ Head (especially crown) and back much darker and underparts and sides of face much whiter than other kingbirds except Eastern (which has prominent white tail-tip band and much smaller bill). Imm: yellower

WESTERN KINGBIRD [27] Tirano Pálido *Tyrannus verticalis*
Range Can–CRic, exc Blz. Sum/win Mex (sum nBajCal, nPac, nHi; tr/win csPac, csHi + adj Atl), Guat (Pac + adj Hi), ElSal.
Habitat Tree-dotted or brushy fields, savannas, borders, partial clearings.
Field Marks 8″ Like Tropical Kingbird, but paler; bill shorter; sides of square tail whitish-bordered.

EASTERN KINGBIRD [20] Tirano Viajero *Tyrannus tyrannus*
Range AK–SAm. Tr Mex (sPac, sHi, Atl + adj Hi, Yuc; cas/acc sBajCal, nPac, cHi), Blz, Guat, ElSal.
Habitat Flocks in trees in pastures, savannas, borders, hedgerows, clearings, or flying 50 to 300 feet above ground.
Field Marks 8″ Upperparts blackish to blackish gray; underparts and tail-tip band white.

GRAY KINGBIRD [20] Tirano Gris *Tyrannus dominicensis*
Range US, Mex, Blz. Tr Mex (e Yuc), Blz (cayes). Rare.
Habitat Overgrown brushy fields, clearings, borders, utility wires.
Field Marks 8.5″ Mostly medium gray above, with browner wings; pale gray to whitish below; darker ear patch and area around eye; tail notched.

SCISSOR-TAILED FLYCATCHER [27] Tirano Tijereta *Tyrannus forficatus*
Range US–Pan. Sum/win Mex (sum ne.nHi, nAtl; tr/win csPac, cHi, csAtl; very rare/cas BajCal, nPac, Yuc), Blz, Guat (Pac), ElSal.
Habitat Tree-dotted pastures, brushy grasslands, hedgerows, utility poles, wires, tops of small trees; flocks overhead.
Field Marks 14″ M: bluish gray above, pale pink and whitish below; red-orange sides. F+Imm: paler below; tail shorter. See Fork-tailed Flycatcher.

FORK-TAILED FLYCATCHER [26] Tirano Tijerilla *Tyrannus savana*
Range Mex–SAm, exc ElSal. Res Mex (se.cAtl+w.sAtl; cas Yuc), Blz (n), Guat (irr e Hi, Atl). Rare, irregular.
Habitat Humid to dry pastures, shrubby grassland, hedgerows; atop weeds, shrubs, fence wires.
Field Marks 16″ Tail, wings, and upper part of head black; back pale gray; underparts white; body smaller, appears more delicate than Scissor-tailed Flycatcher, but tail longer. Imm: tail much shorter, deeply forked.

BECARDS, MOURNERS—CABEZONES, LLORONAS—(FAMILY?)

CINNAMON BECARD [26] Cabezón Canelo *Pachyramphus cinnamomeus*
Range Mex–SAm. Res Mex (extreme se.cAtl–sc.sAtl), Blz (s), Guat (Atl). Rare.
Habitat Upper branches in humid forest, small openings, partial clearings.
Field Marks 5.5″ Medium tawny brown above, pale tawny brown below. Much smaller and paler below than Rufous and Speckled Mourners, Rufous Piha, and Ruddy Leafgleaner.

WHITE-WINGED BECARD [48] Cabezón Aliblanco *Pachyramphus polychopterus*
Range Mex–SAm, exc ElSal. Res Mex (cas/very rare sc.sAtl), Blz (s), Guat (Atl). Rare.
Habitat Open woods, humid forest, borders, partial clearings.
Field Marks 6″ Like more northerly ranging Gray-collared Becard, but collar does *not* extend around hindneck; M: *no* whitish line from bill to just over eye; F: plain dull brownish head; *no* black or rufous on crown.

GRAY-COLLARED BECARD [26] Cabezón Mexicano *Pachyramphus major*
Range Mex–Nic. Res Mex (irr Pac + adj Hi, Atl + adj Hi, Yuc), Blz, Guat (Pac+Atl + adj Hi), ElSal. Rare.
Habitat Cloud forest, other humid woods, dry scrubby woods, gardens, orchards.
Voice A quiet, musical *dewt-tew-tewt.*
Field Marks 5.5″ Bobs head often. Tail graduated; whitish line from bill to just above eye (not shown in illustration). M: black or dark gray and white above, with medium gray underparts and collar (including hindneck); tail feathers broadly white-tipped. F: mostly rufous above; collar and underparts pale buff to white; crown black or reddish brown with black border; tail feathers broadly tipped pale buffy rufous.

ROSE-THROATED BECARD [21] Cabezón Degollado *Pachyramphus aglaiae*
Range US–Pan. Res Mex (Pac, w+e.nHi+csHi, Atl, Yuc), Blz, Guat, ElSal.
Habitat Scrubby woods, borders, openings, overgrown pastures, wooded river borders; builds a bulky hanging nest, one- to two-foot diameter.
Voice A very high-pitched extended note; also a chatter.
Field Marks 6″ Tail *not* graduated; crown blackish; races vary otherwise. M: in most of Mexico, medium gray above; pale gray below, with bushy blackish head and rose-red throat; in Belize, Guatemala (Atl), and Mexico (sAtl) much darker

gray with little or no red on throat. F: in most of Mexico grayish brown above, with pale buff collar and underparts; in Belize, Guatemala (Atl), and Mexico (sAtl) mostly tawny rufous above, with pale tawny collar and underparts.

MASKED TITYRA [26] Titira Puerquito *Tityra semifasciata*
Range Mex–SAm. Res Mex (c.nPac–sPac, s.nAtl+csAtl + adj sHi, Yuc), Blz, Guat (Pac, Atl), ElSal. Rare.
Habitat Grassy forest remnants, partial clearings, river-border woods, borders, openings; usually in pairs, often seen near cavities in dead trees (nests or potential nest sites).
Voice A rasping, gruntlike *kiddit, kiddit.*
Field Marks 8″ M: mostly pearly gray, but forehead and forecrown, patch around eye, outer part of wing, and broad tail band black; eye ring and base of bill red. F: back, crown, nape, and ear patch dark grayish brown.

BLACK-CROWNED TITYRA [26] Titira Piquinegra *Tityra inquisitor*
Range Mex–SAm, exc ElSal. Res Mex (csAtl, Yuc), Blz, Guat (Atl). Rare.
Habitat Upper branches, humid forest borders, openings, partial clearings, river-border woods; often seen in dead trees, in pairs.
Voice A rasping *sik.*
Field Marks 8″ Flies long distances. Like Masked Tityra, but *no* red on head; M: crown all black; F: crown blackish, forehead buff; ear patch rufous.

RUFOUS PIHA [26] Alazán Mayor *Lipaugus unirufus*
Range Mex–SAm, exc ElSal. Res Mex (se.cAtl+sAtl), Blz (s), Guat (Atl). Rare.
Habitat Middle branches, dense humid forest, overgrown partial clearings.
Voice A very loud whistle, *wheet-a-weet.*
Field Marks 10″ Dark reddish brown above and below, paler and tawnier on throat and belly; larger, larger-billed, and more two-toned than Rufous and Speckled Mourners.

THRUSH-LIKE MOURNER [24] Saltarín Tontillo *Schiffornis turdinus*
Range Mex–SAm, exc ElSal. Res Mex (se.cAtl+sAtl, s+c Yuc), Blz, Guat (Atl). Rare.
Habitat Undergrowth in dense humid forest.
Field Marks 7″ Darker and much more olive-brown than other mourners, pihas, and female becards.

GRAY-HEADED PIPRITES [48] Turquito Cabecigrís *Piprites griseiceps*
Range Guat, Hon, Nic, CRic. Res Guat (e Atl). Very rare.
Habitat Humid forest, borders.
Field Marks 4.5″ Yellowish olive above; yellow below with grayish wash across breast; white eye ring; short tail is dark olive; bill short, rather thick.

SPECKLED MOURNER [26] Llorona Manchada *Laniocera rufescens*
Range Mex–SAm, exc ElSal. Res Mex (se.cAtl–sc.sAtl), Blz (s), Guat (Atl). Very rare.
Habitat Dense humid forest; moves slowly.
Voice A whistled *peet-a-weet.*

Field Marks 9″ Like Rufous Mourner and Rufous Piha, but darker brown; two dull spotty wing bars; faint breast bars or scallops; yellow patch on each side of chest, often hidden.

COTINGAS—COTINGAS—COTINGIDAE

LOVELY COTINGA [26] Cotinga Azuleja *Cotinga amabilis*
Range Mex–CRic, exc ElSal. Res Mex (se.cAtl–sc.sAtl), Blz (s), Guat (Atl). Rare, irregular.
Habitat Middle to upper branches in dense humid forest, small openings, borders, partial clearings.
Field Marks 8″ M: cobalt blue; throat and belly patch purple, may look black; wings and tail black. F: speckled and scalloped blackish brown above, spotted pale gray below.

MANAKINS—SALTARINES—PIPRIDAE

WHITE-COLLARED MANAKIN [24] Saltarín Cuelliblanco *Manacus candei*
Range Mex–Pan, exc ElSal. Res Mex (se.cAtl–se.sAtl), Blz, Guat (Atl). Rare.
Habitat Undergrowth in humid forest, shrubby borders, overgrown partial clearings.
Voice Short notes or trills. Also makes loud snapping sounds with wings.
Field Marks 4.5″ M: Mostly black, white, and yellow. F: belly yellower, legs brighter orange than those of other female manakins.

LONG-TAILED MANAKIN [24] Saltarín Toledo *Chiroxiphia linearis*
Range Mex–CRic, exc Blz. Res Mex (sPac), Guat (Pac), ElSal. Rare, irregular.
Habitat Ravines, thickets, undergrowth in humid to rather dry woods.
Voice A loud, mellow *taw-eet-oo* or *to-le-do*.
Field Marks 10″, 5″ M: black, with scarlet crown, pale blue back, central tail feathers very long, black. F: greenish olive above, dull buffy greenish below; central tail feathers noticeably elongated.

RED-CAPPED MANAKIN [24] Saltarín Cabecirrojo *Pipra mentalis*
Range Mex–SAm, exc ElSal. Res Mex (csAtl, Yuc), Blz, Guat (Atl). Rare.
Habitat Undergrowth in dense humid forest.
Voice A series of short and long high-pitched notes.
Field Marks 4″ Makes abrupt short flights or jumps, also snapping, whirring, or buzzy noises. M: black, with mostly red head; yellow thighs; white eyes. F: much duller and grayer below, much darker legs than female White-collared Manakin. Imm M: may be mostly greenish, but eyes white, thighs yellowish.

SHRIKES—VERDUGOS—LANIIDAE

LOGGERHEAD SHRIKE [40] Verdugo Americano *Lanius ludovicianus*
Range Can–Mex, Guat. Res/win Mex (res BajCal, ncPac, ncHi; win all exc Yuc), Guat (very rare/cas w Hi). Rare.

Habitat Scattered trees in pastures, open dry overgrown fields, hedgerows, borders.
Field Marks 8″ Gray and white, with black mask and mostly black wings and tail; bill short, stout, hooked at tip, black.

VIREOS—VIREOS—VIREONIDAE

SLATY VIREO [34] Vireo Pizarra *Vireo brevipennis*
Range Mex. Res Mex (s.cHi + adj Pac). Very rare, local.
Habitat Dense borders, hedgerows, mixed scrubby woods, low brush.
Field Marks 4.5″ Contrasty dark gray and white, with bright olive-green on wings, rump, tail, and crown; eyes white.

WHITE-EYED VIREO [35] Vireo Ojiblanco *Vireo griseus*
Range Can–Pan, exc ElSal. Res/win Mex (res nAtl+n.cAtl; win se.cPac, sAtl, Yuc), Blz, Guat (Atl).
Habitat Thickets, hedgerows, borders, brushy stream valleys, dense forest undergrowth.
Voice A staccato *chík-per-whéeoo-chík.*
Field Marks 4.5″ Grayish green above; pale yellowish wing bars; yellow eye ring and lores; whitish below with yellow wash; eyes white.

MANGROVE VIREO [34] Vireo Manglero *Vireo pallens*
Range Mex–CRic. Res Mex (s.nPac+se rPac+sPac, Yuc), Blz (n), Guat (Pac, Atl), ElSal (cstl).
Habitat Rare and local in coastal swamps of Pac; common in inland thickets, scrubby woods, hedgerows, and borders of Yuc.
Voice In Yuc, a rolling, rasping *weer, weer, weer* or *jury, jury, jury.*
Field Marks 4.5″ Wing bars and lores pale yellowish to whitish; eyes light brownish. Pacific coast bird illustrated; Yucatan birds are similar, but more yellowish olive above, *not* grayish olive, and much more yellowish below.

COZUMEL VIREO [34] Vireo de Cozumel *Vireo bairdi*
Range Mex. Res Mex (ne Yuc: Cozumel Island).
Habitat Thickets, scrub woods, borders, gardens.
Field Marks 4.5″ Grayish brown above; whitish to pale yellow wing bars and feather edgings on black wings; underparts white with cinnamon sides, flanks, and face.

BELL'S VIREO [35] Vireo de Bell *Vireo bellii*
Range US–Nic, exc Blz. Sum/tr Mex (sum nBajCal, nPac, nHi; tr/win all exc sAtl, Yuc); win Guat (Pac + adj Hi), ElSal. Rare.
Habitat Dry wooded river valleys, brushy arroyos, thickets, overgrown borders.
Voice Dry warbled question-and-answer phrases and pauses.
Field Marks 4.5″ Grayish above; faint wing bars, eye line, and eye ring; whitish below.

BLACK-CAPPED VIREO [35] Vireo Gorrinegro *Vireo atricapillus*
Range US–Mex. Sum/win Mex (sum ne.nHi; win s.nPac+cPac, w.cHi). Rare.
Habitat Large shrubs or small trees in dry scrubby woods, thickets, hedgerows, borders.
Field Marks 4″ M: olive-green above; head and face mostly black with white eye ring, lores, and throat; wing bars pale yellow; underparts white with yellowish wash on flanks. F: paler and duller; head dark gray, *not* black; whitish throat.

DWARF VIREO [34] Vireo Enano *Vireo nelsoni*
Range Mex. Res Mex (s+w.cHi + adj Pac). Very rare.
Habitat Thickets, scrubby hedgerows, brushy hillsides, riverside woods.
Field Marks 4″ Olive-gray above; two narrow white wing bars; partial white eye ring; whitish below with pale olive on sides and flanks.

GRAY VIREO [35] Vireo Gris *Vireo vicinior*
Range US–Mex. Sum/win Mex (sum nBajCal, ne.nHi; win sBajCal, nw.nPac, n.nHi). Rare.
Habitat Brushy areas, piñon-juniper, thickets, chaparral.
Field Marks 4.5″ Bobs tail up and down. Gray above; one faint wing bar; faint white eye ring; gray lores.

BLUE-HEADED VIREO [35] Vireo Cabeciazul *Vireo solitarius*
Range Can–CRic. Win Mex (csAtl, e.nHi+csHi, ncAtl; cas Yuc), Guat, ElSal.
Habitat Pine or pine-oak woods, deciduous forest, second growth.
Field Marks 5″ Mostly olive-green or grayish green above, but top and sides of head bluish gray to slaty gray, contrasting with white "spectacles" and throat; bold pale yellowish or whitish wing bars; white below, with yellow flanks and untacs.

CASSIN'S VIREO Vireo de Cassin *Vireo cassinii*
Range Can–Mex. Res/win Mex (res sBajCal; sum.nBajCal, tr/win BajCal, ncPac+Hi).
Habitat Wooded river valleys, pine or pine-oak forest.
Field Marks 5″ Like Blue-headed Vireo, but upperparts (including top and sides of head) uniform dull gray or greenish gray, with little contrast between sides of head and throat; underparts duller whitish, with duller greenish yellow flanks and untacs.

PLUMBEOUS VIREO Vireo Plomizo *Vireo plumbeus*
Range US–Hon. Res/win Mex (res w.nHi+csHi; tr/win ncHi), res. Blz (s), Guat (Pac, Hi), ElSal (n).
Habitat Dry, brushy woods, pinyon-juniper hillsides, pine or pine-oak forest.
Field Marks 5″ Like Blue-headed Vireo, with prominent "spectacles" and wing bars and wing-feather edgings, but dull gray above and on head; pale gray to whitish below; seldom shows any greenish or yellowish wash on wing bars, upperparts, or underparts.

YELLOW-THROATED VIREO Vireo Pechiamarillo *Vireo flavifrons*
Range Can–SAm. Tr/win Mex (sPac, Atl, Yuc), Blz, Guat (Pac, Atl), ElSal. Rare.
Habitat Open woods, wooded river valleys, borders, partial clearings.
Field Marks 5.5″ Yellow-green above; two white wing bars; yellow spectacles; yellow throat and breast; white belly and untacs.

HUTTON'S VIREO [35] Vireo Reyezuelo *Vireo huttoni*
Range Can–Mex, Guat. Res Mex (mts BajCal, Hi + adj Pac), Guat (Hi).
Habitat Pine, pine-oak, or fir forest or scrubby oak woods; middle or upper branches—other drab, wing-barred vireos usually stay at shrub to low-branch levels.
Voice One- or two-note song, repeated persistently.
Field Marks 4″ Like female Ruby-crowned Kinglet, but heavier bill; doesn't flick wings.

GOLDEN VIREO [34] Vireo Dorado *Vireo hypochryseus*
Range Mex. Res Mex (c.nPac cPac + adj Hi).
Habitat Dry scrubby open woods, hedgerows, brushy arroyos, borders.
Voice *Weer, weer, weer, peek.*
Field Marks 5″ Olive-yellow above; superciliary line and underparts bright yellow.

WARBLING VIREO [35] Vireo Gorjeador *Vireo gilvus*
Range AK–Nic. Sum/win Mex (sum mts BajCal, w.ncHi + adj Pac; tr/win all exc sAtl, Yuc); tr/win Blz, Guat (Pac + adj Hi), ElSal. Sum rare, local; win common.
Habitat Pine-oak forest, river-border forest, openings, borders.
Field Marks 5″ Gray or olive-gray above, including crown; whitish below, with sides tinged greenish olive; gray line through eye; white line over eye; *no* wing bars.

BROWN-CAPPED VIREO Vireo Gorripardo *Vireo leucophrys*
Range Mex–SAm, exc Blz, Nic. Res Mex (e Hi + adj Atl), Guat (Hi + adj Pac?), ElSal (w). Rare, local.
Habitat Cloud forest, partial clearings, small openings, tall trees in lush gardens.
Field Marks 5″ Like Warbling Vireo, but crown much browner; upperparts mostly brownish gray.

PHILADELPHIA VIREO Vireo Filadélfico *Vireo philadelphicus*
Range Can–SAm. Tr/win Mex (Atl + adj Hi, Yuc), Blz, Guat (Pac, Atl), ElSal. Very rare.
Habitat Open woods, borders, partial clearings.
Field Marks 5″ Small-billed like Warbling Vireo, but grayer above; darker line through eye; more yellowish breast.

RED-EYED VIREO [35] Vireo Ojirrojo *Vireo olivaceus*
Range AK–SAm. Tr Mex (sPac, Atl, Yuc), Blz, Guat, ElSal (cas).

Habitat Dense or open forest, wooded riversides, gardens, parks with numerous trees, forest borders.

Field Marks 6" Olive-green above, white below; crown medium gray, narrowly black-bordered; white line over eye; dark line through eye; eyes red (adult) or brownish (immature).

YELLOW-GREEN VIREO Vireo Tropical *Vireo flavoviridis*
Range US–SAm. Sum Mex (Pac, Atl, Yuc), Blz, Guat (Pac, Atl), ElSal.
Habitat Middle and upper branches, wooded riversides, borders, humid forest, partial clearings, parks, swamps.
Field Marks 6" Like Red-eyed Vireo, but only a faint blackish crown border and a faint dark line through eye; sides, flanks, and untacs greenish yellow, *not* whitish.

YUCATAN VIREO [34] Vireo Yucateco *Vireo magister*
Range Mex, Blz, Hon. Res Mex (extreme e.sAtl + Yuc), Blz (cstl).
Habitat Middle or upper branches, scrubby woods or forest borders, mangrove swamps, coastal forests.
Field Marks 6" Like Yellow-green Vireo, but more olive to brownish gray above; darker line through eye; gray, *not* yellow, wash on breast, sides, and flanks; larger bill.

TAWNY-CROWNED GREENLET [34] Vireo Leonado *Hylophilus ochraceiceps*
Range Mex–SAm, exc ElSal. Res Mex (se.cAtl + sAtl, s + e Yuc), Blz, Guat (Atl). Rare.
Habitat Humid forest, forest borders, openings, partial clearings; usually at low or middle levels.
Field Marks 4.5" Brown to rufous above, with tawny rufous crown; gray face and throat; pale tawny breast and sides; white eyes.

LESSER GREENLET [34] Vireo Menor *Hylophilus decurtatus*
Range Mex–SAm. Res Mex (sPac, csAtl, s + e Yuc), Blz, Guat (Pac, Atl), ElSal.
Habitat Humid forest, partial clearings, borders; active in middle branches.
Voice A repeated *pit-chu-lip.*
Field Marks 4" Olive-green above; crown and sides of face gray; eye ring and lores white; white below with yellowish green sides, flanks, and untacs.

CHESTNUT-SIDED SHRIKE-VIREO [34] Vireón Pechicastaño *Vireolanius melitophrys*
Range Mex, Guat. Res Mex (csHi + adj Pac+cAtl), Guat (Hi). Very rare, local, irregular.
Habitat Pine, pine-oak, or fir forest, among upper branches.
Voice A loud, low-pitched *whip, whee-ur.*
Field Marks 6.5" M: grayish olive above, with gray crown and nape; white below, with rufous breast band; face and throat white, black, and yellow; eyes white. F: similar pattern, but paler, duller.

GREEN SHRIKE-VIREO [34] Vireón Verde *Vireolanius pulchellus*
Range Mex–Pan. Res Mex (se.cAtl + sAtl), Blz (s), Guat (Pac, Atl), ElSal (w). Rare.

Habitat Canopy in dense humid forest, rarely lower in forest border, partial clearings.
Voice A loud, persistent *wheet-ur, wheet-ur, wheet-ur.*
Field Marks 6" Bright green above with bluish green crown; duller yellow-green below, with yellow throat.

RUFOUS-BROWED PEPPERSHRIKE [34] Vireón Alegrín *Cyclarhis gujanensis*
Range Mex–SAm. Res Mex (sPac + adj Hi, s.nAtl+csAtl, Yuc), Blz, Guat (Pac, Hi, local Atl), ElSal.
Habitat River-border woods, humid forest, partial clearings, borders, tree-dotted pastures.
Voice A phrase of five or six loud, rather staccato notes, repeated often, then changed and repeated.
Field Marks 6.5" Olive-green above, with gray crown, nape, and side of face; forehead and broad line over eye rufous; bill heavy; eyes reddish. Cozumel Island birds duller below, with grayish wash on breast; whitish belly and untacs.

CROWS, JAYS—URRACAS, CUERVOS—CORVIDAE

STELLER'S JAY [29] Chara Copetona *Cyanocitta stelleri*
Range AK–Nic, exc Blz. Res Mex (irr Hi + adj Pac+Atl; cas BajCal), Guat (Hi), ElSal (n).
Habitat Pine, pine-oak, or fir forests, borders, openings, partial clearings.
Voice A slow, harsh *chaa, chaa, chaa, chaa*
Field Marks 12" Two types. Mex (nHi+n.cHi): head, long crest, breast, and upper back dull blackish blue; lower back, rump, belly, and untacs rich medium blue; wings and tail barred; white above and below eye. Mex (se.cHi+sHi), Guat (Hi), ElSal (n): like the northern type, but darker and more purplish blue all over; crest shorter and often *not* raised.

BLACK-THROATED MAGPIE-JAY [28] Urraca Carinegra *Calocitta colliei*
Range Mex. Res Mex (nPac + adj Hi).
Habitat Open scrubby woods, hedgerows, borders, mixed woods and farmland.
Field Marks 27" Purplish blue above, white below; forward-curling crest, throat, chest, and part of face black; very long slender tail.

WHITE-THROATED MAGPIE-JAY [28] Urraca Cariblanca *Calocitta formosa*
Range Mex–CRic, exc Blz. Res Mex (csPac), Guat (Pac + interior e Atl), ElSal.
Habitat Hedgerows, borders, mixed scrubby woods and farms.
Field Marks 21" Like Black-throated Magpie-Jay, but paler blue above; tail shorter; throat and face white; narrow breast band black.

TUFTED JAY [28] Urraca Pinta *Cyanocorax dickeyi*
Range Mex. Res Mex (local, sw.nHi). Rare.
Habitat Usually humid pine-oak, oak, or oak-fir forests on steep slopes.
Field Marks 15" Spectacular pattern of very dark purplish blue and snowy white; bushy crest mostly on forehead and forecrown; yellow eyes.

GREEN JAY [29] Chara Verde *Cyanocorax yncas*
Range US–Hon, exc ElSal; SAm. Res Mex (csPac + adj Hi, Atl + adj Hi, Yuc), Blz, Guat (Pac, Atl).
Habitat Scrubby open woods, thickets, dense borders, cloud forest and other humid forest.
Field Marks 10″ Greenish above; crown, nape, and part of cheek purplish; throat and rest of cheek black; outer tail feathers broadly yellow. Northern birds: yellowish green underparts and brown eyes. Southern birds: bright yellow below, yellow eyes.

BROWN JAY [28] Urraca Papán *Cyanocorax morio*
Range US–Pan. Res Mex (Atl, Yuc), Blz, Guat (Atl), ElSal (cas).
Habitat Small noisy flocks, in dense forest, river-border woods, partial clearings, borders.
Voice Explosive high-pitched cawing sounds, *kay, kay, kay.*
Field Marks 17″ Plain-tipped morph: dark brown above, with blackish brown head, throat, and chest; whitish or pale brownish gray belly; tail rather long, rounded, all dark brown or brown at base and broadly white-tipped; bill and legs black. Imm (illustrated): bill yellow; eye ring and legs dull yellowish. White-tipped morph: white-tipped tail; more contrasty blackish and whitish.

BUSHY-CRESTED JAY [48] Chara Hondureña *Cyanocorax melanocyaneus*
Range Guat, Nic. Res Guat (Hi + adj Pac+e Atl), ElSal.
Habitat Cloud forest, humid pine-oak forest, borders.
Field Marks 12″ Short, bushy crest; head and underparts black, except dark violet-blue belly; wings, back, and tail blue; eyes pale yellow; bill black. Imm: bill yellow, eyes brown.

SAN BLAS JAY [28] Chara Colimense *Cyanocorax sanblasianus*
Range Mex. Res Mex (extreme s.nPac–c.cPac, south of Purplish-backed Jay's range).
Habitat Small flocks in mangrove swamps or rather dry scrubby woods, thickets, borders, coconut groves.
Field Marks 13″ Black, except blue back, rump, wings, and tail; small forehead crest; black bill, white eyes, blackish legs. Imm+juv: forehead crest much larger; bill yellow, eyes dark brown.

YUCATAN JAY [28] Chara Yucateca *Cyanocorax yucatanicus*
Range Mex, Blz, Guat. Res Mex (sAtl, Yuc), Blz (n), Guat (nw Atl).
Habitat Small flocks or family groups in dense scrubby woods, thickets, borders, hedgerows.
Field Marks 13″ Like San Blas Jay, but *not* crested; yellow legs; eyes brown at all ages; Imm: whitish tail corners and yellow bill; Juv: all-white head and underparts.

PURPLISH-BACKED JAY [28] Chara Sinaloense *Cyanocorax beecheii*
Range Mex. Res Mex (nPac, north of San Blas Jay's range). Rare.
Habitat Scrubby woods, thickets, borders.

Field Marks 16" Black, with dark purplish blue back, wings, rump, and tail; small forehead crest seldom raised; black bill; orange-yellow legs; whitish eyes. F: eyes yellowish. Imm: bill yellowish, eyes dark brown.

AZURE-HOODED JAY [28] Chara Gorriazul *Cyanolyca cucullata*
Range Mex, Guat, Hon, CRic, Pan. Res Mex (csAtl + adj Hi), Guat (Hi + adj Atl). Rare.
Habitat Undergrowth of cloud forest, other humid forest, overgrown *cafetales,* partial clearings, dense borders.
Field Marks 12" Often in small flocks. Mostly black head, back, and breast, but very pale blue (white-bordered) patch from midcrown to lower hindneck; rest of plumage dark purplish blue.

BLACK-THROATED JAY [28] Chara de Niebla *Cyanolyca pumilo*
Range Mex, Guat, ElSal, Hon. Res Mex (sHi), Guat (Hi), ElSal (n). Rare.
Habitat Secluded portions of cloud forest, humid pine forest, overgrown partial clearings.
Field Marks 10" Dark purplish blue, but throat, face, and forehead black, bordered with white line above.

DWARF JAY [28] Chara Enana *Cyanolyca nana*
Range Mex. Res Mex (se.cHi). Rare.
Habitat Humid pine-oak woods, fir forest, piney ridges in cloud forest; middle or upper branches, often in groups.
Field Marks 9" Mostly dark grayish blue, with black sides of face and very pale bluish gray throat.

(WHITE-THROATED) OMILTEMI JAY [28] Chara de Omiltemi *Cyanolyca mirabilis*
Range Mex. Res Mex (c+se.cHi). Rare.
Habitat Secluded humid mountain forests, cloud forest.
Field Marks 10" Mostly dark grayish blue, with white throat and face border; black face, crown, hindneck, and breast band.

WESTERN SCRUB-JAY [29] Grajo Azulejo *Aphelocoma californica*
Range US–Mex. Res Mex (BajCal, ncHi + adj nPac+nAtl).
Habitat Open woods, hedgerows, scrubby woods on rocky hillsides, mixed woods and clearings, borders.
Voice A harsh *chreek* or *chak-chak-chak-chak.*
Field Marks 12" Small flocks. Like Mexican Jay, but somewhat browner above; broadly white throat, irregular dark breast band, and white line over eye.

MEXICAN JAY [29] Grajo Mexicano *Aphelocoma ultramarina*
Range US–Mex. Res Mex (w+e.nHi+cHi).
Habitat Pine, pine-oak, or oak woodland, borders, thickets, mixed woods and clearings.
Voice A loud, questioning, somewhat musical *quenk, quenk.*
Field Marks 12" Grayish blue above; blackish ear patch; whitish below with grayer breast; may be vaguely streaked. See Western Scrub-Jay.

UNICOLORED JAY [28] Grajo Unicolor *Aphelocoma unicolor*
Range Mex, Guat, ElSal, Hon. Res Mex (local sw+e.cHi+sHi), Guat (Hi), ElSal (n). Rare.
Habitat Humid pine, pine-oak, or cloud forest, borders, partial clearings.
Voice A single musical *chwenk.*
Field Marks 13″ Very dark, slightly purplish blue all over; ear patch blackish; throat may be faintly streaked; bill black. Wings and tail *not* barred; *no* white on head. Imm: lower mandible yellowish. See Steller's Jay.

PINYON JAY [29] Chara Piñonera *Gymnorhinus cyanocephalus*
Range US-Mex. Res/vis Mex (n.nBajCal; cas n.nPac, n.nHi).
Habitat Open pine, pine-oak, or juniper woods; in flocks, often on ground.
Field Marks 11″ Bluish gray; throat faintly streaked whitish; tail short; bill pointed, slender.

CLARK'S NUTCRACKER [29] Cascanueces Americano *Nucifraga columbiana*
Range Can-Mex. Res/vis Mex (res n.nBajCal, ne.nHi [Cerro Potosí]; cas/very rare vis nHi). Rare, local.
Habitat Coniferous forest, forest borders, partial clearings, often on ground.
Field Marks 12″ Pale gray, except white face and untacs; black wings with some white; white tail with black central feathers; bill long, pointed.

AMERICAN CROW Cuervo Norteño *Corvus brachyrhynchos*
Range AK-Mex. Res/vis Mex (res n.nBajCal; cas/very rare nw.nPac).
Habitat Grassy fields or mixed woods and farmland, often near woodland borders, hedgerows.
Voice A harsh *kah.*
Field Marks 17″ Often in large flocks. Black; tail square-tipped. Larger than Tamaulipas and Sinaloa Crows; smaller than ravens.

TAMAULIPAS CROW [28] Cuervo Tamaulipeco *Corvus imparatus*
Range US-Mex. Res Mex (nAtl+n.cAtl).
Habitat Open brushy grassland, farm fields, semidesert, river-border woods.
Voice A guttural *boys* or *carrk.*
Field Marks 15″ Black; tail square-tipped. See Sinaloa Crow.

SINALOA CROW Cuervo Sinaloense *Corvus sinaloae*
Range Mex. Res Mex (c+s.nPac).
Habitat Open woods or brushy grassland, borders, mixed woods and farms, often near water.
Voice High-pitched cawing notes, more like Brown Jay's than Tamaulipas Crow's.
Field Marks 15″ Like Tamaulipas Crow, but voice different.

CHIHUAHUAN RAVEN [29] Cuervo Llanero *Corvus cryptoleucus*
Range US-Mex. Res/win Mex (n+c.nPac, nHi+n.cHi, nAtl+n.cAtl).
Habitat Open, dry, brushy grassland or semidesert.
Voice Higher-pitched than Common Raven's.

Field Marks 21" Like Common Raven, but neck feathers white at base (usually concealed); bill shorter; throat feathers *not* as shaggy.

COMMON RAVEN [29] Cuervo Grande *Corvus corax*
Range AK–Nic, exc Blz. Res Mex (BajCal, Pac, Hi), Guat (Hi), ElSal.
Habitat Dry, brushy slopes, mixed farms and dry grassland; seen more often than Chihuahuan Raven on rocky mountainsides with scattered large trees, less often in open desert or semidesert.
Voice A low-pitched *a-a-rk*.
Field Marks 25" Black; throat shaggy; head and bill rather large; tail wedge-shaped.

LARKS—ALONDRAS—ALAUDIDAE

HORNED LARK [21] Alondra Cornuda *Eremophila alpestris*
Range AK–Mex, SAm. Res Mex (BajCal, ncPac, ncHi, nAtl).
Habitat Short-grass fields, dry pastures, open grassy semideserts.
Field Marks 7" M: streaked brownish above; mostly white below, with black breast band and black on face; short black "horns"; tail black below, with white margins. F+win M: duller. Imm: faint face pattern and breast band; tail as in adult; *no* "horns."

SWALLOWS—GOLONDRINAS—HIRUNDINIDAE

PURPLE MARTIN [21] Martín Azul *Progne subis*
Range Can–SAm, exc ElSal. Sum/tr Mex (sum BajCal, n.nPac, irr ncHi, nw.nAtl; tr all), Blz, Guat. Rare.
Habitat Colonies in nest boxes, tree cacti, or large dead trees in grassland, park-like openings, partial clearings; flocks along coast in migration.
Field Marks 8" M: black with purplish gloss. F+imm: dark brown above with slight gloss; pale gray-brown to whitish below, with faint scallops and streaks.

SINALOA MARTIN [28] Martín Bicolor *Progne sinaloae*
Range Mex, Guat. Sum Mex (nPac+nw.cPac, irr w.ncHi; cas/acc sPac), cas/acc Guat (Atl). Very rare.
Habitat Usually colonies in oak groves or scattered pines, near suitable nest holes.
Field Marks 7" M: blackish purple, with white belly and untacs. F+imm: like adult male above, but dark areas below are duller and browner.

GRAY-BREASTED MARTIN [28] Martín Pechigris *Progne chalybea*
Range Mex–SAm. Res/sum Mex (res c.nPac–sPac; sum Atl, Yuc); res Blz, Guat (Pac, Atl), ElSal.
Habitat Usually colonies around buildings, town squares, bridges, partial clearings.
Field Marks 7" M: glossy blackish above, whitish to grayish below. F+imm: browner, not as glossy.

TREE SWALLOW [20] Golondrina Invernal *Tachycineta bicolor*
Range AK–CRic. Tr/win Mex, Blz, Guat (exc Pac?), ElSal (cas). Rare to common.
Habitat Over open areas usually near rivers, lakes, coastal lagoons, marshes, beaches.
Field Marks 5.5″ White below, dark greenish blue above; black wings and tail. Imm: brown above, white below; brown patch on side of breast. See Mangrove Swallow.

MANGROVE SWALLOW [28] Golondrina Manglera *Tachycineta albilinea*
Range Mex–Pan. Res Mex (Pac, Atl, Yuc), Blz, Guat (Pac, Atl), ElSal.
Habitat Over lowland rivers, ponds, lakes, coastal lagoons, marshes, swamps.
Field Marks 5″ Often solitary. Like Tree Swallow, but rump and uptacs white (whitish or pale gray in immature). See Violet-green Swallow.

VIOLET-GREEN SWALLOW [21] Golondrina Verde *Tachycineta thalassina*
Range AK–CRic, exc Blz. Res/win Mex (res BajCal, n.nPac, ncHi; sum nHi; win csPac, sHi), Guat (Pac + adj Hi), ElSal.
Habitat Gardens, orchards, parks, in towns and villages, mixed fields and woods, borders.
Field Marks 4.5″ Like Tree and Mangrove Swallows, but purplish gloss above; sides of face and sides (only) of rump white. Imm: grayish brown above; sides of rump white.

BLACK-CAPPED SWALLOW [28] Golondrina Gorrinegra *Notiochelidon pileata*
Range Mex, Guat, ElSal, Hon. Res Mex (sHi + adj Pac+Atl), Guat (Hi + adj Pac, Atl), ElSal (n). Rare.
Habitat Rocky road cuts or cliffs, borders, partial clearings in pine or pine-oak forest, rarely in towns.
Field Marks 5″ Blackish above and on sides, flanks, and untacs; white throat, breast, and belly; tail rather long, deeply forked.

NORTHERN ROUGH-WINGED SWALLOW [21] Golondrina Gorjicafé *Stelgidopteryx serripennis*
(Does not include Yucatan Swallow; see below)
Range AK–Pan. Res/win Mex (res/sum nBajCal, Pac, w+e.nHi+csHi, Atl; tr/win all), Blz, Guat, ElSal.
Habitat·Near road cuts, riverbanks, arroyos, open archaeological sites.
Field Marks 5″ Dark grayish brown above; whitish below, with brownish wash on throat; tail rather short, slightly forked. See Yucatan and Bank Swallows.

(YUCATAN ROUGH-WINGED) YUCATAN SWALLOW Golondrina Yucateca *Stelgidopteryx ridgwayi*
(The AOU lumps this with Northern Rough-winged Swallow; see above)
Range Mex, Blz, Guat. Res Mex (se.cAtl+sAtl, Yuc), Blz, Guat (Atl).
Habitat Dirt banks, especially along rivers or road cuts, archaeological sites.
Field Marks 5″ Like Northern Rough-winged Swallow, but darker above; longer untacs black-tipped.

BANK SWALLOW [20] Golondrina Ribereña *Riparia riparia*
Range AK–SAm. Sum/win Mex (sum n.nAtl; tr/win all); tr/win Blz, Guat, ElSal.
Habitat Often in flocks, over tree-dotted pastures, lakes, swamps, marshes, coastal lagoons.
Field Marks 5″ Much like Northern Rough-winged Swallow, but throat white; dark band across breast.

BARN SWALLOW [21] Golondrina Tijereta *Hirundo rustica*
Range AK–SAm. Res/win Mex (res/sum ne.nPac, ncHi; tr/win all); win Blz, Guat, ElSal.
Habitat Towns, villages, parks, fields, barns, near bridges or buildings.
Field Marks 6″ Glossy blackish blue above; mostly rufous below, with incomplete blackish breast band; tail long, very deeply forked. Imm: duller; tail shorter.

CLIFF SWALLOW [21] Golondrina Risquera *Petrochelidon pyrrhonota*
Range AK–SAm. Sum/tr Mex (sum n.nBajCal, n.nPac, ncIIi, nAtl; tr all); tr Blz, Guat, ElSal.
Habitat Near bridges, dams, lakes, or in towns.
Field Marks 5.5″ Forehead very pale buff or rufous; much of throat and face rufous, with blackish lower throat; rump buffy; back blackish, with white streaks. Imm: mostly darker and duller, especially on head.

CAVE SWALLOW [21] Golondrina Pueblera *Petrochelidon fulva*
Range US, Mex, ElSal, CRic. Res/sum Mex (sPac, nsHi, Yuc), tr ElSal. Irregular.
Habitat Colonies in towns, old buildings, archaeological sites, caves, sinkholes.
Field Marks 5.5″ Like rufous-foreheaded form of Cliff Swallow, but throat very pale buff, with *no* black patch.

TITMICE, CHICKADEES MASCARITAS—PARIDAE

MOUNTAIN CHICKADEE [29] Mascarita Montañesa *Poecile gambeli*
Range AK–Mex. Res Mex (n.nBajCal).
Habitat Mountain pine and pine-oak forest.
Field Marks 5″ Like Mexican Chickadee, but white line over eye; less black on chest; paler sides, flanks, and untacs.

MEXICAN CHICKADEE [29] Mascarita Mexicana *Poecile sclateri*
Range US–Mex. Res Mex (w.+ne.nHi+cHi).
Habitat Mountain pine, pine-oak, or fir forest.
Field Marks 5″ Grayish above, but crown (broadly), throat, and chest black; belly and sides of face white; untacs, flanks, and sides medium gray.

BRIDLED TITMOUSE [29] Paro con Freno *Baeolophus wollweberi*
Range US–Mex. Res Mex (w+se.nHi+cHi).
Habitat Open oak woods, sometimes pine-oak, in mountains.

Voice *Wheeta-wheeta-wheeta.*
Field Marks 5" Gray above, very pale gray below; black of throat barely reaches chest; black line through eye and bordering ear patch; crest black and gray.

OAK TITMOUSE Paro Occidental *Baeolophus inornatus*
Range US–Mex. Res Mex (mts n.nBajCal+mts s.sBajCal).
Habitat Chaparral, oak groves or pine-oak woodlands.
Voice Variations on a loud, clear *wheeta-wheeta-wheeta.*
Field Marks 5.5" Like Juniper Titmouse (no range overlap in Mex), but smaller, smaller-billed, darker, and browner above (and s.sBajCal birds are whiter-breasted); voice and habitat differ.

JUNIPER TITMOUSE [29] Paro Sencillo *Baeolophus ridgwayi*
Range US–Mex. Res Mex (mts. extreme nw.nHi).
Habitat Juniper, or pinyon-juniper hillsides.
Voice A longer, more rapidly repeated series of notes (*whee-whee-whee-whee-whee-whee-whee*) than that of the Oak Titmouse.
Field Marks 5.5" Gray all over; paler below than above; crested. In Baja California see Oak Titmouse.

TUFTED TITMOUSE [29] Paro Penachudo *Baeolophus bicolor*
Black-crested group [29] Paro Copetinegro *B. b. atricristatus*
Range US–Mex. Res Mex (ncAtl + adj Hi).
Habitat Scrubby woods, hedgerows, borders, dry oak woods.
Field Marks 5.5" Gray above, whitish below; crest black; flanks rufous.
Tufted group Paro Penachudo *B. b. bicolor*
Range Can–US. Not in our area.

VERDINS—BALONCITOS—REMIZIDAE

VERDIN [29] Baloncito *Auriparus flaviceps*
Range US–Mex. Res Mex (BajCal, n.nPac, nHi+n.cHi, n.nAtl).
Habitat Shrubtops, in semidesert or desert scrub.
Field Marks 3.5" Mostly medium gray above, pale gray below, but all or part of head yellow; rufous wrist patch usually hidden. Imm: head and wrist patch gray.

BUSHTITS—SASTRECITOS—AEGITHALIDAE

BUSHTIT [29] Sastrecito *Psaltriparus minimus*
Range Can–Mex, Guat. Res Mex (n.nBajCal+s.sBajCal, w+e.nHi+csHi), Guat (w Hi). Irregular.
Habitat Open oak or pine-oak woods, piñon-juniper, chaparral, borders, hedgerows.
Field Marks 4" Usually in flocks among lower branches. Grayish above, whitish below, with long tail; crown and flanks may be grayish or brownish; ear patches may be grayish, brownish, or black. M: eyes dark. F: eyes white. Most Mexican and Guatemalan birds are black-eared; in northwest Mexico and north of there some juveniles may be black-eared; BajCal birds are *not* black-eared.

NUTHATCHES—SALTAPALOS—SITTIDAE

RED-BREASTED NUTHATCH Saltapalo Canadiense *Sitta canadensis*
Range AK–Mex. Win Mex (n.nBajCal, nHi + adj Pac+Atl). Very rare to casual.
Habitat Mainly in conifers.
Field Marks 4" Like White-breasted Nuthatch, but smaller; rufous below; long black line through eye, white line over eye. F+imm: paler and duller.

WHITE-BREASTED NUTHATCH [29] Saltapalo Blanco *Sitta carolinensis*
Range Can–Mex. Res Mex (n.nBajCal+s.sBajCal, w+e.nHi+cHi). Rare.
Habitat Pine, pine-oak, or fir forest.
Field Marks 5.5" M: gray above; crown and hindneck black; white below; some rufous on thighs, belly, or untacs; white patches on black tail. F: duller; crown gray.

PYGMY NUTHATCH [29] Saltapalo Enano *Sitta pygmaea*
Range Can–Mex. Res Mex (mts n.nBajCal, w+ne.nHi+cHi).
Habitat Pine, pine-oak, and fir forest; low branches to treetops.
Field Marks 4" Usually very active small groups voicing tinkling, chippering notes. Gray above, white below; crown brown; nape spot whitish; tiny tail.

CREEPERS—CORTECERITOS—CERTHIIDAE

BROWN CREEPER [31] Cortecerito *Certhia americana*
Range AK–Nic, exc Blz. Res/win Mex (irr res Hi; win nBajCal, nPac, nAtl), Guat (Hi). Rare.
Habitat Pine, pine-oak, or fir forest.
Field Marks 5" Climbs up trunks and large branches. Brownish colors, streaked head and back, stiffened pointed tail feathers, and its way of climbing trees are reminiscent of woodcreepers, but Brown Creeper is smaller, unstreaked whitish below, with whitish line over eye; wings blackish brown and whitish, *not* rich rufous.

WRENS—SALTAPAREDES—TROGLODYTIDAE

BANDED-BACKED WREN [30] Matraca Tropical *Campylorhynchus zonatus*
Range Mex–SAm. Res Mex (sPac, se.cHi+sHi, csAtl), Blz (s), Guat (exc Pac), ElSal (n).
Habitat Dense humid forest, moist pine or pine-oak forest, partial clearings, borders; small groups, in middle or upper branches.
Voice Rasping notes, *ji-ji-ji-jit, jit, ji-jit,* or harsh *crack.*
Field Marks 7" Barred black and pale buff above, spotted black on whitish below, except mostly unspotted cinnamon belly, flanks, and untacs.

GRAY-BARRED WREN [30] Matraca Serrana *Campylorhynchus megalopterus*
Range Mex. Res Mex (cHi).
Habitat Humid pine-oak or fir forest, partial clearings; small flocks in middle or upper branches.

Voice Very harsh rasping notes.

Field Marks 7″ Appears gray, actually blackish and white; barred above, but streaked on head and neck; spotty streaks and dull bars below.

GIANT WREN [30] Matraca Chupahuevo *Campylorhynchus chiapensis*
Range Mex. Res Mex (sPac).
Habitat Hedgerows, tree-dotted brushy fields, river-border woods, partial clearings.
Voice A rollicking *chort-chort-chort-chort;* also *wock-o, wock-o.*
Field Marks 8″ Mostly plain dark chestnut above; primaries blacker; crown, hindneck, and line through eye black; underparts and sides of face mostly white; wings and tail *not* barred.

RUFOUS-NAPED WREN [30] Matraca Nuquirrufa *Campylorhynchus rufinucha*
Range Mex–CRic, exc Blz. Res Mex (csPac, c.cAtl), Guat (Pac), ElSal.
Habitat Hedgerows, brushy fields dotted with small trees, scrubby open woods, borders, semidesert.
Voice A loud, rollicking *joricky-joricky-joricky.*
Field Marks 6″ Crown mostly black; nape and upper back rufous; whitish line over eye; black line through eye; back and rump streaked or spotted or plain rufous; underparts whitish or dull grayish buff, may be partly spotted or barred; wings and tail heavily barred.

SPOTTED WREN [30] Matraca Manchada *Campylorhynchus gularis*
Range Mex. Res Mex (w+se.nHi + adj Pac+Atl, w.cHi). Rare, irregular.
Habitat Hedgerows, semidesert, scrubby hillsides, open oak or pine-oak woods.
Field Marks 7″ Heavily streaked and spotted black, whitish, and rufous above; brown crown and line through eye; whitish line over eye; mustache mark black; chest, sides, and flanks spotted, but throat and belly mostly unspotted. Imm: *not* spotted below.

BOUCARD'S WREN [30] Matraca Balseña *Campylorhynchus jocosus*
Range Mex. Res Mex (se.cHi + adj Pac). Rare.
Habitat Dense scrubby arid areas or brushy parts of pine-oak woods.
Field Marks 7″ Like Spotted Wren, but more heavily spotted below, including lower throat and belly; noticeable dull bars on flanks; darker brown above, especially on crown. Imm: numerous dull spots and bars below.

YUCATAN WREN [30] Matraca Yucateca *Campylorhynchus yucatanicus*
Range Mex. Res Mex (n Yuc).
Habitat Scrubby woods, hedgerows, overgrown fields, thickets, mainly near coast.
Field Marks 7″ Dark brown above; barred on wings, tail, and rump, and streaked on hindneck and back; line over eye whitish; underparts whitish, with narrow spotty streaks on throat and breast and bars on belly and flanks.

CACTUS WREN [31] Matraca Desértica *Campylorhynchus brunneicapillus*
Range US–Mex. Res Mex (BajCal, n+c.nPac, nHi+n.cHi, n.nAtl).

Habitat Scrubby semidesert, overgrown brushy fields, hedgerows, thickets, borders.
Voice A rasping *cha-cha-cha-cha-cha-cha*.
Field Marks 7.5″ Blackish to reddish brown forehead and crown; white line over eye; dull reddish brown above, streaked with black and white; tail and wings barred; heavy spotting below, especially on chest and lower throat, much less on buffy belly and flanks.

ROCK WREN [31, 33] Saltaladera Roquera *Salpinctes obsoletus*
Range Can–CRic, exc Blz. Res Mex (BajCal, nPac, Hi + adj Pac+Atl), Guat (Hi), ElSal.
Habitat Open dry hillsides, archaeological sites, on ground, rocks, boulders.
Field Marks 5.5″ Grayish above, with narrow spotty whitish streaks; rufous rump; white line over eye; whitish to pale buff below, with narrow streaks on breast and sides. In late summer may be very worn and faded.

CANYON WREN [31, 33] Saltaladera Risquera *Catherpes mexicanus*
Range Can–Mex. Res Mex (BajCal, Pac, ncHi + adj Atl, w.sHi).
Habitat Rocky cliffs, archaeological sites, abandoned buildings, steep rocky hillsides, rock walls, *barrancas*.
Voice A descending series of loud *chu-wee* notes, ending in a buzzy note.
Field Marks 5.5″ Mostly reddish brown above and below, except clear white throat and breast; narrow spotty streaks above; bars on wings, tail, and flanks; *no* whitish line over eye.

SUMICHRAST'S WREN [30] Saltapared Cuevero *Hylorchilus sumichrasti*
Range Mex. Res Mex (c.cAtl). Very rare and local.
Habitat Among large rocks, boulders, and small caves, in dense humid forest.
Voice An abrupt *tink*.
Field Marks 5.5″ Mostly dark brown above and below, except dull tawny face, throat, and chest, with blackish crescent bordering rear of ear patch; faint fine spots and bars below; long bill slightly decurved.

NAVA'S WREN Saltapared de Nava *Hylorchilus navai*
Range Mex. Res Mex (extreme se.cAtl+sw.sAtl). Very rare and local.
Habitat Rocky slopes, outcrops, and small caves, in humid forest.
Field Marks 5.5″ Like Sumichrast's Wren but more heavily scalloped and spotted below; throat and center of chest whitish, *not* tawny; sides of head nearly uniform dull tawny.

SPOT-BREASTED WREN [30] Saltapared Cluequita *Thryothorus maculipectus*
Range Mex–CRic. Res Mex (sPac, c.nAtl–sAtl, Yuc), Blz, Guat (Pac, Atl), ElSal.
Habitat Thickets, hedgerows, forest borders, openings, river-border woods.
Voice A loud, rhythmic *wee-sée, wee-lée-ree*.
Field Marks 5″ Mostly plain reddish brown above, basically whitish to rufous below; the only medium-sized or small wren in Mexico with heavily spotted throat and breast. Imm: few small breast spots.

RUFOUS-AND-WHITE WREN [30] Saltapared Rufiblanco *Thryothorus rufalbus*
Range Mex–Pan, exc Blz. Res Mex (c.+e.sPac), Guat (Pac+ne Atl), ElSal. Rare.
Habitat Brushy woodland borders, undergrowth in forest, *cafetales,* tall grass in weedy fields.
Voice A varied series of mellow low-pitched phrases, like hoots or trills of small owl; also *cho-cho-cho.*
Field Marks 5.5″ Bright rufous above; wings and tail barred; plain white below, except prominently barred untacs.

SINALOA WREN [30] Saltapared Sinaloense *Thryothorus sinaloa*
Range Mex. Res Mex (ncPac + adj Hi).
Habitat Shrubby grassland, brushy gullies, scrubby woods, grassy borders.
Voice Like Banded Wren's, a varied patchwork of loud, clear notes, some trills, hoots, *chew-chew,* and chipping notes.
Field Marks 5.5″ Like Plain Wren, but duller brown above and on flanks; streaked behind ear patch; barred untacs.

BANDED WREN [30] Saltapared Ventribarrado *Thryothorus pleurostictus*
Range Mex–CRic, exc Blz. Res Mex (c.cPac+sPac), Guat (Pac), ElSal.
Habitat Thickets, especially in stream valleys, hedgerows, scrubby woods, grassy borders.
Voice Varied phrases, musical trills, hooting notes, chipping notes; like canary song, lower-pitched.
Field Marks 5.5″ Dark reddish brown above; clear white below, except face and neck streaks extending to heavy black bars on sides, flanks, belly, and untacs.

CAROLINA WREN [31] Saltapared Carolinense *Thryothorus ludovicianus*
(Does not include White-browed Wren; see below)
Range US–Mex. Res Mex (nAtl + adj Hi). Rare.
Habitat Hedgerows, brushy grasslands, open woods, borders.
Voice *Toreetle-toreetle-toreetle.*
Field Marks 5.5″ Like Plain Wren, with *no* prominent streaks on or just behind ear patch, but broadly rich tawny, *not* whitish, on breast; more heavily barred wings and tail; barred untacs.

WHITE-BROWED WREN [30] Saltapared Yucateco *Thryothorus albinucha*
(The AOU lumps this with Carolina Wren; see above)
Range Mex, Blz, Guat, Nic. Res Mex (e.sAtl, Yuc), Blz (n), Guat (nw Atl). Rare.
Habitat Thickets, hedgerows, borders, undergrowth of scrubby woods.
Voice A loud *chortle-dee-chortle-dee-chortle-dee.*
Field Marks 5″ Like Plain Wren, but stripes behind ear patch; darker and grayer above and on tail; paler and duller below; barred untacs.

HAPPY WREN [30] Saltapared Feliz *Thryothorus felix*
Range Mex. Res Mex (ncPac + adj Hi).
Habitat Thickets, hedgerows, borders, scrubby woods, brushy hillsides, forest undergrowth.
Voice Like Spotted-breasted Wren's, *see-sée, wee-lée-vee.*

Field Marks 5″ Like Sinaloa Wren, but more rufous, *less* grayish, above and below; more heavily streaked on and behind ear patch; voice entirely different.

PLAIN WREN [30] Saltapared Sencillo *Thryothorus modestus*
Range Mex–Pan. Res Mex (sPac + adj Hi, s.c.sAtl + adj Hi), Blz (mt pine), Guat (Pac+Atl + adj Hi), ElSal.
Habitat Tall grass or weeds, scrubby woods, hedgerows, borders, weedy road shoulders.
Voice A very high-pitched note or two notes, then usually two loud and mellow low-pitched notes, *see-deet, clu-lu.*
Field Marks 5.5″ Brown above; rump, uptacs, and tail more reddish; white line over eye; *no* prominent streaks on or behind ear patch; whitish throat to pale grayish breast to tawny buff belly and flanks and (unbarred) untacs. Imm: darker and duller below.

BEWICK'S WREN [31] Saltapared Tepetatero *Thryomanes bewickii*
Range Can–Mex. Res Mex (BajCal, ncHi, nAtl).
Habitat Parks, vacant lots, gardens, thickets, woods, borders.
Voice One note, then a trill.
Field Marks 5″ Grayish or brownish above, whitish below; untacs barred; tail sides broadly barred, tail feathers white-tipped. Imm: breast scalloped; untacs brownish, faintly barred.

(HOUSE WREN) NORTHERN HOUSE-WREN [31] Matraquila Norteño
Troglodytes aedon
(The AOU lumps this with the Cozumel Wren and the Southern House-Wren and calls the combined species House Wren; see below)
Range Can–Mex. Res/win Mex (res n.nBajCal, w.+e.nHi+cHi; win BajCal, ncPac, ncHi, ncAtl).
Habitat Hedgerows, borders, overgrown fields, wooded river valleys.
Field Marks 5″ Dull grayish brown to dull reddish brown above; grayish to buffy brown below, with paler belly; wings, tail, flanks, and untacs barred; tail short; buffy line over eye in ncHi birds. Imm: scaly lower throat and breast.

SOUTHERN HOUSE-WREN [30] Matraquita Común *Troglodytes musculus*
(The AOU lumps this and the Cozumel Wren with Northern House-Wren and calls the combined species House Wren; see above and below)
Range Mex–SAm. ResMex (sPac, se.cHi+sHi, se.cAtl+sAtl, Yuc), Blz, Guat, ElSal.
Habitat Brushy fields, partial clearings in forest, hedgerows, suburban yards, vacant lots.
Field Marks 4.5″ Like reddish brown races of Northern House-Wren, but somewhat paler below, with whiter throat and unbarred (or very faintly barred) flanks.

COZUMEL WREN [30] Matraquita de Cozumel *Troglodytes beani*
(The AOU lumps this and Southern House-Wren with Northern House-Wren and calls the combined species House Wren; see above)
Range Mex. Res Mex (ne Yuc: Cozumel Island).

Habitat Thickets, yards, vacant lots, borders, partial clearings.
Field Marks **4.5"** Like Southern House-Wren, but paler and whiter below; slightly larger; only wren occurring regularly on Cozumel Island.

RUFOUS-BROWED WREN [30] Matraquita Cejirrufo *Troglodytes rufociliatus*
Range Mex–Nic, exc Blz. Res Mex (sHi), Guat (Hi), ElSal (w). Rare.
Habitat Humid dense pine or pine-oak forest, high cloud forest; often among epiphytes on trunks, middle branches, or fallen logs.
Field Marks **4.5"** Like Southern House-Wren, but face, breast, and (more prominent) line over eye rich reddish tawny brown; belly and untacs buffy; flanks and untacs heavily barred; tail shorter.

WINTER WREN [33] Matraquita Invernal *Troglodytes troglodytes*
Range AK–Mex. Win Mex (n.nAtl + adj Hi). Very rare.
Habitat Brushy stream valleys, forest undergrowth, dense borders.
Field Marks **4"** Dark brown above, paler brown below; heavily barred belly, flanks, and untacs; very short tail; short bill.

SEDGE WREN [31] Saltapared Sabanero *Cistothorus platensis*
Range Can–SAm, exc ElSal. Res/win Mex (res cHi, se.cAtl+w.sAtl; win n.nHi, nAtl), Blz (s), Guat (local, Hi + adj Pac). Very rare, local.
Habitat Open grassy or sedgy marsh, marshy meadows, dense tall grass.
Voice Metallic, chattering, warbling notes; also a metallic *chep.*
Field Marks **4.5"** Back streaked black and whitish; crown finely streaked brown and buff; underparts whitish, tinged pale rufous on sides, flanks, and untacs; tail and bill short.

MARSH WREN [31] Saltapared Pantanero *Cistothorus palustris*
Range Can–Mex, Blz. Res/win Mex (res ec.cHi; sum ne.nBajCal; win BajCal, ncPac, ncHi, ncAtl), Blz (acc). Rare, local.
Habitat Marshes, marshy borders of ponds, canals, lakes.
Voice A metallic, rattling song and a metallic *chuck.*
Field Marks **5"** Like Sedge Wren, but crown blackish and reddish brown, *not* streaked; back streaks more contrasty; white line over eye much more prominent; bill and tail longer.

WHITE-BELLIED WREN [30] Saltapared Cantarina *Uropsila leucogastra*
Range Mex, Blz, Guat, Hon. Res Mex (nw.cPac, s.nAtl+csAtl, Yuc), Blz (n), Guat (nw Atl). Common Atl, Yuc; rare cPac.
Habitat Scrubby thorny woods, brushy fields, thickets, overgrown clearings.
Voice A rapid, rhythmic *chip-it-ti-pee.*
Field Marks **4"** Grayish brown above; white below, with dull buff flanks and untacs; prominent white line over eye; tail short.

WHITE-BREASTED WOOD-WREN [30] Saltabreña Bajeña *Henicorhina leucosticta*
Range Mex–SAm, exc ElSal. Res Mex (sPac, csAtl), Blz, Guat (Pac, Atl).
Habitat Humid forest undergrowth, borders, partial clearings.
Voice A rhythmic *hur-dée-hur-dée-ho* or *pur-dee.*

Field Marks 4″ Dark reddish brown above; streaked face; white line over eye; white throat and breast; rusty brown belly, flanks, and untacs; barred wings and (very short) tail. Imm: breast gray.

GRAY-BREASTED WOOD-WREN [30] Saltabreña Alteña *Henicorhina leucophrys*
Range Mex–SAm, exc Blz. Res Mex (irr csHi + adj Pac+Atl), Guat (Hi + adj Pac), ElSal (n).
Habitat Cloud forest or other humid forest, thickets in openings, partial clearings, borders.
Voice In csAtl, a rapidly repeated rhythmic *chur-rée-chur-rée*, up then down; on Pacific slope of Oaxaca, more complex, like Spotted-breasted Wren's, *wee-sée, wee-lée-ree*, often sung antiphonally.
Field Marks 4″ Often in pairs. Like White-breasted Wood-Wren, but breast and upper belly dark gray, *not* white; flanks and untacs darker.

NIGHTINGALE WREN [30] Saltabreña Oscura *Microcerculus philomela*
Range Mex–CRic, exc ElSal. Res Mex (sw+sc.sAtl), Blz (s), Guat (Atl). Rare, local.
Habitat Dense humid forest undergrowth.
Voice An intriguing, long, deliberate series of random(?)-pitch musical notes.
Field Marks 4″ Dark brown above; wings and tail blackish; ear patch, throat, and breast medium grayish brown; flanks and untacs darker and more reddish brown; may have scaly throat and barred flanks. Juv: scalier throat, breast, and back.

DIPPERS—TORDOS ACUÁTICOS—CINCLIDAE

AMERICAN DIPPER [31] Tordo Acuático *Cinclus mexicanus*
Range AK–Pan, exc Blz, ElSal. Res Mex (w.nHi+irr csHi), Guat (Hi). Rare.
Habitat Along fast-flowing streams in mountain forest; walking and bobbing on banks, rocks, or in shallow water, or submerging.
Field Marks 7″ Plump body, short tail; dark gray all over except white eyelids, yellowish gray legs.

KINGLETS—REYEZUELOS—REGULIDAE

GOLDEN-CROWNED KINGLET [46] Reyezuelo de Oro *Regulus satrapa*
Range AK–Mex, Guat. Res/win Mex (res cHi; win nBajCal, n.nHi, nAtl), Guat (s Hi).
Habitat Upper branches in dense humid pine-oak or fir forests.
Field Marks 3.7″ Grayish olive above, paler below; two white wing bars; head striped black and white, with crown patch orange (male) or yellow (female); tiny bill.

RUBY-CROWNED KINGLET [46] Reyezuelo de Rojo *Regulus calendula*
Range AK–Mex, Guat. Res?/win Mex (res? Guadalupe Island off nBajCal; win/cas all, exc sPac?), Guat (cas Hi).

Habitat Forest, open woods, tree-dotted fields, thickets, borders.
Field Marks 3.7" Like Golden-crowned Kinglet, but head and face mostly greenish gray, *not* striped; white eye ring; M: red crown patch (usually hidden).

GNATCATCHERS—PERLITAS—SYLVIIDAE

LONG-BILLED GNATWREN [34] Saltón Picudo *Ramphocaenus melanurus*
Range Mex–SAm. Res Mex (sPac, se.cAtl+sAtl, s+e Yuc), Blz, Guat (Pac, Atl), ElSal. Rare.
Habitat Undergrowth of dense forest, forest borders, thickets, partial clearings.
Voice A musical, extended trill, usually rising in pitch.
Field Marks 5" Bill long, slender, straight, dark brown and orange; back grayish olive; crown brown; breast (and sides of neck and face) pale tawny; throat white, usually speckled with black; tail short, graduated, tail feathers white-tipped.

BLUE-GRAY GNATCATCHER [46] Perlita Común *Polioptila caerulea*
Range Can–ElSal, Hon. Res/win Mex, Blz, Guat, ElSal (w).
Habitat Shrub-dotted fields, thickets, open woods, borders, scrubby woods.
Field Marks 4.5" M: pale bluish gray above, white below; white feather edgings on blackish wings; forehead and sides of crown narrowly black; eye ring white; long tail mostly black above, white below. F: paler, duller, *no* black on head.

CALIFORNIA GNATCATCHER Perlita Plomiza *Polioptila californica*
Range US–Mex. Res Mex (w+s.nBajCal+sBajCal).
Habitat Scrubby woods, wooded river valleys, overgrown clearings, borders, brushy semidesert.
Field Marks Like Black-tailed Gnatcatcher, but underparts pale to medium gray, *not* white, and narrowly white tail tip.

BLACK-TAILED GNATCATCHER [46] Perlita Desértica. *Polioptila melanura*
Range US–Mex. Res Mex (ne.nBajCal, n.nPac, nHi+n.cHi).
Habitat Scrubby woods, borders, hedgerows, overgrown fields, partial clearings.
Field Marks 4" Like Blue-gray Gnatcatcher, but tail black with narrow white sides, above and below, and broadly white tip from below; Sum M: entire crown black; Win M: little or no black on sides of crown, forehead, or forecrown.

BLACK-CAPPED GNATCATCHER [34] Perlita Sinaloense *Polioptila nigriceps*
Range US–Mex. Res Mex (nPac+nw.cPac).
Habitat Scrubby woods and borders, river valleys, thickets, hedgerows, tree-dotted brushy fields.
Field Marks 4.5" Like Blue-gray Gnatcatcher, but Sum M: entire crown black; F+win M: like female Blue-gray Gnatcatcher, but eye ring less prominent, tail slightly longer; cheeks may be whiter.

WHITE-LORED GNATCATCHER [34] Perlita Cejiblanca *Polioptila albiloris*
Range Mex–CRic, exc Blz. Res Mex (csPac + adj Hi, n Yuc), Guat (Pac), ElSal.

Habitat Grassy, brushy, open fields, vacant lots, borders, overgrown clearings, thickets.
Field Marks 4.5″ Like Blue-gray Gnatcatcher, but Sum M: entire crown black to eyes; Win M: crown black; lores and line over eye white; F: lores and line over eye white. See Tropical Gnatcatcher.

TROPICAL GNATCATCHER [34] Perlita Tropical *Polioptila plumbea*
Range Mex–SAm, exc ElSal. Res Mex (se.cAtl+sAtl, s+e Yuc), Blz, Guat (Atl).
Habitat Humid forest, forest borders, or humid overgrown clearings; usually middle branches or higher.
Field Marks 4.5″ Like winter White-lored Gnatcatcher, but broader white line over eye, winter and summer; ranges do not overlap.

THRUSHES, ROBINS   ZORZALES, MIRLILLOS—TURDIDAE

EASTERN BLUEBIRD [33] Azulejo Gorjicanelo *Sialia sialis*
Range Can–Nic. Res/win Mex (res ncPac, w.nHi+cshi; res/win nAtl; cas n Yuc), Blz (mt pine), Guat (Hi + adj Pac), ElSal.
Habitat Gardens, parks, villages, borders, partial clearings, open pine woods.
Field Marks 6.5″ M: uniform medium blue above; throat and breast bright rufous; belly and untacs white. F: paler, duller; in worn plumage may appear very drab.

WESTERN BLUEBIRD [33] Azulejo Gorjiazul *Sialia mexicana*
Range Can–Mex. Res/win Mex (res n.nBajCal, ncHi; win n.nPac).
Habitat Tree-dotted grasslands, mountain pine forest, borders, partial clearings.
Field Marks 6.5″ Like Eastern Bluebird, but M: throat broadly purplish blue, *not* rufous; usually some rufous across upper back; F: throat and sides of neck more grayish; back brownish, *not* grayish.

MOUNTAIN BLUEBIRD [33] Azulejo Pálido *Sialia currucoides*
Range AK–Mex. Win Mex (n.nBajCal, n.nPac, nHi+n.cHi). Rare.
Habitat Tree-dotted open areas, junipers, partial clearings, pine woods.
Field Marks 6.5″ M: grayish blue above, pale blue and white below. F: throat and breast usually pale grayish, only slightly tinged rufous, if at all.

TOWNSEND'S SOLITAIRE [31] Clarín Norteño *Myadestes townsendi*
Range AK–Mex. Res/win Mex (res w.nHi; win n.nBajCal, n.nPac, n.nHi).
Habitat Middle or upper branches, large trees in pine or open pine-oak forest.
Field Marks 8″ Perches upright. Plumage mostly medium gray; eye ring and sides of tail whitish; wing patch buffy.

BROWN-BACKED SOLITAIRE [32] Clarín Jilguero *Myadestes occidentalis*
Range Mex–Hon, exc Blz. Res Mex (Pac, Hi, Atl), Guat (Hi), ElSal.
Habitat Humid forest, borders, partial clearings, scrubby woods, forests of pine, pine-oak, or fir.

Voice A remarkable cascade of sibilant yet musical notes.
Field Marks 8″ Grayish above, with brownish rump and scapulars, and mostly rufous wings; black line down side of white throat; eye ring and sides of tail whitish.

SLATE-COLORED SOLITAIRE [32] Clarín Unicolor *Myadestes unicolor*
Range Mex–Nic. Res Mex (e.cHi + adj Atl, n.sHi + adj Pac+Atl), Blz (s), Guat (Atl + adj Hi), ElSal (n).
Habitat Cloud forest, other humid forest.
Field Marks 8″ Nearly uniform dark bluish gray, but eye ring and sides of tail white.

ORANGE-BILLED NIGHTINGALE-THRUSH [32] Zorzalito Piquinaranja *Catharus aurantiirostris*
Range Mex–SAm, exc Blz. Res Mex (Pac, Hi, Atl), Guat (Hi), ElSal.
Habitat Hedgerows, gardens, parks, borders, humid forest.
Field Marks 6.5″ Tawny brown above, whitish below; bill, eye ring, and legs orange.

RUSSET NIGHTINGALE-THRUSH [32] Zorzalito Piquipardo *Catharus occidentalis*
Range Mex. Res Mex (w+e.nHi+s.cHi).
Habitat Pine, pine-oak, or fir forest, borders.
Field Marks 6.5″ Like Ruddy-capped Nightingale-Thrush, but tawnier above; bill darker below; extended wing shows buffy patch; breast obscurely streaked or scalloped.

RUDDY-CAPPED NIGHTINGALE-THRUSH [32] Zorzalito de Frantzius *Catharus frantzii*
Range Mex–Pan, exc Blz. Res Mex (irr csHi), Guat (Hi), ElSal (w).
Habitat Humid mountain forest, forest borders, nearby thickets.
Field Marks 6.5″ Grayish rufous above; throat, but *not* breast, faintly streaked; *no* buffy wing patch; bill orange below. See Russet Nightingale-Thrush.

BLACK-HEADED NIGHTINGALE-THRUSH [32] Zorzalito Solitario *Catharus mexicanus*
Range Mex–Pan, exc Blz, ElSal. Res Mex (irr s.nAtl+csAtl + adj Hi; local w.sPac), Guat (Hi + adj Atl).
Habitat Cloud forest, nearby lush gardens, borders.
Field Marks 6.5″ Dark olive above; top and sides of head black; whitish below with grayish breast; belly and untacs white; bill and eye ring orange.

SPOTTED NIGHTINGALE-THRUSH [32] Zorzalito Pinto *Catharus dryas*
Range Mex–Hon, exc Blz; SAm. Res Mex (sHi + adj Pac+Atl), Guat (Hi), ElSal (n). Rare.
Habitat Cloud forest and other humid forest undergrowth.
Field Marks 7″ Dark bluish gray above; top and sides of head broadly black; whitish below, with dull dark spots on salmon to orange breast; bill, eye ring, and long legs orange.

VEERY [33] Mirlillo Rojizo *Catharus fuscescens*
Range Can–SAm, exc ElSal. Tr Mex (csAtl, Yuc), Blz, Guat (Atl). Rare.
Habitat Thickets, scrubby woods or borders.
Field Marks 7″ Tawny brown above, whitish below; breast lightly spotted dark brown on buff.

GRAY-CHEEKED THRUSH [33] Mirlillo Carigris *Catharus minimus*
Range AK–SAm, exc ElSal, Nic. Tr Mex (csAtl, Yuc), Blz, Guat (Atl). Rare.
Habitat Borders, forest floor, partial clearings.
Field Marks 7″ Like Swainson's Thrush, but grayish cheeks, less noticeable eye ring.

SWAINSON'S THRUSH [33] Mirlillo de Swainson *Catharus ustulatus*
Range AK–SAm. Tr/win Mex, Blz, Guat, ElSal.
Habitat Forest, partial clearings, borders.
Field Marks 7″ Grayish to brownish olive above; prominent buffy eye ring and brownish buff cheeks; whitish below, heavily spotted on buffy breast.

HERMIT THRUSH [33] Mirlillo Colirrufo *Catharus guttatus*
Range AK–Mex, Guat, ElSal. Res/win Mex (res mts n.nBajCal; win BajCal, Pac, Hi, ncAtl), Guat (Ili), ElSal (cas).
Habitat Gardens, borders, dense forest, partial clearings.
Field Marks 6.5″ Like Gray-cheeked Thrush, but browner cheeks and back; contrasty reddish brown rump, uptacs, and tail.

WOOD THRUSH [33] Mirlillo Maculado *Hylocichla mustelina*
Range Can–SAm. Tr/win Mex (sPac, Atl, Yuc; acc nPac), Blz, Guat, ElSal.
Habitat Humid forest, scrubby woods.
Field Marks 7.5″ More boldly spotted and appears heavier than similar thrushes; contrasty bright rufous on head and upper back.

BLACK ROBIN [32] Zorzal Negro *Turdus infuscatus*
Range Mex, Guat, ElSal, Hon. Res Mex (s.csHi + adj Pac, e.ncHi+n.sHi + adj Atl), Guat (Hi), ElSal (w). Rare.
Habitat Cloud forest, humid pine or pine-oak forest.
Field Marks 9″ M: black; narrow eye ring red; bill and legs yellow. F: dark brown, tinged grayish above and reddish below, with buffy, streaked throat. See Mountain and Rufous-collared Robins.

MOUNTAIN ROBIN [32] Zorzal Serrano *Turdus plebejus*
Range Mex–Pan, exc Blz. Res Mex (s.sHi), Guat (Hi), ElSal (n). Rare.
Habitat Humid forest, borders, partial clearings.
Voice A loud *kwang*.
Field Marks 10″ Blackish olive-brown above; underparts paler, but *not* rufous; bill and legs black.

CLAY-COLORED ROBIN [32] Zorzal Merulín *Turdus grayi*
Range US–SAm. Res Mex (sPac + adj Hi, Atl + adj Hi, Yuc), Blz, Guat (Pac, Hi?, Atl), ElSal.

Habitat Gardens, parks, hedgerows, river-border woods, forest borders.
Field Marks 9″ Races vary. Pale grayish olive to olive-buff above; tawny olive to rich buff below; throat pale buff, faintly streaked; bill brownish yellow.

WHITE-THROATED ROBIN [32] Zorzal Gorjiblanco *Turdus assimilis*
Range Mex–SAm. Res Mex (Pac+Atl + adj Hi), Blz, Guat (Pac, Atl + adj Hi), ElSal.
Habitat Dense humid forest, borders, plantations, lush gardens, river-border woods.
Field Marks 9″ Races vary. Buffy olive to dark olive-gray above; pale grayish brown to olive-gray below; most of white throat heavily streaked; narrow eye ring orange; bill and legs yellowish. See Clay-colored Robin.

RUFOUS-BACKED ROBIN [32] Zorzal Chivillo *Turdus rufopalliatus*
(Does not include Grayson's Robin; see below)
Range Mex. Res Mex (ncPac + Mexico City + Oaxaca).
Habitat Gardens, hedgerows, parks, plantations, open or dense woods, borders.
Field Marks 9″ Tawny rufous, with mostly bluish gray tail, wings, and head; belly, untacs, and streaked throat whitish. F: paler and duller than male, but brighter and more contrasty than Clay-colored Robin.

GRAYSON'S ROBIN Zorzal de las Islas *Turdus graysoni*
(The AOU lumps this with Rufous-backed Robin; see above)
Range Mex. Res/vis Mex (res islands off cPac; res/vis s.nPac). Common on islands, very rare on mainland.
Habitat Open or dense forest, plantations, hedgerows, borders, scrubby woods.
Field Marks 9″ Like Rufous-backed Robin, but much duller, grayer, and larger-billed.

RUFOUS-COLLARED ROBIN [32] Zorzal Cuellirrufo *Turdus rufitorques*
Range Mex, Guat, ElSal, Hon. Res Mex (sHi), Guat (Hi), ElSal (w).
Habitat Open or dense pine or pine-oak forest, borders, openings, partial clearings.
Field Marks 10″ Bill and legs yellowish; untacs white-streaked. M: black, except rich rufous breast and broad collar. F: similar pattern, but pale to medium brownish gray, *not* black; pale dull brownish tawny, *not* rufous.

AMERICAN ROBIN [31, 32] Zorzal Real *Turdus migratorius*
American Group [31] Zorzal Real *T. m. migratorius*
Range AK–Mex, Guat? Res/win Mex (res n.nBajCal, w+e.nHi+cHi; win BajCal, n.nPac, nHi, ncAtl; cas Yuc), Guat? (Hi).
Habitat Gardens, parks, hedgerows, borders, pine forest, dense pine-oak woods.
Field Marks 10″ M: blackish and dark gray above; white eye ring; breast broadly brownish orange; throat white, streaked black. F: slightly paler and duller.

San Lucas group [32] Zorzal del Cabo *T. m. confinis*
Range Mex. Res Mex (mts s.sBajCal).
Habitat Woods, borders, partial clearings, openings.
Field Marks 10" Like American group, but much paler gray above, mostly buff below; throat streaks very faint.

VARIED THRUSH Mirlo Pinto *Ixoreus naevius*
Range AK–Mex. Win Mex (n.nBajCal). Rare.
Habitat Woods, borders, partial clearings.
Field Marks 9" M: dark slaty gray above; black breast band and ear patch; rufous wing bars; tawny rufous eye line, malar area, throat, and breast. F: similar pattern, but much duller and paler.

AZTEC THRUSH [32] Mirlo Azteca *Ridgwayia pinicola*
Range US–Mex, ElSal? Res Mex (w+e.nHi, local cHi), acc ElSal. Rare.
Habitat Pine, pine-oak, or fir forest, borders.
Field Marks 8" M: boldly blackish brown and white; upperparts obscurely brown-streaked. F: somewhat paler, duller, and more noticeably streaked than shown.

WRENTITS—CAMEAS—TIMALIIDAE

WRENTIT [31] Camea *Chamaea fasciata*
Range US–Mex. Res Mex (nw nBajCal).
Habitat Dry, dense, scrubby vegetation.
Voice A soft *chirr;* also a loud accelerating series of bouncing, chattering, musical notes.
Field Marks 6" Dark grayish brown; faintly streaked below; eyes white; tail long.

THRASHERS—CUITLACOCHES—MIMIDAE

GRAY CATBIRD [33] Mímido Gris *Dumetella carolinensis*
Range Can–Pan. Win Mex (sPac, Atl, Yuc; cas/acc nBajCal, ncPac), Blz, Guat (Hi, Atl), ElSal (cas w).
Habitat Forest undergrowth, partial clearings, borders, hedgerows.
Field Marks 8" Slate gray, with black cap and dark reddish brown untacs.

BLACK CATBIRD [32] Mímido Negro *Melanoptila glabrirostris*
Range Mex, Blz, Guat, Hon. Res Mex (e.sAtl, Yuc), Blz (n), Guat (nw Atl). Common on Cozumel Island, rare elsewhere.
Habitat Scrubby woods or borders, gardens, hedgerows, thickets, humid forest openings.
Field Marks 8" Glossy black, including bill and legs; eyes dark reddish brown.

NORTHERN MOCKINGBIRD [31] Cenzontle Norteño *Mimus polyglottos*
Range Can–Mex. Res Mex (BajCal, ncPac, ncHi, ncAtl).

Habitat Thickets, hedgerows, tree-dotted pastures, farms, gardens, parks, borders.
Field Marks 9″ Wing bars and sides of tail white; large white wing patch shows in flight. See Tropical Mockingbird.

TROPICAL MOCKINGBIRD [32] Cenzontle Tropical *Mimus gilvus*
Range Mex–SAm, exc Nic, CRic. Res Mex (sPac, sHi, sAtl, Yuc), Blz (n), Guat (w Pac, Hi, e Atl), ElSal.
Habitat Thickets, hedgerows, farmyards, gardens, parks, scrubby woods, borders.
Field Marks 10″ Like Northern Mockingbird, but much less white on extended wing, much more white on tail tip.

SAGE THRASHER [33] Mímido Pinto *Oreoscoptes montanus*
Range Can–Mex. Win Mex (BajCal, nPac, nHi, n.nAtl). Rare.
Habitat Open arid areas, shrub-dotted fields.
Field Marks 8″ Grayer and shorter-billed than other thrashers; tail corners and narrow wing bars white; underparts heavily streaked black on whitish.

BROWN THRASHER Cuitlacoche Rojizo *Toxostoma rufum*
Range Can–Mex. Win Mex (nPac, nAtl). Very rare/casual.
Habitat Hedgerows, borders, scrubby woods, thickets.
Field Marks 11″ Like Long-billed Thrasher, but more reddish above, especially on head; a shorter, straighter bill; yellow eyes.

LONG-BILLED THRASHER [31] Cuitlacoche Piquilargo *Toxostoma longirostre*
Range US–Mex. Res Mex (nAtl+n.cAtl).
Habitat Scrubby woods, thickets, borders.
Field Marks 11″ Grayish rufous above; sides of head pale gray; whitish below with heavy blackish streaks; eyes orange or orange-yellow; bill medium long and decurved.

COZUMEL THRASHER [32] Cuitlacoche de Cozumel *Toxostoma guttatum*
Range Mex. Res Mex (ne Yuc: Cozumel Island)
Habitat Scrubby woods, borders, thickets.
Field Marks 10″ Rufous above; heavy blackish streaks below; eyes red.

GRAY THRASHER [32] Cuitlacoche Peninsular *Toxostoma cinereum*
Range Mex. Res Mex (BajCal).
Habitat Scrubby brushy areas, semidesert.
Field Marks 10″ Brownish gray above; heavy black streaks (made up of triangular spots) on white to pale buff below; eyes orange-yellow.

BENDIRE'S THRASHER [31] Cuitlacoche Sonorense *Toxostoma bendirei*
Range US–Mex. Res Mex (n.nPac; acc ne.nBajCal).
Habitat Open arid country, semidesert, scrubby woods, thickets, brushy fields.
Field Marks 10″ Like Curve-billed Thrasher, but slightly browner above; bill shorter and straighter; streaks finer; eyes paler yellow.

OCELLATED THRASHER [32] Cuitlacoche Manchado *Toxostoma ocellatum*
Range Mex. Res Mex (nc–s.cHi). Rare, local.
Habitat Dense scrubby woods; humid oak, pine-oak, or fir forest; borders, partial clearings.
Field Marks 10″ The spots forming its breast streaks are larger, blacker, and more nearly round than those of any other thrasher.

CURVE-BILLED THRASHER [31] Cuitlacoche Común *Toxostoma curvirostre*
Range US–Mex. Res Mex (nPac, ncHi, nAtl).
Habitat Shrubby gardens, parks, thickets, scrub woods, borders.
Voice A loud *whit-whit.*
Field Marks 11″ Races vary. Especially nondescript in worn plumage; usually some buffy tinge below; spots in breast streaks obscure or rather prominent; tail corners pale buff or whitish; bill medium long and decurved; eyes orange-yellow.

CALIFORNIA THRASHER [31] Cuitlacoche Californiano *Toxostoma redivivum*
Range US–Mex. Res Mex (nw.nBajCal).
Habitat Scrubby woods, chaparral, semidesert.
Field Marks 11″ Like Crissal Thrasher, but breast darker and browner; belly and untacs paler cinnamon-buff, *not* rufous.

CRISSAL THRASHER [31] Cuitlacoche Crisal *Toxostoma crissale*
Range US–Mex. Res Mex (ne.nBajCal, nPac, nHi). Rare, local.
Habitat Arid areas with dense scrubby or thorny vegetation.
Field Marks 11″ Belly and untacs (crissum) rich reddish brown; submalar streak prominent; breast medium gray.

LE CONTE'S THRASHER [31] Cuitlacoche Pálido *Toxostoma lecontei*
Range US–Mex. Res Mex (near sea level BajCal, nPac, Sonora).
Habitat Sparse semidesert or desert.
Field Marks 11″ Paler and more nearly uniform gray than other thrashers; untacs pale tawny.

BLUE MOCKINGBIRD [32] Mulato Común *Melanotis caerulescens*
Range Mex. Res Mex (ncPac, w+se.nHi + cHi + adj Atl). Irregular.
Habitat Cloud forest, other humid forest, borders, thickets, scrub woods.
Field Marks 10″ Dark blue with some pale blue streaks; sides of face black; eyes red. Juv: dull blackish gray to blackish blue.

BLUE-AND-WHITE MOCKINGBIRD [32] Mulato Pechiblanco *Melanotis hypoleucus*
Range Mex, Guat, ElSal, Hon. Res Mex (sHi + adj Pac+Atl), Guat (Hi), ElSal (w).
Habitat Scrubby woods, forest borders, scattered thickets, undergrowth in open woods.
Field Marks 10″ Like Blue Mockingbird, but throat, breast, and upper belly white. Juv: dull blackish, with bluish tinge.

STARLINGS—ESTORNINOS—STURNIDAE

EUROPEAN STARLING [33] Estornino Pinto *Sturnus vulgaris*
Range AK–Mex. Res Mex (BajCal, nPac, ncHi, ncAtl, Yuc). Range expanding.
Habitat Parks, gardens, downtown buildings, suburban areas, pastures, farms.
Field Marks 8″ Basically black; short tail; pointed bill. Win: many small buff spots, which wear away gradually; bill black. Sum: obscurely speckled; bill yellow. Juv: dark brownish gray.

PIPITS—BISBITAS—MOTACILLIDAE

AMERICAN PIPIT [33] Bisbita Americana *Anthus rubescens*
Range AK–Mex, Guat, ElSal. Win Mex (all exc sPac+sHi), Guat (Hi), ElSal (cas). Irregular.
Habitat Short grass or bare open fields, lakeshores, pastures.
Field Marks 6″ Often in flocks, bobs tail as it walks. Grayish olive above; buffy to whitish below, with white outer tail feathers, blackish legs; dark streaks most prominent in fall and winter.

SPRAGUE'S PIPIT [33] Bisbita Llanera *Anthus spragueii*
Range Can–Mex. Win Mex (ncHi + adj Pac, ncAtl). Rare.
Habitat Grassy fields, medium or taller grass.
Field Marks 6″ Like American Pipit, but much more prominent streaks above; legs yellowish to pinkish, *not* blackish.

WAXWINGS—CHINITOS—BOMBYCILLIDAE

CEDAR WAXWING [33] Chinito *Bombycilla cedrorum*
Range AK–Pan. Win Mex, Blz, Guat, ElSal. Irregular.
Habitat Usually in flocks in gardens, parks, open woods, borders, orchards.
Field Marks 6″ Crested. Adt: black throat and mask; yellow-tipped gray and black tail; may have red tips on some wing feathers. Juv: paler and duller; head and underparts streaked.

SILKY-FLYCATCHERS—CAPULINEROS—PTILOGONATIDAE

GRAY SILKY-FLYCATCHER [34] Capulinero Gris *Ptilogonys cinereus*
Range Mex, Guat. Res Mex (w+e.nHi+csHi + adj Pac+Atl), Guat (Hi).
Habitat Pine-oak or fir forest, borders, partial clearings, or pure pine or oak woods; often in flocks eating mistletoe berries or catching insects.
Field Marks 8″ Crested; short black bill. M: mostly pale brownish gray, with tawny flanks, yellow untacs; blackish tail, with broad white crossbar seen from below. F: more cinnamon-gray above and below, including flanks.

PHAINOPEPLA [40] Capulinero Negro *Phainopepla nitens*
Range US–Mex. Res Mex (BajCal, n.nPac, ncHi). Rare; mostly win cHi.

Habitat Sparsely wooded dry shrubby areas or semidesert; perches upright on wires, treetops, shrubtops.
Field Marks 7″ Crested; eyes red. M: glossy black except large white patch in extended wing. F: brownish gray, with darker crest and tail; duller wing patch; untacs scalloped whitish and blackish.

OLIVE WARBLERS—CHIPES OLIVÁCEOS—PEUCEDRAMIDAE

OLIVE WARBLER [35] Chipe Oliváceo *Peucedramus taeniatus*
Range US–Nic, exc Blz. Res Mex (w+ne.nHi+cshi), Guat (Hi), ElSal (n).
Habitat Open pine forest or semihumid pine-oak woods, upper branches.
Voice A musical *wheeta, wheeta, wheeta.*
Field Marks 5″ Grayish above, mostly white below. M: entire head and chest orange-brown except black mask; white wing bars and tail patches. F+imm: head and upper breast yellowish; mask gray; faint wing bars.

WOOD-WARBLERS—CHIPES—PARULIDAE

BLUE-WINGED WARBLER [36] Chipe Aliazul *Vermivora pinus*
Range Can–Pan. Tr/win Mex (se.cPac+sPac, Atl, Yuc), Blz, Guat (Pac, Atl), ElSal (cas). Rare.
Habitat Dense humid forest, open woods, borders.
Field Marks 4.5″ M: hindneck and upperparts brownish gray; head and underparts mostly bright yellow; black line through eye; white bars on bluish wings. F: similar pattern but paler and duller.

GOLDEN-WINGED WARBLER [36] Chipe Alidorado *Vermivora chrysoptera*
Range Can–SAm. Tr/win Mex (cPac, se.cAtl+sAtl, Yuc), Blz, Guat (Atl), ElSal. Very rare.
Habitat Humid forest, borders, partial clearings.
Field Marks 4.5″ M: bluish gray above, with yellow crown; black ear patch and throat; yellow marks on wing. F: similar pattern but paler and duller.

HYBRIDS OF GOLDEN-WINGED WARBLER AND BLUE-WINGED WARBLER [36]
Brewster's Warbler Like Blue-winged, but white mostly replaces yellow.
Lawrence's Warbler Like Golden-winged, but yellow replaces white.

TENNESSEE WARBLER [36] Chipe Peregrino *Vermivora peregrina*
Range AK–SAm. Tr/win Mex (irr all exc nHi), Blz, Guat, ElSal. Rare, except sPac.
Habitat Humid forest, open woods, trees in pastures, borders, hedgerows.
Field Marks 4.5″ Sum M: grayish green above, white below; head pale gray; white throat and line over eye. F+win M+imm: more yellowish overall; faint wing bar.

ORANGE-CROWNED WARBLER [35] Chipe Celato *Vermivora celata*
Range AK–Mex, Blz, Guat, ElSal. Res/win Mex (res nBajCal; win BajCal, Pac, Hi, ncAtl; cas/very rare sAtl, Yuc), Blz (cas), Guat (Hi), ElSal (cas).

Habitat Open pine, pine-oak, or fir forest, thickets, gardens, parks, borders.
Field Marks **4.5″** Races vary. Greenish gray to grayish olive above; yellowish gray to grayish yellow below, with faint dark streaks; faint line over eye; hidden crown patch.

NASHVILLE WARBLER [36] Chipe Gorrigrís *Vermivora ruficapilla*
Range Can–Mex, Blz, Guat, ElSal, Hon. Tr/win Mex (BajCal, Pac, Hi, ncAtl; cas Yuc), Blz (cas), Guat (Pac + adj Hi, cas Atl), ElSal.
Habitat Open or dense woods, thickets, gardens, parks, borders.
Field Marks **4.5″** Greenish olive above; wings darker; white eye ring; gray head with reddish brown crown patch; bright yellow below. F+imm: similar but slightly duller.

VIRGINIA'S WARBLER [35] Chipe de Virginia *Vermivora virginiae*
Range US–Mex, Blz, Guat. Tr/win Mex (ncPac, ncHi), Blz (acc), Guat (acc Atl). Rare.
Habitat Brushy areas, scrubby woods, arroyos, borders.
Field Marks **4.5″** Gray above; crown patch rufous; eye ring white; breast, rump, uptacs, and untacs bright yellow; throat and belly whitish. Imm: crown gray; breast and belly buff.

COLIMA WARBLER [35] Chipe Colimense *Vermivora crissalis*
Range US–Mex. Sum/win Mex (sum ne.nHi; win sw.nHi, cHi). Rare.
Habitat Undergrowth of open or scrubby pine woods, or oak or fir forest.
Field Marks **5″** Like Virginia's Warbler, but browner; untacs, uptacs, and rump buffier; breast whitish.

LUCY'S WARBLER [35] Chipe de Lucía *Vermivora luciae*
Range US–Mex. Sum/win Mex (sum ne.nBajCal, n.nPac; tr/win sBajCal, ncPac).
Habitat Arroyos, river valleys, open or dense woods, borders.
Field Marks **4.5″** Like Colima Warbler, but entirely white below; rump patch rufous, *not* buffy yellow.

NORTHERN PARULA [36] Párula Norteña *Parula americana*
Range Can–CRic. Tr/win Mex (se.cPac, Atl, Yuc; cas/very rare ncHi), Blz (cstl), Guat (Pac, Atl), ElSal (acc). Rare.
Habitat Wooded riversides, dense thorny woods, partial clearings, borders, gardens.
Field Marks **4.5″** M: grayish blue above; yellowish olive back patch; yellow throat and breast, black and reddish patch on lower throat and chest; belly, untacs, partial eye ring, and wing bars white. F: paler and greener above; only a trace of breast patch, or none.

TROPICAL PARULA [36, 38] Párula Tropical *Parula pitiayumi*
Range US–SAm. Res Mex (ncPac + adj Hi, Atl + adj Hi), Blz (cas), Guat (Pac, Atl). Local.

Habitat Humid forest, riverside woods, borders, partial clearings.
Field Marks 4.5″ Like Northern Parula, but throat and upper breast tawnier; *no* eye ring; *no* well-defined breast patch. M: ear patch black.

(CRESCENT-CHESTED) SPOT-BREASTED WARBLER [38] Chipe Cejiblanco *Parula superciliosa*
Range Mex–Nic, exc Blz. Res Mex (w.+e.nHi+csHi), Guat (Hi), ElSal.
Habitat Pine, pine-oak, or fir forest.
Field Marks 4.5″ Greenish olive back; gray head with white line over eye; yellow throat and breast, with chestnut breast patch; belly and untacs white.

YELLOW WARBLER [36] Chipe Amarillo *Dendroica petechia*
(Does not include Mangrove Warbler; see below)
Range AK–SAm. Sum/win Mex (res ne Yuc: Cozumel Island; sum n.nBajCal, n.nPac, w.ncHi; tr/win all); win Blz, Guat, ElSal.
Habitat Gardens, parks, scrubby woods, wooded riversides, scattered trees, borders.
Field Marks 4.5″ M: greenish yellow above (crown rufous in Cozumel Island birds: Golden Warbler); rufous streaks on bright yellow below; tail mostly yellow below. F: unstreaked, yellowish. See also Mangrove Warbler.

MANGROVE WARBLER [38] Chipe Manglero *Dendroica erithachorides*
(The AOU lumps this with Yellow Warbler; see above)
Range Mex–SAm. Res cstl Mex (sBajCal, Pac, Atl, Yuc), Blz (cstl + cayes), Guat (cstl), ElSal (cstl). Local.
Habitat In or near mangroves.
Field Marks 4.5″ Like Yellow Warbler, but M: entire head rufous.

CHESTNUT-SIDED WARBLER [37] Chipe Gorriamarillo *Dendroica pensylvanica*
Range Can–SAm. Tr/win Mex (Atl, Yuc; acc/very rare BajCal, Pac), Blz, Guat (Atl), ElSal (acc). Rare in winter.
Habitat Humid forest, river-border woods, open scrubby woods, borders, hedgerows.
Field Marks 4.5″ Sum adt: back heavily streaked, black on yellowish green; two white wing bars; white below with broad chestnut streak on side; black line through eye. Imm+win adt: bright yellow-green above, white below; wing bars; *no* black on face; may be faintly streaked above; may show trace of rufous on sides.

MAGNOLIA WARBLER [36] Chipe Colifajado *Dendroica magnolia*
Range AK–Pan. Tr/win Mex (csPac, csHi, Atl, Yuc), Blz, Guat, ElSal.
Habitat Open woods, borders, wooded riversides, lush gardens, orchards, overgrown clearings.
Field Marks 4.5″ Much like Yellow-rumped Warbler, heavily streaked, but basically yellow below, *not* white; broad white midtail bar, most of tail white from below; entire crown grayish.

CAPE MAY WARBLER [36] Chipe Atigrado *Dendroica tigrina*
Range Can–Pan. Tr/win Mex (cstl e.sAtl, e Yuc; acc/very rare Pac, Hi, c+w Yuc), Blz (cstl + cayes); cas/acc Guat, ElSal (cas). Rare.
Habitat Dense scrubby woods, borders, partial clearings.
Field Marks 4.5″ Sum M: black-streaked olive above, with yellow rump; side of head yellow, with chestnut ear patch; yellow below with heavy black streaks. F+win M: paler and duller; sides of head mostly gray; yellow patch on side of neck. Imm: still paler and duller; no yellow except on rump; trace of pale color on side of neck.

BLACK-THROATED BLUE WARBLER [36] Chipe Azuloso *Dendroica caerulescens*
Range Can–Mex, Blz, Guat, CRic, SAm. Win Mex (e.sAtl, e Yuc; cas/acc BajCal, nPac, sHi), Blz (cstl + cayes), Guat (Hi?, Atl). Very rare.
Habitat Humid forest, drier woods, borders, partial clearings.
Field Marks 5″ M: grayish blue above; black face, throat, and sides; rest of underparts and spot on wing white. F: greenish to brownish gray; small spot on wing and line over eye white; ear patch blackish.

YELLOW-RUMPED WARBLER [35] Chipe Común *Dendroica coronata*
Myrtle group Chipe Común *D. c. coronata*
Range AK–Pan. Win Mex, Blz, Guat, ElSal.
Habitat Pine-oak or oak woods, forest borders, semidesert, overgrown clearings, gardens.
Field Marks 5″ Sum M: streaked bluish gray above; rump, crown, and side patch yellow; face black and white; breast black and sides streaked black; throat, belly, and untacs white. Sum F: duller; brownish; streaked above and below. Imm+ win adt: duller, not as much yellow.
Audubon's group [35] Chipe de Audubón *D. c. auduboni*
Range AK–Mex, Guat, Hon. Res/win Mex (res mts n.nBajCal, w.nHi; win BajCal, ncPac, Hi, nAtl), Guat (res Hi).
Habitat Pine-oak, pine, or fir forest, borders, overgrown fields, hedgerows.
Field Marks 5″ Like Myrtle group, but throat usually yellow(ish); lacks white line over eye; Sum M: more broadly black breast.

BLACK-THROATED GRAY WARBLER [35] Chipe Negrigrís *Dendroica nigrescens*
Range Can–Mex, Guat. Sum/win Mex (mts n.nBajCal, n.nPac; tr/win BajCal, ncPac, ncHi, ncAtl), acc Guat (Pac).
Habitat Open pine or pine-oak woods, borders, scrubby woods, partial clearings.
Field Marks 4.5″ Like Blackpoll and Black-and-white Warblers, but faint, *not* bold, streaks above; blackish ear patch; usually small yellow spot in front of eye.

TOWNSEND'S WARBLER [36] Chipe Negriamarillo *Dendroica townsendi*
Range AK–CRic, exc Blz. Tr/win Mex (BajCal, Pac, Hi), Guat (mostly Pac, Hi), ElSal.
Habitat Pine, pine-oak, or fir forest, scrubby woods.
Field Marks 4.5″ M: crown, throat, and extensive ear patch black; breast and

sides yellow, with black streaks on sides. F+imm: duller overall; throat yellow, *not* black; dark ear patch prominent.

HERMIT WARBLER [36] Chipe Coronado *Dendroica occidentalis*
Range Can–Nic. Tr/win Mex (nBajCal, Pac, Hi), Blz (acc), Guat (Hi), ElSal (cas).
Habitat Pine or pine-oak woods, fir forest.
Field Marks 4.5″ Like Townsend's Warbler, with black throat and rear crown, but *no* yellow below; forecrown and sides of face yellow, *not* black.

BLACK-THROATED GREEN WARBLER [36] Chipe Dorsiverde *Dendroica virens*
Range Can–Pan. Win Mex (csPac, csHi, Atl, Yuc), Blz, Guat, ElSal.
Habitat Humid forest, borders, pine-oak woods.
Field Marks 4.5″ Sum M: forehead yellow, but entire crown and back unstreaked olive green; white wing bars; yellow face, with faint ear patch; throat black, sides streaked black; breast, belly, and untacs white. F+imm+win M: chin and upper throat yellow or whitish; lower throat streaked or blotched with black or gray.

GOLDEN-CHEEKED WARBLER [36] Chipe Dorsinegro *Dendroica chrysoparia*
Range US–Nic. Tr Mex (e Hi + adj Atl); win Blz (?), Guat (Hi), ElSal (cas). Rare.
Habitat On migration in open pine woods, borders, or mixed pine and oak woods.
Field Marks 4.5″ Like Black-throated Green Warbler, but M: entire crown and back black; F+imm: darker olive above; more black on lower throat, chest, and sides.

BLACKBURNIAN WARBLER [37] Chipe Gorjinaranja *Dendroica fusca*
Range Can–SAm. Tr Mex (sPac, sHi, Atl + adj Hi, Yuc; acc nBajCal), Blz, Guat, ElSal. Rare.
Habitat Wooded river valleys, humid forest, scattered trees in pastures, borders.
Field Marks 5″ M: black-and-white streaked above; orange face, throat, and chest, with black ear patch; white wing patch, belly, and untacs. F+imm: duller; orange-tinged face, throat, and upper breast; dark ear patch; whitish scapulars and back streaks.

YELLOW-THROATED WARBLER [37] Chipe Domínico *Dendroica dominica*
Range US–Pan. Tr/win Mex (csPac, sHi, Atl, Yuc; cas/acc sBajCal, s.nPac), Blz, Guat, ElSal (cas).
Habitat Pine woods, palm forest, borders.
Field Marks 5″ Like Grace's Warbler, but blacker face patch; white neck patch and line over eye; plain gray back.

GRACE'S WARBLER [35] Chipe Pinero *Dendroica graciae*
Range US–Nic. Res Mex (w Hi + adj Pac), Blz (pine), Guat (Pac, Hi, Atl?), ElSal (n).
Habitat Open pine woods, borders, or pine with scattered oaks; middle or upper branches.

Field Marks **4.5″** Bluish gray above; streaked back; gray cheeks and sides of neck; yellow throat, chest, and line over eye; white belly, untacs, and wing bars; streaked sides.

PINE WARBLER [36] Chipe Nororiental *Dendroica pinus*
Range Can–Mex. Win Mex (nAtl). Very rare.
Habitat Pine or mixed pine and deciduous trees.
Field Marks **5″** Olive above, unstreaked; two white wing bars; faint line over eye; yellow throat and breast faintly streaked; white belly and untacs. Imm: whitish throat and breast.

PRAIRIE WARBLER [37] Chipe Galán *Dendroica discolor*
Range Can–Hon, exc Guat. Tr/win Mex (e.sAtl, e Yuc; cas/acc ncPac, nHi, ncAtl), Blz (cstl + cayes), ElSal (cas). Rare.
Habitat Scrubby woods, borders.
Field Marks **4.5″** Rufous streaks on greenish above; black-bordered yellow ear patch; all yellow below with heavy black side streaks. F: duller. Imm: much duller.

PALM WARBLER [37] Chipe Playero *Dendroica palmarum*
Range Can–Mex, Blz, Hon, Nic. Win Mex (e.sAtl, n+e Yuc; cas/acc BajCal, ncPac, cAtl), Blz (cstl + cayes).
Habitat On ground or low shrubs, in openings, grassy areas, open shores, stream banks, clearings.
Field Marks **5″** Bobs tail persistently. Rump greenish yellow, untacs yellow; faint wing bars. Races vary, from rufous streaks on yellow below, rufous cap, and yellow line over eye, to mostly gray streaks on whitish below, grayish cap, and white line over eye.

BAY-BREASTED WARBLER [37] Chipe Castaño *Dendroica castanea*
Range Can–SAm. Tr Mex (Atl, Yuc; cas BajCal, ncPac), Blz (n), Guat (Atl), ElSal (acc). Rare.
Habitat Humid forest, borders, hedgerows.
Field Marks **5″** White wing bars; black legs; streaked black on brownish or greenish above; belly white. Sum M: black mask; buff neck patch; chestnut crown and throat. F+win M: whitish throat; only faintly rufous on sides. Imm: faint streaks above, fainter below; untacs whitish or buff. See immature Black-poll Warbler.

BLACKPOLL WARBLER [37] Chipe Gorrinegro *Dendroica striata*
Range AK–Mex, Blz, CRic–SAm. Tr Mex (ne Yuc; cas/acc BajCal, csPac, nHi), Blz (n). Very rare.
Habitat Semihumid forest, open woods, borders.
Field Marks **5″** White wing bars; pale legs. Sum M: streaked black on pale olive above; white below with sides streaked black; black crown; white cheeks and throat. F+win M: streaked above and below on whitish or pale yellow. Imm: heavier streaks, whiter untacs than immature Bay-breasted Warbler; yellowish legs and feet. See Black-throated Gray and Black-and-white Warblers.

CERULEAN WARBLER [37] Chipe Cerúleo *Dendroica cerulea*
Range Can–SAm, exc ElSal. Tr Mex (Atl, Yuc; cas/acc BajCal), Blz, Guat (Atl).
Very rare.
Habitat Forest, open woods, borders.
Field Marks 4.5″ White wing bars. M: blue crown; black streaks on bluish above and on white below; black lower-throat band. F+imm: bluish gray or olive-gray above; may be bluer on crown; faint streaks on buffy yellowish below.

BLACK-AND-WHITE WARBLER [36] Chipe Trepador *Mniotilta varia*
Range Can–SAm. Tr/win Mex, Blz, Guat, ElSal.
Habitat Humid and semihumid forest, pine-oak woods, borders, partial clearings.
Field Marks 5″ M: striped black and white; plain white belly; white stripe down center of crown; black throat. F: fainter streaks below; white throat. See Blackpoll Warbler.

AMERICAN REDSTART [37] Pavito Migratorio *Setophaga ruticilla*
Range AK–SAm. Tr/win Mex, Blz, Guat, ElSal.
Habitat Humid forest, pine-oak woods, mangroves, borders.
Field Marks 5″ Adt M: black, with white belly and untacs; orange patches on sides, wings, and tail. F: grayish above, with yellow patches. 1st-yr M: like female, but darker, patches more orange.

PROTHONOTARY WARBLER [36] Chipe Protonotario *Protonotaria citrea*
Range Can–SAm, exc ElSal. Tr/win Mex (Atl, Yuc; cas/acc nBajCal, ncPac), Blz, Guat (Pac, Atl). Very rare.
Habitat Scrubby woods, forest borders, moist hedgerows, other wet, low-lying wooded areas.
Field Marks 5.5″ Bill black, pointed. M: entire head, breast, and sides orange-yellow; belly and untacs white; wings and tail mostly blue-gray. F: duller.

WORM-EATING WARBLER [36] Chipe Vermívoro *Helmitheros vermivorus*
Range Can–Pan. Tr/win Mex (csPac, Atl, Yuc), Blz, Guat (Pac, Atl), ElSal. Rare.
Habitat Humid forest, wooded riversides, deciduous woods.
Field Marks 5″ Brownish gray above, whitish with buff wash below; head striped black and tawny buff; bill pointed.

SWAINSON'S WARBLER [36] Chipe de Swainson *Limnothlypis swainsonii*
Range US–Mex, Blz, Guat? Tr/win Mex (tr Atl, Yuc; win sAtl, s+e Yuc); win Blz, Guat? (Atl?). Very rare.
Habitat Humid forest, dense scrubby woods, thickets.
Field Marks 5″ Like Worm-eating Warbler, but much paler streak through eye; crown reddish brown, *not* striped black and buff.

OVENBIRD [37] Chipe Suelero. *Seiurus aurocapillus*
Range Can–SAm. Win Mex (s.nPac+csPac, csHi, Atl, Yuc; cas/acc n.nPac), Blz, Guat, ElSal. Rare.
Habitat Undergrowth of dense forest, scrubby woods, wooded riversides.

Field Marks 6″ Greenish brown above; broad, black-bordered, orange center-crown streak; white below with heavy black streaks; legs pink; tail rather short.

NORTHERN WATERTHRUSH [37] Chipe Charquero *Seiurus noveboracensis*
Range AK–SAm. Tr/win Mex (win all, exc nHi where tr); win Blz, Guat, ElSal.
Habitat Swamps, borders of ponds, lakes, streams, pools.
Field Marks 6″ Bobs tail and body as it walks. Like Louisiana Waterthrush, but underparts and line over eye yellowish (to whitish in some races); throat speckled.

LOUISIANA WATERTHRUSH [37] Chipe Arroyero *Seiurus motacilla*
Range Can–SAm. Tr/win Mex (Pac, w+e.ncHi, Atl, Yuc; cas BajCal), Blz, Guat, ElSal.
Habitat Shores or banks of freshwater lagoons, ponds, streams, swamps.
Voice Often a sharp *chip.*
Field Marks 6″ Bobs tail and body as it walks. Like Ovenbird, with heavy black streaks on white below (*no* throat speckles, flanks usually buffy), but crown and back plain dark brown; white line over eye is broader behind eye; legs pinkish.

KENTUCKY WARBLER [37] Chipe Cachetinegro *Oporornis formosus*
Range Can–SAm. Tr/win Mex (sPac, Atl, Yuc; cas/very rare ncPac), Blz, Guat, ElSal. Rare.
Habitat Forest undergrowth, thickets, overgrown clearings.
Field Marks 5″ Yellowish green above; yellow spectacles and long black vertical line below eye; bright yellow below. Imm: duller; line below eye shorter.

MOURNING WARBLER [37] Chipe Llorón *Oporornis philadelphia*
Range Can–SAm. Tr Mex (sPac, csHi, Atl; cas/acc sBajCal, csPac), Blz, Guat, ElSal. Rare.
Habitat Undergrowth of humid forest, borders, overgrown clearings, thickets.
Field Marks 5.5″ Adt: yellowish olive above, yellow below; head and throat medium to dark bluish gray; M: throat-chest mark blackish. Imm: throat tinged yellowish; faint eye ring. See MacGillivray's Warbler.

MACGILLIVRAY'S WARBLER [35] Chipe de Tolmie *Oporornis tolmiei*
Range AK–Pan, exc Blz. Res/win Mex (res ne.nHi; tr/win all exc sAtl+Yuc), Guat (Pac, Hi), ElSal. Res rare and local; tr more common.
Habitat Gardens, humid forest, thickets, borders, scrubby woods.
Field Marks 5″ Like Mourning Warbler, but partial white eye ring prominent above and below eye.

COMMON YELLOWTHROAT [38] Mascarita Común *Geothlypis trichas*
Common group [38] Mascarita Común *G. t. trichas*
Range AK–Pan. Res/win Mex (res nBajCal, ncPac, w.nHi+cHi, n.nAtl; win all); win Blz, Guat, ElSal.
Habitat Marshes, wet tall-grass meadows, grassy thickets.
Field Marks 4.5″ M: black mask with grayish or white border; underparts yellow, except whitish belly; upperparts medium olive. F: *no* mask; top and sides of head yellowish green.

Chapala group Mascarita de Chapala *G. t. chapalensis*
Range Mex. Res Mex (w.cHi, especially Lake Chapala).
Habitat Marshes bordering large lakes.
Field Marks 4.5" Like Altamira Yellowthroat (but no range overlap).

BELDING'S YELLOWTHROAT [38] Mascarita Peninsular *Geothlypis beldingi*
Range Mex. Res Mex (sBajCal).
Habitat Marshes, marshy river valleys, lagoons.
Field Marks 5" Like Common group of Common Yellowthroat, but M: border of mask yellow (*G. b. beldingi*) or broad gray (*G. b. goldmani*); underparts mostly bright yellow; belly whitish in some.

ALTAMIRA YELLOWTHROAT [38] Mascarita de Altamira *Geothlypis flavovelata*
Range Mex. Res Mex (s.nAtl+n.cAtl).
Habitat Brackish or freshwater marshes, marshy lagoons, partly flooded fields.
Field Marks 5" Like Common group of Common Yellowthroat, but underparts all yellow; M: very broad yellow border behind mask.

BLACK-POLLED YELLOWTHROAT [38] Mascarita Transvolcánica *Geothlypis speciosa*
Range Mex. Res Mex (c.cHi). Irregular and local.
Habitat Large freshwater marshes or marshy areas near lakes, ponds, slow-moving water.
Field Marks 5" Like Common group of Common Yellowthroat, but darker and more olive-green above, mostly golden yellow below; M: mask larger, merging into blackish crown.

HOODED YELLOWTHROAT [38] Mascarita Matorralera *Geothlypis nelsoni*
Range Mex. Res Mex (e.ncHi). Rare, local.
Habitat Weedy, brushy, rather dry slopes, brushy undergrowth in open pine or pine-oak woods.
Field Marks 5" Like Common group of Common Yellowthroat, but darker gray mask border in male; M+F: darker and greener above; all yellow below, with darker wash on sides and flanks.

GRAY-CROWNED YELLOWTHROAT [35] Mascarita Piquigruesa *Geothlypis poliocephala*
Range Mex Pan. Res Mex (s.nPac+csPac, s.nAtl+csAtl, Yuc), Blz, Guat (Pac, Atl), ElSal. Rather common, but irregular.
Habitat Tall-grass fields, other dense tall herbaceous growth, thickets, weedy hedgerows.
Field Marks 5.5" M: dull medium olive above, but forehead and lores black; crown and nape gray; bright yellow below; partial eye ring; bill thick, yellowish. F: duller; head less contrasty.

HOODED WARBLER [37] Chipe de Capucha *Wilsonia citrina*
Range Can–Pan. Tr/win Mex (Atl, Yuc; cas/acc Pac), Blz, Guat (Atl), ElSal. Rare.
Habitat Humid forest undergrowth, borders, partial clearings.
Field Marks 5.5" White tail patches. M: yellow face; black hood, including

throat; yellowish olive above, yellow below. F: *no* hood; olive crown, yellow throat. See Wilson's Warbler.

WILSON'S WARBLER [37] Chipe Pelucillo *Wilsonia pusilla*
Range AK–Pan. Tr/win Mex, Blz, Guat, ElSal.
Habitat Humid forest, scrubby woods, partial clearings, borders, lush gardens.
Field Marks **4.5″** Like Hooded Warbler, but *no* white tail patches; M: circular black cap; sides of neck and throat yellow, *not* black.

CANADA WARBLER [37] Chipe Collarejo *Wilsonia canadensis*
Range Can–SAm. Tr Mex (sPac, Atl + adj Hi; cas/very rare Yuc), Blz, Guat (Hi + adj Pac+Atl), ElSal. Rare.
Habitat Dense forest undergrowth, thickets, borders.
Field Marks **5″** M: dark bluish gray above; yellow spectacles; yellow below, with white untacs; black streaky necklace. F+imm: duller; necklace faint or absent.

RED-FACED WARBLER [35] Chipe Coloradito *Cardellina rubrifrons*
Range US–Mex, Guat, ElSal, Hon. Sum/win Mex (sum w.nHi; win s.nHi+ csHi), Guat (Hi), ElSal (cas). Rare.
Habitat Pine, pine-oak, or fir forest, scrubby oak woods.
Field Marks **5″** Gray back; white nape, rump, and underparts, except red throat and chest; forehead and forecrown red; hindcrown black.

RED WARBLER [38] Chipe Rojo *Ergaticus ruber*
Range Mex. Res Mex (w.nHi+cHi).
Habitat Mostly fir forest, but also dense humid pine-oak or pine woodland; lower to middle branches.
Field Marks **5″** Adt: red, with pale silvery gray ear patch (blackish in northwestern birds). Imm: dull red; dark ear patch.

PINK-HEADED WARBLER [38] Chipe Rosado *Ergaticus versicolor*
Range Mex, Guat. Res Mex (sHi), Guat (Hi).
Habitat Open pine woods or rather humid pine-oak or oak woods.
Field Marks **5″** Much of plumage dark red to brownish red, but entire head, throat, and chest silvery pink.

PAINTED REDSTART [35] Pavito Aliblanco *Myioborus pictus*
Range US–Nic, exc Blz. Res/sum Mex (w+e.nHi+csHi + adj Pac, Atl), Guat (Hi), ElSal (n).
Habitat Pine or pine-oak woods, borders, partial clearings.
Field Marks **5″** Mostly black, but breast broadly red; white wing patch, outer tail feathers, and center of belly and untacs.

SLATE-THROATED REDSTART [38] Pavito Selvático *Myioborus miniatus*
Range Mex–SAm, exc Blz. Res Mex (w+e.nHi+csHi + adj Pac+Atl), Guat (Hi + adj Pac), ElSal (w).
Habitat Cloud forest, humid lowland forest, mountain pine-oak or fir forest.
Field Marks **5″** Dark blue-gray above; chestnut crown; mostly red below or

orange-red in Guatemala (Pac) and El Salvador, with blackish throat and white untacs; tail long, white-cornered, often fanned.

FAN-TAILED WARBLER [38] Pavito Roquero *Euthlypis lachrymosa*
Range Mex–Nic, exc Blz. Res Mex (Pac + adj Hi, s.nAtl+cAtl), Guat (Pac), ElSal. Rare.
Habitat Humid forest, borders, wooded riversides, rocky wooded hillsides.
Field Marks 6″ Often on ground, fans and droops tail. Bluish gray above; black-bordered yellow crown; white tail corners; dull tawny below with yellow throat and white untacs.

GOLDEN-CROWNED WARBLER [38] Chipe Rey Gorridorado *Basileuterus culicivorus*
Range Mex–SAm. Res Mex (cspac, Atl, s+e Yuc), Blz, Guat (Pac, Atl), ElSal (w).
Habitat Cloud forest and other humid forest, borders, overgrown clearings.
Voice A loud, deliberate *weety, weety, wítchu.*
Field Marks 5″ Greenish olive above, yellow below; black-bordered orange crown stripe; pale yellow eye ring.

RUFOUS-CAPPED WARBLER [38] Chipe Rey Mexicano *Basileuterus rufifrons*
Rufous-capped group [38] Chipe Rey Mexicano *B. r. rufifrons*
Range Mex, Blz, Guat. Res Mex (Pac, w+e.nHi+cshi, ncAtl), Blz (s), Guat (Atl).
Habitat Borders, scrubby open woods, overgrown clearings, hedgerows.
Field Marks 5″ Adt: crown, nape, and ear patch rufous, with white line above and below ear patch; throat and breast yellow, belly and untacs white, or all-yellow underparts in Mex (sAtl), Blz, Guat (Atl). Juv: much duller, browner; buffy wing bars; head pattern olive-brown and whitish; underparts buffy.
Chestnut-capped group [38] Chipe Rey de Delattre *B. r. delattrii*
Range Mex–SAm, exc Blz. Res Mex (e.sPac), Guat (Pac), ElSal.
Habitat Humid forest, borders.
Field Marks 5″ Like southeastern race of Rufous-capped group (all yellow below), but *no* white line below ear patch; nape olive, *not* rufous.

GOLDEN-BROWED WARBLER [38] Chipe Rey Cejidorado *Basileuterus belli*
Range Mex, Guat, ElSal, Hon. Res Mex (w+e.ncHi+sHi + adj Pac+Atl), Guat (Hi), ElSal (n).
Habitat Humid pine-oak or fir forest, cloud forest, borders, partial clearings, in shrubby undergrowth or lower tree branches.
Voice A rasping *zi-zi-zi,* like katydid call; also a song.
Field Marks 5″ Adt: like Chestnut-capped group of Rufous-capped Warbler, but crown narrowly black-bordered; line over eye yellow; colors seem more intense. Juv: olive-brown above; two buff wing bars; duller face pattern; mostly dark brownish olive below.

YELLOW-BREASTED CHAT [37] Chipe Arriero *Icteria virens*
Range Can–Pan. Sum/win Mex (sum nBajCal, nPac, ncHi; tr/win all); win Blz, Guat, ElSal.
Habitat Borders, hedgerows, brushy fields, low shrubby vegetation, overgrown clearings.

Field Marks 7″ Olive above; white spectacles; bright yellow throat and breast; white belly and untacs; rather thick black bill.

RED-BREASTED CHAT [38] Rosillo Occidental *Granatellus venustus*
Range Mex. Res Mex (c.nPac–inland sPac). Rare.
Habitat Scrubby woods, thickets, overgrown clearings, borders.
Field Marks 5.5″ White outer tail feathers and tail corners. M: blue-gray above; head, underparts, and tail black and white, with red chest patch and untacs. F: grayish above; conspicuous buffy line over and behind eye; underparts buff with slightly paler throat and belly, pink untacs; tail tip and outer tail feathers white.

GRAY-THROATED CHAT [38] Rosillo Oriental *Granatellus sallaei*
Range Mex, Blz, Guat. Res Mex (se.cAtl+sAtl, Yuc), Blz, Guat (Atl). Rare.
Habitat Scrubby woods, thickets, undergrowth, overgrown clearings.
Field Marks 5″ M: head, throat, and upperparts bluish gray, with white line behind eye; breast, belly, and untacs red; sides and flanks white. F: like female Red-breasted Chat (ranges *do not* overlap), but may be slightly paler below; untacs buff, *not* pink; outer tail feathers gray, *not* white; tail tip narrowly white.

BANANAQUITS—PLATANERAS—COEREBIDAE

BANANAQUIT [35] Platanera Común *Coereba flaveola*
Range Mex–SAm, exc ElSal. Res Mex (se.cAtl+s.sAtl, ne Yuc), Blz (s), Guat (Atl).
Habitat Humid forest, partial clearings, borders, scrubby woods, gardens, hedgerows.
Field Marks 4.5″ Mostly blackish above with yellowish rump patch; white line over eye; small white wing spot; mostly yellow below, with white or pale gray throat and white untacs. Imm: duller.

TANAGERS—TANGARAS, PIRANGAS—THRAUPIDAE

COMMON BUSH-TANAGER [39] Chinchinero Común *Chlorospingus ophthalmicus*
Range Mex–SAm. Res Mex (s+e.cHi+sHi + adj Pac, Atl), Blz (s), Guat (Hi), ElSal (n).
Habitat Undergrowth in humid forest, dense hedgerows and borders, lush gardens.
Field Marks 5.5″ Mostly yellowish olive, brighter below; throat, belly, and large eye patch white to grayish; crown and ear patch grayish brown to blackish.

ROSY THRUSH-TANAGER [39] Tangara Cuitlacoche *Rhodinocichla rosea*
Range Mex, CRic–SAm. Res Mex (s.nPac+nw.cPac).
Habitat Scrubby woods, borders, thickets, hedgerows; on or near ground.
Voice A loud *chor-ee-cho* or *chu-wee-oo-bar.*
Field Marks 8″ M: dark gray above, with blackish wings, crown, ear patch, and flanks; underparts and line over eye mostly rosy red. F: dark brownish gray and tawny; *not* blackish and rosy red.

GRAY-HEADED TANAGER [39] Tangara Cabecigrís *Eucometis penicillata*
Range Mex–SAm, exc ElSal. Res Mex (se.cAtl+sAtl, e Yuc), Blz, Guat (Atl). Rare.
Habitat Dense humid forest undergrowth, overgrown small openings.
Field Marks 6.5" Olive-green above, bright yellow below, but entire head gray.

BLACK-THROATED SHRIKE-TANAGER [39] Acalandriado Cabecinegro *Lanio aurantius*
Range Mex, Blz, Guat, Hon. Res Mex (se.cAtl+sAtl), Blz, Guat (Atl). Rare.
Habitat High branches, dense humid forest.
Field Marks 8" Bill heavy, flattened, hook-tipped. M: mostly tawny yellow, but tail, wings, and entire head black; small white patch near wrist. F: rich olive-brown above; rump tawnier; head more grayish olive; belly yellow; untacs tawny.

RED-CROWNED ANT-TANAGER [39] Tangara Hormiguera *Habia rubica*
Range Mex–SAm. Res Mex (cSPac, s.nAtl+csAtl, s+e Yuc), Blz, Guat (Pac, Atl), ElSal.
Habitat Thickets, dense undergrowth of humid forest, wooded riversides, overgrown clearings; often follows ant swarms.
Field Marks 7" M: plumage brownish red (noticeably browner than shown), paler below, with pinkish red throat and chest; red crown patch black-bordered. F: dull olive-brown, paler below; throat slightly more yellowish; crown patch tawny, black-bordered; lower mandible pale.

RED-THROATED ANT-TANAGER [39] Tangara Selvática *Habia fuscicauda*
Range Mex–SAm. Res Mex (sPac, s.nAtl+csAtl, Yuc), Blz, Guat (Pac, Atl), ElSal.
Habitat Humid forest, thickets, overgrown clearings, brushy borders.
Field Marks 7" Like Red-crowned Ant-Tanager, but M: throat patch more sharply defined; crown patch less obvious; F: throat patch contrasty buffy; crown patch obscure or absent.

ROSE-THROATED TANAGER [39] Tangara Yucateca *Piranga roseogularis*
Range Mex, Blz, Guat. Res Mex (e.sAtl, s+e Yuc), Blz (n), Guat (n Atl). Rare.
Habitat Partly overgrown clearings, scrubby woods, humid forest, borders.
Field Marks 6" M: gray, paler below, with red crown, wings, and tail; throat and untacs pink; eye ring whitish. F+imm: no red; throat and untacs pale buff-yellow.

HEPATIC TANAGER [40] Piranga Encinera *Piranga flava*
Range US–SAm. Res Mex (w+e.nHi+csHi + adj Pac+Atl), Blz (pine), Guat, ElSal (n).
Habitat Open pine or pine-oak woods, borders.
Field Marks 7.5" Bill blackish gray; no crest. M: dull red, with grayish cheek patch. F+imm: grayish to yellowish green above, yellow below; grayish cheek patch.

SUMMER TANAGER [40] Piranga Avispera *Piranga rubra*
Range US–SAm. Sum/win Mex (sum ne.nBajCal, nPac, nHi; tr/win all); win Blz (s), Guat, ElSal.

Habitat Humid forest, pine-oak woods, borders, gardens, orchards; middle to upper branches.
Field Marks 7" Like Hepatic Tanager, but bill brownish yellow; *no* gray cheek patch; M: paler and brighter red; F+imm: brighter yellowish below, paler yellowish green above.

SCARLET TANAGER Piranga Olivácea *Piranga olivacea*
Range US–SAm, exc ElSal. Tr Mex (sAtl, Yuc; cas nBajCal), Blz, Guat (Atl). Very rare.
Habitat Dense forest, scrubby woods, borders.
Field Marks 7" Bill pale brownish yellow. Sum M: scarlet, with black wings and tail. Win M: like female Summer Tanager, but slightly more greenish, wings and tail blackish. F+imm: like winter male, but wings and tail duller (but darker than those of female and immature Summer Tanager). See White-winged Tanager.

WESTERN TANAGER [40] Piranga Occidental *Piranga ludoviciana*
Range AK–SAm. Sum/win Mex (sum n.nBajCal, extreme n.nPac; tr/win all exc Yuc), Blz, Guat, ElSal.
Habitat Pine, pine-oak, or fir forest, wooded riversides, gardens, borders, orchards.
Field Marks 7" Sum M: yellow, with red head; black back, tail, and wings; two prominent wing bars, one yellow and one white. Win M: like summer male, but duller and greener yellow; head yellowish, *not* red, with faint red wash around base of bill. F+imm: like winter male, but more grayish green above.

(FLAME-COLORED) STRIPED TANAGER [39] Piranga Rayada *Piranga bidentata*
Range Mex–Pan, exc Blz. Res Mex (w+e.ncHi+sHi + adj Pac+Atl), Guat, ElSal.
Habitat Cloud forest, pine-oak woods, partial clearings, borders.
Field Marks 7" M: red or orange-red, with heavy black streaks on back; two white bars on black wings; white corners on black tail. F: like male, but basically yellowish, *not* red.

WHITE-WINGED TANAGER [39] Piranga Tropical *Piranga leucoptera*
Range Mex–SAm. Res Mex (c.cPac, sPac + adj Hi, s.nAtl+cAtl+s.sAtl + adj Hi), Blz, Guat (Pac, Atl), ElSal.
Habitat Cloud forest, other humid forest, borders, partial clearings, *cafetales*.
Voice A quiet, buzzy *wheet-wheet*.
Field Marks 5.5" Bill black; two white wing bars. M: scarlet, with black mask, tail, wings, and bill. F: yellowish, *not* red, with dark wings and tail.

RED-HEADED TANAGER [39] Piranga Cabecirroja *Piranga erythrocephala*
Range Mex. Res Mex (ncHi + adj Pac). Rare.
Habitat Open grassy pine-oak woods, pure oak woods, mixed scrubby woods, borders.
Field Marks 6" M: dull yellowish green above, yellow below, with red crown, face, and throat. F: duller yellowish, with gray cheeks, no red.

CRIMSON-COLLARED TANAGER [39] Tongonito Real *Ramphocelus sanguinolentus*
Range Mex–Pan, exc ElSal. Res Mex (se.cAtl–sc.sAtl), Blz (s), Guat (Atl). Rare.

Habitat Humid forest openings, partial clearings, mixed farms and second growth, borders.
Field Marks 7.5" Black, with red rump, uptacs, untacs, hindcrown, nape, and broad collar; whitish bill.

PASSERINI'S TANAGER [39] Tangara Terciopelo *Ramphocelus passerinii*
Range Mex–Pan, exc ElSal. Res Mex (sw+sc.sAtl), Blz (s), Guat (Atl).
Habitat Humid forest borders, partial clearings, gardens, orchards.
Field Marks 7" Bill whitish. M: velvety black, with scarlet rump patch. F: mostly dull grayish orange, browner and brighter below and on rump; wings and tail blackish; head grayer.

STRIPED-HEADED TANAGER [39] Cuadrillero Pintado *Spindalis zena*
Range Mex (+ Antilles). Res Mex (ne Yuc: Cozumel Island).
Habitat Scrubby woods, borders, orchards, partial clearings.
Field Marks 6.5" M: gaudy black-and-white head, wings, and tail, yellow throat and tawny rufous chest and collar. F: olive-gray above, paler below; white wing spot.

BLUE-GRAY TANAGER [45] Tangara Azul Gris *Thraupis episcopus*
Range Mex–SAm. Res Mex (sPac, csAtl, Yuc [established?]), Blz, Guat (Pac, Atl), ElSal.
Habitat Partly wooded pastures, mixed farms and woods, borders, gardens, orchards.
Voice A high-pitched chipping song; a very high-pitched *wees*.
Field Marks 6.5" Usually in pairs. Pale bluish gray, with darker blue wings and tail.

YELLOW-WINGED TANAGER [39] Tangara Aliamarilla *Thraupis abbas*
Range Mex–Nic. Res Mex (sPac, csAtl, Yuc), Blz, Guat (Pac, Atl), ElSal.
Habitat Humid forest, borders, partial clearings, wooded riversides, orchards.
Field Marks 7" Head, throat, chest, and back purplish blue, merging into grayish olive breast, belly, untacs, and rump; blackish scallops on back; wings and tail mostly black, with bright yellow spot that becomes stripe on extended wing.

SCRUB EUPHONIA [39] Monjita Gorjinegra *Euphonia affinis*
Scrub group [39] Monjita Gorjinegra *E. a. affinis*
Range Mex–CRic. Res Mex (se.cPac+sPac, s.nAtl+csAtl, Yuc), Blz, Guat (Pac, Atl), ElSal.
Habitat Wooded river valleys, partial clearings, humid forest, borders, gardens, orchards; often in mistletoe.
Field Marks 4" M: forehead broadly yellow; breast, belly, and untacs rich yellow; throat and upperparts blackish blue. F: grayish green above, with grayer forecrown; yellowish forehead, belly, and rump; mostly dull yellowish green below.
Godman's group Monjita de Godman *E. a. godmani*
Range Mex. Res Mex (nPac+nw.cPac). Rare.
Habitat Borders, scrubby woods, partial clearings.

Field Marks 4″ Like Scrub group, but M: more lemon-yellow; untacs white; F: gray hindcrown and nape.

YELLOW-THROATED EUPHONIA [39] Monjita Gorjiamarilla *Euphonia hirundinacea*
Range Mex–Pan. Res Mex (sPac, s.nAtl+csAtl, Yuc), Blz, Guat (Pac, Atl), ElSal (w).
Habitat Humid forest, borders, partial clearings, wooded riversides, gardens.
Field Marks 4″ Like Scrub group of Scrub Euphonia, but M: throat yellow; F: whitish below, with yellow sides.

ELEGANT EUPHONIA [39] Monjita Elegante *Euphonia elegantissima*
Range Mex–Pan. Res Mex (w+e.nHi+csHi + adj Pac+Atl), Blz, Guat (Hi + adj Pac+Atl), ElSal.
Habitat Cloud forest, other humid forest, pine-oak or fir forest, lush gardens; middle or upper branches, often in mistletoe.
Field Marks 4.5″ Crown and nape broadly bright light blue. M: blackish violet above and on throat and face; rich brownish orange below. F: mostly pale olive above, pale dull yellowish below; throat dull tawny.

OLIVE-BACKED EUPHONIA [39] Monjita Olivácea *Euphonia gouldi*
Range Mex–Pan, exc ElSal. Res Mex (se.cAtl+s.sAtl), Blz, Guat (Atl). Rare.
Habitat Dense humid forest, small openings, partial clearings.
Field Marks 4″ M: mostly bluish green to grayish green; forehead yellow; belly and untacs tawny brown; sides speckled yellow. F: duller; forehead dark rufous; breast, belly, and flanks yellowish gray.

WHITE-VENTED EUPHONIA Monjita Chiquita *Euphonia minuta*
Range Mex–Blz, Guat, Nic–SAm. Res Mex? (sc.sAtl?), Blz (s), Guat (Atl). Very rare.
Habitat Dense humid forest, partial clearings, borders.
Field Marks 3.5″ Like Godman's group of Scrub Euphonia (untacs white), but M: orange-yellow, *not* lemon-yellow; F: darker yellowish gray breast contrasts more with pale gray throat and white belly.

BLUE-CROWNED CHLOROPHONIA [39] Cilindro *Chlorophonia occipitalis*
Range Mex–Nic, exc Blz. Res Mex (se.cHi+sHi + adj Pac+Atl), Guat (upper slopes Pac, Atl), ElSal (w). Rare.
Habitat Humid forest, openings, partial clearings, *cafetales,* borders; middle or upper branches, often in flocks in or near mistletoe.
Field Marks 5.5″ M: rich yellowish green, including throat and flanks, with bright yellow breast, most of belly, and untacs; crown pale blue; narrow breast band brown. F: duller; *no* breast band.

(AZURE-RUMPED) CABANIS'S TANAGER [39] Tangara Chiapaneca *Tangara cabanisi*
Range Mex, Guat. Res Mex (se.sPac), Guat (w Pac). Very rare and local.
Habitat Humid mountain forest, partial clearings, borders; upper branches.
Field Marks 6″ Pale blue back (may be scalloped) and rump; purplish blue

crown; black wings and tail, with blue feather edgings; whitish blue below; scalloped black partial collar.

GOLDEN-HOODED TANAGER [39] Tangara Dorada *Tangara larvata*
Range Mex–SAm, exc ElSal. Res Mex (se.cAtl–sc.sAtl), Blz (s), Guat (Atl). Rare.
Habitat Humid forest, partial clearings, borders, lush gardens.
Field Marks 5.5″ Black, with pale blue rump, wrist patch, and flanks; golden tawny hood; black-and-blue mask; white belly.

GREEN HONEYCREEPER [47] Mielero Verde *Chlorophanes spiza*
Range Mex–SAm, exc ElSal. Res Mex (se.cAtl+s.sAtl), Blz (s), Guat (Atl). Rare.
Habitat Humid forest, borders, lush gardens, partial clearings.
Field Marks 5.5″ Bill decurved. M: bright bluish green, with black crown and mask; mostly yellowish bill; red eyes. F: medium green all over, including crown and mask.

SHINING HONEYCREEPER [47] Mielero Patiamarillo *Cyanerpes lucidus*
Range Mex–SAm, exc ElSal. Res Mex (sc.sAtl), Blz (s), Guat (Atl). Rare, local.
Habitat Dense humid forest.
Field Marks 4.5″ Like Red-legged Honeycreeper, but M: throat black; crown and back violet-blue; legs bright yellow; F: more heavily streaked below; throat buff; legs dull yellow.

RED-LEGGED HONEYCREEPER [47] Mielero Patirrojo *Cyanerpes cyaneus*
Range Mex–SAm. Res/sum Mex (sum se.cPac, cAtl; res/sum sPac, sAtl, s+e Yuc); res Blz, Guat (Pac, Atl), ElSal.
Habitat Humid forest, borders, lush tall hedgerows, gardens, partial clearings.
Field Marks 4.5″ M: mostly violet-blue, with black back, wings, and tail; crown pale blue; legs bright red. F+win M: dull yellowish green above; pale greenish yellow below, faintly streaked; legs duller red. Molting males dappled, red-legged.

BRUSH-FINCHES, SPARROWS, TOWHEES—SALTONES, GORRIONES—EMBERIZIDAE

BLUE-BLACK GRASSQUIT [41] Semillerito Brincador *Volatinia jacarina*
Range Mex–SAm. Res Mex (s.nPac+csPac, csAtl, Yuc), Blz, Guat (Pac, Atl), ElSal.
Habitat Overgrown fields, weedy hedgerows, cornfields, shrubby vacant lots, borders.
Field Marks 4″ Courting male repeatedly flutters into the air two or three feet above an open perch, then back down, voicing a sibilant *si-ew*. Bill rather small. Sum M: glossy black, with small white patch on side under wing. Win M: brown above, whitish below; heavily mottled and scaled with blackish. F: brown; paler and streaked below. Imm M: like female, but breast streaks, tail, and wings blacker.

SLATE-COLORED SEEDEATER [48] Semillerito Gris *Sporophila schistacea*
Range Mex?–SAm. Res Mex? (cAtl?), Blz (n), Guat (ne Atl). Very rare.
Habitat Humid forest borders, partial clearings, dense undergrowth.
Field Marks 4.5″ M: dark gray, with white belly, untacs, and wing spot; may have small white wing bar and neck patch; bill yellow; legs greenish. F: olive-brown above; pale olive-brown below to more buffy or whitish on belly and untacs; bill dark.

VARIABLE SEEDEATER [41] Semillerito Puntiblanco *Sporophila americana*
Range Mex–SAm, exc ElSal. Res Mex (se.cAtl–sc.sAtl), Blz (s), Guat (Atl). Rare.
Habitat Tall grass, weedy overgrown fields, humid forest borders, openings.
Field Marks 4.5″ M: like Blue-black Grassquit, but bill heavier; white spot on base of primaries (may be hidden) and white wing linings. F: greenish brown above; paler and buffier below, unstreaked; wing linings white.

WHITE-COLLARED SEEDEATER [40] Semillerito Collarejo *Sporophila torqueola*
Cinnamon-rumped group [40] Semillerito Occidental *S. t. torqueola*
Range Mex. Res Mex (s.nPac+cPac + adj Hi).
Habitat Brushy fields, weedy grassy borders, gardens, hedgerows.
Field Marks 4″ M: back, wings (with white spot but no wing bars), and tail brownish gray; rump, belly, and untacs rich orange-buff; head and breast band black, except pale buff throat; broad white partial collar. F: grayish brown above, pale yellowish buff below.
White-collared group Semillerito Común *S. t. morelleti*
Range Mex–Pan. Res Mex (se.cAtl+sAtl + adj Hi, Yuc), Blz, Guat, ElSal.
Habitat Overgrown fields, weedy borders, hedgerows, vacant lots.
Field Marks 4″ M: black, but wing bars, wing spot, throat, partial collar, belly, and untacs whitish; rump pale. F: grayish brown above, with buff wing bars, rump, underparts.
Sharpe's group [40] Semillerito de Sharpe *S. t. sharpei*
Range US–Mex. Res Mex (nAtl+n.cAtl + adj nHi).
Habitat Overgrown pastures, borders, grassy areas, farmyards.
Field Marks 4″ M: black or brown head and back; pale gray or buffy rump; whitish partial collar and throat; whitish or buffy below, with blotchy chest band or none; white wing bars and wing spot. F: like White-collared group, but browner, duller-rumped.

RUDDY-BREASTED SEEDEATER [41] Semillerito Pechicanelo *Sporophila minuta*
Range Mex–SAm, exc Blz. Res Mex (s.nPac+csPac), Guat (Pac), ElSal.
Habitat Tall-grass fields, tall-grass or sedge marshes, weedy vacant lots, weedy orchards.
Field Marks 3.7″ Sum M: blue-gray above, rufous below and on rump. F+win M: brownish above, buff and brownish buff below; two pale gray wing bars.

THICK-BILLED SEED-FINCH [41] Semillerito Piquigrueso *Oryzoborus funereus*
Range Mex–SAm, exc ElSal. Res Mex (se.cAtl–sc.sAtl), Blz (s), Guat (Atl). Rare.
Habitat Wet grassy overgrown clearings, humid forest borders, ditch banks.

Field Marks 4.5″ Like Variable Seedeater of our area, but bill much larger, very heavy at base; F: much darker richer brown.

BLUE SEEDEATER [41] Semillerito Azul *Amaurospiza concolor*
Range Mex–SAm, exc Guat? Res Mex (w+s.cHi+shi + adj Pac), Blz (acc), Guat (Hi?), ElSal (acc n). Very rare, local.
Habitat Thickets, brushy undergrowth, in or near humid forest or scrubby woods.
Field Marks 5.5″ M: dull slaty blue or dark rich blue. F+imm: gray-brown; paler below.

YELLOW-FACED GRASSQUIT [41] Semillerito Oliváceo *Tiaris olivacea*
Range Mex–SAm. Res Mex (ncAtl+s.sAtl + adj Hi, Yuc), Blz (s), Guat (Atl), ElSal.
Habitat Grassy fields, pastures, suburban lawns, hedgerows, borders.
Field Marks 4″ M: mostly grayish olive; head and breast (broadly) black; throat and line over eye bright yellow. F: dull gray-green; chin and short line over eye dull yellow.

SLATY FINCH [42] Semillerito Pizarra *Haplospiza rustica*
Range Mex–SAm, exc Blz, Guat? Res Mex (e.cHi + adj Atl, sPac + adj Hi), Guat? (Hi?), ElSal (cas n). Very rare.
Habitat Dense humid mountain forest, or small openings in brushy scrubby woods.
Voice A weak musical *chew, chew, pee-toot.*
Field Marks 5″ Tail short, notched; bill black and sharp-pointed with a straight culmen, longer than but *not* as heavy as that of Blue Seedeater. M: dark slate-gray. F: dark brown above, faintly streaked; paler below with more prominent streaks.

CINNAMON-BELLIED FLOWERPIERCER [47] Piquichueco Mexicano *Diglossa baritula*
Range Mex, Guat, ElSal, Hon, Nic. Res Mex (csHi + adj Pac+Atl), Guat (Hi), ElSal (w). Rare.
Habitat Pine-oak or fir forests, borders, gardens, partial clearings, openings.
Field Marks 4.5″ Tip of upper mandible hooked down over up-curved lower mandible. M: blackish gray to bluish gray above and on throat; mostly rufous below. F: olive-gray above; mostly buffy brown below, faintly streaked. Imm M: like adult male, but duller.

GRASSLAND YELLOW-FINCH [41] Semillero Amarillo *Sicalis luteola*
Range Mex–SAm, exc Guat?, ElSal. Res Mex (c.cHi + adj Pac, se.cAtl+w.sAtl), Blz (acc), Guat? Rare, local.
Habitat Wet grassy fields, wet pastures, sugarcane or rice fields.
Field Marks 5″ Often in flocks. M: plain rich yellow below; streaked blackish gray on greenish yellow above; yellow line over eye. F: duller; browner above, grayer below.

WHITE-NAPED BRUSH-FINCH [42] Saltón Cerquero *Atlapetes albinucha*
White-naped group [42] Saltón Cerquero. *A. a. albinucha*
  Range Mex. Res Mex (e.cHi+n.sHi + adj Atl). Rare.
  Habitat Overgrown fields, partial clearings, thickets at forest borders, brushy fields near forest.
  Field Marks 7″ Olive-gray above; head mostly black, with broad white stripe in center of crown; throat broadly bright yellow; underparts otherwise yellowish to grayish olive.
Yellow-throated group [42] Saltón Gorjiamarillo *A. a. gutturalis*
  Range Mex–SAm, exc Blz. Res Mex (se.sHi), Guat (Hi), ElSal (w).
  Habitat Forest borders, thickets, partial clearings, mixed overgrown fields and woods.
  Field Marks 7″ Like White-naped Brush-Finch, but only throat yellow; breast pale gray; center of belly white; flanks and untacs dark brownish gray.

RUFOUS-CAPPED BRUSH-FINCH [42] Saltón Gorrirrufo *Atlapetes pileatus*
  Range Mex. Res Mex (w+e.nHi+cHi + adj Pac, Atl).
  Habitat Pine, pine-oak, or other mountain forest undergrowth, borders, weedy clearings.
  Field Marks 5.5″ Seems excitable, moving tail abruptly and chipping rapidly when alarmed. Gray-brown above; crown rufous; blackish eye patch; yellow to yellowish gray below.

CHESTNUT-CAPPED BRUSH-FINCH [42] Saltón Collarejo *Buarremon brunneinucha*
(Does not include Tuxtla Brush-Finch)
  Range Mex–SAm, exc Blz. Res Mex (s+e.cHi+sHi + adj Pac, Atl), Guat (Hi + adj Pac), ElSal (n).
  Habitat Undergrowth in humid forest, dense borders, partial clearings, thickets.
  Field Marks 7″ Bright olive-green above; crown and nape rich reddish brown; extended black mask; black throat-chest band; dark sides, flanks, and untacs.

(PLAIN-BREASTED) TUXTLA BRUSH-FINCH [42] Saltón de Tuxtla *Buarremon apertus*
(The AOU lumps this with Chestnut-capped Brush-Finch; see above)
  Range Mex. Res Mex (cAtl: Sierra de Tuxtla).
  Habitat Brushy undergrowth in humid forest, borders, partial clearings.
  Field Marks 7″ Like Chestnut-capped Brush-Finch, but *no* black throat-chest band.

GREEN-STRIPED BRUSH-FINCH [42] Saltón Verdirrayado *Buarremon virenticeps*
  Range Mex. Res Mex (wc.nHi+cHi).
  Habitat On ground in dense pine-oak or fir forest, dense borders, thickets in open woods.
  Field Marks 7″ Olive-green above; crown and nape striped black and yellow-green; extended black mask; throat white; breast, sides, and flanks dark gray.

ORANGE-BILLED SPARROW [42] Rascadorcito Piquinaranja *Arremon aurantiirostris*
Range Mex–SAm, exc ElSal. Res Mex (se.cAtl–sc.sAtl), Blz (s), Guat (Atl).
Habitat Thickets and other dense undergrowth of humid forest.
Field Marks 6.5″ White throat, belly, and line over eye, on black head and underparts; dark olive-green above; may show yellow wrist patch; bill bright orange.

OLIVE SPARROW [44] Gorrión Oliváceo *Arremonops rufivirgatus*
Range US, Mex, Blz, Guat, CRic. Res Mex (c.nPac–sPac, ncAtl, Yuc), Blz (n), Guat (nw Atl).
Habitat Thickets and undergrowth in humid forest or scrubby woods, hedgerows, overgrown clearings.
Field Marks 6″ Dull olive above; head striped reddish brown and gray, including center-crown stripe and stripe through eye; whitish and pale olive-gray below.

GREEN-BACKED SPARROW [42] Gorrión Talero *Arremonops chloronotus*
Range Mex, Blz, Guat, Hon. Res Mex (sAtl, s+e Yuc), Blz, Guat (Atl).
Habitat Humid forest undergrowth, border, thickets, grassy shrubby overgrown clearings.
Field Marks 6″ Like Olive Sparrow, but brighter olive-green above; crown stripes and eye stripes blackish brown and dull gray; untacs pale pinkish salmon.

RUSTY-CROWNED GROUND-SPARROW [42] Rascadorcito Coronirrufo *Melozone kieneri*
Range Mex. Res Mex (c.nPac–cPac + adj Hi).
Habitat Dense shrubby dry woods, thickets, rocky grassy slopes, overgrown clearings.
Field Marks 6.5″ Head pattern dark gray, white, and mostly rufous; large black breast spot on white below; dark olive-green above.

PREVOST'S GROUND-SPARROW [42] Rascadorcito Chiapaneco *Melozone biarcuatum*
Range Mex–CRic, exc Blz, Nic. Res Mex (e.sPac+sc.sAtl + adj Hi), Guat (Hi + adj Pac+Atl), ElSal.
Habitat Weedy, shrubby overgrown clearings, hedgerows, humid forest borders.
Field Marks 6.5″ Like Rusty-crowned Ground-Sparrow, but much more white on face; no black breast spot.

WHITE-EARED GROUND-SPARROW [42] Rascadorcito Orejiblanco *Melozone leucotis*
Range Mex–CRic, exc Blz, Hon. Res Mex (e.sPac + adj Hi), Guat (Pac), ElSal (w).
Habitat Humid forest, brushy borders, wooded riversides, partial clearings.
Field Marks 6.5″ Head black, except gray center-crown stripe, white spot before eye and on ear, and yellow line behind eye; mostly gray-brown above; white below, with black breast spot and rich brown flanks and untacs.

GREEN-TAILED TOWHEE [43] Rascadorcito Migratorio *Pipilo chlorurus*
Range US–Mex. Res/win Mex (res n.nBajCal; win nPac+n.cPac, ncHi, nAtl). Rare.
Habitat Overgrown fields, gardens, borders, scrubby woods, partial clearings.
Field Marks 7″ Olive-green above; crown rufous; ear patch gray with white line below that, then black line, then white throat; breast and sides olive-gray.

COLLARED TOWHEE [42] Rascador Collarejo *Pipilo ocai*
Range Mex. Res Mex (w+e.+s.cHi).
Habitat Thickets at borders of pine, pine-oak, and fir forest, forest undergrowth or partial clearings, hedgerows.
Field Marks 8.5″ Eyes red. Yellow-olive above; whitish below, with buffy olive flanks; head and broad collar black, with rufous crown and nape; white throat and line over eye; bill black; iris red. See following Hybrids discussion.

HYBRIDS OF COLLARED TOWHEE AND SPOTTED TOWHEE [42]
A great variety of plumage patterns and colors, apparently intermediate between those of the Collared Towhee and the Spotted Towhee, occur mostly in the western and southeastern central Highlands. Most authorities consider them hybrids between the Collared and Spotted species. Other authorities, however, treat them as intergrades between two groups (the Collared group and the Spotted group) of a single species, the Spotted Towhee. Still others consider them distinct races of either the Collared or the Spotted species. Six representative plumage types are shown in small figures on Plate 42.

EASTERN TOWHEE Rascador Nororiental *Pipilo erythrophthalmus*
Range Can–Mex. Win Mex (n.nAtl). Very rare.
Habitat Hedgerows, dense borders, undergrowth in deciduous woods, brushy overgrown fields.
Field Marks Like Spotted Towhee, but *no* white spots or bars on wings and scapulars.

SPOTTED TOWHEE [42] Rascador Común *Pipilo maculatus*
Range Can–Mex, Guat. Res Mex (BajCal, Hi), Guat (Hi).
Habitat Thickets, borders, undergrowth in pine forest or pine-oak woods.
Field Marks 8″ Eyes red. M: upperparts, entire head, throat, and chest black, with two white wing bars, white spots on scapulars, and white tail corners; breast and belly white; sides, flanks, and untacs rufous. F: like male, but dark brown replaces black. See Hybrids discussion above.

CALIFORNIA TOWHEE [44] Rascador Pardo *Pipilo crissalis*
Range US–Mex. Res Mex (BajCal).
Habitat Brushy open areas with scattered trees, dry rocky hillsides, gardens, hedgerows, borders.
Field Marks 8″ Like Canyon Towhee, but darker overall; crown duller and more olive-brown; *no* central chest spot on necklace.

CANYON TOWHEE Rascador Cañonero *Pipilo fuscus*
Range US–Mex. Res Mex (nPac, ncHi).

Habitat Scrubby semidesert; dry, rocky, brushy hillsides; hedgerows, thickets.
Field Marks 8″ Gray-brown above; crown dull rufous; underparts whitish to pale gray to buffy brown untacs; necklace of dark spots around buffy throat, with larger central spot.

ABERT'S TOWHEE [44] Rascador Desértico *Pipilo aberti*
Range US–Mex. Res Mex (extreme ne.nBajCal + extreme nw.nPac).
Habitat Brushy undergrowth in scrubby woods, dry stream valleys.
Field Marks 8.5″ Like California Towhee, but *no* necklace or central spot on chest; black area all around base of thick bill; eyes pale brownish.

WHITE-THROATED TOWHEE [42] Rascador Oaxaqueño *Pipilo albicollis*
Range Mex. Res Mex (se.cHi + adj Pac).
Habitat Thickets in shrubby grassy areas, hedgerows, dry rocky hillsides, borders, gardens, parks.
Field Marks 7.5″ Like California Towhee, but throat contrasty white between tawny midthroat band and faint spotty throat-chest band; fresh plumage shows faint, narrow wing bars.

BRIDLED SPARROW [45] Zacatonero Patilludo *Aimophila mystacalis*
Range Mex. Res Mex (se.cPac + adj Hi).
Habitat Semidesert, rocky hillsides with mixed scrubby trees, thorny shrubs, patchy short grass, cactus.
Field Marks 6″ Black chin and upper throat with white-line border; rufous above and on flanks and untacs; black-streaked back; white wing bars.

BLACK-CHESTED SPARROW [45] Zacatonero Pechinegro *Aimophila humeralis*
Range Mex. Res Mex (w+c.cPac).
Habitat Brushy semidesert, thorny scrubby woods, borders.
Field Marks 6″ White throat, with black border and broad breast band; head mostly dark gray-brown; white mustache mark and spot in front of eye; streaked back; pale wing bars.

STRIPED-HEADED SPARROW [45] Zacatonero Charralero *Aimophila ruficauda*
Range Mex–CRic, exc Blz. Res Mex (s.nPac+cPac), Guat (se Pac, e Atl), ElSal.
Habitat Thickets in dry overgrown fields or pastures, hedgerows, scrubby woods, vacant lots, borders.
Voice A series of sharp, high pitched notes in chorus or duet, *pich-ee-pich-ee-pich-ee-pich-ee.*
Field Marks 6.5″ Black-and-white crown, line over eye, and ear patch; streaked back; whitish below; birds from Mex (extreme se.cPac), Guat (Pac), and ElSal have spotty pale gray chest band.

(CINNAMON-TAILED) SUMICHRAST'S SPARROW [45] Zacatonero Ístmico
Aimophila sumichrasti
Range Mex. Res Mex (extreme se.cPac + adj sPac). Rare, local.
Habitat Borders, hedgerows, scrubby thorny woods, patchy short grass.
Field Marks 6.5″ Crown and back striped dark brown, with whitish center stripe and line over eye; front of face whitish with black-bordered white mus-

tache mark; lower mandible pale yellowish, tail cinnamon-rufous. See Rusty and Rufous-winged Sparrows.

BOTTERI'S SPARROW [44] Zacatonero de Botteri *Aimophila botterii*
Range US–CRic, exc ElSal. Sum Mex (Pac, ncHi, Atl, w+nw Yuc), Blz (cas), Guat (Pac). Irregular.
Habitat Pastures, weedy fields, grassy plains with scattered pines and palmettos.
Field Marks 5.5" Grayish above with dark rufous stripes on back; fine streaks on rufous crown; sides of head and underparts grayish buff, with slightly darker line through eye; tail rounded, grayish brown. See Cassin's Sparrow.

CASSIN'S SPARROW [44] Zacatonero de Cassin *Aimophila cassinii*
Range US–Mex. Res/win Mex (nPac, nHi, nAtl). Rare, local.
Habitat Open grassy plains, mesquite grassland, short-grass pastures.
Field Marks 5.5" Like Botteri's Sparrow, but more scalloped than streaked above; faint flank streaks; outer tail feathers pale-tipped.

RUFOUS-WINGED SPARROW [44] Zacatonero Sonorense *Aimophila carpalis*
Range US–Mex. Res/win Mex (nPac).
Habitat Dry grassy plains with shrubs and small trees, grassy openings or borders, scrubby overgrown fields.
Field Marks 5.5" Like Sumichrast's Sparrow (no range overlap), but tail gray, *not* rufous; more fine streaks in broad crown stripes; wrist patch brighter rufous.

RUFOUS-CROWNED SPARROW [44] Zacatonero Coronirrufo *Aimophila ruficeps*
Range US–Mex. Res Mex (nBajCal, w+e.nHi+cHi + adj Pac+Atl).
Habitat Dry to semidesert scrub, rocky slopes with patchy shrubs and short grass.
Field Marks 6" Grayish brown above, with dull rufous streaks; crown and line through eye plain rufous; line over eye, sides of face, and underparts pale brownish gray, with slightly darker breast; black streak below faint whitish mustache mark; *no* rufous wrist patch.

OAXACA SPARROW [45] Zacatonero Oaxaqueño *Aimophila notosticta*
Range Mex. Res Mex (se.cHi). Rare, local.
Habitat Dry brushy hillsides or ravines, with patchy grass, thorny shrubs, small trees.
Field Marks 6.5" Back brownish with blackish brown streaks; crown rufous, may be finely streaked; sides of head gray with contrasty black-and-white streaks; underparts pale gray to grayish buff; bill black. See Rusty Sparrow.

RUSTY SPARROW [45] Zacatonero Rojizo *Aimophila rufescens*
Range Mex–CRic. Res Mex (Pac + adj Hi, s.nAtl–w.sAtl + adj Hi), Blz (local), Guat, ElSal.
Habitat Thickets, weedy undergrowth in pine or pine-oak woods, borders, hedgerows, partial clearings, drier piney ridges in cloud forest.
Field Marks 7" Races vary. Typically brownish above, with black-streaked back; crown rufous, may be finely streaked or mottled, or have grayish partial center

stripe; blackish line through eye; black streak below dull whitish mustache mark; tail dark rufous; lower mandible pale grayish. See Sumichrast's and Oaxaca Sparrows.

FIVE-STRIPED SPARROW [45] Gorrión Cincorrayas *Aimophila quinquestriata*
Range US-Mex. Sum/win Mex (nPac).
Habitat Densely shrubby areas, dry brushy slopes, dry weedy overgrown fields.
Field Marks 5.5" Dark grayish brown above, with dark brown, black, and white head; medium gray breast, sides, and flanks, with black spot on chest.

STRIPED SPARROW [42] Gorrión Rayado *Oriturus superciliosus*
Range Mex. Res Mex (w.nHi+cHi).
Habitat High-mountain bunchgrass fields, grassy open pine woods, grassy borders.
Field Marks 6.5" Heavily striped above, pale gray below; crown rufous, with finely black-streaked gray center stripe; whitish line over eye; black ear patch and bill.

CHIPPING SPARROW [43] Chimbito Común *Spizella passerina*
Range AK-Nic. Res/win Mex (BajCal, nPac, Hi, nAtl), Blz, Guat (Pac, Hi, Atl), ElSal (n).
Habitat Open pine woods, grassy woods borders, clearings; in flocks in dry grassland.
Field Marks 5" Sum adt: back heavily streaked; crown rufous, sharply bordered by white line over eye; black line through eye; black bill; pale gray nape, cheeks, rump, and underparts. Imm+win adt: crown fine-streaked; superciliary line and ear patch brownish gray; bill yellowish.

CLAY-COLORED SPARROW [44] Chimbito Pálido *Spizella pallida*
Range Can-Mex, Guat. Res/tr Mex (BajCal, ncPac, ncHi, ncAtl; cas/acc Yuc), Guat (cas Hi).
Habitat Dry grassy fields, borders, parks, grassy hedgerows.
Field Marks 5" Heavily streaked black on buffy brown back; crown finely black-streaked, with gray center stripe; nape grayish; ear patch buff-brown; rump grayish tan like back color; whitish below. See Chipping and Brewer's Sparrows.

BREWER'S SPARROW [44] Chimbito Desértico *Spizella breweri*
Range Can-Mex. Win Mex (BajCal, n.nPac, nHi).
Habitat Dry short-grass fields, semidesert with patchy grass and thorny shrubs.
Field Marks 5" Like Clay-colored Sparrow, but white eye ring; *no* center crown stripe.

FIELD SPARROW [43] Chimbito Llanero *Spizella pusilla*
Range Can-Mex. Win Mex (ne.nHi, n.nAtl). Rare.
Habitat Grassy plains, grassy overgrown clearings, borders, hedgerows.
Field Marks 5" Heavily streaked black and rufous on buff back and scapulars; crown, nape, and line behind eye rich dark rufous; white eye ring and wing bars; breast pale gray; rufous wash on sides and flanks; bill pinkish.

WORTHEN'S SPARROW [45] Chimbito Altiplanero *Spizella wortheni*
Range Mex. Res Mex (se.nHi+n.cHi). Very rare.
Habitat Dry grassy weedy fields with thickets, hedgerows, grassy openings in dense brushy areas.
Field Marks 5″ Like Field Sparrow, but somewhat paler overall; *no* dark rufous line behind eye; more prominent eye ring.

BLACK-CHINNED SPARROW [44] Chimbito Carbonero *Spizella atrogularis*
Range US–Mex. Res/win Mex (sum n.nBajCal, n.nPac; res/win BajCal, n.nPac, ncHi).
Habitat Grassy scrubby slopes, semidesert, patchy grass and thorny shrubs.
Field Marks 5″ M: dark gray; streaked brown and blackish back; black upper throat and narrow eye patch; whitish belly, untacs, and wing bars; pinkish bill. F+imm: little or no black or blackish gray on throat and around eye.

VESPER SPARROW [43] Gorrión Torito *Pooecetes gramineus*
Range Can–Mex, Guat. Win Mex (BajCal, ncPac, ncHi, ncAtl; cas/very rare sHi, Yuc), Guat (Hi).
Habitat Tree-dotted grassland, grassy borders and hedgerows, overgrown brushy fields.
Field Marks 6″ Streaked above and below with blackish brown; tail notched, with white outer feathers; brownish ear patch against whitish background; white eye ring.

LARK SPARROW [44] Gorrión Arlequín *Chondestes grammacus*
Range Can–ElSal, Hon. Res/win Mex (res nBajCal, nPac, nHi; tr/win all); win Guat (Pac), ElSal (cas).
Habitat Pastures, grassy fields, farmyards, hedgerows, overgrown fields, borders.
Field Marks 6″ Entire head striped contrasty black, chestnut, and white; underparts whitish, with black spot on breast; tail rounded; outer tail feathers black, broadly white-cornered. Juv: head much duller; breast streaked.

BLACK-THROATED SPARROW [44] Chiero Gorjinegro *Amphispiza bilineata*
Range US–Mex. Res Mex (BajCal, nPac, nHi+n.cHi, nAtl).
Habitat Brushy, thorny semidesert, dry scrubby fields.
Field Marks 5.5″ Crown, nape, and ear patch black and gray; throat to upper breast black; white line over eye and below ear patch; mostly white below, brownish gray above; white tail sides. Juv: streaked above and below; *no* black on throat.

SAGE SPARROW [44] Chiero de Lunar *Amphispiza belli*
Range US–Mex. Res/win Mex (res nBajCal+nw.sBajCal; win nPac, nHi).
Habitat Dry scrub, semidesert, dry slopes with thorny shrubs and small trees.
Field Marks 5.5″ Black streaks on gray above, with blackish or gray crown, nape, and sides of head; white line over eye; fine streaks and a black breast spot on white underparts.

LARK BUNTING [43] Gorrión Alipálido *Calamospiza melanocorys*
Range Can–Mex. Win Mex (BajCal, n.nPac, nHi+n.chi, n.nAtl).
Habitat Open grassy plains, roadsides, dry brushy fields.
Field Marks 7" Sum M: black; large white wing patch; white tail-tip spots; bill dark, rather heavy. F: finely streaked black on dark brown above, brown on whitish below; pale buffy stripes above and below ear patch; wing patch buffy or whitish. Win M: like female, but much more contrasty; spotty or blotchy black throat.

SAVANNAH SPARROW [44] Gorrión Sabanero *Passerculus sandwichensis*
Range AK–ElSal, Hon. Res/win Mex (res BajCal, nPac + adj Hi, chi; tr/win all exc sPac, shi); cas Blz, Guat, ElSal.
Habitat Grassy fields, marshes, grassy borders of marshes, hedgerows.
Field Marks 5" Races vary, but all are streaked above (sometimes only faintly) and below; may have central breast spot; tail notched; may have yellow above eye.

BAIRD'S SPARROW Gorrión de Baird *Ammodramus bairdii*
Range Can–Mex. Win Mex (n.nHi). Rare.
Habitat Tree-dotted grassy plains, dry grassy rocky slopes.
Field Marks 5" Crown and nape finely black-streaked, with tawny buff center stripe; face buffy; underparts whitish, with chest band made up of short streaks; short, notched tail. Much like Grasshopper Sparrow, but white and streaked below, *not* buff and unstreaked.

GRASSHOPPER SPARROW [44] Gorrión Chapulín *Ammodramus savannarum*
Range Can–SAm. Res/win Mex (res nBajCal, nPac, nchi, se.cAtl+sAtl; win all); res Blz; win Guat (Pac, Atl), ElSal. Sum rare, local; win common.
Habitat Grassy meadows, grassy borders of farm fields, mixed grass, weeds, and low shrubs.
Field Marks 5" Rich buff throat, breast, sides, untacs, may have faint streaks; crown striped black on buff; back striped black, rufous, and buff; tail short, feather tips pointed.

SIERRA MADRE SPARROW [42] Gorrión Serrano *Xenospiza baileyi*
Range Mex. Res Mex (sw.nHi + c.chi) Very rare, local.
Habitat Lush grass, often bunchgrass, on open slopes or among scattered pines, or grassy, brushy thickets in mountain meadows.
Field Marks 5" Heavily streaked black on rufous above; sides of head (including line over eye) gray with fine black streaks; heavy black streaks on whitish below. Somewhat like a dark-streaked Song Sparrow (may have central breast spot), but smaller, more delicate and slender; more rufous above; shorter-tailed.

FOX SPARROW [43] Gorrión Rascador *Passerella iliaca*
Range AK–Mex. Win Mex (n.nBajCal; cas nPac).
Habitat Thickets, forest undergrowth and borders, hedgerows, gardens.
Field Marks 6.5" Races visiting Mexico may have unstreaked blackish brown,

brown, or gray crown, sides of head, and back; rufous or brownish rump and tail; pale gray mustache mark; speckled throat; heavily streaked breast, sides, and flanks.

SONG SPARROW [44] Gorrión Cantor *Melospiza melodia*
Range AK–Mex. Res/win Mex (res BajCal, n.nPac, w.nHi+cHi; win n.nPac, n.nHi). Local and irregular.
Habitat Gardens, parks, woodland borders, thickets, dense marshes, marshy ponds.
Field Marks 6″ Races vary from pale rufous and gray, only lightly streaked (BajCal+nPac), to dark brownish, rather heavily streaked, above and below, to almost blackish brown and heavily streaked (ncHi). All have rather long, rounded tail, moved up and down in flight, and most have large central breast spot.

LINCOLN'S SPARROW [43] Gorrión de Lincoln *Melospiza lincolnii*
Range AK–Pan. Tr/win Mex (all, but very rare sAtl, Yuc), Blz (s), Guat (Hi), ElSal.
Habitat Thickets, undergrowth in pine, pine-oak, fir forests, shrubby borders, hedgerows.
Field Marks 5″ Fine blackish streaks on rich buff breast and sides; lower breast, belly, and untacs white; center crown stripe gray, lateral crown stripes black and reddish brown; sides of face, including line over eye, gray; black-streaked back and scapulars.

SWAMP SPARROW [43] Gorrión Pantanero *Melospiza georgiana*
Range Can–Mex. Win Mex (ncHi, nAtl+n.cAtl; cas/very rare nw.nPac). Rare.
Habitat Marshes, swamps, flooded woods, bogs.
Field Marks 5.5″ Sum adt: streaked brown and black back; wings and rump mostly rufous; *no* distinct wing bars; crown rufous, partly edged black; center of forehead gray; throat distinctly whitish; breast, ear patch, and line over eye gray; may be faintly streaked below, especially in winter. Win adt: crown finely streaked black, brown, and gray. Imm: ear patch buffy.

(RUFOUS-COLLARED) ANDEAN SPARROW [45] Gorrión Chingolo *Zonotrichia capensis*
Range Mex–SAm, exc Blz, Nic. Res Mex (sHi + adj Pac, Atl), Guat (Hi + adj Pac, Atl), ElSal.
Habitat Parks, gardens, orchards, patios, hedgerows, borders, partial clearings.
Voice Two or three loud and musical extended notes.
Field Marks 5.5″ Back heavily streaked brownish and black; top and sides of head boldly striped black and gray; throat and face below ear patch white; throat-chest patch black; partial collar rufous; belly, flanks, and untacs pale dull brownish.

WHITE-THROATED SPARROW [43] Gorrión Gorjiblanco *Zonotrichia albicollis*
Range Can–Mex. Win Mex (n.nAtl; cas/very rare nBajCal, n.nPac). Very rare.
Habitat Thickets, hedgerows, borders, brushy clearings.

Field Marks 6" Adt: streaked above; head stripes black and white or blackish brown and dull buff; ear patch gray; distinct white throat; bright or dull yellow spot in front of eye; white wing bars; breast plain pearly gray or faintly to rather heavily streaked dull gray; belly and untacs pale gray to whitish.

WHITE-CROWNED SPARROW [43] Gorrión Coroniblanco *Zonotrichia leucophrys*
Range AK–Mex. Win Mex (BajCal, ncPac, nHi+nw.cHi, nAtl; cas/very rare n Yuc).
Habitat Thickets, hedgerows, overgrown clearings, borders.
Field Marks 6" Adt: contrasty black-and-white crown pattern and line through eye; breast and sides of head pearly gray; throat, belly, and untacs whitish; bill pinkish or yellowish; back streaked black, brown, and whitish; two white wing bars. Imm: stripes on crown brown, buff, and whitish.

GOLDEN-CROWNED SPARROW [43] Gorrión Coronidorado *Zonotrichia atricapilla*
Range AK–Mex. Win Mex (nBajCal; cas/very rare sBajCal, nw.nPac).
Habitat Thickets, hedgerows, gardens, borders, brushy vacant lots.
Field Marks 6.5" Streaked above; crown patch dull yellow, with broad black borders; wing bars white; throat, sides of head, breast, and sides pale gray and brownish gray. Imm: crown fine-streaked, with trace of yellow and black pattern or not; browner face.

DARK-EYED JUNCO [44] Carbonero Apizarrado *Junco hyemalis*
Slate-colored group [44] Carbonero Apizarrado *J. h. hyemalis*
Range AK–Mex. Win Mex (nBajCal, n.nPac, n.nHi, nAtl). Rare.
Habitat Overgrown clearings, brushy open woods, hedgerows, borders.
Field Marks 6" M: dark gray, with white belly, untacs, and outer tail feathers; bill pale. F: duller.
Oregon subgroup [44] Carbonero Pinto *J. h. oreganus*
Range AK–Mex. Res/win Mex (res n.nBajCal; win nBajCal, n.nPac, n.nHi; cas/very rare s.sBajCal, n.nAtl).
Habitat Borders, brushy open woods, hedgerows.
Field Marks 6" M: entire head and chest black; back rusty brown; belly and outer tail feathers white; sides rufous; bill pale. F: duller.
Pink-sided subgroup Carbonero Rosado *J. h. mearnsi*
Range Can–Mex. Win Mex (n.nHi).
Habitat Borders, open woods, hedgerows.
Field Marks 6" Head pale gray; back dull brown; sides and flanks pinkish; outer tail feathers white.
Gray-headed group [44] Carbonero Viejo *J. h. caniceps*
Range US–Mex. Win Mex (nPac, nHi).
Habitat Thickets, hedgerows, borders.
Field Marks 6" Rump and top and sides of head pale to medium gray; back bright rufous; very pale gray below; outer tail feathers white; bill typically pale.

YELLOW-EYED JUNCO [44] Carbonero Ojilumbre *Junco phaeonotus*
Mexican group Carbonero Mexicano *J. p. phaeonotus*
   Range US–Mex. Res Mex (w+e.nHi + adj Pac+Atl+cHi).
   Habitat Undergrowth or partial clearings in pine forest, pine-oak woods, or fir forest, borders.
   Field Marks 6″ Head and rump mostly medium gray; lores black; throat, breast, and sides pale gray; back rich reddish brown; outer tail feathers white; iris yellow; bill blackish above, yellowish below.
Baird's group Carbonero del Cabo *J. p. bairdi*
   Range Mex. Res Mex (s.sBajCal).
   Habitat Mountain forest undergrowth, openings, borders.
   Field Marks 5.5″ Like Mexican group, but paler head; less contrast between paler, duller back and browner rump; pale rufous sides and flanks; paler breast.
Chiapas group Carbonero Chiapaneco *J. p. fulvescens*
   Range Mex. Res Mex (nw.+c.sHi).
   Habitat Partial clearings or undergrowth in pine or pine-oak forest, borders, roadsides.
   Field Marks 6″ Like Mexican group, but darker below; back duller; rump less contrasty.
Guatemala group Carbonero Guatemalteco *J. p. alticola*
   Range Mex, Guat. Res Mex (se.sHi), Guat (Hi).
   Habitat Openings or undergrowth in pine or pine oak forest, overgrown clearings, borders.
   Field Marks 6.5″ Like Chiapas group, but larger and much duller and darker above.

MCCOWN'S LONGSPUR [43] Arnoldo de McCown *Calcarius mccownii*
   Range Can–Mex. Win Mex (n.nPac, n.nHi).
   Habitat Treeless short-grass plains, dry open fields, pastures, bare cultivated fields.
   Field Marks 5.5″ Tail white with central, inverted black T. Sum M: streaked above; black crown; white line over eye; gray ear patch with black lower border; throat broadly white; black chest patch; white belly and gray sides and flanks; rufous wrist patch. F+win M: rufous wrist patch, often concealed; crown finely streaked; throat, sides of face, and line over eye buffy, with grayish brown ear patch; breast patch brownish, scaly, may be faint or absent.

CHESTNUT-COLLARED LONGSPUR [43] Arnoldo Ventrinegro *Calcarius ornatus*
   Range Can–Mex. Win Mex (n.nPac, nHi+n.cHi; cas/very rare sBajCal, c.cHi, c.cPac).
   Habitat Grassy plains, large open fields, lakeshores.
   Field Marks 5.5″ Tail white with broad, black inverted V. Sum M: heavily streaked above; black-and-white head, with pale yellow on throat and ear patch; chestnut hindneck to side of neck; mostly black below, with white belly. F: like McCown's Longspur, but see tail pattern; also more heavily streaked be-

low; *no* trace of rufous wrist patch. Win M: head and throat mostly buffy whitish, with scaled blackish and buffy or whitish crown and underparts; may have pale tawny collar.

GROSBEAKS, BUNTINGS—PICOGRUESOS, COLORINES—CARDINALIDAE

(GRAYISH) GRAY SALTATOR [41] Saltador Gris *Saltator coerulescens*
Range Mex–CRic, SAm. Res Mex (s.nPac+cspac, Atl, Yuc), Blz, Guat (Pac, Atl), ElSal.
Habitat Partial clearings, mixed farms and scrubby woods, hedgerows, gardens, orchards, borders.
Voice A loud slow *chew-chew-wheet.*
Field Marks 9" Gray to brownish gray above; white line over eye; grayish buff below; throat white, black-bordered.

BUFF-THROATED SALTATOR [41] Saltador Brincón *Saltator maximus*
Range Mex–SAm, exc ElSal (acc). Res Mex (se.cAtl+sAtl), Blz, Guat (Atl), ElSal (acc).
Habitat Humid woods, forest borders, hedgerows, partial clearings.
Voice Gentle, musical, mellow warbling sounds.
Field Marks 9" Like buff-throated race of Black-headed Saltator, but smaller; nape medium gray, *not* mostly black.

BLACK-HEADED SALTATOR [41] Saltador Chorcha *Saltator atriceps*
Range Mex–Pan. Res Mex (csPac, s.nAtl+csAtl, Yuc), Blz, Guat (Pac, Atl), ElSal.
Habitat Thickets at forest borders, open woods, tree-dotted fields, wooded riversides, hedgerows.
Voice A shrill descending chatter, *chut-chut-chut-chut-chut;* a shrill *chreet.*
Field Marks 10" Very noisy, in small flocks or family groups. Rich yellow-green above, crown and nape broadly black; sides of head black or blackish gray; throat white with broad black border, or (in Sierra de Tuxtla, cAtl) throat buffy; breast and belly gray; untacs rufous. See Buff-throated Saltator.

BLACK-FACED GROSBEAK [41] Picogrueso Carinegro *Caryothraustes poliogaster*
Range Mex–Pan, exc ElSal. Res Mex (sc.cAtl+sAtl), Blz, Guat (Atl).
Habitat Dense humid forest, in middle and upper branches.
Voice An unmusical note, then a loud doubled whistle.
Field Marks 7" Very active, often in flocks. Yellow-green wings, tail, and back; pale gray rump; very pale gray or whitish belly and untacs; bright greenish yellow all around black face and throat.

CRIMSON-COLLARED GROSBEAK [41] Picogrueso Cuellirrojo *Rhodothraupis celaeno*
Range Mex. Res Mex (s.nAtl+n.cAtl). Rare.
Habitat Wooded riversides, humid forest, borders, tree-dotted overgrown fields, lush hedgerows.

Field Marks 8″ M: black, with broadly red full collar, breast, and belly; medium to dark gray bill. F: dull yellowish olive, brighter below; black crown, face, and throat.

NORTHERN CARDINAL [40] Cardenal Común *Cardinalis cardinalis*
Range Can–Mex, Blz, Guat. Res Mex (sBajCal, ncPac, Atl, Yuc), Blz (n), Guat (nw Atl). Irregular.
Habitat Scrubby woods, borders, brushy overgrown fields, hedgerows, thickets.
Field Marks 8″ Crested; heavy bill red in adult. M: bright red; black around base of bill. F: grayish brown and buffy brown, with red tinge on wings, tail, and crest; dark gray around base of bill. Imm: dull dark brown, including bill.

PYRRHULOXIA [40] Cardenal Torito *Cardinalis sinuatus*
Range US–Mex. Res Mex (sBajCal, nPac, nHi+n.cHi, nAtl). Irregular.
Habitat Arid brushy areas, semidesert, thickets, mesquite grassland.
Field Marks 8″ Heavy pale dull yellow bill, with curved culmen. M: grayish, with rosy red face-throat-breast patch, tail, part of wings, and tip of crest. F: duller, more olive-gray; no red on throat or breast. Compare with Northern Cardinal.

YELLOW GROSBEAK [41] Picogrueso Amarillo *Pheucticus chrysopeplus*
Range Mex, Guat. Res Mex (nPac+nw.cPac+sPac + adj Hi), Guat (Pac).
Habitat Dense scrubby woods, borders, hedgerows, partial clearings.
Field Marks 9″ M: breast, belly, back, and entire head and throat bright yellow, or orange in Mex (sPac) and Guat (Pac); wings and tail black and white; bill very heavy and black (any bright Mexican oriole will have a much smaller bill and some black on head or throat). F: duller; heavily streaked above; two white wing bars.

ROSE-BREASTED GROSBEAK [43] Picogrueso Pechirrosa *Pheucticus ludovicianus*
Range Can–SAm. Tr/win Mex (cSPac, sHi, Atl, Yuc; cas/very rare BajCal, nPac, ncHi), Blz, Guat, ElSal.
Habitat River-border woods, parks, gardens, orchards, humid forest, borders.
Field Marks 7.5″ Heavy dull yellowish bill. Sum adt M: black head and back; black-and-white wings and tail; red breast patch and underwing; mostly white belly and rump. Imm M+win M: much like summer adult male, but dark areas browner, pale areas duller, streaked or mottled. F: heavily streaked dark brown and pale buff on upperparts, head, and most of underparts; wing bars and line over eye whitish; resembles female Purple Finch, but larger and larger-billed.

BLACK-HEADED GROSBEAK [40] Picogrueso Tigrillo *Pheucticus melanocephalus*
Range Can–Mex. Res/win Mex (res/sum nBajCal, n.nPac, ncHi; tr/win BajCal, ncPac, ncAtl).
Habitat Pine, pine-oak, or fir forest, borders, gardens, wooded riversides.
Field Marks 7.5″ Yellow underwing. Adt M: black head; orange-brown breast and partial collar, shading to yellowish buff to whitish untacs; heavily streaked back; wings and tail black and white. F+imm M: like female Rose-breasted

Grosbeak, but rich brownish buff below, not whitish, with fewer and finer streaks.

BLUE-BLACK GROSBEAK [41] Picogrueso Negro *Cyanocompsa cyanoides*
Range Mex–SAm, exc ElSal. Res Mex (se.cAtl+sAtl), Blz, Guat (Atl). Rare.
Habitat Humid forest undergrowth, borders, weedy forest openings, thickets.
Voice Rasping, clinking call notes.
Field Marks 6.5″ Very heavy dark bill. M: appears black; actually blackish blue with slightly paler forehead, sides of crown, and wrist patch. F: dark, rich chocolate-brown.

BLUE BUNTING [41] Azulejito *Cyanocompsa parellina*
Range Mex–Nic. Res Mex (c.nPac–cPac, s.nAtl+csAtl, Yuc), Blz (n), Guat (Pac, Atl), ElSal.
Habitat Scrubby woods, undergrowth of wooded riversides, weedy borders and thickets, overgrown fields.
Field Marks 5.5″ M: dark blue, except powder-blue forehead, malar streak, rump, and wrist patch. F: brown; paler and buffier below.

BLUE GROSBEAK [40] Piquigordo Azul *Guiraca caerulea*
Range US–CRic. Res/win Mex (res/sum nBajCal, nPac, Hi, ncAtl; tr/win BajCal, Pac, Atl, Yuc), win Blz, res/win Guat, res ElSal.
Habitat Scattered thickets in open, dry, rocky, grassy fields, scrubby woods borders, weedy grassy hedgerows.
Field Marks 6″ Heavy bill. Adt M: dark violet-blue, with black-streaked back; black wings with rufous wing bars and feather edgings; bill contrasty whitish. F: brownish, with brownish bill; streaked above; buffy below, with some faint streaks; buff wing bars; rump may be bluish.

(ROSE-BELLIED) ROSITA'S BUNTING [41] Colorín de Rosita *Passerina rositae*
Range Mex. Res Mex (border of cPac with sPac). Rare, local.
Habitat Dense scrubby woods, thickets, dry brushy hillsides.
Field Marks 5.5″ M: medium blue, darker and richer on head; patchy red and blue breast; rose-pink belly and untacs. F: brown, blue tinged above, pink-tinged below.

LAZULI BUNTING [40] Colorín Aliblanco *Passerina amoena*
Range Can–Mex, Blz? Sum/win Mex (sum n.nBajCal; tr/win BajCal, nPac+ n.cPac, w.ncHi), Blz (cas/acc?).
Habitat Tree-dotted brushy fields, weedy hedgerows and thickets, open scrubby woods, borders.
Field Marks 5″ Whitish wing bars; bluish rump. M: blue head; streaked back; tawny breast; white belly and untacs. F: brown head and back; paler and buffier below; two buffy wing bars.

INDIGO BUNTING [43] Colorín Azul *Passerina cyanea*
Range Can–SAm. Tr/win Mex (cspac, csHi, Atl, Yuc; cas/very rare BajCal, nPac, nHi), Blz, Guat, ElSal.

Habitat Short-grass fields with scattered shrubs, hedgerows, thickets or scrubby woods, borders.
Field Marks 5" Sum M: rich dark blue. Win M: dark brown above, whitish below; rump and breast tinged blue. F+imm: brown above; paler below, faintly streaked.

VARIED BUNTING [40] Colorín Morado *Passerina versicolor*
Range US–Mex, Guat. Res/sum Mex (sBajCal, Pac, ncHi, ncAtl), Guat (Atl).
Habitat Dense scrubby woods, semidesert scrub, overgrown fields, borders.
Field Marks 5" M: may appear black; actually purple, with bluish rump, red nape patch, and blackish wings; somewhat mottled or scaly in winter. F: grayish brown, paler below; *not* streaked.

ORANGE-BREASTED BUNTING [41] Colorín Ventridorado *Passerina leclancherii*
Range Mex. Res Mex (cPac).
Habitat Open scrubby woods, woodland borders, dry brushy hillsides, partial clearings, hedgerows.
Field Marks 5" M: bright blue above, rich bright yellow and orange below. F: dull gray-green above; wings and tail tinged bluish; much brighter yellow below than other buntings.

PAINTED BUNTING [40] Colorín Sietecolores *Passerina ciris*
Range US–Pan. Sum/win Mex (sum nc.+ne.nHi; tr/win all exc BajCal; cas/acc sBajCal); win Blz, Guat (mainly Pac, Atl), ElSal.
Habitat Weedy fields, borders, openings in forest, partial clearings, thickets.
Field Marks 5" M: red below and on rump; dark violet-blue head; bright yellow-green back. F+imm: distinctive lime-green above, with darker wings; dull pale greenish gray below.

DICKCISSEL [43] Espiza *Spiza americana*
Range Can–SAm. Tr/win Mex (s.nPac+csPac, sHi, Atl, Yuc; cas/acc sBajCal, nPac, nHi), Blz, Guat, ElSal. Irregular.
Habitat Grassy fields with weedy thickets, hedgerows among farm fields and pastures.
Field Marks 6" Yellowish line over eye; rufous wrist patch. M: black or dark gray throat patch; yellow breast; streaked back. F+imm: much duller; *no* black throat patch; underparts buffy or partly yellow, finely streaked or plain.

BLACKBIRDS, ORIOLES—TORDOS, BOLSEROS—ICTERIDAE

BOBOLINK Tordo Migratorio *Dolichonyx oryzivorus*
Range Can–SAm. Tr Mex (e Yuc; cas/acc BajCal), Blz (cstl + cayes), Guat (Atl). Rare.
Habitat Hay fields, rice fields, fields of tall grass and weeds.
Field Marks 7" Sum M: underparts, crown, and sides of head black; scapulars, rump, and uptacs white; nape and hindneck broadly pale buffy yellow. F+win

M: like a large sparrow, with dark streaks on buff to tawny buff background, especially on head, back, and flanks; darker above, paler below.

RED-WINGED BLACKBIRD [46] Tordo Sargento *Agelaius phoeniceus*
Range AK–CRic. Res/win Mex (res nBajCal, csPac, w+e.nHi+chi, Atl, Yuc; win BajCal, npac); res Blz (n), Guat (Pac, Atl), ElSal.
Habitat Marshy areas, moist grassy fields, hay fields, pastures, cropland.
Field Marks 9", 7.5" Often in single-sex flocks in winter. M: black; red wrist patch, bordered yellowish or whitish. F: dark gray or blackish; heavily streaked below; may show trace of red on wrist patch and pinkish on throat. Imm M: blackish, scaled or mottled; dull red wrist patch.

TRICOLORED BLACKBIRD [46] Tordo Capitán *Agelaius tricolor*
Range US–Mex. Res Mex (nw nBajCal). Local.
Habitat Pastures, grassy fields, open cropland; nests in large colonies in marshy areas.
Field Marks 8.5", 7.5" Like Red-winged Blackbird, but M: wrist patch broadly bordered white; F: trace of red on wrist patch (but less than on immature male Red-winged Blackbird).

EASTERN MEADOWLARK [46] Pradero Común *Sturnella magna*
Range Can–SAm. Res Mex (nPac, Hi, ncAtl+w.sAtl, n Yuc), Blz (s), Guat (Hi, Atl), ElSal (w).
Habitat Grassy fields, partly overgrown pastures, hay fields, openings in mesquite grassland.
Voice A slurred whistle, *chee-wee, chee-wee.*
Field Marks 9" Streaked above; streaked head; mostly bright yellow below, with black breast patch and side streaks; white outer tail feathers; some races paler. See Western Meadowlark.

WESTERN MEADOWLARK Pradero Gorjeador *Sturnella neglecta*
Range Can–Mex. Res/win Mex (res nBajCal, n.nPac, nHi; win BajCal, nPac, ncHi, nAtl).
Habitat Open grassy areas, dry grassy plains, hay fields, pastures.
Voice Abrupt, mellow, chortling, descending series.
Field Marks 9" Like Eastern Meadowlark, but usually more yellow on malar area; slightly less white on tail; best identified by song

YELLOW-HEADED BLACKBIRD [46] Tordo Cabeciamarillo *Xanthocephalus xanthocephalus*
Range Can–Mex, CRic, Pan. Res/win Mex (res n.nBajCal, n.nAtl; tr/win sBajCal, ncPac, ncHi, nAtl; cas/very rare cAtl, Yuc). Irregular.
Habitat Usually cattail or bulrush marshes, hay fields, pastures, cropland.
Field Marks 9", 8" M: black; yellow head and breast; white wing patch. F+imm: dark brown above; head brown and yellowish; chest dull yellow; belly streaked dark and whitish.

(MELODIOUS) SINGING BLACKBIRD [47] Tordo Cantor *Dives dives*
Range Mex–Nic. Res Mex (s.nAtl+csAtl, Yuc), Blz, Guat (Atl), ElSal.
Habitat Humid forest borders, open woodlots, lush hedgerows, orchards, tree-dotted pastures.
Voice A loud, whistled note, then one or two lower-pitched notes; often sung antiphonally and in rounds.
Field Marks 11″ Usually in pairs, in small loose flocks. Black; green gloss on male; eyes dark brown.

BREWER'S BLACKBIRD [46] Tordo Ojiclaro *Euphagus cyanocephalus*
Range Can–Mex, Guat. Res/win Mex (n.nBajCal; win BajCal, nPac+nw.cPac, ncHi, nAtl+n.cAtl), very rare Guat (Hi).
Habitat Farmyards, corrals, cropland, pastures, parks, gardens, vacant lots.
Field Marks 9″ Often in flocks. M: iridescent black; eyes yellow. F: gray-brown; eyes brown.

GREAT-TAILED GRACKLE [46] Zanate Mexicano *Quiscalus mexicanus*
Range US–SAm. Res Mex (nBajCal, Pac, Hi, Atl, Yuc), Blz, Guat, ElSal.
Habitat Suburban areas, city parks, plazas, farmyards, pastures, cropland, orchards.
Field Marks 17″, 13″ Yellow eyes. M: iridescent black; tail long, keel-shaped. F: blackish brown; paler on face, throat, and breast; tail rather long, somewhat keel-shaped.

BRONZED COWBIRD [46] Tordo Ojirrojo *Molothrus aeneus*
Range US–Pan. Res Mex (Pac, Hi, Atl, Yuc; cas nBajCal), Blz, Guat, ElSal.
Habitat Farms, tree-dotted pastures, open woods, borders.
Field Marks 8″, 7″ Courting male hovers a few feet above female on ground. Glossy black; eyes red; ruff may show on hindneck. F: duller.

BROWN-HEADED COWBIRD [46] Tordo Cabecicafé *Molothrus ater*
Range AK–Mex. Res/win Mex (BajCal, ncPac, ncHi, ncAtl).
Habitat Scrubby woods, partial clearings, borders, grassy hedgerows.
Field Marks 7.5″, 6.5″ M: glossy black, with entire head dark brown; tail short; bill black, short. F: dull brownish gray; somewhat paler and faintly streaked below.

GIANT COWBIRD [47] Tordo Gigante *Scaphidura oryzivora*
Range Mex–SAm, exc ElSal. Res Mex (se.cAtl+sAtl), Blz, Guat (Atl). Rare.
Habitat Tall trees in partial clearings or openings, or projecting above the canopy, in humid forest, borders, or tree-dotted pastures.
Field Marks 14″, 12″ Often in loose flocks on high, exposed branches, in or near oropendola colonies. M: glossy black, with prominent neck ruff and red eyes. F: duller; ruff small or absent. Imm: eyes whitish.

BLACK-COWLED ORIOLE [47] Bolsero de Sureste *Icterus dominicensis*
Range Mex–Pan, exc ElSal. Res Mex (se.cAtl+sAtl, Yuc), Blz, Guat (Atl). Rare.

Habitat Humid forest openings, partial clearings, borders, overgrown plantations.
Field Marks 7.5" M: black, except bright yellow belly, untacs, rump, uptacs, and wrist patch. F: like male, but crown and back yellowish olive. Imm: like female, but wings mostly blackish brown; tail dark brownish olive.

(BLACK-VENTED) WAGLER'S ORIOLE [47] Bolsero de Wagler *Icterus wagleri*
Range Mex–Nic, exc Blz. Res Mex (Pac, w+se.nHi+csHi), Guat (Hi + adj Pac+Atl), ElSal (n). Local.
Habitat Scrubby woods, hedgerows, around palms in gardens, parks, fields.
Field Marks 8" M+F: like male Black-cowled Oriole, but more orange tinge; orange-yellow rump patch smaller; uptacs and untacs black, *not* yellow. Imm: bright yellow below, including most of throat, face, and untacs; faintly streaked or mottled yellowish olive crown, back, wings, and tail.

BAR-WINGED ORIOLE [47] Bolsero Guatemalteco *Icterus maculialatus*
Range Mex, Guat, ElSal. Res Mex (sPac + adj IIi), Guat (Pac + adj Hi), ElSal. Rare, local.
Habitat Scrub woods, forest borders, overgrown clearings.
Field Marks 8" One white wing bar. M: black, with yellow belly, untacs, rump, and wrist patch. F: mostly olive, yellower below; face and throat black.

ORCHARD ORIOLE [46] Bolsero Castaño *Icterus spurius*
(Does not include Ochre Oriole; see below)
Range Can–SAm. Sum/win Mex (sum n.nPac, ncHi, n.nAtl; tr/win s.nPac+ cspac, Hi, Atl, Yuc; cas/acc BajCal); win Blz, Guat, ElSal. Sum rare.
Habitat Tree-dotted fields, borders, hedgerows; also marshes, weedy fields.
Field Marks 6.5" M: dark reddish brown below, also on rump and wrist patch; black wings (one white bar), tail, back, and entire head. F: greenish olive above, yellowish below; belly yellower than in Bullock's Oriole; paler and bill straighter than in Hooded Oriole; two white wing bars. Imm M: like female, but throat-to-eye black.

OCHRE ORIOLE [47] Bolsero Ocráceo *Icterus fuertesi*
(The AOU lumps this with Orchard Oriole; see above)
Range Mex. Res Mex (s.nAtl+n.cAtl). Rare, local.
Habitat Grassy, brushy fields, hedgerows, tree dotted wet meadows and marshes.
Field Marks 6.5" Like Orchard Oriole, but M: pale orange-brown replaces dark reddish brown; F+imm: buffier yellow below.

HOODED ORIOLE [46] Bolsero Zapotero *Icterus cucullatus*
Range US–Mex, Blz. Sum/win Mex (res/sum BajCal, n.nPac, Atl, Yuc; tr/win s.nPac+cPac, ncHi), Blz (n).
Habitat Semidesert, farmyards, gardens, palm groves, orchards, borders.
Field Marks 7.5" Bill appears slightly more slender and decurved than that of other orioles. M: orange-yellow (northwest Mexico) to bright reddish orange

(southeast Mexico and north Belize), except black back, tail, wings (two white bars), and chest-to-eye patch; in northwest Mexico, back may be heavily scaled with pale olive in fall and early winter. F+imm: like Orchard Oriole, but somewhat more orange.

YELLOW-BACKED ORIOLE [47] Bolsero Dorsidorado *Icterus chrysater*
Range Mex–SAm, exc CRic. Res Mex (sHi + adj Pac, se.cAtl+e.sAtl, Yuc), Blz, Guat, ElSal (n).
Habitat Humid forest, openings, partial clearings, open mountain pine or pine-oak forest, borders.
Field Marks **8.5″** *No* white wing bar; yellow to orange-yellow all over except black tail, wings, and chest-to-eye patch. Imm: like adult, but duller; chest-to-eye patch may be complete, partial, or absent.

YELLOW-TAILED ORIOLE [47] Bolsero Coliamarillo *Icterus mesomelas*
Range Mex–SAm, exc ElSal. Res Mex (se.cAtl+sAtl, Yuc), Blz, Guat (Atl).
Habitat Humid forest openings, partial clearings, borders, wooded riversides.
Field Marks **8″** Chest-to-eye patch, back, wings (except long yellow bar), and central tail feathers black; otherwise bright yellow, including outer tail feathers; tail appears yellow from below. Imm: mostly pale yellowish olive above, yellow below; may have blackish chest-to-eye patch; tail mostly greenish yellow.

STREAKED-BACKED ORIOLE [47] Bolsero de Fuego *Icterus pustulatus*
Range Mex–CRic, exc Blz. Res Mex (Pac + adj Hi), Guat (interior Atl?, se Pac), ElSal.
Habitat Scrubby woods, borders, tree-dotted brushy slopes, gardens, orchards; often hangs nest on utility wires.
Field Marks **8″** M: bright red-orange to yellow-orange; black tail and chest-to-eye patch; black-and-white wings; black-streaked back, streaks wider and heavier in southern Mexico, Guatemala, and El Salvador; may seem as black on back as Hooded or Altamira Oriole, but bill slightly larger and straighter, wrist patches more orange than Hooded's, and bill smaller than the heavier-bodied Altamira's. F: dull yellow-orange below, with black chest-to-eye patch; pale olive above with darker wings. Imm: like female, but duller and may lack black chest-to-eye patch.

ORANGE ORIOLE [47] Bolsero Yucateco *Icterus auratus*
Range Mex, Blz. Res Mex (ne.sAtl, Yuc), Blz (n). Rare.
Habitat Scrubby woods, borders, partial clearings, mixed farms and thorny woods.
Field Marks **7.5″** M: bright orange; black wings (one bar), tail, and breast-to-eye patch; back *not* black. F+imm: duller, especially pale olive-yellow back, which may have faint streaks, but still brighter above and below than similar species (Hooded, Altamira, etc).

SPOTTED-BREASTED ORIOLE [45] Bolsero Pechimanchado *Icterus pectoralis*
Range US–CRic, exc Blz. Res Mex (csPac), Guat (Pac + interior Atl), ElSal.

Habitat Scrubby woods, borders, tree-dotted brushy fields, lush hedgerows, orchards, gardens.

Field Marks 10″ Orange, with black back, wings, tail, chest-to-eye patch, and chest spots; white patch on wing, but *no* white wing bar. Imm: duller; breast spots may wear off, but usually a trace remains; back may wear to obscurely spotted brownish olive.

ALTAMIRA ORIOLE [46] Bolsero Campero *Icterus gularis*

Range US–Nic. Res Mex (c.cPac–sPac, Atl, Yuc), Blz (n), Guat (Pac, Atl), ElSal.

Habitat Partial clearings, open woods, hedgerows, borders, roadsides; often hangs nest on utility wires.

Field Marks 10″ Heavy-bodied; white wing bar. M: orange, with black back, tail, and breast-to-eye patch; black wings with white bar and orange wrist patch. Hooded Oriole smaller, with black-and-white wrist patch and slender, curved bill. F: duller. Imm: like adult male, but yellow, *not* orange.

AUDUBON'S ORIOLE [46] Bolsero de Audubón *Icterus graduacauda*

Range US–Mex, Blz? Res Mex (extreme s.nPac+cPac, s+e.cHi, nAtl+n.cAtl), Blz (acc?). Rare, local.

Habitat Tree-dotted pastures, gardens, parks, orchards, borders, open woods.

Field Marks 9″ Yellowish green or bright yellow above; lemon-yellow below, except entire head, chest, wings, and tail black; streaky white wing bar (northeast Mexico) or none. See Scott's Oriole.

BALTIMORE ORIOLE [46] Bolsero Norteño *Icterus qalbula*

Range Can–SAm. Tr/win Mex (csPac, s.cHi+shi, Atl), Blz, Guat, ElSal.

Habitat Borders, gardens, parks.

Field Marks 7.5″ M: bright orange, including much of tail and wrist patch, but entire head and upper breast, back, wings (one white bar), and center of tail black. F+imm: grayish green above; dark mottling on crown, back, face, and throat; dull yellowish orange below, with whitish belly; two white wing bars.

BULLOCK'S ORIOLE [46] Bolsero de Bullock *Icterus bullockii*

Range Can–Mex, Guat, ElSal. Sum/win Mex (sum n.nBajCal, n.nPac, n.nHi; tr/win csPac, cshi, ncAtl), Guat (Hi), ElSal (cas w).

Habitat River-border woods, open pine-oak woods, borders, orchards.

Field Marks 8″ M: like Baltimore Oriole, but face and sides of neck broadly orange, *not* black; large white wing patch. F: dull yellowish gray above; two white wing bars; belly and untacs whitish, not yellowish or pale dull orange of Orchard and Hooded Orioles. Imm M: like female, but black throat.

(BLACK-BACKED) ABEILLE'S ORIOLE [47] Bolsero de Agua *Icterus abeillei*

Range Mex. Res Mex (s.nHi+n.cHi). Rare.

Habitat Mixed farms and small woodlots, tall hedgerows or borders, especially near water.

Field Marks 8″ Like Bullock's Oriole, but M: cheeks, sides, flanks, rump, and uptacs black, *not* orange; F: more likely to have trace of black on throat; Imm: darker olive ear patch, crown, and back.

SCOTT'S ORIOLE [46] Bolsero Tunero *Icterus parisorum*
Range US–Mex. Sum/win Mex (res/sum BajCal, s.nHi+cHi + adj Pac; tr/win ncPac).
Habitat Grassland with scattered large trees or hedgerows, semidesert scrub, prickly pear cactus, borders.
Field Marks 8″ M: lemon-yellow, but entire head, chest, back, much of tail, and wing black; white bar, yellow wrist patch on wing. Imm M: much duller; crown and back olive, scalloped and spotted with black; black face patch and throat, *not* entire head; wings and tail grayish olive; two whitish wing bars. F: like immature male, but ear patch pale olive; throat dull yellow, spotted with dark gray.

YELLOW-BILLED CACIQUE [47] Zanate Piquiclaro *Amblycercus holosericeus*
Range Mex–SAm. Res Mex (sPac, s.nAtl+csAtl, Yuc), Blz, Guat (Pac, Atl), ElSal.
Habitat Very secretive; dense undergrowth of humid forest, thickets, dense hedgerows near forest.
Voice A loud, mellow *whee-haw* or *wa-wee-a,* somewhat like Northern Bobwhite's call, or high-pitched *eek,* followed by rasping trill, *br-r-r-r-r-r* (may be from different individual).
Field Marks 9″ Black; bill pale yellow (appears white); eyes white. Imm: eyes pale brown.

(YELLOW-WINGED) MEXICAN CACIQUE [47] Zanate de Oro *Cacicus melanicterus*
Range Mex, Guat, ElSal. Res Mex (c.nPac–sPac), Guat (local Pac), ElSal (cas/acc?).
Habitat Open woods, wooded stream valleys, mixed farms and small woodlots, orchards, borders.
Field Marks 12″, 10″ Strong musky odor. M: black, including floppy, ragged crest, except yellow rump, wing patch, outer tail feathers, and untacs; bill pale yellow, pointed. F: duller.

(CHESTNUT-HEADED) WAGLER'S OROPENDOLA [47] Zacua Montañera *Psarocolius wagleri*
Range Mex–SAm, exc ElSal. Res Mex (se.cAtl–sc.sAtl), Blz (s), Guat (Atl). Rare, local.
Habitat Tree-dotted pastures, partial clearings, openings in humid forest, tall trees above forest canopy; nests in colonies.
Field Marks 14″, 11″ Black and dark reddish brown, tail yellow below; bill pale greenish, pointed, swollen base forms shield on top of head. See Montezuma Oropendola.

MONTEZUMA OROPENDOLA [47] Zacua de Moctezuma *Psarocolius montezuma*
Range Mex–Pan, exc ElSal. Res Mex (csAtl), Blz, Guat (Atl). Local.
Habitat Large trees in partial clearings, openings, or along borders, tall trees above forest canopy.
Voice Many odd snapping, squeaking, popping, or gurgling sounds, and distinctive rasping, resonant *chock* note.

Field Marks 20″, 17″ Much larger than Wagler's Oropendola and colors mostly reversed; head black, *not* reddish brown; breast, belly, and wings reddish brown, *not* black; tail yellow below; blue skin and pink wattles around bill base; bill black, orange-tipped.

FINCHES, SISKINS—DOMINIQUITOS—FRINGILLIDAE

PURPLE FINCH [40] Carpodaco Purpúreo *Carpodacus purpureus*
Range Can-Mex. Win Mex (nw.nBajCal).
Habitat Pine-oak woods, wooded stream valleys, weedy borders.
Field Marks 5.5″ M: raspberry red, except whitish belly and untacs; back streaked; head, underparts, and rump unstreaked. F: heavily streaked whitish and dark brownish gray; mustache mark and line behind eye whitish; ear patch and streak on side of throat blackish. See House and Cassin's Finches.

CASSIN'S FINCH [40] Carpodaco de Cassin *Carpodacus cassinii*
Range Can-Mex. Res/win Mex (res n.nBajCal; win nHi+n.cHi). Rare.
Habitat Upper branches in mountain pine or pine-oak forest, borders, tree-dotted openings, clearings.
Field Marks 6″ Like Purple Finch, but untacs streaked, *not* plain; M: crown brighter red, more contrasty with streaked grayish brown nape and back; paler and less extensively pink on breast, F: more narrowly streaked, face pattern less contrasty. See House Finch.

HOUSE FINCH [40] Carpodaco Común *Carpodacus mexicanus*
Range Can-Mex. Res Mex (BajCal, nPac, ncHi; local Spac, sHi).
Habitat Vacant lots, suburban gardens, mixed farms and overgrown fields or open woodlots, parks, semidesert, weedy borders.
Field Marks 5.5″ Culmen of bill slightly curved. M: rump and most of head and breast rosy red; nape and back brownish gray, streaked above and below. F: streaked above and below, but *no* contrasting face streaks. See Purple Finch.

RED CROSSBILL [44] Piquituerto Común *Loxia curvirostra*
Range AK-Nic. Res Mex (n.nBajCal, w.nHi+csHi + adj Pac+Atl), Blz (mt pine), Guat (Hi), ElSal (cas n). Rare, irregular.
Habitat Open pine or pine-oak forest, borders, scattered pines on rocky, grassy slopes.
Voice Call in flight, *dip-dip* or *clip-clip*.
Field Marks 6″ Bill crossed; wings and forked tail black. M: brick red. F: dull yellow-green; back and crown streaked. Imm M: mottled red and yellowish green.

PINE SISKIN [40] Pinero Rayado *Carduelis pinus*
Range AK-Mex, Guat. Res/win Mex (res n.nBajCal, w.nHi+cHi+n.sHi; win nPac, nHi, nAtl), Guat (w Hi).
Habitat Pine, pine-oak, or fir forests, openings, partial clearings, borders.
Voice A buzzy *zree-ee-ee*.
Field Marks 4.5″ Streaked blackish brown on pale grayish brown (sHi birds

have fewer and fainter streaks above and below); wings and forked tail blackish with yellow patch; bill small and pointed. See Black-capped Siskin.

BLACK-CAPPED SISKIN [41] Pinero Gorrinegro *Carduelis atriceps*
Range Mex, Guat. Res Mex (n+se.sHi), Guat (Hi). Rare.
Habitat Open pine or pine-oak forest, borders, partial clearings, small grassy openings.
Field Marks **4.5"** Often in flocks. Adults *not* streaked, except on untacs. M: wings and forked tail blackish with yellow patch; crown black; grayish olive-green above, paler grayish green below. F: duller; crown dark grayish olive. Imm: heavily streaked, like Pine Siskin, but darker above, paler and more yellowish below.

BLACK-HEADED SISKIN [41] Pinero Encapuchado *Carduelis notata*
Range Mex–Nic. Res Mex (w+e.nHi+csHi + adj Pac, Atl), Blz (mt pine), Guat (Hi + adj Pac+Atl), ElSal (n).
Habitat Pine or pine-oak mountain forest, deciduous woods on lower slopes, tree-dotted suburban gardens, parks, borders.
Field Marks **4.5"** M: black wings, tail (with yellow patch), most of crown, face, throat, and chest; bright yellow below; back dull yellow-green. F: duller. Imm: dull yellow-olive above, paler and more yellowish below; *little or no* black on head, throat, or chest.

LESSER GOLDFINCH [44] Dominiquito Dorsioscuro *Carduelis psaltria*
Range US–SAm. Res/win Mex (res BajCal, Pac, Hi, Yuc; win nAtl), Guat (Hi + adj Pac+Atl), ElSal.
Habitat Open pine or pine-oak woods, partial clearings, borders, weedy fields, vacant lots, gardens.
Field Marks **4"** M: black above, bright yellow below (except northwest Mexico birds, Green-backed group, have black crown, streaked olive-green back and rump); tail black above, white below; wings black with white patch and wing bar. F: dull olive-green above, faintly streaked; yellow below; wings blackish with two white bars. Imm: like adult female, but duller.

LAWRENCE'S GOLDFINCH [44] Dominiquito Gris *Carduelis lawrencei*
Range US–Mex. Res/win Mex (res n.nBajCal; win n.nPac). Rare.
Habitat Brushy fields, open oak or pine-oak woods, borders, hedgerows, gardens.
Field Marks **4"** Sum M: pale gray above, mostly whitish below, except black throat, face, and forecrown and olive-yellow chest; tail black above, white below; wings black with broad yellow wing bars and patches. Win M: browner above, duller below. F: like winter male, but *no* black on head, throat, or chest.

AMERICAN GOLDFINCH [43] Dominiquito Canario *Carduelis tristis*
Range Can–Mex. Win Mex (n.nBajCal, n.nPac, nw+ne.nHi, nAtl+n.cAtl). Rare.
Habitat Tree-dotted brushy fields, borders, hedgerows, weedy overgrown fields.
Field Marks **4.5"** Sum M: bright yellow, with black crown patch, wings, and

tail; white untacs and uptacs; yellowish wrist patch, white wing bar. F+win M: mostly olive-green or buffy olive, with whitish belly and untacs; blackish wings, with white wing bars; *no* black on crown.

HOODED GROSBEAK [41] Pepitero Encapuchado *Coccothraustes abeillei*
Range Mex, Guat, ElSal. Res Mex (w+se.nHi, cHi, se.sHi + adj Pac I Atl), Guat (Hi), ElSal (n). Rare, local.
Habitat Cloud forest, humid pine-oak or fir forest, lush gardens, partial clearings, borders.
Voice A loud, mellow *tyew-tyew* or *clew, clew.*
Field Marks **6.5″** Bill very heavy, pale greenish. M: greenish yellow, but entire head, throat, wings (with whitish patch), and tail black. F: yellow-olive, with black crown; wings (with pale gray patch) and tail black; outer tail feathers partly white-tipped.

EVENING GROSBEAK [40] Pepitero Vespertino *Coccothraustes vespertinus*
Range Can–Mex. Res Mex (w.nHi, c.cHi). Very rare.
Habitat Mountain pine or pine-oak forest, partial clearings.
Voice A rolling, musical *chir-r-rp.*
Field Marks **7″** Like Hooded Grosbeak, but M: head blackish brown with broadly yellow forehead; F: much duller; gray top of head; *no* yellow on head.

HOUSE SPARROWS—GORRIONES—PASSERIDAE

HOUSE SPARROW [33] Gorrión Doméstico *Passer domesticus*
Range AK–SAm, exc Blz? Res Mex (BajCal, Pac, Hi, ncAtl+w.sAtl), Blz (s?), Guat, ElSal.
Habitat Cities, villages, suburban areas, farmyards, parks.
Field Marks **6″** M: gray, chestnut, and whitish head pattern; throat and chest gray, gradually becoming black as pale gray feather tips wear off; pale gray breast, belly, and untacs; streaked black-and-brown back. F: mostly brownish gray; back streaked blackish and brown; buffy line over eye.

Accidental, Casual, or Very Rare and Local Species

LIST A

Accidental or casual species; species probably extinct in or extirpated from our area of coverage (Mexico, Belize, Guatemala, El Salvador); or species proven to occur *regularly* on islands or waters within 200 miles of the mainland (or on the Revillagigedo Islands, Mexico) but only accidentally or casually, or not at all, within three miles of the mainland coast, Cozumel Island (Mexico), or the readily accessible cayes of Belize. (For accidental or casual species within our area but *not* occurring on the mainland or within the above-mentioned three-mile zone, see List B below. Species considered by some authors to occur in our area solely because of their occurrence on or near Clipperton Island are not included anywhere in this book.)

YELLOW-BILLED LOON *Gavia adamsii*
Range Acc nBajCal.

ATITLAN GREBE *Podilymbus gigas*
Range Was (?) res Guat (Hi: Lake Atitlan). Extinct (?).

LAYSAN ALBATROSS *Phoebastria immutabilis*
Range Res Mex (islands off BajCal, cPac); cas/acc in 3-mile waters.

DARK-RUMPED PETREL *Pterodroma phaeopygia*
Range Vis Mex (off cPac).

JUAN FERNANDEZ PETREL *Pterodroma externa*
Range Vis Mex (off cPac).

TAHITI PETREL *Pterodroma rostrata*
Range Vis Mex (off cPac).

KERMADEC PETREL *Pterodroma neglecta*
Range Vis Mex (off cPac).

COOK'S PETREL *Pterodroma cookii*
Range Vis Mex (off BajCal+ncPac).

PARKINSON'S PETREL *Procellaria parkinsoni*
Range Vis Mex (off csPac), Guat (off Pac), ElSal (off Pac).

CORY'S SHEARWATER *Puffinus diomedea*
Range Vis Mex (off Yuc).

FLESH-FOOTED SHEARWATER *Puffinus carneipes*
Range Vis Mex (off BajCal+ncPac).

GREATER SHEARWATER *Puffinus gravis*
Range Acc Mex (Yuc: Quintana Roo).

BULLER'S SHEARWATER *Puffinus bulleri*
Range Vis Mex (off BajCal+ncPac).

CHRISTMAS SHEARWATER *Puffinus nativitatus*
Range Vis Mex (off csPac), Guat (off Pac).

MANX SHEARWATER *Puffinus puffinus*
Range Acc Blz.

WILSON'S STORM-PETREL *Oceanites oceanicus*
Range Vis Mex (off csPac, cAtl), Guat (Pac).

LEACH'S STORM-PETREL *Oceanodroma leucorhoa*
Range Res/vis Mex (res off BajCal; vis off csPac), vis Guat (Pac).

(WEDGE-RUMPED) GALAPAGOS STORM-PETREL *Oceanodroma tethys*
Range Vis Mex (off BajCal, Pac), Guat (off Pac), ElSal (off Pac).

ASHY STORM-PETREL *Oceanodroma homochroa*
Range Res/vis Mex (off w.nBajCal).

WHITE-TAILED TROPICBIRD *Phaethon lepturus*
Range Cas/acc Mex (sPac; Yuc), Blz (cstl)? Guat (Atl)?

RED-TAILED TROPICBIRD *Phaethon rubricauda*
Range Res/vis Mex (off BajCal+cPac).

GREAT FRIGATEBIRD *Fregata minor*
Range Res Mex (off cPac: Revillagigedo Islands).

GARGANEY *Anas querquedula*
Range Acc Mex (s.nPac).

HARLEQUIN DUCK *Histrionicus histrionicus*
Range Cas/acc Mex (nw.nPac).

OLDSQUAW [3] Pato Viejo *Clangula hyemalis*
Range Cas/acc Mex (nBajCal, ncPac).

BARROW'S GOLDENEYE *Bucephala islandica*
Range Cas/acc Mex (nBajCal?, n.nHi?).

RED-THROATED CARACARA *Daptrius americanus*
Range Extirpated from Mex, Blz, Guat, ElSal.

CHUKAR *Alectoris chukar*
Range Introduced (established?) (very rare/cas?) Mex (n.nBajCal).

RING-NECKED PHEASANT *Phasianus colchicus*
Range Established? (very rare/cas?) Mex (n.nBajCal).

YELLOW RAIL [9] *Coturnicops noveboracensis*
Range Mex (c.cHi), extirpated?

WHOOPING CRANE [9] *Grus americana*
Range Cas Mex (nHi, nAtl).

ESKIMO CURLEW *Numenius borealis*
Range Extinct? Formerly cas/acc Mex, Guat.

RUFF *Philomachus pugnax*
Range Acc Guat (Pac).

AMERICAN WOODCOCK *Scolopax minor*
Range Cas/acc Mex (nAtl, Yuc).

GREAT SKUA *Catharacta skua*
Range Acc Blz (cstl).

SOUTH POLAR SKUA *Catharacta maccormicki*
Range Extremely rare/cas near shore Mex, Guat (Pac), ElSal.

LONG-TAILED JAEGER *Stercorarius longicaudus*
Range Very rare/cas 3-mile waters Mex (BajCal, Pac), Guat (Pac).

LITTLE GULL *Larus minutus*
Range Acc/cas Mex (c.cAtl).

BLACK-HEADED GULL *Larus ridibundus*
Range Acc/cas Mex (s.cAtl).

BLACK-TAILED GULL *Larus crassirostris*
Range Acc/cas Blz (cstl).

LESSER BLACK-BACKED GULL *Larus fuscus*
Range Very rare/cas Mex (n.nAtl, n Yuc).

KELP GULL *Larus dominicanus*
Range Acc/cas Mex (n Yuc).

GLAUCOUS GULL *Larus hyperboreus*
Range Very rare/cas Mex (nBajCal, n.nPac).

GREAT BLACK-BACKED GULL *Larus marinus*
Range Acc/cas Blz (cstl).

ARCTIC TERN [II] *Sterna paradisaea*
Range Offshore Mex (BajCal, Pac), Guat (Pac), ElSal.

BLACK NODDY *Anous minutus*
Range Acc Mex (off ne Yuc).

PIGEON GUILLEMOT   Cepphus columba
Range Cas Mex (off nw.nBajCal).

ANCIENT MURRELET   Synthliboramphus antiquus
Range Cas/acc Mex (off nw.nBajCal).

CRESTED AUKLET   Aethia cristatella
Range Acc/cas Mex (off nw.sBajCal).

HORNED PUFFIN   Fratercula corniculata
Range Acc Mex (nBajCal).

SOCORRO DOVE [12]   Zenaida graysoni
Range Wild birds probably extinct. Was in Mex (cPac: Revillagigedo Islands).

DOWNY WOODPECKER   Picoides pubescens
Range Cas/acc? Mex (n.nBajCal).

IMPERIAL WOODPECKER [45]   Campephilus imperialis
Range Probably extinct; was res Mex (w.ncHi).

BLUE-AND-WHITE SWALLOW   Pygochelidon cyanoleuca
Range Cas/acc Mex (sPac), Guat (Pac).

SOCORRO WREN [30]   Thryomanes sissonii
Range Res Mex (off cPac: Socorro Island).

CLARION WREN [30]   Troglodytes tanneri
Range Res Mex (off cPac: Clarion Island).

SONG WREN   Cyphorhinus phaeocephalus
Range Cas/acc ElSal.

DUSKY WARBLER   Phylloscopus fuscatus
Range Acc Mex (nBajCal).

ARCTIC WARBLER   Phylloscopus borealis
Range Acc Mex (sBajCal).

NORTHERN WHEATEAR   Oenanthe oenanthe
Range Acc Mex (n Yuc).

SOCORRO MOCKINGBIRD [32]   Mimodes graysoni
Range Res Mex (off cPac: Socorro Island).

WHITE WAGTAIL   Motacilla alba
Range Acc Mex (s.sBajCal).

RED-THROATED PIPIT   Anthus cervinus
Range Cas/acc Mex (BajCal, cPac).

BLACK-WHISKERED VIREO   Vireo altiloquus
Range Cas/acc Mex (ne Yuc), Blz (cayes).

CONNECTICUT WARBLER *Opornis agilis*
Range Cas/acc Blz (cstl + cayes).

LAPLAND LONGSPUR *Calcarius lapponicus*
Range Cas/acc Mex (sBajCal, c.cAtl, nw Yuc).

LE CONTE'S SPARROW *Ammodramus leconteii*
Range Cas/acc Mex (nw.nAtl).

NELSON'S SHARP-TAILED SPARROW *Ammodramus nelsoni*
Range Cas/acc Mex (n.nBajCal).

SEASIDE SPARROW *Ammodramus maritimus*
Range Cas/very rare Mex (extreme ne.nAtl).

DARK-EYED JUNCO (Guadalupe group) *Junco h. insularis*
Range Res (?) Mex (off nBajCal: Guadalupe Island).

RUSTY BLACKBIRD *Euphagus carolinus*
Range Cas/acc Mex (n.nBajCal, nw.nPac).

LIST B

Species that have not been shown to occur on the mainland or on the islands or cayes mentioned in List A, or within the 3-mile near-shore zone, and are only accidental or casual in our area outside the 3-mile near-shore zone. (Species considered by some authors to occur in our area solely because of their occurrence on or near Clipperton Island are not included anywhere in this book.)

SHORT-TAILED ALBATROSS *Diomedea albatrus*
Range Cas Mex (off cPac: Revillagigedo Islands).

BAND-RUMPED STORM-PETREL *Oceanodroma castro*
Range Acc Mex (off cPac: Revillagigedo Islands).

WHITE TERN *Gygis alba*
Range Acc/cas Mex (off cPac: Revillagigedo Islands).

Bibliography

Alvarez del Toro, Miguel. *Lista de las aves de Chiapas*. Tuxtla Gutiérrez: Instituto de Ciencias y Artes de Chiapas, 1964.

American Ornithologists' Union. *Check-list of North American Birds*. 6th ed. 1983.

———. 35th–40th supplements to the *Check-list of North American Birds*, 6th ed. *Auk* 102(1985), 104(1987), 106(1989), 108(1991), 110(1993), 112(1995).

Blake, Emmet R. *Birds of Mexico*. Chicago: University of Chicago Press, 1953.

Cicero, Carla. "Sibling Species of Titmice in the *Parus inornatus* Complex." *University of California Publications in Zoology* 128(1966): 1–217.

Davis, L. Irby. *A Field Guide to the Birds of Mexico and Central America*. Austin: University of Texas Press, 1972.

Eaton, Stephen W., and Ernest P. Edwards. "The Mangrove Cuckoo in Interior Tamaulipas, Mexico." *Wilson Bull.* 59(1947): 110–111.

———. "Notes on Birds of the Gomez Farias Region of Tamaulipas." *Wilson Bull.* 60(1948): 109–114.

Edwards, Ernest P. *Finding Birds in Mexico*. 1st ed. Sweet Briar, Va.: Ernest P. Edwards, 1955.

———. "Nesting of the Lesser Swallow-tailed Swift, *Panyptila cayennensis*, in Guatemala." *Auk*, July 1959.

———. *A Field Guide to the Birds of Mexico*. 1st ed. Sweet Briar, Va.: Ernest P. Edwards, 1972.

———. *1976 Supplement to Finding Birds in Mexico*. Sweet Briar, Va.: Ernest P. Edwards, 1976.

———. "Hummingbirds Feeding on an Excretion Produced by Scale Insects." *Condor* 84(1982): 122.

———. *1985 Supplement to Finding Birds in Mexico*. Sweet Briar, Va.: Ernest P. Edwards, 1985.

———. *A Field Guide to the Birds of Mexico*. 2nd ed. Sweet Briar, Va.: Ernest P. Edwards, 1989.

Edwards, Ernest P., and Frederick K. Hilton. "*Streptoprocne semicollaris* in the lowlands of Sinaloa and Nayarit." *Auk* 73 (January 1956).

Edwards, Ernest P., and Robert B. Lea. "Birds of the Monserrate Area, Chiapas, Mexico." *Condor* 57(1955): 31–54.

Edwards, Ernest P., and Paul S. Martin. "Further Notes on Birds of the Lake Patzcuaro Region, Mexico." *Auk* 72(1955): 174–178.

Edwards, Ernest P., and Richard E. Tashian. "The Prothonotary and Kentucky Warblers on Cozumel Island, Quintana Roo, Mexico." *Wilson Bull.* 68(1956): 73.

———. "Avifauna of the Catemaco Basin of Southern Veracruz, Mexico." *Condor* 61(1959): 325–337.

Friedmann, Herbert, Ludlow Griscom, and Robert T. Moore. *Distributional Checklist of the Birds of Mexico: Part 1.* Pacific Coast Avifauna No. 29. Cooper Ornithological Society, 1950.

Howell, Steve N. G., and Sophie Webb. *A Guide to the Birds of Mexico and Northern Central America.* New York: Oxford University Press, 1995.

Lea, Robert B., and Ernest P. Edwards. "Notes on Birds of the Lake Patzcuaro Region, Michoacan, Mexico." *Condor* 52(1950): 260–271.

Miller, Alden H., Herbert Friedmann, Ludlow Griscom, and Robert T. Moore. *Distributional Checklist of the Birds of Mexico: Part 2.* Pacific Coast Avifauna No. 33. Cooper Ornithological Society, 1957.

National Geographic Society. *Field Guide to Birds of North America.* Washington, D.C.: National Geographic Society, 1983.

Peterson, Roger Tory, and Edward L. Chalif. *A Field Guide to Mexican Birds.* Boston: Houghton Mifflin, 1973.

———. *Aves de México.* Translated by Mario Ramos and María Isabel Castillo. Mexico, D.F.: Editorial Diana, 1989.

Phillips, Allan R. *The Known Birds of North and Middle America: Part 1.* Denver: Allan R. Phillips, 1986.

Ridgely, Robert S. *A Guide to the Birds of Panama.* Princeton, N.J.: Princeton University Press, 1976, 1981.

Ridgely, Robert S., and John A. Gwynne. *A Guide to the Birds of Panama with Costa Rica, Nicaragua, and Honduras.* Princeton, N.J.: Princeton University Press, 1989.

Ridgely, Robert S., and Guy Tudor. *The Birds of South America, Vol. 1.* Austin: University of Texas Press, 1989.

Ridgway, Robert (also Herbert Friedmann, author of parts 9–11). *Birds of North and Middle America.* U.S. National Museum Bulletin 50, pts. 1–11. Washington, D.C., 1901–1950.

Robbins, Chandler S., Bertel Bruun, and Herbert S. Zim. *Birds of North America.* New York: Golden Press, 1983.

Sutton, George M. *Mexican Birds: First Impressions.* Norman: University of Oklahoma Press, 1951.

Sutton, George M., Robert B. Lea, and Ernest P. Edwards. "Notes on the Ranges and Breeding Habits of Certain Mexican Birds." *Bird-Banding* 21(1950): 45–59.

Sutton, George M., and Olin S. Pettingill, Jr. "Birds of the Gomez Farias Region, Southwestern Tamaulipas." *Auk* 59(1942): 1–34.

Wilson, Richard G., and Hector Ceballos-Lascurain. *The Birds of Mexico City.* Burlington, Ontario: BBC Printing and Graphics, 1986.

Also numerous articles, mostly by S. N. G. Howell, Sophie Webb, A. M. Sada, and John Arvin, in *Mexican Birds Newsletter, Aves Mexicanas* (and *MBA Bulletin Board*), and *Euphonia.*

Index of English Names, Spanish Group Names, and Generic Names

References to plate illustrations are in **boldface**